HOLOCAUST CINEMA IN THE TWENTY-FIRST CENTURY

Holocaust Cinema
IN THE TWENTY-FIRST CENTURY
MEMORY, IMAGES, AND THE ETHICS OF REPRESENTATION

Edited by **OLEKSANDR KOBRYNSKYY** & **GERD BAYER**

WALLFLOWER PRESS

A Wallflower Press Book
Published by
Columbia University Press
Publishers Since 1893
New York • Chichester, West Sussex
cup.columbia.edu

Copyright © Columbia University Press 2015
All rights reserved.
Wallflower Press® is a registered trademark of Columbia University Press

Cover image: *Ida* (2014)
© Opus Films/Phoenix Film/Sylwester Kazimierczak

A complete CIP record is available from the Library of Congress

ISBN 978-0-231-17422-0 (cloth : alk. paper)
ISBN 978-0-231-17423-7 (pbk. : alk. paper)
ISBN 978-0-231-85091-9 (e-book)

Columbia University Press books are printed on permanent
and durable acid-free paper.
This book is printed on paper with recycled content.
Printed in the United States of America

Contents

Notes on Contributors vii

INTRODUCTION
The Next Chapter in the History of Holocaust Cinema
Oleksandr Kobrynskyy and Gerd Bayer 1

PART ONE: THE PAST AND ITS PRESENCE

1 TRANSFORMATIONS OF HOLOCAUST MEMORY
 Frames of Transmission and Mediation
 Aleida Assmann 23

2 SUPPLEMENTING *SHOAH*
 Claude Lanzmann's *The Karski Report* and *The Last of the Unjust*
 Sue Vice 41

3 THE ACT OF DIGGING
 Archaeology, Photography and Forensics in *Birthplace* and *Holocaust by Bullets*
 Brad Prager 59

4 THE WILLING AMNESIA
 The Holocaust in Post-Soviet Cinema
 Olga Gershenson 76

5 WILHELM BRASSE'S PHOTOGRAPHS FROM AUSCHWITZ
 Testimony and Photography in Irek Dobrowolski's *The Portraitist*
 Tomasz Łysak 95

PART TWO: THE ETHICS OF MEMORY

6 **THE SINGULAR JEW**
   Representing National Socialism's Jewish Victims in Recent Historical Cinema
   Jennifer M. Kapczynski 117

7 **LOCKED DOORS AND HIDDEN GRAVES**
   Searching the Past in *Pokłosie*, *Sarah's Key* and *Ida*
   Tobias Ebbrecht-Hartmann 141

8 **THE ETHICS OF PERSPECTIVE AND THE HOLOCAUST ARCHIVE**
   Spielberg's List, *The Boy in the Striped Pyjamas* and *Fateless*
   Martin Modlinger 161

PART THREE: THE LEGACY OF EVIL

9 **'THE DOCTOR IS DIFFERENT'**
   Ambivalent Ethics, Cinematic Heroics and the Figure of the Jewish Doctor
   in Tim Blake Nelson's *The Grey Zone*
   Erin McGlothlin 183

10 **ON THE CINEMATIC NAZI**
   Aaron Kerner 203

11 **THE HOLOCAUST AS CASE STUDY**
   Universalist Rhetoric and National Memory in Stefan Ruzowitzky's
   Radical Evil
   Oleksandr Kobrynskyy 221

12 **TV AS A HISTORICAL ARCHIVE?**
   How Epic Family Series Memorialise the Holocaust
   Marcus Stiglegger 242

Index 260

Notes on Contributors

ALEIDA ASSMANN is Professor emerita for English Literature at the University of Konstanz. The recipient of numerous international fellowships, awards and honours, she has written widely on cultural memory, including *Erinnerungsräume: Formen und Wandlungen des kulturellen Gedächtnisses* (1999; English translation 2011) and the co-edited anthology *Memory in a Global Age: Discourses, Practices and Trajectories* (2010).

GERD BAYER is a tenured faculty member (Akademischer Oberrat & Privatdozent) in the English Department at the University of Erlangen-Nürnberg. He has written on Holocaust literature and film, on early modern and contemporary fiction, on various aspects of popular culture, on mockumentary film and on postcolonial fiction.

TOBIAS EBBRECHT-HARTMANN is Lecturer of Film- and German Studies in the Department of Communication and Journalism and the DAAD Center for German Studies at the Hebrew University in Jerusalem. He is the author of *Geschichtsbilder im medialen Gedächtnis: Filmische Narrationen des Holocaust* (2011) and *Übergänge: Passagen durch eine deutsch-israelische Filmgeschichte* (2014).

OLGA GERSHENSON is Professor of Judaic and Near Eastern Studies at the University of Massachusetts Amherst. She is the author of *Gesher: Russian Theater in Israel* (2005), *The Phantom Holocaust: Soviet Cinema and Jewish Catastrophe* (2013), and articles on culture, history and film. Her most recent work deals with new Jewish museums in postcommunist Europe.

JENNIFER KAPCZYNSKI is Associate Professor of German and Film Studies at Washington University in St. Louis. She is the author of *The German Patient: Crisis and Recovery in Postwar Culture* (2008) and co-editor, with Paul Michael Lützeler, of *Die Ethik der Literatur* (2011) and, with Michael D. Richarsdon, of *A New History of German Cinema* (2014).

TOMASZ ŁYSAK is Assistant Professor in the Department of Applied Linguistics at the University of Warsaw. The recipient of a National Science Centre grant ("From Newsreel to Post-Traumatic Film: Documentary and Artistic Films on the Holocaust"), he has published research on Holocaust representations in *Polin: Studies in Polish Jewry*, *Kwartalnik Filmowy*, *Slovo* and in various edited volumes.

ERIN MCGLOTHLIN, Associate Professor of German and Jewish Studies at Washington University in St. Louis, has published on Holocaust literature and film, including *Second Generation Holocaust Literature: Legacies of Survival and Perpetration* (2006). Her current project is a monograph entitled *Constructing the Mind of the Holocaust Perpetrator in Fictional and Documentary Discourse*.

AARON KERNER is a Professor at the School of Cinema at San Francisco State University. Amongst other publications, he is the author of *Film and the Holocaust* (2011) and *Torture Porn in the Wake of 9/11* (2015).

OLEKSANDR KOBRYNSKYY is Lecturer in the English Department at the University of Erlangen-Nürnberg. His current research focuses on representations of the Holocaust in Anglophone literatures and European cinema. He holds degrees in English and History from Erlangen and an MA in Holocaust Studies from Royal Holloway, University of London.

MARTIN MODLINGER completed a PhD at the University of Cambridge and was a research fellow at the University of Bremen. The co-editor of *Other People's Pain: Narratives of Trauma and the Question of Ethics* (2011), he has since escaped academia and is now Director of Science and Culture at the Renewable Freedom Foundation.

BRAD PRAGER is Professor of Film Studies and German Studies at the University of Missouri. He is the author of *The Cinema of Werner Herzog: Aesthetic Ecstasy and Truth* (2007), *Aesthetic Vision and German Romanticism: Writing Images* (2007) and *After the Fact: The Holocaust in Twenty-First Century Documentary Film* (2015).

MARCUS STIGLEGGER teaches film and cultural studies at the University of Mainz, having held visiting professorships at the Universities of Clemson, Wroclaw, and various German universities. He has authored eight monographs, including *Auschwitz-TV: Reflexionen des Holocaust in Fernsehserien* (2014) and *SadicoNazista: Geschichte, Film und Mythos* (1999/2015).

SUE VICE is Professor of English Literature at the University of Sheffield. Her authored books include *Holocaust Fiction* (2000), *Children Writing the Holocaust* (2004) and *Shoah* (2011), and she has edited *Representing the Holocaust: Essays in Honour of Bryan Burns* (2003) and, with Jenni Adams, *Representing Perpetrators in Holocaust Literature and Film* (2013).

INTRODUCTION

The Next Chapter in the History of Holocaust Cinema

Oleksandr Kobrynskyy and Gerd Bayer

As the twenty-first century gathers momentum, ostensibly moving the traumatic legacy of World War II into an ever more distant past, the production of Holocaust films proliferates.[1] While the number of witnesses to the atrocities perpetrated by Nazi Germany is dwindling, there seems to be an uninterrupted, even growing interest in this particular set of historical events and their cultural and ethical implications. The preservation of Holocaust memory is without doubt one of the dominant ethical imperatives of our time; archival sources become more accessible,[2] and a plethora of new studies deals with Nazi Germany's attempt to exterminate the Jews of Europe, as well as with the cultural aftermath of the Holocaust.[3] However, the dissemination of Holocaust memory is mainly taking place outside the realm of academia. Since the 'communicative memory' (see Assmann 2008) of the Holocaust is dying with the last eyewitnesses, widely available media, in particular film, are assuming an increasingly significant part in the transmission of what Joshua Hirsch has aptly termed 'a form of posttraumatic historical memory' (2004: 3). The question of how mediated representations can deal responsibly and effectively with the memories of the past has therefore to be asked anew. And it has to be asked in a transnational context that is inclusive of different traditions:[4] Holocaust remembrance exists at the intersection of national cultures, aesthetic conventions and, at least in the context of film, the inner logic of popular forms of entertainment. The detailed study of Holocaust cinema closes the gap between archive and cultural practice, and the resulting broadening of perspectives allows for a more comprehensive understanding of the different strategies used to remember past atrocities.

For many decades after the end of World War II, critics and the general audience have debated whether art can ever provide an appropriate environment for representing the Holocaust. Elie Wiesel has famously noted that 'A novel about Auschwitz is not a novel – or else it is not about Auschwitz' (2006: x), suggesting that art and Auschwitz cannot meet.[5] For this reason, amongst others, representations of the Holocaust have always existed in a state of tension between truthful commitment to first-hand testimony and the possibility of art to evoke ethical and aesthetic response through a wide range of representational techniques, what Michael Rothberg (2000) has analysed under the term 'traumatic realism'. Departing from Wiesel's hamstringing syllogism, Rothberg discusses literary and cinematic representations of the Holocaust that daringly address in their mimetic programme the tension between the demand for historic truthfulness and the epistemological doubt inherent in representations of traumatic events. Critical discourse (and artistic practice) in the twenty-first century has accordingly moved from asking whether it is right to produce aesthetic renderings of the Holocaust to the question of what the formal and ethical parameters of these representations should be to keep the traumatic memory of the Holocaust alive.[6] The risks involved in Holocaust representation include exploitation, numbing, commercialisation and outright falsification. Just as written forms of representation have to face 'the potential futility of literature' when faced with the Holocaust (Spargo 2010: 1), films dealing with the Holocaust need to decide '*how* to represent it' and critics should therefore study '*how* it has been represented' (Kerner 2011: 1).

The possible benefits of such a critical investigation derive from a more comprehensive understanding of the immersive nature of film and its widespread use in segments of society that might be averse to other forms of artistic and intellectual memory work. Eventually, as Eva Hoffman has argued so powerfully in *After Such Knowledge* (2004), new forms of cultural remembering will have to be found as historical distance grows (see also Bayer 2010). Filmmakers thus face the same challenges as historians when they encounter what Dominick LaCapra discusses as the difficult balance between objectification and ethical engagement that is posed by 'the diachronic weight of the past' (2001: 39). What these various critical positions emphasise is that only a broad analysis of cinematic forms of Holocaust representations – that is to say, an analysis that ventures across national and linguistic boundaries and proceeds without limiting itself to particular cinematic genres – provides insight into how diversely cultural renderings of the Holocaust engage with the past. Such an approach needs to be aware, furthermore, that the political unconscious of any form of cultural representation exists always already as a complex historical moment, one that is determined by the generational affiliations of those involved in its production and consumption as well as by various aspects of popular culture.[7]

Holocaust films are doubly entwined in the dynamic of memories. As cultural artefacts that come into being within a specific production context, these films shed light on how communities deal with or fail to come to terms with the legacy of the Holocaust. In doing so, they reflect past and present strategies of representation, as well as their limits. In the introduction to their collection of essays about Holocaust narratives, Jakob Lothe, Susan Rubin Suleiman and James Phelan point to a similar temporal duality when they write that their title, *After Testimony*, refers both to the historical moment after the last witnesses will have died and to the fact that all contemporary narratives about the Holocaust 'must in some way come to terms with the historical reality that the accounts of survivors have tried to communicate' (2012: 2); that is to say, they always include palimpsestic qualities.[8] On a separate temporal level, they assume a significant part in the way traumatic memories are kept alive, providing visual instances of what Cathy Caruth has described as 'the literal return of the event against the will of the one it inhabits' (1995: 5).

This two-fold temporal entanglement of Holocaust cinema is illustrated in numerous contemporary Holocaust films, for instance in Władysław Pasikowski's *Aftermath* [*Pokłosie*] (2012) and its reception in Poland. The film presents a riveting narrative of two men fighting a memory war against a rural community committed to oblivion. Franciszek Kalina, who had lived in Chicago for many years, returns to his home village in Poland to find his brother Józef collecting tombstones which, after the local Jewish community had been extinguished during World War II, were removed from the Jewish cemetery and used to pave roads. As the archaeological documents of a troublesome past are unearthed and publicly displayed – Józef is setting up the tombstones on his farmland – this endeavour triggers growing opposition and hostility. Franciszek discovers a hidden archive, and his homecoming turns into a series of uncanny revelations bringing to light gruesome details about the implication of Gentile Poles, including his own father, in the extermination of the local Jews. The brothers' efforts to establish by means of cultural artefacts and archival material what Aleida Assmann (2011) calls 'cultural memory' stems from a self-imposed ethical obligation to revive the commemoration of an event suppressed in the collective memory of the local community. Containing references to the by now well-documented Jedwabne massacre of 1941, in which Poles played an active part, the film was charged by Polish nationalist groups with falsification of history. The filmmakers were accused of anti-Polish sentiments, the film was banned from some local cinemas and one actor allegedly even received death threats.[9] This circumstance testifies both to the continuous controversial nature of films with Holocaust references and to the unremitting presence of the past in present discourses. The film not just reveals troubling facets of a national past but also exemplifies how this knowledge implicates viewers in their historical present.

As this example shows, Holocaust cinema in the twenty-first century covers historical ground far beyond the period of Nazi rule, asking at times uncomfortable questions about memory and forgetting. One development illustrated by *Aftermath*, a film that does not contain any direct representations of the historical events, is the growing interest in the cultural repercussions of the Holocaust. While the history of persecution and destruction continues to inform cinematic imagination, filmmakers' attention increasingly turns to issues of how communities in the immediate post-war time have dealt with the legacy of the then recent past. Giulio Ricciarelli's *Labyrinth of Lies* [*Im Labyrinth des Schweigens*] (2014) explores German post-war amnesia and the dominating practice in the 1950s of covering up crimes committed under the Nazi regime. Fighting cartels of silence, a young lawyer, supported by chief state attorney Fritz Bauer, finally succeeds in collecting evidence against former concentration camp officials and in filing a class action lawsuit leading to the Frankfurt Auschwitz trials of 1963–65. The trial of Adolf Eichmann in 1961, widely acknowledged as a pivotal milestone in the history of discourses about the Holocaust, provides the backdrop for Margarethe von Trotta's *Hannah Arendt* (2012), a film which traces Arendt's coverage of the proceedings against Adolf Eichmann in Jerusalem and touches upon her controversial ideas about the logistician of the 'Final Solution' and the phenomenology of evil in totalitarian states. Both films also invite allegorical readings that address twenty-first-century viewers and the political realities in which they live.

While ethical implications of what it means to represent perpetrators have yet to be fully grasped, critics have raised the broader issue of how Holocaust films shape their objects of representation. This debate goes back at least to Gillian Rose's influential essay about the ethics of reception in Holocaust cinema, and it is comprehensively addressed in the contributions to Jenni Adams and Sue Vice's volume *Representing Perpetrators in Holocaust Literature and Film* (2012) as well as in Matthew Boswell's *Holocaust Impiety in Literature, Popular Music and Film* (2012). Writing about Claude Lanzmann's *Shoah* (1985), Rose voices her concern that this film, like others at the time, 'is not self-referentially sceptical about its own means and forms of representation' (1996: 49). Rose was clearly unhappy with how cinema avoided asking the most probing questions about representing the Holocaust. Echoing the point made by Fredric Jameson when he opens his book on visual culture with the statement that 'The visual is *essentially* pornographic' (1992: 1), Rose proposed: 'Let us make a film in which the representation of Fascism would engage with the fascism of representation' (1996: 50). In other words, Rose insisted that Holocaust cinema needs to be more aware of the power and dominance that visual representations yield over what they represent. It is precisely these 'self-referential' aspects that feature prominently in recent Holocaust films. Potentially in response to this academic debate, contemporary cinema is not just approaching the mind and psyche of the perpetrators, but it also increasingly pays attention to the capacity of films to create, in their own historical contexts, stereotypical images of evil. As recent documentaries like Yael Hersonski's *A Film Unfinished* (2010) or Andre Singer's *Night Will Fall* (2014) make clear, the very images that have survived from the concentration camps and ghettos also always exist within the limitations that pertain to all forms of visual representation (see also Michalczyk 2014). It is arguably only within the most recent wave of Holocaust cinema, explicitly asking about the role that film played as a medium of communication, that one of the major concerns expressed by Rose has finally been addressed.

This new self-reflexivity is notably allied with cinema's ambition to contribute to righting the wrongs of the past. The Kalina brothers' frantic search for historical truth in *Aftermath* is symptomatic for the sad insight that, with some remarkable exceptions, judicial systems worldwide had largely missed earlier opportunities to bring to court former Nazis, their collaborators as well as other individuals involved in violent crimes during the war. As long as prosecutors, continuing the mission of Fritz Bauer and the 'Nazi hunter' Simon Wiesenthal, pursue their search for surviving perpetrators, there is a chance that delayed justice still be done. Yet where real-life justice cannot be achieved, poetic justice in the fictional story-world of film steps in. In Quentin Tarantino's *Inglourious Basterds* (2007), a troop of Jewish avengers specialising in hunting down Nazis in war-struck Europe end up massacring the inner circle of the Nazi party along with Hitler himself.[10] Notably, the place chosen for the bloodbath by the ruthless anti-Nazi task force is a cinema, in which the upper echelon of the Nazi party gathers for the screening of a propaganda movie. In Tarantino's highly self-referential engagement with issues of retribution and representation, cinema both metaphorically and literally provides a setting for belated justice.

Inglourious Basterds distinctly displays two strands of contemporary cinematic discourse about the Holocaust. Firstly, the stereotype of the passive Jewish victim, which to no small degree was advanced by Hannah Arendt, is challenged by feature films premised upon historical instances of armed Jewish resistance. Tim Blake Nelson's *The Grey Zone* (2001) depicts both the work of the so-called 'Sonderkommando', which was responsible for the burning of corpses in Auschwitz crematoria, and their heroic, albeit doomed, uprising against the SS guards. The same reversal of power is also at the heart of Claude Lanzmann's *Sobibór, October 14, 1943, 4pm* (2001), which combines an interview with Yehuda Lerner, one of the survivors of the camp uprising, with recent footage from the location. To mention just one further example, the fierce struggle of Jewish partisans against German occupation forces in the woods of Belarus provides the historical backdrop for Edward Zwick's *Defiance* (2008). The supposed passivity of the Holocaust victims undergoes a thorough revision in these films, and the discursive tradition that rests on an almost exclusive focus on victimisation is countered with accentuations of a more active historical role of Jews.

Secondly, numerous intertextual references in *Inglourious Basterds* to earlier filmic representations of war and Nazism are symptomatic for the rise of a meta-cinematic discourse in Holocaust cinema.[11] While Rose's point about a lack of self-reflexivity invites films to reflect on their own status as representation, this aspect of twenty-first-century Holocaust cinema addresses the role of earlier films in shaping the popular imagination of the Holocaust and influencing subsequent cinematic productions. Recent Holocaust cinema indeed has to be seen as engaging not just with the historical reality of the Holocaust and its repercussions but also with the quite substantial body of Holocaust cinema to date, so well described in Annette Insdorf's ground-breaking study, *Indelible Shadows* (2003), and more recently updated by Lawrence Baron's *Projecting the Holocaust into the Present* (2005) or Axel Bangert's *The Nazi Past in Contemporary German Film* (2005).[12] In the light of this research it becomes clear that the first decade and a half of the twenty-first century has seen a new quality of cinematic engagement with the Holocaust, one that responds to the changing historical setting as well as to the manner in which mediated memory replaces communicative memory. The various releases from Claude Lanzmann's original *Shoah* material over the past ten years demonstrate, for instance, how Holocaust cinema exists as an intertextual network of visualised memories that frequently adds to and cites from earlier documents. Lanzmann's recent films accordingly raise questions about the historical environment in which particular filmic images are released. They suggest that, even in the highly intellectualised documentary context of the filmmaker's original mode of production, various ethical choices (like deleting particular material) were made that he is now reversing (see Prager 2015). As a result of these tendencies, Holocaust cinema has by now started to reflect its own position towards documenting and representing the past.

This cinematic engagement with the visual legacy of the archive is not limited to moving images. As the contributions to Axel Bangert, Robert Gordon and Libby Saxton's *Holocaust Intersections* (2013) demonstrate, the field of visual culture has contributed significantly to how the Holocaust and other forms of genocide are represented in an aesthetic context. In recent Holocaust films, photographs are saliently used, which draws our attention to intermedial relations between cinema and photography.[13] There are significant areas of overlap between these two largely separate semiotic traditions, for instance when portraits of perpetrators, bystanders and victims appear in films as intermedial reproductions of archival images. The proliferation of these images in recent Holocaust films can at least in part be explained by photography's mimetic qualities that assign to black-and-white photographs, appearing on cinema screens, a sense of referential authenticity. The practice of German occupiers to take, often against orders, remembrance photos has left us with a number of images first-handedly documenting crimes against civilians.[14] While there are very few surviving photographs of the extermination procedure in the camps (see Didi-Huberman 2008), mug shots of prisoners and photographs of victims of medical experiments are occasionally used in recent films. Where photography enters the film as a conceptual pattern rather than as physical presence, such as the recreation of the atelier situation in *The Portraitist* [*Portrecista*] (2006), or when it echoes the photographic technique of double exposure in *Radical Evil* [*Das radikal Böse*] (2013), the role played by such intermedial references is further emphasised. What such strategies reveal is that Holocaust cinema starts to admit to the medial nature of its form of commemoration.

Family album photographs appear in films as artefacts of a troubled past. Displaying yellowish stains, worn edges and other irregularities, or going up in flames, as in *Lore* (2012), photographs become witnesses of volatile histories of commemoration and forgetting. The inclusion of photographs in works of literature has been discussed by Marianne Hirsch, who aims at 'exploring affiliative structures of memory beyond the familial' (2012: 21). In the process of generational and affiliative remembrance, photography appears as a kind of a memory anchor. Hirsch discusses the palimpsestic qualities of double exposure photography, which reveals the 'shadow archive that haunts the intimacy of family pictures' (2012: 158). The tentative use of animated family pictures in the Academy-Award-winning short documentary *The Lady in Number 9: Music Saved My Life* (2013) reflects the realisation of filmmakers that the corporeal presence of the eyewitness becomes less available in its indexical function. Holocaust survivor Alice Herz-Sommer, whose astonishing life story the film narrates, sadly passed away shortly after its completion, as if the point needed emphasis that photography only ever attempts to replace lived and embodied memory (see also Kaplan 2011). While work by photographers creates multiple points of reference for filmmakers, film, conversely, leaves its mark on photographical practices. Film sets for *Schindler's List* (1993) have become popular tourist destinations, and it is often photos of Spielberg's sets rather than those of the remains of the original Płaszów camp that make it into contemporary family albums.

As the World Wide Web increasingly makes porous the divide between private and public memories, online social networks and video sharing websites are turning into public archives of Holocaust-related visual material. The democratisation of filmmaking and film consumption enabled by digital technology is changing the way moving images are created, distributed and viewed. At the same time, viewers gain access to multiple levels of production and reception contexts. Some of these online films have reached large audiences. For instance, a four-minute video showing a survivor visiting with his grandchildren and great-grandchildren sites of his Holocaust past was viewed on YouTube hundreds of thousands of times. What generated attention was the video's music clip aesthetic: the footage is set to Gloria Gaynor's disco classic 'I Will Survive', and the family is seen dancing at various iconic places, including the gate of the Auschwitz concentration camp.[15] Even before being watched, the video appears already contextualised by the number of views, user rating and comments. The YouTube sidebar suggests thematically related videos such as Associated Press interview footage that includes a critical response by the head of the Anti-Defamation League and an apologetic comment by the survivor's daughter, a filmmaker, who had uploaded the video on YouTube, justifying her intention to raise awareness for the Holocaust.[16] Much of the video clip's controversial potential indeed derives from the fact that it is made publicly available. In an essay for the online version of German magazine *Der Spiegel*, Henryk M. Broder praises the video as 'a clever response to the question of how one can commemorate something that has long since been ground into historic gravel in the quarry of the "culture of remembrance"' (2010). He furthermore sees in it 'an attempt to offer an approach to counter the mindless rituals, one that celebrates the power of life' (ibid.).[17] Irrespective of what one may think about the video's ethics, or its aesthetic qualities, it offers one of multiple entry points into the complex of mediated Holocaust memories, an almost globally available digital storehouse of archival footage and full films, including the classics of the genre, like Lanzmann's *Shoah*, and shorter clips from films and video testimonies of survivors. This storehouse has become a rich resource for filmmakers and students of Holocaust film alike.

Discussing cultural developments in the digital age, Andrew Hoskins (2007) coins the term of a 'connective turn'. Memory is not collective or re-collective anymore but constituted 'through the flux of contacts between people and digital technologies and media' (quoted in Hirsch 2012: 22). Unless access to video sharing platforms is restricted by government regulations in certain countries, Internet users can extend their knowledge of both the historical events surrounding the Holocaust and their visual representations. Digital technology gradually dissolves the distinction between producer and consumer, between television and cinema, between still and moving images; and it changes the generic territory of the increasingly self-reflexive Holocaust film within formerly more tightly-drawn thematic boundaries.

Debates taking place in the realm of Holocaust studies are connected in various ways to the larger concerns within the neighbouring academic discourses of postmodern and postcolonial studies. While, as Robert Eaglestone has powerfully demonstrated, postmodernism has 'an origin in the Holocaust' (2004: 343), much recent criticism, such as Michael Rothberg's *Multidirectional Memory* (2009), has demonstrated the benefits of considering both the Holocaust and the legacy of colonialism simultaneously. Within Holocaust cinema, a similar tendency is gathering momentum in that a number of recent films set out to move beyond the associative value that Auschwitz has acquired as a symbol for the totalitarian violence of the twentieth century as a whole. One German film, Robert Thalheim's *And Along Came Tourists [Am Ende kommen Touristen]* (2007), even addresses the question of how the city of Oświęcim, known around the world for the adjacent site of the former Auschwitz concentration camp, and the people who live there can combine memory and everyday life in a manner that is not necessarily and at all times determined by the horrific past.

As Jeffrey Skoller (2005) has shown, some avant-garde filmmakers have addressed the spectral quality of ghosts of the past that were haunting Holocaust film. Yet it was relatively late into the history of Holocaust cinema, with films like Leszek Wosiewicz's *Kornblumenblau* (1988) and Tim Blake Nelson's *The Grey Zone*, that the ethics of spectatorship allowed for what Libby Saxton (2008) discusses as the view 'through the spyhole' and into the gas chambers. Once this final taboo was lifted and the mechanisation of destruction has been put on the screen, the recent tendency seems to be to broaden the viewers' understanding of how and where the mass destruction of European Jewry took place. While in the understanding of many non-experts the Holocaust occurred primarily in gas chambers at places like Auschwitz, recent films draw attention again to the fact that before the implementation of industrialised mass killing in extermination camps, sweeping mass shootings were carried out by mobile death squads in Eastern Europe. This mass murder, accounting for a large portion of total Holocaust victims, is addressed in films like Stefan Ruzowitzky's *Radical Evil* or *Holocaust by Bullets* (2008), a documentary based on Patrick Desbois' investigations aimed at localising all sites in Eastern Europe where Jews were rounded up and shot.

Traces of this chapter in the history of the attempted extermination of the Jews of Europe reach across what Timothy Snyder (2010) has dubbed 'bloodlands', territories in Eastern Europe suffering alternately from the genocidal practices of Stalinism and Hitlerism. It is only recently that a scholarly debate about the geographical reaches of the Holocaust is gathering momentum, for instance in the various maps and graphs to be found in the contributions to Anne Kelly Knowles, Tim Cole and Alberto Giordano's edited volume, *Geographies of the Holocaust* (2014).

Another aspect of the history of the Holocaust remains largely unwritten, and unfilmed: while murder by gassing began in the euthanasia programmes at mental hospitals, another step towards the development of concentration camp gas chambers was the systematic use of hermetically sealed vans for mass killings, starting in 1941. The memory of this practice has largely faded from cultural and public memory, over-determined as it is by images of concentration camps and gas chambers. What David Albahari has so provocatively and brilliantly portrayed in his historical novel *Götz and Meyer* (1998), which evokes the ethical mind-set of the perpetrators through two drivers of gas vans, has as yet to be included in the larger framework of Holocaust representation. In the light of how early twenty-first-century Holocaust cinema has aimed to extend the way in which viewers reflect about and remember the Holocaust, one can expect future films to move further away from what Insdorf describes as 'images – of smoke, of barbed wire, of sealed train cars, of skeletal bodies – that now function as synecdoches' (2003: 248) and be more inclusive of lesser-known aspects of the Nazi crimes.

* * *

This collection of essays concentrates on a fairly narrow historical slice, studying only the most recent chapter in the history of Holocaust cinema, namely those films produced since the turn of the millennium. The contributions in this volume nevertheless embrace all forms of film, from fiction to documentary; they analyse Holocaust imagery in big-budget Hollywood productions as well as its exploitative uses in B-movies; and they explore avant-garde films alongside poetic meditations on memory and forgetting.

To address such a diverse corpus of recent Holocaust cinema, this volume brings together scholars from a broad range of humanities disciplines to discuss how twenty-first-century cinematic representations of the Holocaust live up to their difficult tasks of keeping memories alive, of dealing with atrocities in an ethically responsible manner, and of finding a visual language to which their viewers can relate. Throughout, the focus lies on recent films from across Europe and beyond. The essays collected here accordingly range from theoretical discussions of ethical issues to the role of public memory, from the formal quality of individual films to the specificity of particular cinematic genres, such as documentary or feature film. Starting with a discussion of the roles of archives, the pliability of material objects in the cinematic context and their re-workings through time, they also address questions of ethics as they relate to the unique situation of films produced in nations like Germany, France or Russia. They furthermore discuss the role played by monolingual and multilingual scripts in an increasingly global and always already diasporic framework of Holocaust memories.

The volume opens with an essay by Aleida Assmann in which she describes three different stages through which memory culture moved following the Holocaust. While an initial period reacted with silence and an attempt at forgetting, Assmann points to Hannah Arendt's work as a philosophical turning point that adjusted the manner in which, starting in the 1980s, memory work could and should respond to shameful events like the Holocaust. The new forms of transmitting history relied on principles of identification, ethics and empathy, which resulted in an attitude towards the past that also allowed for the admittance of wrong-doing and suggested forms of ethical engagement. Assmann proposes that, at the contemporary historical moment she terms 'post memory', the dwindling numbers of direct witnesses will lead to a situation where secondary witnesses bear the brunt of Holocaust memory. For this form of indirect or adopted memory work, film and other media play a crucial role, since it is through their forms of representation that secondary witnessing can relate to the past.

The first group of essays, under the heading 'The Past and Its Presence', discuss how contemporary Holocaust films rely on the historical past as well as on cinematic precursors, at times even engaging in active self-referential discussions of how these two aspects relate to each other. Sue Vice's contribution returns to Claude Lanzmann's *Shoah*, in particular to the release of two films in which Lanzmann re-edits archival material or intercuts it with recent footage as a means both to contribute to the contemporary debate about the ethics of memorialisation and to re-engage with his earlier film project. The first film, *The Karski Report* (2010), is devoted to how the Western world was unwilling to listen to reports about the Nazi atrocities. The interview with Jan Karski demonstrates how, in his retelling of the past, the witness has to re-experience his shock at how little value is assigned to his report; and it thereby also addresses how Lanzmann sees his own role in representing this history truthfully. In *The Last of the Unjust* (2013), Lanzmann engages with Benjamin Murmelstein twice, once during the original making of *Shoah*, and in a second persona as the elder statesman of Holocaust cinema. Both Lanzmann and Murmelstein, suggests Vice, use this film to reflect on how ethics, memory and representation can be brought into alignment within the Holocaust discourse, at least implicitly admitting to the insufficiency of cinema.

Brad Prager's essay is built around the notion of digging, taking from archaeology and forensic sciences the interest in retrieving information from the earth. He begins by discussing the limitations of forensic sciences and its need to rely on narrative and interpretation, but he also stresses that evidential material dug from the earth, such as bullet casing or bones, can at times add to our knowledge about aspects of the Holocaust only poorly understood so far. Both films analysed by Prager, *Birthplace* (1992) and *Holocaust by Bullets*, deal with scenes of murder that occurred outside the well-researched sites of concentration camps and gas chambers. As Prager shows, recent documentary films aim to bring to light information about both the mass murder in Eastern Europe and about individual biographies. He emphasises that the matter of culpability frequently complicates the search for truth, as when witnesses fear that their speaking about the past will incriminate themselves or those close to them. What the films discussed here show forcefully is how the Holocaust continues to inhabit the European landscape, with numerous sites of atrocities remaining unidentified or unmarked.

Covering adjacent geographical spaces, Olga Gershenson traces the continuities between the dominating refusal in the Soviet Union to treat the Holocaust as a unique and separate phenomenon and what she describes as 'willing amnesia' in present-day Russia. Popular historical drama series broadcast on Putin's state television use triumphalist images of a heroic past to gloss over inconvenient aspects of national history. Marginalised on Soviet screens, the Holocaust has become a more prominent subject in recent Russian productions.[18] These films navigate a difficult territory between melodramatic exaggeration and the attempt to create empathy with the Jewish victims of what discourse in Russia continues to refer to as the Great Patriotic War. By focusing on the films *Holocaust: Is it Wallpaper Paste?* [*Kholokost – Klei dlia oboev*] and *Shoes* [*Tufel'ki*] (both 2013), Gershenson demonstrates how filmmakers, in their effort to establish an alternative memorial discourse in Russian film, use a broad range of cinematic devices between emotional closeness and visual abstraction.

Images of children subjected to medical experiments haunt the visual legacy of Auschwitz, and they appear prominently in *Holocaust: Is it Wallpaper Paste?* Shot by the Polish inmate Wilhelm Brasse, these photographs occupy an ethical middle ground between their exploitative purpose and their function of preserving visual memory of individual victims. In his discussion of *The Portraitist* (2005), Irek Dobrowolski's benevolent cinematic portrayal of the Auschwitz photographer, Tomasz Łysak elucidates discursive grounds where photography, testimony, biography and film meet. Łysak describes the practice of identification photography in Auschwitz and pinpoints how Dobrowolski uses the spatial arrangement of portrait photography as an aesthetic template for his film. Whereas instances of Brasse's immoral behaviour were variously reported by his biographers and appear in earlier video testimonies, Dobrowolski chose to leave out footage that testifies to ethically problematic traits of his 'model'. Constructing a spotless image of a morally intact patriot, the film falls into a strand in Polish film that propagates a nationalist narrative of World War II.

The second part of this book consists of three essays that address 'The Ethics of Memory', focusing on the various points where cinematic commemoration and philosophical enquiry meet. In her essay, Jennifer Kapczynski discusses two filmic examples of what she defines as the 'Singular Jew', a character prototype employed in film to single-handedly represent the fate of all of Central Europe's murdered Jews. Writing about the German television mini-series *Generation War* [*Unsere Mütter, unsere Väter*] (2013), Kapczynski shows how such a character's involvement in a love plot and his eventual survival raise ethical issues: on the one hand, the survival plot effaces the actual murder of the majority of Jews; on the other it allows viewers to empathise with the rare survivor, making this particularly troublesome when a film at the same time, and to a greater degree, evokes pity and sympathy for the death of German characters. Turning to *Lore*, the essay explores a more creative and productive use of the 'Singular Jew'. It shows how by undermining the representational value of such a singular character, and in particular by stressing the way that media are employed to nurture such a narrative, cinema can actively invite its viewers to question the manner in which film frequently simplifies and, at least ethically, falsifies the historical facts.

Tobias Ebbrecht-Hartmann's contribution to this volume echoes Tony Judt's proposition that the Holocaust has become a 'contemporary European entry ticket' (2005: 803) for countries striving to join the European Union. Ebbrecht-Hartmann links up a historical outline of European memory of the Holocaust with a close reading of how inconvenient aspects of national histories resurface in recent European Holocaust films. With important political speeches as milestones, Ebbrecht-Hartmann traces a historical paradigm change in European post-war history from forgetting and covering up crimes of the past towards the establishment of a more or less reconciled European Union which chose the Holocaust as its historical foundation. In the film analyses, Ebbrecht-Hartmann examines the literal and metaphorical excavation of Polish pasts in Władysław Pasikowski's *Aftermath*, shows how history is made usable for the present in Gilles Paquet-Brenner's *Sarah's Key* (2010) and depicts how Polish and Jewish identities are renegotiated in Paweł Pawlikowski's *Ida* (2013). Addressing the differences between these films, Ebbrecht-Hartmann argues that in all three the theme of uncovering, which is typical for the horror genre, is productively employed to renegotiate within ethical frameworks different national narratives of the Holocaust.

Martin Modlinger's essay begins with a comprehensive review of the current scholarly debate regarding the ethical implications of the historical moment when direct experience, as described by witnesses, is increasingly replaced by mediated forms of imagination. He demonstrates that, in a media-saturated culture of virtual communication, memory about the Holocaust takes on a new quality, one that increasingly relies on references not to the still growing archive of historical data and material, but to the field of aesthetic representation itself. The visual archive of the Holocaust thus becomes more and more self-referential. Modlinger, for instance, discusses an installation/film project that reveals how successful Holocaust films can influence the manner in which visitors relate to historical sites. This shift in focus is then applied to a close analysis of two films, *The Boy in the Striped Pyjamas* (2008) and *Fateless* (2005), both of which apply child-protagonists in order to address the limitations of any form of gaze when it comes to the Holocaust.

Essays in the third and final part, entitled 'The Legacy of Evil', turn to films that deal with perpetrators, asking questions about the ethics of representation. This section begins with a contribution by Erin McGlothlin on the character of the doctor in *The Grey Zone*. While doctors in films and TV series usually represent heroic figures who take on the characteristics of saviours, the perverse logic of medical experiments at Auschwitz reverse this situation. McGlothlin contrasts two aspects of the film: the (ultimately failed) uprising of the *Sonderkommando* that aimed to destroy the gas chambers and crematoria, and the discovery of a girl who had survived the gas chamber and was smuggled out by Dr Miklós Nyiszli, the Jewish doctor working for Mengele. The essay carefully discusses the ethical choices Nyiszli and the members of the *Sonderkommando* have to make, showing how complex the assigning of guilt and the workings of atonement are. McGlothlin demonstrates that *The Grey Zone* avoids simple redemptive strategies and instead confronts readers with the full force of the death camps and their deadly efficiency.

In his contribution to this volume, Aaron Kerner argues that cinema has so far been mostly unable to represent Nazi characters in a manner that does not automatically turn them into inhuman monsters. Kerner draws attention to the tendency of Holocaust films to extrapolate Nazi evil, and thereby to lose sight of the perpetrators' more or less ordinary human nature. He suggests that this defence mechanism, which allows filmmakers and viewers alike to keep the horrors of Nazism at bay, falls short of powerful ethical obligations since it pretends that the Holocaust stands as an aberration with little chance of being repeated. Calling for new strategies of representing perpetrators, Kerner discusses a few cinematic, photographic and television examples that partly succeed in a more nuanced engagement with perpetrators. While Juraj Herz's *The Cremator* (1969) constructs the Nazi as a mentally and sexually deviant figure, Vicente Amorim's *Good* (2008) abandons the dominant ethical dualism, which Kerner diagnoses in the genre of Holocaust cinema.

Radical Evil seems to respond to the desideratum formulated by Kerner by entirely abandoning a Manichean representation of perpetrators in favour of a differentiating exploration of how 'ordinary men' turn into mass murderers. In his analysis of Stefan Ruzowitzky's documentary, Oleksandr Kobrynskyy discusses the ethical implications of the turn towards a dehistorising use of the Holocaust as an example within the broader framework of future-oriented human rights education. Kobrynskyy argues that the film's universalist rhetoric and its aesthetics, such as the peculiar use of re-enactment and split screens in representations of perpetrators, are strongly informed by the subjectivities of German post-war generations. Whereas mass shootings of Jewish civilians on Soviet territories occupied by Nazi Germany have been represented in earlier films, Ruzowitzky's essayistic approach uses the massacres as argumentative material for a socio-psychological case study of human evil. Kobrynskyy suggests that *Radical Evil* represents a new tendency in German and Austrian filmmaking about the Holocaust that ushers in a gradual departure from the paradigm of national memory.

The volume ends with an essay by Marcus Stiglegger that discusses the extent to which cinema remains the main place where visual culture and moving images memorialise the Holocaust. By turning to television, Stiglegger demonstrates that, within this widely consumed media context, visual representations of the Holocaust are not so much concerned directly with the historical events but, at least in terms of the iconographic value, reuse at times excessively the images and tropes first introduced in influential documentary and fiction films like Alain Resnais' *Night and Fog* [*Nuit et brouillard*] (1955) or Spielberg's *Schindler's List*. Turning next to recent television series, the essay establishes how such films reflect the political realities of the cultural spheres where they are produced. For instance, German series tend to take a specific view of how memory, culpability and historical depth are employed; and an example from Iran shows how the Holocaust can be enlisted for propagandistic uses, leaving little room for historically accurate or ethically responsible engagement with the past.

By studying twenty-first-century Holocaust cinema, the essays collected here add to a number of related discourses, whose global significance is underlined by the omnipresence of genocidal incidents.[19] The inclusion of films produced in different countries and using many different languages further testifies to the fact that representations of the Holocaust in the form of moving images have indeed become a global phenomenon.

Notes

1. An extensive – but, due to permeable generic boundaries, necessarily incomplete – filmography of Holocaust films screened before 2004 is Caroline Joan Picart's two-volume *Holocaust Film Sourcebook*.
2. In 2007, the archive of the International Tracing Service in the German town of Bad Arolsen was opened to historical research. In 2014, a digital copy of the U.N. War Crimes Commission Archive was made publicly accessible by the United States Holocaust Memorial Museum. The EHRI Online portal, launched in 2015 by the European Holocaust Research Infrastructure, provides search access to Holocaust archives in over fifty countries.
3. To give but two examples for the tendencies in recent scholarship: one trend is that genocidal violence in Eastern Europe under the Nazi occupation has recently received more attention by historians, for instance in Timothy Snyder's *Bloodlands: Europe Between Hitler and Stalin* (2010); another development is that the previously dominant hypothesis about an alleged posttraumatic silence of survivors in the post-war time is increasingly questioned. On the magnitude of practices of Holocaust commemoration in the immediate post-war period, see David Cesarani and Eric Sundquist's *After the Holocaust: Challenging the Myth of Silence* (2012), as well as Laura Jockusch's research on Jewish historical commissions in *Collect and Record!: Jewish Holocaust Documentation in Early Post-war Europe* (2012).
4. As Lawrence Baron observes: 'Around 20 percent of the Holocaust films made in the 1990s were multinational endeavors, and that rate has climbed to nearly 40 percent for movies released between 2000 and 2004' (2005: 11). Although we have not set up a statistical database for the time after 2004, the films discussed in this volume suggest that the percentage of internationally produced Holocaust films remains high.
5. On Theodor Adorno's famous – and much misquoted – dictum about the barbarity of writing a poem after Auschwitz, and on various related issues, see Freiburg and Bayer's introduction to their edited anthology *Literatur und Holocaust* (2009).
6. See, for instance, the contributions to Jean-Michel Ganteau and Susana Onega's collection *Trauma and Romance in Contemporary British Literature* (2013).
7. On the at times difficult assigning of generational affiliation, see also Suleiman (2002).
8. In this sense, Holocaust cinema projects memory into the future, influencing – through what Daniel Levy and Natan Sznaider term 'future oriented memories' (2006: 23) – both future forms of public commemoration on the national and global level and subsequent aesthetic forms of representation.
9. For the controversy the film caused, see Grollmus (2013).
10. For discussion of Tarantino's film, see the volume edited by Robert von Dassanowsky (2012).
11. The frequent cross-references in *Inglourious Basterds* include allusions to World War II movies like *The Dirty Dozen* (1967) and *The Big Red One* (1980) and to Charlie Chaplin's Hitler satire, *The Great Dictator* (1940).
12. Cinematic approaches to the Holocaust almost seem to preclude generic innovation, as shown in the debates following Roberto Benigni's *Life Is Beautiful* [*La vita è bella*] (1997); see Mitchell (2000).
13. On how cinematic and photographic images, both historical and staged, relate to the Holocaust, see Kramer (2003).
14. On the extensive amount of studies about photography and the Holocaust, see Milton (1999).

15 Dancing in the context of Holocaust commemoration also plays a significant role in Marceline Loridan-Ivens' *The Birch Tree Meadow* [*La petite prairie aux bouleaux*] (2004).
16 Adolek Kohn, having left his native Poland after surviving Auschwitz, moved to Australia. The video, made by his daughter Jane Korman, is part of her 'Dancing Auschwitz' art project, and documents the family's trip to memorial sites in Europe.
17 For an analysis of non-traditional approaches to Holocaust commemoration and their problems in the context of collective memory in Israel, see Zandberg (2006).
18 For representation of Jewish life in Soviet films see Lilia Antipow, Jörn Petrick and Matthias Dornhuber's volume, *Glückssuchende?: Conditio Judaica im sowjetischen Film* (2011).
19 For a geographical and historical survey of academic discussions of genocide, see Adam Jones' *Genocide: A Comprehensive Introduction* (2011).

Filmography

And Along Came Tourists [*Am Ende kommen Touristen*]. Dir. Robert Thalheim. Germany, 2007.
Aftermath [*Pokłosie*]. Dir. Władysław Pasikowski. Poland, 2012.
The Birch Tree Meadow [*La petite prairie aux bouleaux*]. Dir. Marceline Loridan-Ivens. France/Germany/Poland, 2004.
The Big Red One. Dir. Samuel Fuller. USA, 1980.
Birthplace [*Miejsce urodzenia*]. Dir. Paweł Łoziński. Poland, 1992.
The Boy in the Striped Pyjamas. Dir. Mark Herman. UK/USA, 2008.
The Cremator [*Spalovač mrtvol*]. Dir. Juraj Herz. Czechoslovakia, 1969.
Defiance. Dir. Edward Zwick. USA, 2008.
The Dirty Dozen. Dir. Robert Aldrich. UK/USA, 1967.
Fateless. Dir. Lajos Koltai. Hungary/Germany/UK/Israel, 2005.
A Film Unfinished. Dir. Yael Hersonski. Israel/Germany, 2010.
Generation War [*Unsere Mütter, unsere Väter*]. Dir. Philipp Kadelbach. Germany, 2013.
The Grey Zone. Dir. Tim Blake Nelson. USA, 2001.
Good. Dir. Vicente Amorim. UK/Germany, 2008.
The Great Dicator. Dir. Charlie Chaplin. USA, 1940.
Hannah Arendt. Dir. Margarethe von Trotta. Germany, 2012.
Holocaust by Bullets [*La Shoah par balles: l'histoire oubliée*]. Dir. Romain Icard. France, 2008.
Holocaust: Is it Wallpaper Paste? [*Kholokost – klei dlia oboev*]. Dir. Mumin Shakirov. Russia, 2013.
Inglourious Basterds. Dir. Quentin Tarantino. USA, 2007.
The Karski Report [*Le rapport Karski*]. Dir. Claude Lanzmann. France, 2010.
Kornblumenblau. Dir. Leszek Wosiewicz. Poland, 1989.
Labyrinth of Lies [*Im Labyrinth des Schweigens*]. Dir. Giulio Ricciarelli. Germany, 2014.
The Lady in Number 9: Music Saved My Life. Dir. Malcolm Clarke. Canada/USA/UK, 2013.
The Last of the Unjust [*Le dernier des injustes*]. Dir. Claude Lanzmann. France, 2013.
Life Is Beautiful [*La vita è bella*]. Dir. Roberto Benigni. Italy, 1997.
Lore. Dir. Cate Shortland. Germany, 2012.
Night and Fog [*Nuit et brouillard*]. Dir. Alain Resnais. France, 1953.
Night Will Fall. Dir. Andre Singer. UK/Germany, 2014.

The Portraitist [*Portrecista*]. Dir. Irek Dobrowolski. Poland, 2006.
Radical Evil [*Das radikal Böse*]. Dir. Stefan Ruzowitzky. Germany/Austria, 2013.
Sarah's Key [*Elle s'appelait Sarah*]. Dir. Gilles Paquet-Brenner. France, 2010.
Ida. Dir. Paweł Pawlikowski. Poland/Denmark/France/UK, 2013.
Schindler's List. Dir. Steven Spielberg. USA, 1993.
Shoah. Dir. Claude Lanzmann. France, 1985.
Shoes [*Tufel'ki*]. Dir. Costa Fam. Russia, 2012.
Sobibór, October 14, 1943, 4 p.m. Dir. Claude Lanzmann. France, 2001.

Bibliography

Adams, Jenni and Sue Vice (eds) (2012) *Representing Perpetrators in Holocaust Literature and Film*. London: Vallentine Mitchell.

Albahari, David ([1998] 2004) *Götz and Meyer*, trans. Ellen Elias-Bursać. London: Harvill.

Antipow, Lilia, Jörn Petrick and Matthias Dornhuber (eds) (2011) *Glückssuchende?: Conditio Judaica im sowjetischen Film*. Würzburg: Königshausen & Neumann.

Assmann, Aleida (2011) *Cultural Memory and Western Civilization: Arts of Memory*. Cambridge: Cambridge University Press.

Assmann, Jan (2008) 'Communicative and Cultural Memory', in Astrid Erll and Ansgar Nünning (eds) *Cultural Memory Studies: An International and Interdisciplinary Handbook*. Berlin: de Gruyter, 109–18.

Bangert, Axel (2014) *The Nazi Past in Contemporary German Film: Viewing Experiences of Intimacy and Immersion*. Rochester, NY: Camden House.

Bangert, Axel, Robert S. C. Gordon and Libby Saxton (eds) (2013) *Holocaust Intersections: Genocide and Visual Culture at the New Millennium*. London: Legenda.

Baron, Lawrence (2005) *Projecting the Holocaust into the Present: The Changing Focus of Contemporary Holocaust Cinema*. New York: Rowman & Littlefield.

Bayer, Gerd (2010) 'After Postmemory: Holocaust Cinema and the Third Generation', *Shofar*, 28, 4, 116–32.

Boswell, Matthew (2012) *Holocaust Impiety in Literature, Popular Music and Film*. Basingstoke: Palgrave.

Broder, Henryk M. (2010) '"Dancing Auschwitz": Holocaust Survivor Becomes YouTube Star', *Spiegel Online*. Online: www.spiegel.de/international/world/dancing-auschwitz-holocaust-survivor-becomes-youtube-star-a-711247.html

Caruth, Cathy (1995) 'Introduction', in Cathy Caruth (ed.) *Trauma: Explorations in Memory*. Baltimore, MD: Johns Hopkins University Press, 3–12.

Cesarani, David, and Eric Sundquist (2012) *After the Holocaust: Challenging the Myth of Silence*. New York: Routledge.

Dassanowsky, Robert von (ed.) (2012) *Quentin Tarantino's Inglourious Basterds: A Manipulation of Metacinema*. London: Continuum.

Didi-Huberman, George (2008) *Images in Spite of All: Four Photographs from Auschwitz*, trans. Shane B. Lillis. Chicago: University of Chicago Press.

Eaglestone, Robert (2004) *The Holocaust and the Postmodern*. Oxford: Oxford University Press.

____ (2012) 'Avoiding Evil in Perpetrator Fiction', in Jenni Adams and Sue Vice (eds) *Representing*

Perpetrators in Holocaust Literature and Film. London: Vallentine Mitchell, 13-24.

Freiburg, Rudolf and Gerd Bayer (2009) 'Introduction', in Gerd Bayer and Rudolf Freiburg (eds) *Literatur und Holocaust*. Würzburg: Königshausen & Neumann, 1–38.

Ganteau, Jean-Michel and Susana Onega (eds) (2013) *Trauma and Romance in Contemporary British Literature*. New York: Routledge.

Grollmus, Denise (2013) 'In the Polish *Aftermath*: In a Public Debate over a Controversial New Holocaust Film, Poland Faces up to a Complicated Past', *Tablet: A New Read on Jewish Life*. Online: http://www.tabletmag.com/jewish-arts-and-culture/129082/in-the-polish-aftermath

Hirsch, Joshua (2004) *Afterimage: Film, Trauma, and the Holocaust*. Philadelphia, PA: Temple University Press.

Hirsch, Marianne (2012) *The Generation of Postmemory: Writing and Visual Culture After the Holocaust*. New York: Columbia University Press.

Hoffman, Eva (2004) *After Such Knowledge: Memory, History, and the Legacy of the Holocaust*. New York: Public Affairs.

Hoskins, Andrew (2011) '7/7 and Connective Memory: Interactional Trajectories of Remembering in Post-Scarcity Culture', *Memory Studies*, 4, 3, 269–80.

Insdorf, Annette (2003) *Indelible Shadows: Film and the Holocaust*. 3rd ed. Cambridge: Cambridge University Press.

Jameson, Fredric (1992) *Signatures of the Visible*. London: Routledge.

Jockusch, Laura (2012) *Collect and Record!: Jewish Holocaust Documentation in Early Post-war Europe*. New York: Oxford University Press.

Jones, Adam (ed.) (2011) *Genocide: A Comprehensive Introduction*. 2nd ed. New York: Routledge.

Judt, Tony (2005) *Post-war: A History of Europe Since 1945*. New York: Penguin.

Kaplan, Brett Ashley (2011) *Landscapes of Holocaust Postmemory*. New York: Routledge.

Kerner, Aaron (2011) *Film and the Holocaust: New Perspectives on Dramas, Documentaries and Experimental Films*. London: Continuum.

Knowles, Anne Kelly, Tim Cole and Alberto Giordano (eds) (2014) *Geographies of the Holocaust*. Bloomington, IN: Indiana University Press.

Kramer, Sven (ed.) (2003) *Die Shoah im Bild*. Munich: text + kritik.

Lothe, Jakob, Susan Rubin Suleiman and James Phelan (2012) 'Introduction: "After" Testimony – Holocaust Representation and Narrative Theory', in Jakob Lothe, Susan Rubin Suleiman and James Phelan (eds) *After Testimony: The Ethics and Aesthetics of Holocaust Narrative for the Future*. Columbus, OH: Ohio State University Press, 1–19.

Michalczyk, John (2014) *Filming the End of the Holocaust*. London: Bloomsbury.

Milton, Sybil (1999) 'Photography and the Holocaust: A Select Bibliography', *History of Photography*, 23, 4, 379–82.

Mitchell, Vallentine (2000) '"Don't touch my Holocaust": Responding to *Life Is Beautiful*,' *Holocaust Studies: A Journal of Culture and History*, 9, 1, 19–32.

Picart, Caroline Joan (ed.) (2004) *The Holocaust Film Sourcebook*. 2 vols. Westport, CO: Praeger.

Prager, Brad (2015) *After the Fact: The Holocaust in Twenty-First Century Documentary Film*. New York: Bloomsbury.

Rose, Gillian (1996) *Mourning Becomes the Law: Philosophy and Representation*. Cambridge: Cambridge University Press.

Rothberg, Michael (2009) *Multidirectional Memory: Remembering the Holocaust in the Age of Decolonization*. Stanford, CA: Stanford University Press.

Rothberg, Michael (2000) *Traumatic Realism: The Demands of Holocaust Representation*. Minneapolis, MN: University of Minnesota Press.

Saxton, Libby (2008) *Haunted Images: Film, Ethics, Testimony and the Holocaust*. London and New York: Wallflower Press.

Snyder, Timothy (2010) *Bloodlands: Europe Between Hitler and Stalin*. New York: Basic Books.

Spargo, R. Clifton (2010) 'Introduction: On the Cultural Continuities of Literary Representation', in R. Clifton Spargo and Robert M. Ehrenreich (eds) *After Representation: The Holocaust, Literature, and Culture*. New Brunswick, NJ: Rutgers University Press, 1–22.

Skoller, Jeffrey (2005) *Shadows, Specters, Shards: Making History in Avant-Garde Film*. Minneapolis, MN: University of Minnesota Press.

Suleiman, Susan Rubin (2002) 'The 1.5 Generation: Thinking about Child Survivors and the Holocaust', *American Imago*, 59, 3, 277–95.

Wiesel, Elie (2006) *Day*, trans. Anne Borchardt. New York: Hill & Wang.

Zandberg, Eyal (2006) 'Critical Laughter: Humor, Popular Culture and Israeli Holocaust Commemoration', *Media Culture Society*, 28, 4, 561–79.

PART ONE

THE PAST AND ITS PRESENCE

CHAPTER ONE

Transformations of Holocaust Memory
FRAMES OF TRANSMISSION AND MEDIATION

Aleida Assmann

The Holocaust has changed the world beyond recognition. This happened not only when it occurred but also in the various steps in which its memory was formed and transformed until today. In this essay, I will attempt a sweeping overview, looking at three stages of transformation of Holocaust memory, beginning roughly in the years 1945, 1985 and 2015. The first stage relates to the memory of the victims that emerged after 1945 in a culture of forgetting; the second stage started in 1985 when a new 'memory culture' was developed as a public and institutional context that established different frames of transmission; and a third stage concerns the current transformation of Holocaust memory confronting us with new challenges as we move across the shadow line of an embodied memory of survivors to an exclusively mediated memory.

AFTER 1945: THE MEMORY OF HOLOCAUST VICTIMS IN A CULTURE OF FORGETTING

Right after World War II, some survivors – like Primo Levi, Elie Wiesel or Robert Antelme – felt an intense obligation evoked by their unlikely survival; namely, to tell their stories. It became their mission as survivors to become witnesses for those who had died disgraced, abused, exploited and unnamed in the camps. More often than not, however, these acts of witnessing occurred against a backdrop of silence that was hard to penetrate as it was woven out of the texture of ignorance, denial and indifference. The eager would-be witnesses had to face the fact that they were addressing a society that had no place for their testimonies. The nightmare that had already haunted the inmates of the camps in their dreams indeed became true after the war, when they discovered that their friends and neighbours were unwilling to listen and preferred to move ahead and leave the past behind.

In her memoir *Still Alive*, Ruth Klüger tells an incident with her American aunt who instructs her about the proper conduct of an immigrant to the US: '"You have to erase from your memory everything that happened in Europe. You have to make a new beginning. You have to forget what they did to you. Wipe it off like chalk from a blackboard." And to make me understand better, she gestured as if wiping a board with a sponge' (1992: 177). When she proved recalcitrant to this injunction, she was sent to a psychoanalyst who was to help her to forget. When this incident happened in the late 1940s or early 1950s, America was still in the grip of the enforced assimilation policy of the melting-pot ideology which was itself dictated by the 'time regime of modernity' (Assmann 2013). This temporal orientation, which was unconsciously lived and supported as a cultural norm, demanded from the members of the American society to look forward into the future and to leave the past behind. Geared exclusively towards the future, this time regime prevented the possibility of publicly communicating and sharing the memory of the Holocaust. There was as yet no social frame for paying attention to the traumatic past as a vital ingredient of the present and for acknowledging the experience of the victims as an urgent element of their identity. Adhering to the past was generally considered to impede the principle of progress. Progress in the sense of moving on to a better world after having closed the darkest chapter of European history was certainly what was aspired by many. This conviction prevailed not only in the US but also in Europe during the Cold War. It was already expressed clearly by Winston Churchill in 1946 in a speech that he gave in Zurich. Addressing the students of the university, he admonished the European states to put an 'end to reckoning' and to wipe the slate clean:

> We must all turn our backs upon the horrors of the past. We must look to the future. We cannot afford to drag forward across the years that are to come the hatreds and revenges which have sprung from the injuries of the past. If Europe is to be saved from infinite misery, and indeed from final doom, there must be an act of faith in the European family and an act of oblivion against all the crimes and follies of the past. (1948: 200)

This temporal orientation of modernisation created a cultural frame that had no place for remembering the Holocaust. The result was that in Western countries, Holocaust survivors who were intent on acting as witnesses or wanted to talk about their past found themselves cut off from the societies in which they lived. This silence, as Saul Friedlander rightly emphasised, 'did not exist within the survivor community. It was maintained in relation to the outside world' (1994: 259). Annette Wieviorka (1994) has shown how in the first decade after the war Holocaust memory remained largely confined to victim groups. Living estranged from the rest of society in pockets of a counter-culture the survivors were left alone with their memories, sharing them only with family members and other survivors with whom they also commemorated their dead. The Eichmann Trial was an important event in authorising the witnesses and their testimonies, but it did not immediately break up the enclaves of Jewish communication about the Holocaust. This only happened with the American TV miniseries *Holocaust* (1978), which reached and moved members of the whole society.

Four principles of a new culture of remembering

Five years after Churchill's speech, Hannah Arendt questioned the normative implications of the modernist time regime, replacing them with a configuration of new ethical values. In her foreword to *The Origins of Totalitarianism* she made four influential statements that we can identify today as the foundation of a new memory culture that was realised only four decades later.

1. Facing the horrors of World War II, Arendt marked a deep caesura which, however, was the opposite of the performative act of closure, the 'Schlussstrich' (finishing line) called for by Churchill. At this point in history, she states that 'all hopes have died'. This can be read as an explicit reference to the progress-oriented time regime of modernity, which through the massive crime and rupture of the genocide had lost the lure of its (false) promises. With the experience of the Holocaust, a new era begins in which 'the essential structure of all civilizations is at the breaking point' (1966: vii).

2. Arendt argued that in its final stage, totalitarianism had produced 'an absolute evil', absolute in the sense that 'it can no longer be deduced from humanly comprehensible motives' (1966: viii, ix). Not only for those who had been targeted by the violence that had been unleashed, this experience has culminated in a *negative revelation*, which Arendt qualified as the beginning of a new era: the era of knowing 'the truly radical nature of Evil' (1966: ix). Yosef H. Yerushalmi and others have later elaborated the metaphysical nature of the event, which had caused mankind to eat a second time from the tree of knowledge, this time the fruit being bitter ashes: 'Out of the ashes of the extermination camps a grotesque new tree of realization has grown. [...] All of us have tasted of its bitter fruit and know what our predecessors did not know. If this is possible, anything is possible. We all, not just Jews and Germans, but the whole world has lost the last trace

of naiveness' (1995: 55). With this interpretation and evaluation, the event was elevated from the level of contingent history to a concern for universal humanity.

3. This negative revelation urgently required an answer in the shape of a practical response. This meant, for Arendt, the *safeguarding of human dignity* on a new political, legal and universal level: 'human dignity needs a new guarantee which can be found only in a new political principle, in a new law on earth, whose validity this time must comprehend the whole of humanity while its power must remain strictly limited, rooted in and controlled by newly defined territorial entities' (1966: ix).

4. Arendt also demanded a further response consisting in a changed value of memory. She referred to remembering as a new form of ethical obligation:

> We can no longer afford to take that which was good in the past and simply call it our heritage, to discard the bad and simply think of it as a dead load which by itself time will bury in oblivion. The subterranean stream of Western history has finally come to the surface and usurped the dignity of our tradition. This is the reality in which we live. And this is why all efforts to escape from the grimness of the present into nostalgia for a still intact past, or into the anticipated oblivion of a better future, are vain. (1966: xi)

The guiding principle of this new ethical stance combines a new attitude to time with a new form of remembering. It goes with the conviction that the past does not automatically dissolve and disappear as it is left behind in our emphatic orientation towards the future. On the contrary, the weight of the past has become a continuing challenge which requires retrospective attention, 'examining and bearing consciously the burden which our century has placed on us' (1966: viii). Arendt's four principles – the caesura created by a rupture in civilisation, the negative revelation of an absolute Evil, the necessity of a new human rights policy and the claim for an ethical form of remembering – are indeed the foundation on which a new memory culture was finally established. These principles created a new frame of transmission of Holocaust memory, which, however, was not established until the 1980s and 1990s. It took three to four decades before Arendt's statement that 'this is the reality in which we live' was generally acknowledged and her principles were finally embraced.

AFTER 1985: THE EMERGENCE OF A NEW MEMORY CULTURE

What are the salient features of the new 'memory culture' that evolved after this time lag? It is based on a new awareness of the violent rupture and ongoing impact of a traumatic past. In the wake of the memory of the Holocaust, other traumatic memories relating to genocides and crimes against humanity were recovered within the framework, retelling, among others, the histories of slavery and colonialism from the point of view of the victims. In the context of identity politics, this gave rise to much antagonistic discourse and a competition of victimhood. In the long run, however, the social and political prominence of the memory of the Holocaust was not only eliding other memories but was also enabling them by providing a new sensibility and language (see Rothberg 2009). This has led to a radical transformation of the Western view of history with its long tradition and emphasis on victory and progress. This caesura was famously marked by Jean-François Lyotard's formula of 'the end of grand narratives' in the late 1980s. Instead of arriving at 'the end of history', however, as Francis Fukuyama had it, we could witness the recovery of a hitherto neglected history in the form of previously unheard voices of women, socially inferior actors and victims of state violence which, by and by, were included into a revised official historiography. The specific innovation that distinguishes the new memory culture from previous shapes of cultural memory consists in the fact that for the first time in history a self-critical 'negative memory' of political actors was formed that acknowledged the experience of the victims, adopting its perspective and integrating it into the framework of a more self-conscious national memory. By integrating negative episodes into their memory and giving voice to historical experience of their own subcultures and minorities, Arendt's words were finally heeded: 'We can no longer afford to take that which was good in the past and simply call it our heritage' (1966: xxxi) while at the same time discarding the legacy of shameful episodes and burying them in oblivion. It is this ethical turn towards responsibility and accountability that characterises the new approach to the past and its frames of transmission.

The centre of this new memory culture is a new commitment to human rights. Although a new Declaration of Human Rights was drafted and adopted by the United Nations in 1948 as a response to World War II, the successful claiming of these rights on behalf of Holocaust victims became an effective legal resource only in the 1980s and 1990s. With the help of world-wide access to digital communication it became possible to put pressure on the claims of victims by publicising their testimonies in a global arena. In this way, the transnational space of non-hierarchical and decentralised mutual awareness of human rights claims and violations came to be connected with a new world ethos. Under these circumstances, the new ethical stance towards one's past became 'epidemic' and triggered what has been appropriately termed 'a politics of regret' (Olick 2007; see also Torpey 2003; and Assmann and Shortt 2012). Former colonial empires, dictatorships and other autocratic regimes adopted this new approach towards facing their criminal pasts. Historical commissions were established by the respective governments to recover the truth of a preceding history of violence and to channel the transitional processes from autocratic regimes into democracies. From the 1990s onward, the 'politics of regret' stimulated a flood of public apologies issued by high officials and statesmen. These incidents had one thing in common: people were no longer selecting only the good things in the past and calling them their 'heritage', but, for the first time, focused also on a legacy of 'negative memory' which until then had no chance ever to be registered in the annals of history. In spite of all the shortcomings connected with the pragmatic realisation of these principles and the shortcomings in bureaucratic processes of restitution, the successors of former perpetrators and Nazi collaborators acknowledged past injustices, respected the testimony of the victims and rehabilitated their perspective. While the violence of extermination and oppression perpetrated in the past cannot be undone, what can at least be undone in the present is an oppressive political climate prolonging the attitude of denial and indifference. By developing a culture of empathy with the victims and by taking responsibility for the crimes, memory thus became an important therapeutic mode of restoring a link in time between the victims and the successors of the perpetrators.

THREE FRAMES OF TRANSMISSION: IDENTIFICATION, ETHICS, EMPATHY

In the new memory culture, remembering became a collective political and therapeutic project of reaching out across the rift between former perpetrators and victims to bridge the gap between a repressed past and the present. But this remembering was by no means a homogeneous activity. Little attention has so far been paid to various 'frames of transmission' within which individuals perceive their past, depending on the ways in which they are personally anchored and position themselves vis-à-vis a violent history.[1] 'If ... we consider both German and Jewish contemporaries of the Nazi period – contemporary adults, adolescents, or children, even the children of these groups – what was traumatic for the one group was obviously not traumatic for the other. [...] The victims of Nazism cope with a fundamentally traumatic situation, whereas many Germans have to cope with a widening stain, with potential shame or guilt' (Friedlander 1994: 257) – and, as I would like to add in updating this statement, the breaking of the silence. I will discuss here three frames of transmission that are all part of our contemporary memory culture but defined by different sites, perspectives and national contexts: the identification mode relating to the victims, the ethical mode relating to the former perpetrators and the empathy mode relating to the bystanders.

The identification mode

From the Jewish point of view, the frame of transmission is that of individual and collective identification. In this frame, the process of transmission is based on genealogical links and guided by the principle of identification with the victims connecting the past of those who died and suffered with the future of succeeding generations. As these victims were not targeted for what they had done but for who they were, the genocidal violence of the Nazis hit all European Jews irrespective of the nations of which they were part, with a special aim of destroying also their future. This further explains why individual remembering is closely connected to the collective Jewish history of family, diaspora community and the nation of Israel.

There are different forms in which identification can shape the process of transmission. A prominent example is the children of Holocaust survivors who refer to themselves as '2G' ('second generation'), defining themselves as a group with seminal common features and a collective identity. These children (over-)identified with their parents by not only sharing their history but also their trauma, appropriating it unconsciously as part of their own self. In their collective psychological anamnesis they discovered that their generation had from early on been implicated into the trauma of their parents, who had re-enacted their trauma and transmitted it to their children unconsciously in the embodied symbiotic relationship of everyday life (see Epstein 2010). The distinctive and liberating move of the 2Gs was to transform the unconscious imprint of the trauma that they had come to share viscerally into a conscious *identification* and thus into a central feature of their identity. More generally speaking, 'identification' is a form of relating to other persons in real life, but also when viewing films or reading books, in which the distinction between 'self' and 'other' is blurred or bracketed. Identification in the case of the members of 2G meant that the borderline between the identity of the parent and that of the child had become porous and that this was later on acknowledged not only as a handicap but also as an individual asset. We are dealing here not only with the generally acknowledged syndrome of 'trans-generational trauma' but with a more general condition for which Marianne Hirsch has supplied the important term 'postmemory' (see Hirsch 2009, 2012). By including into her term both identification and disidentification, by moving between filial and affiliative positions and by transforming what had been dealt with as a psychological and genealogical topic into an issue of aesthetic practices she has opened up this discourse for new approaches to Holocaust literature and art.

Identification, however, does not only relate to a specific group among the second generation of Holocaust survivors but also applies more generally to Jewish remembering and acts of commemoration across generations. One example is that of taking on the name of a child that died in the Holocaust as a symbolic sibling in the religious ceremony of Bar or Bat Mizvah. This symbolic gesture confirms not only the personal identification with an individual child victim but also in a more general way the integration of the dead into the living memory of the community. Another collective formative experience is the 'march of the living', an educational tour that brings Israeli schoolchildren to Auschwitz where they re-enact and re-experience culturally the collective trauma of their families and the nation by personally connecting with their historical site of suffering and death. In this case, the flag is used very much like a prayer shawl, providing protection from the trauma that is personally reenacted at the historical site and, at the same time, symbolising the community of the living that survived the threat of total extinction. A third example is the reenactment of 'living history', a new form of teaching and learning history via identification that was developed in the United States and has spread to many countries. In some Israeli schools, children are asked to dress in a particular way to resemble, for instance, the children of the Warsaw Ghetto. By reenacting the iconic photo of the young boy and other families harassed by German SS officers in Warsaw, the past is brought to life in the class-room via identification and embodied personification. The boys and girls are not only 'remembering' the past event but are also staging and feeling it themselves in their own flesh and blood as re-experienced annually in the ritual of Pessach. Examples of the identification mode could be multiplied. They are – in different forms and expressions – a defining trait of Israeli and Jewish memory culture.

The ethical mode

Identification along the lines just indicated is the prerogative of the succeeding generations of Jewish victims and not accessible to other groups. For these, other meaningful links to connect to the traumatic event have been created. There is another frame of transmission of Holocaust memory that I will refer to as the ethical mode. This form of memory was developed by and for those who are genealogically and historically connected to the country of the perpetrators. In Germany, as Raul Hilberg has emphasised, the Holocaust was family history. This means that the children of the generation of World War II were also intensely linked to the event, but this time through feelings and concepts such as (belated) guilt, shame, responsibility and regret. While in the families of survivors, the Holocaust was firmly embedded in the communicative memory of families, anchored in the society and supported by long entrenched cultural patterns, in German and Austrian families it was for decades passed over in silence. Recovering this memory for the second generation of Germans involved the very opposite of an act of identification; it required, rather, a conscious facing and working through this history, along with the breaking with oppressive family ties that had reinforced complicity and denial. This is exactly what the ethical mode makes possible: recovering a new and independent stance from both German silence and communicative memory by creating a 'negative memory' that is rooted in a new self-critical memory culture.

In Germany, the second generation descending from the perpetrators wanted to break as thoroughly away from their own parents as the children of the survivors wanted to merge with them. Longing to distance themselves from their own family background, their country and its history, some of them took a short cut and, bypassing the ethical mode, identified directly with the Jewish victims. In psychoanalytic terms, this move has been called 'counter-identification'. Again we are dealing with a merging of self and other in a strategy that denies one's own history in an attempt to partake of the identity of the innocent victim. For some members of the German '2G' this act of over- or counter-identification was a welcome way of bypassing and eliding their own history. It was supported by a strong will to break away from an evil past by radically cutting the bonds of family and history. Fantasising a new identity was an act of emotional and moral rebellion verging on conversion, which, however, did not allow for any personal working through or cognitive historical self-orientation. Among Germans, this 'emotional fallacy' has become the topic of extensive reflection and criticism (see Jureit and Schneider 2010).[2] Historian Reinhart Koselleck also emphasised the important difference between the identification mode and the ethical mode when he commented on the new Holocaust memorial in Berlin:

> We Germans must not hide behind the various groups of victims, least of all behind the Jews, as if we were entitled to a Holocaust Memorial just like other countries in the world. This is something that we as Germans have no access to. We are different in that we need to include the perpetrators into our memory. As we must position ourselves in relation to the perpetrators, we are not entitled to focus exclusively on positive heroes like the resisters. (2002: 28)

Denying any historical link to the perpetrators is exactly what the Germans of the GDR did: they focused exclusively on the heroes of resistance, thus imagining themselves exclusively as victims of the Nazi regime without any necessity of taking responsibility for German atrocities. The dimension of perpetration was 'externalised' onto the other Germany in order not to taint the heroic national self-image. Their paradigm, again, was that of identification; this time not with Jewish victims, however, which were generally bypassed, but with communist resistance fighters.

As the identification paradigm was ruled out for Germans (except for Neo-Nazis, who identify with the perpetrators), they created a new mode: the ethical stance. The succeeding generations of Germans have developed the ethical mode, adopting the emotional complex of guilt, shame, responsibility, remorse and mourning. As the perpetrators themselves tenaciously preferred to forget, to deny and to justify themselves, succeeding German generations who are no longer tainted with guilt, are taking up in a vicarious position a stance that had been totally inaccessible to the perpetrators themselves. This self-critical stance that consists in addressing a guilty past and accepting responsibility for it is at the heart of the new memory culture that has been built into the foundations of the German state. The message of official commemoration includes three dimensions: first, honoring the victims; second, preserving the memory of this darkest chapter of German history; and third, citizenship education: respecting human rights and the principles of democracy.

With the growing temporal distance to the historic events the strong sense of guilt that had dominated the emotions of the first and the discourse of the second generation has been translated half a century after the end of the war into notions of responsibility and political vigilance. Remembering in the German case connects 'anamnetic solidarity' with the victims with a 'politics of regret' regarding the historical connection with the perpetrators. It combines historical consciousness (it was in this country where these events happened) with democratic education (this state will actively oppose discrimination and exclusion of minorities). In Germany, the frame of transmission of Holocaust memory is thus considered as an antidote, working in the form of vaccination that helps to make the patient immune to a dangerous disease: never again! This sense of accountability combining the memory of the past with a sense of vigilance towards the future is the core of the ethical paradigm. Remembering in this frame is therefore also a pedagogical tool that is saturated with instructions, admonitions and warnings.

The empathy mode

The first two frames of transmission have made us aware that the 'we' of the group remembering the Holocaust is not necessarily all-inclusive but marked by distinctive filiations and affiliations. The 'we' of these frames is defined by the boundaries of the intergenerational embodied memories that are transmitted within the family and shaped by the collective self-image of a nation. The third frame of transmission offers the possibility to transcend such distinctions and categories. It brackets the historically prescribed affiliations and creates a stance that provides at the same time more distance than the identification frame and more proximity than the ethical frame. It does not emerge from group relations, starting with the family and extending these ties to the diasporic group or nation, but from a self and its individual stance, thus bracketing the constraints of a collective 'we'. The empathic mode is not a distinctly separate frame of transmission but one that is also inscribed into the identification mode and the ethical mode. It differs from these frames, however, in offering an individual approach to the atrocities and trauma of the Holocaust that is based on maintaining a conscious distinction between self and other.

Empathy is a complex emotion that is constituted by both cognition and imagination, combining intellect and knowledge with feelings and a concern for others. It has been discovered and redefined by neuroscientists who have taught us in studies emerging since the year 2000 that this pro-social emotion is a general human endowment, developing together with the human brain from early on (see Gintis and Bowles 2009; Rifkin 2009). The possibility of empathy arises at the age of two and a half years when children are able to acquire a sense of their individual self and its distinctness from another human being. Empathy makes it possible for humans to think in the minds of others and to imagine the suffering of another person. It differs from compassion, which is strongly coloured by Christian cultural traditions, but also from sympathy or identification because it involves a consciousness of the difference between self and other. It is elicited not only in personal interaction but also through the media, which have a great potential for staging impressive images of suffering but also for presenting information and knowledge that can serve as a basis or trigger for empathy. Knowledge is of paramount importance to consolidate a mere affective state into a conscious subjective stance. In spite of its promising universal quality, it should not be forgotten that empathy can easily be blocked, be it through a surfeit of images without a clear personal connection, or because of a selective perspective that restricts it exclusively to what Avishai Margalit, referring to the ties within one's in-group, terms 'thick relations'; these 'are grounded in attributes such as parent, friend, lover, fellow-countryman [and] are anchored in a shared past or moored in shared memory. Thin relations, on the other hand, are backed by the attribute of being human' (2003: 7). The question of similitude between the person who suffers and the person who experiences the emotion was an important criterion for Aristotle's definition of compassion. As Martha Nussbaum has convincingly argued, this emotion was clearly restricted, because 'all kinds of social barriers – of class, religion, ethnicity, gender, sexual orientation – prove recalcitrant to the imagination, and this recalcitrance impedes emotion' (2001: 317). Empathy clearly exceeds the culturally defined and highly gendered range of compassion. It builds a bridge between self and other by creating a sensibility for the suffering of others under the premise that the observer could be subject to the same pain. The affirmation of the other can include also distant groups and individuals, provided that they are judged to be 'significant others', not in the sense of G. H. Mead but in the sense of Nussbaum, who defines these as being 'an important part of one's own scheme of goals and projects, important as ends in their own right' (2001: 320). Only when the other is recognised as part of 'my circle of concern' can attention be invested and empathy be released. The political and cultural framework of a memory culture but also media representations channel and stimulate empathy by bringing others into one's circle of concern, turning them into 'grievable victims' (see Butler 2009).

Thus the trans-generational transmission of Holocaust memory is not a purely individual affair, but a process framed by historical affiliations, political contexts and cultural traditions. While in the identification mode, which is focused on the victims, the roles between the self and other are blurred in order to generate a sense of belonging to a group and to affirm a collective cultural identity, they are clearly accentuated in the ethical mode that maintains a link to the perpetrators and the responsibility for the historical crimes, thus connecting the commemoration of the Holocaust today with political messages such as 'never again', civil education, protection of minorities or the prevention of anti-Semitism. The empathy mode once again reconstructs the trauma of the Holocaust from the perspective of the victims. Empathy with the victims is of course also present in the identification mode and in the ethical mode, but the empathy mode is possible without any personal connection to either the victims or the perpetrators. It is the most subjective and generalisable mode that, however, does not give up the basic distinction between self and other. That this mode is especially geared to media representations was proved, for instance, by the overwhelming effect of the American TV series *Holocaust*, which reached a transatlantic audience and moved the hearts of the people when it was broadcasted in the US, across Europe and, specifically, Germany in 1978/79.

Since the beginning of the new millennium, framing a long-term transmission of Holocaust memory has become a concrete project of politicians, survivors and professional experts. On 27 January 2000, the foundations to a new Holocaust memory community were laid in Stockholm, when, in a highly symbolic act, forty states signed a declaration to take Holocaust memory across the threshold of the twenty-first century and to safeguard it for the future. In 2005 the community of Holocaust memory was further enlarged when the member states of the European Union and the United Nations adopted 27 January as Holocaust Remembrance Day. Continuing the Stockholm Declaration, an official transnational frame of transmission for these different countries has been created by the International Holocaust Remembrance Alliance (IHRA), a network consisting of 31 states and eight observer countries, most of them from Europe. In this transnational frame, which includes programmes for museums, monuments, commemoration dates, scholarship and education, the empathic mode of Holocaust remembrance has been adopted both as a foundational myth of Europe and as a universally accessible memory. In this process, it has received a normative and inclusive institutional framework and achieved a trans-national status with a growing uniformity at the expense of historical specificity. Although Holocaust museums are now being built in Central and Eastern European countries, this does not necessarily imply that the new transnational memory community initiated from above has penetrated all regions and is all-encompassing. There are still pockets of silence, denial or indifference in Europe where a self-critical approach to one's own history is still rejected and the national narrative of pride or suffering excludes or covers up the local history of Jewish victims and other minorities.

There are other effects of the official memory frame that could be mentioned. In Germany, for instance, a transnational frame of memory is generally welcomed because it replaces the ethnic and genealogical frames. More than seventy years after the historical events, the link connecting succeeding generations with the guilt of their (grand) fathers and (grand)mothers is becoming ever more tenuous. As Holocaust memory is becoming more and more homogeneous, differences in terms of familial and historical legacies are losing their sharp contours and affective energy. Germany today ranks behind the United States and Russia as the most attractive immigration country. More than 15 million people, amounting to 19 per cent of its population, have their roots and historical background in other countries. How are these newcomers to be integrated into a 'German' frame of transmission? While family affiliations were once more activated as the most loaded and direct approach to the Nazi past in the German TV miniseries *Generation War [Unsere Mütter, unsere Väter]* (2013), this frame of transmission can no longer serve as a normative model in an ethnically diverse German society. From this point of view, a more transnational framework seems necessary, one that opens up new points of access and creates space for diverse perspectives. But there is also a backlash built into the growing uniformity of Holocaust memory: in this narrative the Germans remain tied to the emblematic position of the perpetrators. A German boy with Turkish roots recently discovered this dilemma when he joined a group of adolescents travelling to Auschwitz to learn about the history of his country.[3] At the historic site, he had to experience that simply by speaking the language of the perpetrators he felt automatically stigmatised and was therefore inscribed into this history.

While guidelines for collective commemorations can and have to be assigned and installed from above, remembering is something that cannot be delegated to politicians or other professional groups. Nor is it something that can be merely continued. As the historical event of the Holocaust is rapidly receding into the past, an urgent question is whether it will become *history* and thus be only the concern of a few historians or whether it will retain the quality of *memory* that has to be transmitted to succeeding generations. Such an affective, living connection to the past will have to be reignited from below by sparking new attention, interest, empathy and commitment of *individuals*.

AFTER 2015: THE ERA OF 'POST MEMORY' AND THE CONCEPT OF 'SECONDARY WITNESS'

'We who come after do not have memories of the Holocaust.' When Eva Hoffman wrote this, she was referring to her own 'generation of postmemory' (2004: 6). Her 'we' was clearly defined: she spoke for the children of the survivors, the second generation. We can, however, also read this statement as a valid description for a much more general 'we'; namely, the inclusive community of Holocaust memory from the point of view of all succeeding generations. This means that we have arrived at a temporal threshold when the concept of 'postmemory' needs to be revised and enlarged. From the highly specific generation marking the hinge between the survivors and their children, it is becoming a general condition and predicament. Moving along the temporal axis from second to third and fourth generation, the condition of 'postmemory' is becoming a condition of 'post memory' (which I prefer to write in two words so as to distinguish it from Marianne Hirsch's term).

There are considerable differences concerning Holocaust memory when comparing the situation of the second generation and the problems facing us today. Even though the second generation was belated, its state of post-ness was qualified by the continuity of an embodied memory that unconsciously carried the affective charge of the traumatic impact across the gap between one generation and the other. This experiential link with an 'internalised' and 'strangely unknown' past can hardly be prolonged in a world that is teeming with symbolic representations, frames of commemoration and a plethora of external images of the Holocaust. What had been embodied by the survivors and to some extent prolonged by the second generation in the era of 'postmemory' will have to be created anew in the era of 'post memory'. This means that the link to this event will have to be reconstructed without the help of an indexical 'umbilical chord' (Hirsch 2009: 111) that had been a significant trope of the generation postmemory, but will have to rely solely on external and material forms, frames and genres of mediation.

How do the frames of transmission change with the rapidly growing temporal distance from the historical events and generation of the survivors? Next to historic sites and material objects, media will now define the frame of transmission. In a few years' time, the memory of the Holocaust will have to rely on images, narratives and information circulating across the globe along the channels of analogue and digital communication. In view of such a 'popularisation' and 'trivialisation', theorists of the older generation speak with bitterness of 'the end of the Holocaust' (see Rosenfeld 2011). For theorists of the younger generation such as Natan Sznaider and Daniel Levy, on the other hand, this is a source of optimism. They argue that thanks to the transmission of Holocaust memory through the channels of popular culture in the last decades of the twentieth century, it has acquired the status of a global, universal or cosmopolitan memory.

The urgent question, however, is: what will be the quality of this memory in the future? Is it still possible and justified to apply the term 'memory' in the era of 'post memory'? How can memory create 'an affective link' to a more and more distant past in the true sense of 'an embodied "living connection"' (Hirsch 2009: 111)? Since there is no possibility to prolong, extend or transfer existing memories, the only alternative is to *recreate* as memory what already exists in a mediated form in the archives. Memory, in other words, will become a project of revival through production and reception in the domain of cultural media (see Bayer 2010). This is the context in which a new notion of the 'secondary witness' comes into play.

'The passing of the survivor does not mean the passing of witness' (1998: 39). Using this quote from Geoffrey Hartman, we can reintroduce the concept of the secondary witness as an important figure in the long-term guardianship of Holocaust memory. As the survivor who had been a primary witness disappears as a living resource and point of reference, the act of witnessing has to be transferred to secondary witnesses who can take shape in flesh and blood in generations to come. The term 'secondary witness' without a generational limit was first introduced by Terrence Des Pres and Lawrence Langer (see Hartman 1998: 38). While the primary witness is severely damaged by what he or she witnesses, the secondary witness is an onlooker who is exposed only to media representations that stimulate his or her imagination. This contact to the trauma does not take place in a (belated) real life context but in the mediated shape of a symbolic and artistic form that does not endanger the physical integrity of the spectator. In the absence of living testimonies, the secondary witness is only confronted with symbolic representations. This position is open to any person. What counts is the mode of reception in which this encounter takes place. According to Hartman, a secondary witness deals with the Holocaust not as an event in *history* that is receding into a more and more distant past, but as an event in *memory* that retains its charge in the present and into the future. Receiving it as a memory means that it is received in the modes of identification, ethics or empathy with consequences for one's own life, value system and actions. *Receiving* in this sense means *responding* to a representation of the Holocaust. The important hypothesis is here that a 'punctum', in Roland Barthes' sense of an affective link between the viewer and the image, can be recreated and re-experienced in a new media setting. This experiential quality can indeed occur when viewing a film, reading a book or paying attention to a video testimony. In the era of post memory, writes Hartman, 'so much of value that had been build up cannot be recovered or transmitted. The novel, the memoir, the oral testimony must then supplement history writing, help it to become the bearer of a retrospective "thick description," saving bits and pieces that could seed a renewal' (2007: 24). In such a situation the secondary witness recasts his or her relation between the present and the past, between documentation and projection, between internal and external images, and between the self and others who are enlarging the circle of concerns. Through such a punctum, new mnemonic energy is injected into the stream of transmission. It is such creative and receptive acts of which the 'living chain of transmission' could be composed in the era of post memory.

From the start, creating and referring to representations and mediation had been an integral part of Holocaust memory. After the passing of the survivors, however, the future of the Holocaust will *solely* be grounded in symbolic representations such as books and performances, films and exhibitions. Will these texts and images be perceived as passing history or as an abiding memory, and what will determine the difference? It is a specific form of empathy that will turn the mere spectator into a secondary witness. This response is based on intellectual interest, active imagination, emotional investment and ethical engagement. The empathic listener and spectator assume the role of a 'witness for the witness' who 'actively receives words that reflect the darkness of the event' (Hartman 1998: 48). Participation in such a memory creates an 'affective community' (see Halbwachs 1992: 30–3) that is independent from the filiations created by blood or nation or religion. Dominick LaCapra speaks in this context of the 'labor of listening and attending that exposes the self to empathetic understanding and hence to at least muted trauma' (1992: 40). Empathy is an imaginative act that works on the level of media presentations, creating the human possibility to think and feel in the position of another without blurring the distance between self and other. Empathy can be blunted, worn out and blocked, but it can also be trained and cultivated by visual and verbal art to expand the realm of experience of the self to include into our circle of concern the suffering and experience of others who are not like us.

CONCLUSION

'No one bears witness for the witness' ('Niemand / zeugt für den / Zeugen'). This verse from 'Aschenglorie', a poem by Paul Celan (1967: 68), describes the situation of the 1950s and 1960s when the survivors were left alone with their trauma and testimonies. The future transmission of Holocaust memory is again precarious; it depends on secondary witnesses who create and receive texts, images and performances that elicit responses and resonance within the framework of an affective community. In doing so, secondary witnesses have both the potential and responsibility to transform the symbolic archive of representations into a living memory; they are a link, a hinge and a relay in the chain of transmission.

Saul Friedlander, a child survivor, has repeatedly referred to the 'deep memory' of the Holocaust as a persistent legacy. With this term he refers to the affective legacy of the traumatised survivor and to the generation of postmemory that prevents the possibility of closure. He sees the problem of the future of Holocaust memory in the threat of closure: 'The question remains whether at the collective level as well an event such as the Shoah may, after all the survivors have disappeared, leave traces of a deep memory beyond individual recall, which will defy any attempt to give it meaning' (1994: 254). We have ample reason to assume that this deep memory will motivate generations of writers, readers, artists and viewers in the future to confront the insuperable moral outrage and unsolvable conundrum of the Holocaust as an ongoing emotional, aesthetic and intellectual challenge.

Notes

1 Dominick LaCapra (1992) comments on the different subject positions depending on historical affiliations when he emphasises that the same statement can take on different meanings if uttered by people with different connections to the events.
2 Martin Walser also distanced himself repeatedly from the hypocritical desire to change sides

from perpetrator to victim in the emotional framing of personal memory. Could it be possible, he asked in his speech delivered 1998 in the Frankfurt Paulskirche, that those 'after having worked in the gruesome service of memory work, feel a little less guilty and a bit closer to the victims than to the perpetrators? A momentary suspension of the inexorable contrast between victims and perpetrators. I have never thought it possible to leave the side of the guilty' (1988: 4; my translation).

3 *Junge Muslime in Auschwitz: Dem Antisemitismus entgegentreten.* Documentary, shown by WDR Television on 21 October 2014; see http://www1.wdr.de/fernsehen/kultur/west-art-magazin/sendungen/jungenprojektduisburg100.html

Bibliography

Arendt, Hannah (1966) *The Origins of Totalitarianism*. New York: Harcourt, Brace & World.

Assmann, Aleida (2013) *Ist die Zeit aus den Fugen? Aufstieg und Niedergang des Zeitregimes der Moderne*. Munich: Hanser.

Assmann, Aleida and Linda Shortt (eds) (2012) *Memory and Political Change*. London: Palgrave Macmillan.

Bayer, Gerd (2010) 'After Postmemory: Holocaust Cinema and the Third Generation', *Shofar*, 28, 4, 116–32.

Butler, Judith (2009) *Frames of War: When is Life Grievable?* New York: Verso.

Celan, Paul (1967) *Atemwende*. Frankfurt: Suhrkamp.

Churchill, Winston (1948) *The Sinews of Peace: Post-War Speeches*, ed. Randolph S. Churchill. London: Cassell.

Epstein, Helen ([1979] 2010) *Children of the Holocaust: Conversations with Sons and Daughters of Survivors*. Lexington, MA: Plunkett Lake Press.

Friedlander, Saul (1994) 'Trauma, Memory, and Transference', in Geoffrey H. Hartman (ed.) *Holocaust Remembrance: The Shapes of Memory*. Oxford: Blackwell, 252–63.

Gintis, Harold and Samuel Bowles (2009) *A Cooperative Species: Human Reciprocity and its Evolution*. Princeton, NJ: Princeton University Press.

Halbwachs, Maurice (1992) *On Collective Memory*, ed. and trans. Lewis A. Coser. Chicago: Chicago University Press.

Hartman, Geoffrey H. (1998) 'Shoah and Intellectual Witness', *Partisan Review*, 65, 1, 37–48.

____ (2007) *A Scholar's Tale. Intellectual Journey of a Displaced Child of Europe*. New York: Fordham.

Hirsch, Marianne (2009) 'The Generation of Postmemory,' *Poetics Today*, 29, 1, 103–28.

____ (2012) *The Generation of Postmemory: Writing and Visual Culture after the Holocaust*. New York: Columbia University Press.

Hoffman, Eva (2004) *After Such Knowledge: Memory, History, and the Legacy of the Holocaust*. New York: Public Affairs.

Jureit, Ulrike and Christian Schneider (2010) *Gefühlte Opfer: Illusionen der Vergangenheitsbewältigung*. Stuttgart: Klett.

Klüger, Ruth (2001) *Still Alive: A Holocaust Girlhood Remembered*. New York: Feminist Press.

Koselleck, Reinhart (2002) 'Formen und Traditionen des negativen Gedächtnisses', in Volkhart Knigge and Norbert Frei (eds) *Verbrechen erinnern: Die Auseinandersetzung mit Holocaust und*

Völkermord. Munich: Beck, 21–33.

LaCapra, Dominck (1992) 'Representing the Holocaust: Reflections on the Historians' Debate,' in Saul Friedlander (ed.) *Probing the Limits of Representations: National-Socialism and the 'Final Solution'*. Cambridge, MA: Harvard University Press, 108–27.

Levy, Daniel and Natan Sznaider (2006) *The Holocaust and Memory in the Global Age*. Philadelphia, PA: Temple University Press.

Margalit, Avishai (2003) *The Ethics of Memory*. Cambridge, MA: Harvard University Press.

Nussbaum, Martha (2001) *Upheavals of Thought: The Intelligence of Emotions*. Cambridge: Cambridge University Press.

Olick, Jeffrey (2007) *The Politics of Regret: On Collective Memory and Historical Responsibility*. New York and London: Routledge.

Rifkin, Jeremy (2009) *The Empathic Civilization: The Race to Global Consciousness in a World in Crisis*. Cambridge: Polity Press.

Rosenfeld, Alvin (2011) *The End of the Holocaust*. Bloomington, IN: Indiana University Press.

Rothberg, Michael (2009) *Multidirectional Memory: Remembering the Holocaust in the Age of Decolonization*. Stanford, CA: Stanford University Press.

Torpey, John (ed.) (2003) *Politics of the Past: On Repairing Historical Injustices*. Lanham, MD: Rowman & Littlefield.

Walser, Martin (1998) 'Erfahrungen beim Halten einer Sonntagsrede,' Reception Speech of the Peace Price in the Frankfurt Paul's Church, October 11. Online: http://opus.bsz-bw.de/hdms/volltexte/2005/488/pdf/walserRede.pdf

Wieviorka, Annnette (1994) 'On Testimony', in Geoffrey H. Hartman (ed.) *Holocaust Remembrance: The Shapes of Memory*. Oxford: Blackwell, 23–32.

Yerushalmi, Yosef H. (1995) *Diener von Königen und nicht Diener von Dienern*. Munich: Siemens Stiftung.

CHAPTER TWO

Supplementing *Shoah*:
CLAUDE LANZMANN'S *THE KARSKI REPORT* AND *THE LAST OF THE UNJUST*

Sue Vice

The two most recent releases of edited material from the outtakes of Claude Lanzmann's 1985 film *Shoah*, which are available to view in their entirety at the United States Holocaust Memorial Museum in Washington, seem to be at odds with each other in filmic and conceptual terms. In this essay, I will consider whether the concerns of *The Karski Report* (2010) and *The Last of the Unjust* (2013) are in fact so different, or whether they represent both a specific kind of meditation on the memory of the Holocaust, and a self-reflexive consideration of that memory as it is represented in *Shoah* itself.

The Karski Report is a focused, 48-minute long presentation of discarded material from Lanzmann's 1978 interview with the Polish envoy, extracts from which are among the best known of the encounters in *Shoah*. Jan Karski joined the Polish resistance in 1939 and acted clandestinely as a courier for the Polish government in exile. From 1942 onwards he reported to the Polish, British and US governments on the situation in Poland, including the destruction of the Warsaw Ghetto and the genocide of Poland's Jewish population. While the extracts in *Shoah* focus on the details of what Karski witnessed in the Ghetto and Izbica Lubelska, a satellite camp for Bełżec, into which he was smuggled, *The Karski Report* centres on the reception of his report by the Allied governments. Unlike the material in *Shoah*, the newly released film does not show any location other than that of the interview setting itself, in Karski's home in Washington. In *Shoah*,

Karski recounts, at some emotional cost, what he saw and heard in the Warsaw Ghetto and Izbica Lubelska, and, as he speaks, we see footage of New York Harbor and the Statue of Liberty; while in *The Karski Report*, constituted from footage shot on the following day, he is more composed in telling Lanzmann how he passed on this eyewitness account to Franklin D. Roosevelt and Roosevelt's confidant, Felix Frankfurter. The focus of *The Karski Report* is almost claustrophobically limited to shots of varying length of Karski seated in his living-room and close-ups on what Lanzmann calls his 'extraordinary' face, interleaved with occasional two-shots in which the director is visible seated opposite him.

Fig. 1 Lanzmann and Karski: a formal interview

Fig. 2 Lanzmann and Murmelstein: an informal interview

By contrast, *The Last of the Unjust* consists of over three-and-a-half hours edited down from a ten-hour encounter with Benjamin Murmelstein from 1975, the very first interview ever undertaken by Lanzmann. In the released film, this material is extensively intercut with present-day and even archive film footage and photographs. None of the material from the encounter with Murmelstein appears in *Shoah*. Indeed, it is an interview with a kind of witness that is almost entirely absent from the 1985 film, since Murmelstein was one of the heads of wartime Jewish Councils. Such an encounter appears in *Shoah* only in its invocations of Adam Czerniakow, the leader of the Warsaw Ghetto Jewish Council who killed himself in 1942. Murmelstein, who had been a rabbi in Vienna before the war, became in December 1944 what turned out to be the last Jewish 'Elder' at Theresienstadt, a term arising, as the film's prologue has it, from a Nazi vocabulary of 'contempt and fear' possessing 'tribal' connotations. After the war, Murmelstein was exonerated of any misdeed by a Czech tribunal, although the prologue points out that 'the hatred of some of the survivors came to be focused upon him'.

Despite the two films appearing to be so different, *The Karski Report* and *The Last of the Unjust* have significant elements in common. In particular, they present a cinematic meditation on forms of knowledge about the Holocaust as these existed during World War II and afterwards, as well as a consideration of temporal distance which augments that in *Shoah*. Such a concern with modes of knowledge as they change over time is also evident metatextually, since both films' origins lie in Lanzmann's decision to return to

Shoah's outtakes in response to specific instances of contemporary cultural debate about the Holocaust's legacy. Thus, the new releases rely upon but also exceed the preoccupations and techniques of the earlier film.

THE KARSKI REPORT

The impetus for the release of *The Karski Report* lies in Lanzmann's response to Yannick Haenel's prize-winning novel *Jan Karski*, which draws upon the interview in *Shoah* and other documentary material, including Karski's own writings. The novel's third section features 'scenes, phrases and thoughts' which Haenel has 'invented' and attributed to Karski (2009: vii), including details that Lanzmann describes as filling him with 'shame and anger' (2010b). These moments include the fictional Karski accusing the director of 'injustice' in his representation of the Polish people, as well as the 'complete alteration' of the meaning of the envoy's own words, since *Shoah* includes 'only forty minutes' of the two-day interview (Haenel 2009: 179). Haenel's fictional Karski decides that Lanzmann must have moved the focus of his film away from that of the 'saving of the Jews', since only the account of his experience in the Ghetto, and not his invitation to report to Franklin Roosevelt and Felix Frankfurter in Washington, remains in the original film's final version; there is 'nothing' on his efforts to 'transmit the message' from the Jewish leaders to the Allies, nor about 'American indifference' to it (ibid.). Haenel is in part drawing on Karski's account of viewing *Shoah* on its release, in which the former envoy describes his regret at the omission from the film of any expression of the indifference of the 'leaders of nations', and the contrasting efforts of 'ordinary people', particularly in Poland, to save the Jews (1986: 174). Lanzmann's critical view of what Haenel describes as a 'homage' to *Shoah* is clear in his published comments (see Lanzmann 2010a and 2010b), but also in the film itself. Naturally, *The Karski Report*'s meaning is not confined to answering back to Haenel. However, in a sense it can be considered to have done so, since the film's structure and technique convey a preoccupation with meta-questions about the nature of understanding and knowledge of the Holocaust, as much as the specific possibility of rescue in the face of the indifference on which Haenel focuses: a rescue which Lanzmann states in the prologue to have been in any case 'impossible'.

The Karski Report opens on a close-up of Jan Karski's face, in a short sequence reproduced from *Shoah*, and we hear again the words from the conclusion to his interview there: 'But I reported … what I saw.' Lanzmann says of this moment in *Shoah* that it was the interview's only possible conclusion, since 'Everybody knows that the Jews were not rescued. [Karski] didn't need to say more. It was very strong to end that way' (quoted in Jeffries 2011). *The Karski Report* is thus both an edited version of the second day's interview (see Besson 2011), the absence of which Haenel's Karski laments, and a supplement to *Shoah*, following Jacques Derrida's sense in *Of Grammatology*, in that it is an addition to the film as well as an element crucial to understanding it. As Karski himself puts it, due to its 'self-limitation', *Shoah* 'has created the need for the next movie, equally great, equally truthful' (1986: 174). It is tempting to see *The Karski Report* as that 'next movie'. Karski's words imply both senses of supplementarity: that it might be an addition, 'a plenitude enriching another plenitude', or a substitute, one which 'adds only to replace' (Derrida 1974: 144). In an analogous manner, the later film self-consciously refers back to *Shoah* and appears to fulfil Karski's words from it ('I reported … what I saw'), yet has its own, supplementary meaning. In the prologue to *The Karski Report*, which takes the form of a scrolling text in English which is also read out by Lanzmann, we learn that the second day's material was omitted from *Shoah* 'for the properly artistic reasons of dramatic tension', since otherwise the section featuring Karski would have been too long, and because the latter 'acted very differently on the second day'. We see the truth of the latter observation in the brief, contrasting moment taken from *Shoah*, in which the close-up on Karski's face reminds us that his anguish was evident in a way it is not in the later film. The title *The Karski Report* itself has a double meaning, since it refers both to the report that the courier imparted in 1943, and to the account that we hear him give to Lanzmann. Although in the present we may possess the historical knowledge of genocide that Roosevelt and his confidant Frankfurter could not take in, it remains the case that, as Karski puts it, 'healthy humanity, rational humanity, who did not see it with their own eyes' cannot understand. The position of the audience of the past, including Roosevelt and Frankfurter, is taken up by the film's spectators in the present.

As Lanzmann claims, Karski's demeanour is different in this new film from that in *Shoah*, a difference not only embodied but perhaps maintained by his altered and even more formal attire. In *The Karski Report*, he is able to describe more objectively the response which overwhelmed him in *Shoah* – 'I am much weaker emotionally. I break down,' as he puts it of his post-war life – although even here his eyes glisten with unshed tears. For the most part, however, Karski has regained his composure, and the comforting hand on his shoulder, that of his wife, Pola Nirenska, which was visible in *Shoah*, is no longer present; indeed, Karski describes how, 'unable to bear it, she left the house' during the interview (1986: 174). His remarks are punctuated by cynical, mirthless laughter, a performative, and seemingly self-protective, mannerism that is not present in *Shoah*. This repeated quirk is evident, for instance, when Karski describes Roosevelt's offer of part of East Prussia to Poland in a post-war settlement, a suggestion which, he claims, the Polish ambassador, Jan Ciechanowski, 'loved' since he wished Poland to have it all. Karski's recounting the ambassador's words of advice about how to conduct himself in Roosevelt's presence has a metacinematic effect, in a film all about talking and listening. An auditory connection is established between the two moments of the delivery of the report and the time of the interview, some 35 years later, by Karski's account of the 'most intimate' moments in 1943 that passed between him and the ambassador when the latter walked his dog Groszek at night; in the present, Karski's own pet dog can be heard, although is never seen, shaking itself and panting, in a belated version of the past.

During their evening walks, Ciechanowski advised Karski to be very precise; not to talk too much, as was the latter's habit; and to attend to Roosevelt's questions, a piece of advice that has an ironic resonance for the spectator, since in the present Karski does not always answer Lanzmann but prefers to narrate his own story, and we discover that the President put no questions to the envoy. As he does in relation to the Jewish leaders in *Shoah*, here Karski reinhabits the persona of his interlocutor Roosevelt, and reproduces his words in a slow, deep voice, giving what one reviewer describes as 'a fair imitation of Roosevelt's pronunciation' of the word 'war': 'The Allied nations are going to win this war. No more wars. Justice will be done [...] The United States will not abandon your country.' Yet we learn that 'not a single' question followed Karski's words on the subject of the 'Jewish problem', although he phrased this in incontrovertible terms: 'Mr President, the situation is horrible. Without the outside help, the Jews will perish in Poland.' Karski replies to Lanzmann's response, 'Did he understand the fantastic emergency?', with just the kind of concision that Ciechanowski urged: 'I think [he] did not.' Instead, Roosevelt asked his visitor about different matters, and suggested that Karski deliver his report to other individuals, one of whom was Frankfurter, an Associate Justice of the Supreme Court and Roosevelt's close colleague. Unlike his fictional counterpart in Haenel's novel, Karski interprets these referrals to imply that Roosevelt was 'interested in the Jewish problem' but that it was 'not of his direct jurisdiction'.

Yet the centre of the film is not Karski's encounter with the President, as Haenel's version implies, although the notion of failing to understand what one has heard appears here for the first time. The time devoted to recounting this meeting is in the manner of an anticipatory prelude to that with Frankfurter. Karski describes the latter twice as a 'small man', in contrast to Roosevelt, who 'looked like a world leader' and one who became perceptibly 'smaller and smaller' as Karski repeated his report about the 'Jewish leaders, the Ghetto, Bełżec'. Such is the significance of this remembered scene that Karski allows Frankfurter to inhabit his own body as he gives a kinetic account of the Justice's response. First Karski casts his eyes to the floor, as Frankfurter did on hearing his story, then enacts the latter's standing up in order to declare that he 'must be totally honest' with the young man whose report he has just heard, of which he declares: 'I do not believe you!' Ciechanowski takes Frankfurter's words to cast doubt on Karski's reliability as a witness, for which the ambassador's presence was to vouch. However, it is not the envoy but his message to which Frankfurter refers, as he clarifies with formal precision, in a manner we perceive by means of Karski's reenactment: 'Mr. Ambassador, I did not say that he is lying. I said that I don't believe him. These are different things.' It is this utterance, in the form of Frankfurter's words ventriloquised by Karski, with its separation of knowledge and belief, that lies at the heart of *The Karski Report*, and constitutes the burden of its report to us as its spectators. We are far from Haenel's claim that footage of the second day's interview with Karski would offer a factual or moral counterbalance to that in *Shoah* by revealing Karski's own efforts to 'save the Jews', as his eponymous protagonist puts it. As Annette Wieviorka has argued, Haenel's Karski gives the Holocaust an 'a posteriori' central role in the encounter between Karski and Roosevelt which it did not have in 1943 (quoted in Dupuis 2010). In the film Karski makes a similar point, in observing that, at the time of his meeting, 'For me, the Jewish problem was not the only problem. For me, the key problem was Poland ... what was going to happen to the Polish nation?' As we saw in *Shoah*, it is with the hindsight of almost forty years that the 'Jewish problem' has assumed such a significance for Karski that, he claims here, 'I cannot handle it'. He expresses his own version of Frankfurter's inability to reconcile information with acceptance, even in his position as a firsthand witness. Now Karski speaks for himself: 'What I saw in this respect, Jewish extermination, is incomprehensible for me.' The tenses of Karski's utterance embody a psychic accuracy: despite his own act of witnessing in the past, the events remain incomprehensible in the present.

The moment of Frankfurter's supplemental utterance in *The Karski Report* offers not just a philosophical but a temporal challenge to the spectator, insisting on a belated return to a moment where the 'obscenity' of understanding, in Lanzmann's celebrated phrase, seemed first to be acknowledged (1991). In concluding this scene, Karski takes his head in his hands to reincarnate the Justice's own act of matching gesture to repudiation, and ventriloquises the latter's words: 'My mind, my heart, they are made in such a way that I cannot accept it. No! No!' In the interview's present, Karski's verdict on these words – 'It was a shock to me' – is matched by his action of sitting down, as if in defeat: we witness the abandonment of the persona of Frankfurter by means of the 'shock' of Karski's return to his seat and to his own first-person utterance. The film's temporal significance, and its efforts to retrieve the moment of 1943 in the present, is apparent in Lanzmann's response to Karski after his reenactment has ended. The director's question, 'Did you remember Warsaw when you were here in Washington?' uses the adverb 'here' to both geographical and temporal effect, referring not to the present moment of 1978 but to Karski's visit in 1943. Even more ambiguously, Lanzmann's question, 'Is it possible to grasp the destruction of the Jews, when one lives in Washington?' refers to Roosevelt and Frankfurter in wartime Washington, but also to the audience, in the present, watching this scene in the capital. Karski simply replies: 'At that time: probably not.'

Fig. 3 Karski acts out Felix Frankfurter's words

THE LAST OF THE UNJUST

The spare and apparently unified nature of *The Karski Report* is a contrast to the elaborately staged and stylised work that is *The Last of the Unjust*. While the former appeared very quickly after Lanzmann's broadside against Haenel's novel, *The Last of the Unjust* involved many months of shooting in different countries, work which was, as Lanzmann puts it, 'cinematographically difficult, and morally very trying' (quoted in Cannes Film Festival 2013). This film's title quotes Murmelstein's own self-designation, citing and reversing that of André Schwarz-Bart's 1959 novel, *The Last of the Just*, whose eponymous righteous men are to justify humanity's actions to God. Yet the title is ironised by the words we hear from Murmelstein during the film's duration and by their framing, implying that he is, rather, justifying himself to human judges. The original interview with Murmelstein was recorded in Rome, as the first of Lanzmann's decade-long efforts to collect the material that went to constitute *Shoah*. In this sense *The Last of the Unjust* is a fitting late release in 'coming full circle' (Macnab 2014) back to the director's earliest work, following Derrida's argument that a supplementary entity might precede what it supplements, belatedly 'taking the place' of a film that is 'already significant' (1974: 281). In *The Last of the Unjust* the process of editing has produced a sense of formal and verbal 'circling' around its protagonist and his experiences. The interview took place before any other material for *Shoah* was gathered, and certainly long before the process of cutting for that film made clear that its 'organising principle' would be that of 'death' and 'the process of extermination', as Lanzmann's editor puts it (Postec 2011). Thus, the interview with Murmelstein 'did not fit with the rest of the film' in its focus on the difficulty of survival (Lanzmann quoted in Macnab 2014), and, in 1980s France, on the spectre of collaboration (see Wildmann 2011: 123).

Lanzmann appears in two guises in *The Last of the Unjust*; as the young, 'fashionably coiffed' interviewer who is for the most part located just off-screen, sometimes apparent in a two-shot, and, in the present, visible as the 'silver-haired eminence' and narrator (see Hoberman 2014), his lone presence in the frame emphasising Murmelstein's absence almost forty years on. Murmelstein likewise appears in two visual guises, as a young man in the past, and his present-day aged self. For most of the film's duration, the camera's focus is on the former Elder's seventy-year-old yet 'cherubic' face (see Scott 2014) as he speaks in fast, high-pitched bursts. Lanzmann and the translator Angelika Schrobsdorff are sometimes visible sitting beside him, or reflected in Murmelstein's dark glasses when the camera closes in on him. The contrast this structure offers to the shot/reverse-shot representation of interviewer and subject in *The Karski Report*, where the former envoy sits by himself opposite Lanzmann, sums up the difference in the latter's interrogative personae. Where he is conventionally attired and formal in his dealings with Karski,

Lanzmann is informal in both dress and manner with Murmelstein, to whom he reacts with a sense of humour and warmth.

Murmelstein also appears in the film as the youthful Deputy to Paul Eppstein, his predecessor as the Elder of the Jews, in a photograph taken during the war at a Theresienstadt council meeting. At this meeting Eppstein gave a speech about the 'embellishment' ('*Stadtverschönerung*') of the ghetto, planned by the Nazis as a way of convincing a delegation of the Danish Red Cross during their visit in June 1944 that Theresienstadt was a 'model ghetto'. Murmelstein describes himself as 'listening attentively' to Eppstein's speech, and indeed this seems to be what we see of him in the photograph. In its context here, this image stands in for footage cut from the 1944 propaganda film *The Führer Gives the Jews a City*, extracts from which are included in *The Last of the Unjust*. Although the presence of such material, alongside the reproductions of inmates' drawings of the camp and photographs, may appear to fly in the face of Lanzmann's much-debated repudiation of the visual archive, what we see is not given the status of documentary imagery. The film extracts and drawings are clearly marked as representations, used as cinematic signifiers to varied effect as the narratorial Lanzmann speaks in the present. While extracts from *The Führer Gives the Jews a City* lay bare Nazi deception even as they show the prisoners' faces, the drawings represent the 'reverse world' of the camp as those prisoners experienced it. Murmelstein was included in the Nazis' film along with Eppstein, but this material was excised after the latter's execution, since, in Murmelstein's sardonic words, 'a dead Elder of the Jews can't be used for propaganda'. Thus the presence of the photograph signifies not just a past moment, but stands for the atrocities that underlay the 'mask' of the camp.

Since Lanzmann appears in *The Last of the Unjust* in footage taken both at the beginning of his career and towards its end, the film is in part a meditation on his own status as an auteur. Indeed, the impetus to make the film came from Lanzmann's presence at an unauthorised screening at the Austrian Film Museum in Vienna in 2007 of some of the unedited material from Murmelstein's interview, which he claims made him feel as if he had been 'robbed', a response akin to his accusing Haenel and his novel of being 'parasites' on *Shoah* (see Lanzmann 2010b; Cannes Film Festival 2013). *The Last of the Unjust* is the outcome of his assertion of ownership by making 'a proper cinematic work' out of the footage which had been shown in its unedited, and thus unsupplemented, state, transforming it into 'art', in Richard Brody's term (2013). Thus the epithet 'unjust' comes to refer to the director as well as his interlocutor, as the film's closing sequence suggests in showing the two men walking away arm-in-arm from the camera. The film as released by Lanzmann exhibits a tension between its documentary, or even polemical, qualities, and those which are cinematic and philosophical, and is at its most striking when the two are blended together. In relation to its historical significance, the press release for the Cannes Film Festival describes the film as offering an 'unprecedented insight into the genesis of the Final Solution. It reveals the true face of Eichmann', whom Murmelstein describes as 'demonic, not banal', and 'exposes without artifice the savage contradictions of the Jewish Councils' (2013). Some critics even took Lanzmann to task for not releasing the film during Murmelstein's lifetime since it would have helped in rehabilitating his reputation (see Scott 2014). In aesthetic terms, the process of transforming 'raw' interview material into a self-contained film becomes clear if we contrast elements of the original ten hours of footage with the present version, which has been cut, refashioned and supplemented with other material.

Time and the process of aging are concerns that unite the historical and aesthetic elements of *The Last of the Unjust*, while also continuing *Shoah*'s efforts to reveal the existence of the past in the present moment. Such a preoccupation is evident in the film's structuring by means of a visual contrast between places and faces, as the press release puts it: it does not hide 'anything of the passage of time on men, but show[s] the incredible permanence of the locations' (Cannes Film Festival 2013). Thus we see present-day footage of Nisko in Poland, Vienna, Prague and Jerusalem shot at the time of Lanzmann's editing in the new millennium, as well as the skyline of Rome, in material from the original interview. The film's central geographical contrast is between Theresienstadt and Rome, and, in the mise-en-scène, tyrannies from different millennia appear in the form of their characteristic buildings. Among Lanzmann's first words to Murmelstein is his wish to use their conversation about Theresienstadt 'to return to this past'. However, a new topical concern emerges here in relation to the passage of time as it affected the human victims and witnesses of Nazi atrocity. In his introduction to the screenplay for *Un vivant qui passe* (1997), repeated in the prologue to *The Last of the Unjust*, Lanzmann notes that many of the prisoners in Theresienstadt were from the 'Grand Reich': those who, 'too old to begin their lives anew', relied for protection in Theresienstadt upon their status as *'Prominenten'*; that is, German or Austrian heroes of World War I, former government functionaries, well-known lawyers, doctors or artists. Murmelstein presents himself as having a particular concern for the old, in contrast to the first of Theresienstadt's three Elders, Jacob Edelstein, who 'cherished youth'. Murmelstein's comprehension of genocide was formed through witnessing the fate of these individuals. In 1939 he had to accompany an investigatory Nazi visit to the town of Nisko, as part of a projected plan of forced Jewish 'resettlement' to this area of southern Poland, where he saw at first hand 'the problem of the elderly' among the Viennese deportees. During the experimental Nisko episode, Murmelstein came to understand that deportation amounted to 'a death march' for the older evacuees, who, unlike those who were 'young and healthy', could not move quickly or for long distances, nor carry luggage through the muddy terrain, an 'image' which, as Murmelstein says some thirty years on, is 'still with me now'. A version of such an 'image' is shared with the spectator. Murmelstein's words are accompanied by a tracking shot of a path winding among trees in the environs of present-day Nisko, the pace

Fig. 4 Lanzmann in the Nisko forest

of the hand-held tracking shot imitating the slow steps of individuals who are necessarily absent. As Brett Ashley Kaplan argues, such imagery in a Holocaust context succeeds in transforming even a forest into a 'signifier of lost witnessing' (2008: 110).

In the interview's present moment, the seventy-year-old Murmelstein does not just recall his earlier interest in the fate of the old, but identifies himself with them, in a version of the 'reincarnation' which Lanzmann sought throughout *Shoah*. The interview opens with a wide panoramic shot of Rome which is accompanied by Lanzmann's remark to Murmelstein that it was hard to find him, as if we are seeing the very streets among which the director searched, and that he was told the former Elder was 'dead or very old'. Murmelstein's response – 'He is!' – is characteristically wry, but also reveals the dual nature of the threat to which he was exposed during the Holocaust years. The very possibility of surviving into a natural old age was a liability for the Elders, almost all of whom 'met a tragic end'. It is not simply that Murmelstein considers himself to be old, although he makes reference to his age matching the Biblical span of seventy years, and, apparently inaccurately, to his fading memory. As well as this, his status as not just the 'last' but the 'only one alive' among all of Europe's Holocaust-era Elders goes to the heart of the film's concern with Murmelstein's wartime role. Murmelstein's repeating the question put to him at Pankratz Prison in Prague after the war, where he freely submitted to imprisonment and trial, 'How come you're alive?', sums up the implication that the fact of survival itself might hint at collaboration or corruption. Thus the question posed by the officer at Pankratz addresses not just Murmelstein's age but also his behaviour, in a version of Lanzmann's query to the former Elder about whether saving himself and saving the ghetto were really 'the same thing', as Murmelstein claims, or if the former took precedence.

The moment of editing is also characterised by an identificatory link to the Nazis' victims, in the form of Lanzmann's implicitly likening himself to the older inmates of Theresienstadt. In the film's opening moments, the director reads extracts about the experience of new arrivals from Murmelstein's book, *Terezin: Il Ghetto-Modello di Eichmann* (1961), while standing on the platform at Bohušovice, the station which served the camp. Rather than the 'thermal spa with hotels and pensions' which the old people had been led to expect, they were met at Bohušovice with SS brutality and the theft of their belongings. Lanzmann's reading out the description of the passengers' 'hoary heads' as they anxiously 'peered out' of the train as it drew into the station associates the arrival of the old people with his own 'silver-haired' presence on the same platform. The next scene shows the remaining camp buildings and equally links the director with the old people of the past. His slow and cautious ascent of a flight of worn wooden stairs into a dark attic is followed by his continuing to read from Murmelstein's book about the fate of the aged, who had to sleep in such quarters under the roof and could only reach the washing facilities by means of an 'endless flight of stairs', an 'impossible enterprise' which left these former surgeons and lawyers 'lying in the dust and in their own excrement'. The camera, in its slow pan around the interior of the dark and deserted buildings, invites us to relive the horrified gaze of the people who arrived there.

Fig. 5 Lanzmann at Bohušovice station

However, such a process of associative identification on Lanzmann's part is not entirely the same as the 'reincarnation' that takes place in *Shoah*, by means of which individuals re-inhabit their own past, but represents an empathy that is shown to us cinematically as Lanzmann 'films himself into' this history (Brody 2013). The director's climbing the stairs, as we see and hear him do in the present, reenacts and echoes the deathly events of the past. Indeed, Lanzmann's ascent constitutes another anticipatory foreshadowing, of a moment that occurs at the film's end but which took place earlier in his personal history. As Lanzmann and Murmelstein walk down a flight of steep wooden steps near Titus Arch in Rome, the younger man tries to help the elder by taking his arm, but Murmelstein gestures at Lanzmann to take his hand away. By the time of editing, it is Lanzmann who has assumed the mantle of age. The presence of these older men in the mise-en-scène conveys not just the invisibility of the murdered old people at Theresienstadt, whose 'prominent' status was not enough to save their lives, but constitutes the very embodiment of the passage of time and the fact that its retrieval is possible only filmically.

The interview's circling shape itself provides a formal answer to the question about Murmelstein's time at Theresienstadt, in its imitating the basis of his explanation: he claims that he survived 'because I had a tale to tell'. This phrasing is ambivalent, since the act of telling took place in the past, yet, like Karski's report, it continues into the present time of the interview, where Murmelstein is giving another account. Murmelstein describes himself, in one of his gender-shifting comparisons, as telling stories 'like Scheherazade' by making himself crucial to the illusion of Theresienstadt as a 'model ghetto'. His assertion that he and the other leading 'Prominenten' were 'weaving the thread of the ghetto' hints at another mythological figure, that of Penelope, who deferred an unwanted outcome by making sure that her act of weaving had no end. Soon after the execution of Eppstein at Theresienstadt in late September 1944, a mass transport 'to the East' of five thousand working men was demanded by the camp commandant in order, according to Lanzmann, to ensure that no revolt took place. Murmelstein's commentary on this takes place in terms of the notion of the spinning and weaving of a falsely positive narrative directed at the outside world, one that was crucial in preventing the ghetto's liquidation: 'When the thread of stories was broken by the October transports we had to mend it.' Such a necessity – 'we had to' – arises from the Nazis' imperatives as well as those of self-preservation.

Lanzmann, in the present, emphasises the horror of life at Theresienstadt, just that aspect which he accuses Murmelstein of omitting from his account in the interview, and describes existence at the camp as the product of a combination of 'deception and raw violence'. Like Scheherazade, whose stories staved off the threat of execution, Murmelstein's life depended on how crucial he could make himself to this imposture. The speech that he, as Elder, was asked to prepare for the Red Cross visit of April 1944, one which had to be approved by Himmler, seemed to mean that Murmelstein 'could not be so easily killed', as was the usual fate of the Elders. However, the SS, in any case in a state of confusion as the war's ending neared, were faced with the dilemma of whether to make him the object of the camp's savage reality or to keep him as an element of its façade: 'either to gas me or to present me to the Red Cross', in Murmelstein's phrasing. As Lanzmann drily responds, 'That's quite a choice.' Murmelstein claims that the SS could not decide and gave up.

Indeed, the image of the thread or string is itself woven throughout Murmelstein's account, as a figure for malign manipulation by the Fates as well as one for narrative itself. He disputes Gideon Hausner's description at the Eichmann Trial of the Elders as simple tools, suggesting that if they were marionettes, they had to 'pull [their] own strings'. In dialogue from the ten-hour version of the interview, but cut from *The Last of the Unjust*, Murmelstein invokes the knots in *tzitzit*, that is, the fringes of a *tallit*, or prayer-shawl, as another kind of symbolic 'thread'. Like Theresienstadt itself, the very name of which, as Murmelstein puts it, constituted a 'camouflage word' for extermination, the *tzitzit* signified on two levels. In the present, Murmelstein interprets the prayer shawl, with its blending of cotton and wool, as a kind of 'knot writing' about peace between the different constituencies of settled farmer and nomadic shepherd, an implicit reference to the rivalry that led to Cain's murder of Abel. By shocking contrast, he describes a wartime incident in which the Nazis took a shawl's knotted fringes to be a kind of 'pigeon post' of secret communication, and executed a Jew simply for being in possession of a *tallit*. Murmelstein's characterisation of his outraged response to this news – 'It was too much!' – shows that, for the Jews under Nazi rule, such threads could become simply another occasion for atrocity. Thus the extreme battle for meaning and interpretation during the Holocaust years continues into the present for the spectator, who is invited by the former Elder himself to 'condemn' yet not to 'judge'. While such a distinction has puzzled the film's reviewers, since condemnation is hard to arrive at in the absence of judgement (see, for instance, Scott 2014), Murmelstein's remark seems to be a challenge, like Karski's more meditative one, arising from the inability of those on the outside of events to comprehend them.

The Last of the Unjust, like *The Karski Report* and the whole of *Shoah* itself, consists of material that has been edited from the original eleven-minute reels of interview footage in order to constitute an artistic whole. As Daniel Wildmann (2011) argues, in an article published before the film's release, many different works with varying significance could be created from the unedited material. This is evident in the present film in the supplementation of interview material with such historical documents as drawings by Theresienstadt inmates, chosen to accompany Lanzmann's voiceover about, for instance, the use of hearses to serve the living in this 'world upside-down'. The film's sequences have been structured to conclude on significant moments, isolated from their earlier unedited context. For example, Murmelstein's ironic quotation of Eichmann's horribly bathetic warning at Nisko, that because the water was contaminated new wells had to be dug, 'otherwise ... it means dying', has been edited to act as the conclusion to a sequence. Murmelstein's citation of this utterance is followed by a cut to present-day footage of the town and its nearby fields. In the original interview, by contrast, even Murmelstein's twice quoting Eichmann's words does not make them stand out from the surrounding anecdotes about individuals and comments on his own memory, all of which has been omitted from *The Last of the Unjust*.

The present film's ending, in which Lanzmann and Murmelstein walk through Titus Arch together, takes a more definitive form in *The Last of the Unjust* than in the original interview, where it also occurred on the last day of the two men's encounter but did not constitute its final moment. Critics have responded in varying ways to the artistically crafted version, which is notable for ending in Rome and not returning to Lanzmann's commentary in the present. Geoffrey Macnab argues that the final shot, in which Lanzmann has his arm around the former Elder as they walk away from the camera, their conversation now inaudible, resembles that showing 'Claude Rains and Humphrey Bogart at the end of *Casablanca*' (2014). This implies that the 'beautiful friendship' between Lanzmann and Murmelstein – the director has since described how he 'came to love' his interviewee (quoted in Jeffries 2011) – arises, like that between Louis and Rick in Michael Curtiz's 1942 film, as the result of both men having renounced the personal for the sake of the political. Scott sees in the 'final gesture' of Lanzmann's film a different, metatextual connection between the former Elder and his interviewer, that of the recognition of 'one wily, ambitious adventurer' by another, one which is hinted at in the film's title. While the black leather jackets worn by both men make this similarity a visual one, considering Lanzmann in such a light in 1975 is to 'project our knowledge backwards', to quote Murmelstein.

Fig. 6 Lanzmann and Murmelstein walk towards Titus Arch

Yet such a reliance on present knowledge is hard to avoid. The conclusion to *The Last of the Unjust* may seem elegiac to a contemporary audience, in its appearance and in the dialogue. The 1970s film stock intensifies the impression of autumnal Roman sunshine with its nostalgically grainy, low-contrast look, particularly when set against the sharply defined, dark-hued sequences from the wintry present. Murmelstein's final words in this setting are a reference to himself as an individual and as a historical anachronism: he claims that the Jewish Elder is 'like a dinosaur on the highway', and the 'problem' of such a phenomenon will be solved when the dinosaur vanishes and the highway is left 'free for cars'. Only the knowledge that Lanzmann and Murmelstein are walking on the Via Sacra, itself a Roman version of a 'highway', could make us question whether the former Elder is right to associate the road with the future and himself with oblivion. The spectator might rather conclude that, like the thread, the road is a figure for narrative and history as they carry such figures as the former Elder, and the film's director, into the future. But the apparently teleological road represents another circling shape, since the past is visually rewound for us in the form of the old film footage.

A return to the original footage may also supplement what critics have taken to be the film's omissions. J. Hoberman takes Lanzmann to task for 'mak[ing] no mention [of] Murmelstein's well-known identification with the first-century historian and erstwhile priest Flavius Josephus, who was at once a Jewish patriot and a Roman collaborator' (2014). Such an observation implies that the explicit discussion of Josephus from the original interview should not have been edited out of the released version, since, in the outtakes, Murmelstein declares that the historian Zdenek Lederer called him 'the second Josephus' (1953: 167), perhaps in reference to the Roman-Jewish historian's seeming to benefit personally from the suffering of his people. This is an argument that Murmelstein naturally repudiates. Yet the setting, with the arch in prolonged view, makes the spectator keep this likeness in mind throughout the film's conclusion (see Wildmann 2011: 116). In the outtakes, Lanzmann introduces the sequence set on the Via Sacra by asking of Murmelstein's choice of location, 'Why Titus Arch? What is the symbolism?' In *The Last of the Unjust*, the visual has come to stand in for the verbal, since this question has not been included. Instead, we see the first-century arch itself, which commemorates the Roman destruction of the second Temple in Jerusalem, an action led by the very Emperor Titus for whom Josephus acted as translator. Although a large *menorah* features in relief in one of the arch's friezes depicting Roman plunder, we do not see it. Both the notion of theft and the image of the *menorah* are visually emphasised in the film, in relation to the Roman and also the more recent past. For Murmelstein, Nazi plunder is a 'red thread' that runs throughout the 'whole story' of Theresienstadt, since the 'emigration funds' associated with the camp were crucial in allowing Eichmann and its other overseers to amass independent funds. A large commemorative *menorah* of a different kind has already appeared in the mise-en-scène, represented in a tracking shot of the graveyard at present-day Theresienstadt. In the twenty-first-century present, the *menorah* does not glorify but laments Jewish destruction.

CONCLUSION

Both *The Karski Report* and *The Last of the Unjust* present cinematic acts of utterance in a way that implies, as *Shoah* did on its release in 1985, that documentary evidence is not sufficient in considering in the present the significance of wartime genocide. Eric Kohn describes *The Karski Report* as 'weighted with psychological intrigue' (2011), and this is true of *The Last of the Unjust* too: each represents an epistemological conundrum, in relation to outsiders' varying ability to comprehend the reality of mass murder, of which the experience of the former Jewish leaders is one element. While the 'report' of the one film's title assumes the burden of knowledge of genocide, the 'unjust' in the other is an ambiguous and ironic designation. Such commonality is striking despite the films' formal differences. Both have been edited to offer a particular look. In the case of *The Karski Report* the interview footage has been 'remodeled', in Rémy Besson's phrase (2011), to appear as a real-time meditation returning us to the moment of learning about genocide. Thus it includes no landscape footage or narration, apart from a prologue which concludes with the words of Raymond Aron, on being asked if he knew what was happening in the East: 'I knew, but I didn't believe it, and because I didn't believe it, I didn't know.' *The Last of the Unjust* is more self-consciously mediated, as a film which layers more kinds of visual material from a greater range of temporal and historical sources than does any other of Lanzmann's works, yet it presents analogous questions. Both films are portraits of the artist as well as of their protagonists, by reason of the impetus for their release and the explicit framing of each in terms of Lanzmann's contemporary role, paratextually in

The Karski Report's title crawl, intradiegetically in his role as character-narrator in *The Last of the Unjust*.

These recently released films are entirely fitting supplements to *Shoah*, and it might be that Lanzmann will be inspired or provoked to release more films consisting of other, currently unedited, footage from the outtakes. These might include, for instance, material which seems to represent failed or unconventional encounters. Examples of such material could be the footage of Leib Garfunkel, which shows this extraordinarily surviving member of the Judenrat from the Kovno Ghetto in an interview which proceeds by means of Lanzmann's interpreter, Corinna Coulmas, reading from a book, Garfunkel's *The Destruction of Kovno's Jewry* (1959). By contrast, Lanzmann could not interview Rabbi Michael Weissmandl, who had died in 1957, and has to attempt a triangulated reconstruction of his voice and experience of escape from a train bound for Auschwitz, and efforts to bargain for the lives of Slovakian Jews in the face of Allied inaction, through the indirect testimony of others, including the scholars Siegmund Forst and Hermann Landau. Lastly, Lanzmann's attempt to speak to Gustav Laabs, one of his perpetrator interviewees, was thwarted because the one-time gas van operative who had worked at Chełmno was either not at home or not answering the door when the director called on him. In the place of an interview, in the outtakes we see Lanzmann reading from the transcript of Laabs' 1963 trial in Bonn, in accompaniment to the camera zooming in slowly to the curtained window of his apartment. Such a camera movement implies revelation, yet this is impossible. The window is an enigmatic reflective surface, the opacity of which is more obvious the closer we get, in another image of what Lanzmann calls, in the prologue to *The Karski Report*, the 'illegibility' of past events.

Notes

1. Karski believed that the camp into which he moved was Bełżec, but it has since been identified as Izbica Lubelska, a smaller death- and transit-camp nearby; see Karski, *Story of a Secret State*, editor's note, 446. Thanks for their help in completing this article to James Bell, André Bonzel, Tomasz Łysak, Beate Müller and Daniel Wildmann.
2. See such histories of the Judenräte as Isaiah Trunk's *Judenrat: The Jewish Councils in Eastern Europe Under Nazi Occupation* and, on Theresienstadt itself, Ruth Bondy's *'Elder of the Jews': Jacob Edelstein of Theresienstadt*.
3. Lanzmann's phrase 'the destruction of the Jews' has been substituted here for the original's 'Bełżec' in the soundtrack, presumably, as Besson argues, because it has now been established that this was not the camp that Karski visited (Besson 2011, n. 31).
4. For a discussion of this topic, see for instance Libby Saxton's *Haunted Images: Film, Ethics, Testimony and the Holocaust*.
5. A greater degree of ambivalence on the subject of age is expressed in the original interview, where, for instance, Murmelstein dismissively describes Leo Baeck as 'senile'.

6   We might think of another testifier's invocation of the *Iliad*, in Primo Levi's citation of Dante's 'Canto of Ulysses' in *If This Is a Man* (1947).
7   The outtakes were created by Claude Lanzmann during the filming of *Shoah* and are used and cited by permission of the United States Holocaust Memorial Museum and Yad Vashem, the Holocaust Martyrs' and Heroes' Remembrance Authority, Jerusalem.

Filmography

The Karski Report. Dir. Claude Lanzmann. France, 2010.
The Last of the Unjust. Dir. Claude Lanzmann. France/Austria, 2013.
Shoah. Dir. Claude Lanzmann. France, 1985.

Bibliography

Besson, Rémy (2011) '*The Karski Report*', Études photographiques, 27 May. Online: http://etudes-photographiques.revues.org/3467
Brody, Richard (2013) 'Claude Lanzmann's *The Last of the Unjust*', *New Yorker*, 27 September. Online: http://www.newyorker.com/culture/richard-brody/claude-lanzmanns-the-last-of-the-unjust
Cannes Film Festival (2013) Press release. Online: http://www.festival-cannes.com/assets/Image/Direct/048627.pdf
Derrida, Jacques (1974) *Of Grammatology*. Baltimore, MD: Johns Hopkins University Press.
Dupuis, Jérôme (2010) 'Pourquoi Lanzmann s'en est-il pris au Karski de Haenel?', *L'Express*, 10 February. Online: http://www.lexpress.fr/culture/livre/pourquoi-lanzmann-s-en-est-il-pris-au-karski-de-haenel_845729.html
Garfunkel, Leib (1959) *Kovnoh Hayehudit Behurbanah* [*The Destruction of Kovno's Jewry*]. Jerusalem: Yad Vashem.
Haenel, Yannick (2009) *Jan Karski: Roman*. Paris: Gallimard.
Hoberman, J. (2014) '*The Last of the Unjust*, the New Film by the Director of *Shoah*, is a Moral and Aesthetic Blunder', *Tablet*, 5 February. Online: http://tabletmag.com/jewish-arts-and-culture/161448/last-of-the-unjust-lanzmann-hoberman82
Jeffries, Stuart (2011) 'Claude Lanzmann on why Holocaust Documentary *Shoah* Still Matters', *The Guardian*, 9 June, 14.
Kaplan, Brett Ashley (2008) 'Exposing Violence, Amnesia and the Fascist Forest through Susan Silas and Collier Schorr's Holocaust Art', *Images: A Journal of Jewish Art and Culture*, 2, 110–28.
Karski, Jan ([1986] 2007) '*Shoah*', in Stuart Liebman (ed.) *Claude Lanzmann's 'Shoah': Key Essays*. New York: Oxford University Press, 171–4.
____ (2012) *Story of a Secret State: My Report to the World*. 1946. Trans. Krystyna Sokolowska. London: Penguin.
Kohn, Eric (2011) 'Claude Lanzmann Revisits Jan Karski in *The Karski Report*', *Indiewire*, 3 March. Online: http://www.indiewire.com/article/review_the_karski_report
Lanzmann, Claude (1991) '"The Obscenity of Understanding": An Evening with Claude Lanzmann',

American Imago, 48, 473–95.

____ (1997) *Un vivant qui passe: Auschwitz 1943 – Theresienstadt 1944*. Paris: Gallimard.

____ (2010a) 'Jan Karski de Yannick Haenel: un faux roman.' *Marianne* 23 January. http://www.marianne.net/Jan-Karski-de-Yannick-Haenel-un-faux-roman_a184324.html.

____ (2010b) 'Non, Monsieur Haenel, je n'ai en rien censuré le témoinage de Jan Karski', *Le Monde*, 30 January. Online: http://www.lemonde.fr/idees/article/2010/01/30/non-monsieur-haenel-je-n-ai-en-rien-censure-le-temoignage-de-jan-karski_1298986_3232.html

Lederer, Zdenek (1953) *Ghetto Theresienstadt*. New York: Howard Fertig.

Murmelstein, Benjamin (1961) *Terezin: Il Ghetto-Modello di Eichmann*. Bologna: Cappelli.

Macnab, Geoffrey (2014) 'Return to *Shoah*: Claude Lanzmann's New Film *The Last of the Unjust* Revisits Holocaust Epic', *The Independent*, 14 March, 29.

Postec, Ziva (2011) 'Le montage du film *Shoah*', *Kef Israël*, 26 January. Online: http://kefisrael.com/2011/01/26/le-montage-du-film-shoah-ziva-postec/

Saxton, Libby (2008) *Haunted Images: Film, Ethics, Testimony and the Holocaust*. London and New York: Wallflower Press.

Scott, A. O. (2014) 'Eichmann's Rabbi Gazes Backward', *New York Times*, 6 February. Online: http://www.nytimes.com/2014/02/07/movies/lanzmanns-the-last-of-the-unjust-hears-a-wily-survivor.html?_r=0

Schwarz-Bart, André (1959) *The Last of the Just*, trans. Stephen Becker. New York: Atheneum.

Wildmann, Daniel (2011) 'Emotionen, Körper, Mythen: Lanzmann interviewt Murmelstein', in Ronny Loewy and Katharina Rauschenberger (eds) *'Der Letzte der Ungerechten': Der 'Judenälteste' Benjamin Murmelstein in Filmen 1945–1975*. Frankfurt: Campus Verlag, 101–24.

CHAPTER THREE

The Act of Digging:
ARCHAEOLOGY, PHOTOGRAPHY AND FORENSICS IN *BIRTHPLACE* AND *HOLOCAUST BY BULLETS*

Brad Prager

Excavation is a practice associated with archaeology, and contemporary Holocaust documentaries now and again centre on the process of digging. As a discipline, archaeology is associated chiefly with ancient history, and it deals in general with prehistoric societies, ones that left only fragmentary traces behind. In this sense, one might similarly describe the last moments of Holocaust victims with reference to a deficit of written records. The practices of archaeology can, for this reason, be central. Particularly when one considers the atrocities in the East – the murderous work of the *Einsatzgruppen* and the mass killings at the Operation Reinhard camps – as cases in which large numbers of people were executed, and much of the evidence was wiped away. The goal is not to misconstrue the word archaeology, which is primarily concerned with the distant past, but rather to analyse Holocaust excavations and the search for traces as, in some sense, archaeological pursuits. In a number of contemporary Holocaust documentaries unearthed objects, especially the bones of victims, are given an ostensibly authentic status parallel to that of archival photographs. Contemporary portraits of human remains compete with archival images for predominance. Where have documentary films situated themselves in relation to these forensic displays?

Forensics is, in part, about establishing truth, which is a particularly weighted enterprise where the Holocaust and Holocaust denial are concerned. Excavations can unearth incontrovertible forensic evidence, yet legal scholars have suggested that we suffer from an overinvestment in that science. Today, forensics has a unique epistemological status, owing in some measure to its expanded employment in the popular imagination, for example, in CBS's popular media franchise *CSI* (*Crime Scene Investigation*), which depicts a world in which all crimes can be solved and prosecuted forensically. Some theorists have been troubled by that television programme's impact on how potential jurors rely on particular kinds of evidence. N. J. Schweitzer and Michael Saks offer the hypothesis that programmes of that sort have 'raised the public's expectations for the kind of forensic-science evidence that could and should be offered at trials' such that jurors are 'disappointed by the real evidence with which they are presented'; they argue that jurors may end up acquitting more defendants because 'in court they are not seeing enough forensic science to persuade them of guilt' (2007: 358). Moreover, *CSI* may have 'fooled the public into thinking that forensic science is far more effective and accurate than it actually is' (ibid.). Along similar lines, Simon Cole and Rachel Dioso-Villa worry that forensic science may 'tempt jurors to abandon law as a truth-making enterprise altogether in favor of science' (2006/7: 469). Central to the latter account is that both law and forensic science are viewed as competing 'truth-making' enterprises. Forensic science may have more than a merely evidentiary value; science itself is viewed as the conveyor of truth.

In June 1985 a skeleton was exhumed in Brazil. According to Rolf Mengele the skeleton belonged to his father Josef, who died there in a swimming accident six years earlier, and forensic data confirmed that the bones belonged to the notorious Nazi experimenter. Thomas Keenan and Eyal Weizman argue that a decisive cultural turn was taking place at that time: 'In the period coinciding with the discovery of Mengele's skeleton, scientists began to appear in human rights cases as expert witnesses, called to interpret and speak on behalf of things – often bones and human remains' (2012: 13). A report about Mengele's bones, signed by experts from the Simon Wiesenthal Center, including Clyde Snow, a renowned specialist in bone analysis, argued that the exhumed skeleton was Mengele's 'within a reasonable scientific certainty' (Blumenthal 1985: 8). The forensic investigators relied on an 'innovative West German photographic comparison in which pictures of the exhumed skull were matched on a video terminal to known photos of Dr. Mengele from his Nazi file in 1938'; the technique was described as 'most convincing' by the expert anthropologist quoted in the *New York Times* (ibid.). Moreover, 'pathological and radiological tests showed an old healed fracture of the right hip, which the experts said may have been the result of a motorcycle accident at Auschwitz that Dr. Mengele was known to have suffered on June 21, 1943'; the article then adds that, 'the actual medical record' of that Auschwitz accident 'has not been located' (ibid.).

To be clear: Mengele was by no means a victim. The story of his skeleton, however, can be understood as symptomatic of a high-profile moment in the history of Holocaust forensics. In 1992 the skeletal remains were retested for DNA, and it was proven, once again, that Mengele died in Brazil more than a decade earlier. The bones were at the centre of that examination. Using DNA fingerprinting, or 'compar[ing] tests from one of the bones with blood samples submitted by Dr. Mengele's son Rolf', scientists were able to deduce with '99.997 percent certainty' that the remains were Josef Mengele's (Anon. 1992: A7). An expert investigator concluded that 'there was no room for doubt in the case' (ibid.). Regardless of how the evidence was interpreted, the testing was taken for dispositive and used to settle accounts. Although witness testimony, that of survivors in particular, arguably became paramount at the time of the Eichmann trial in the early 1960s, and remained so as Claude Lanzmann filmed *Shoah* (1985) in the 1970s and early 1980s, forensic analysis has recently claimed a central place. The tools of archeology, particularly those of excavation and forensic analysis have begun to increase in prominence.

Keenan and Weizman, the authors of *Mengele's Skull*, introduce readers to the term 'osteobiography', which is the addition of narrative language to scientific evidence, or the effort of experts to speak on behalf of human remains. The term was originally associated with Clyde Snow, one of the specialists who identified Mengele. Snow explains the central tenet of his method: 'When we see bones on the table they are dead. But in the living body, the bone is a very dynamic tissue, and it is very responsive to stresses, occupational stress for example, sports, injury, other activities. We take that osteobiography, we compare it with our missing person' (quoted in Keenan and Weizman 2012: 19). Bones are things, and they call for narrative context; experts adduce and recount their stories, speaking in those instances where the witnesses cannot speak for themselves. Such declarations are conditional and contextual; the objects, the bones, about which the experts speak, are silent. In the case of the Holocaust, the victims were often unable to tell their stories. Where mass killings occurred in the East, few obvious markers remain, and, with only one or two key exceptions, no filmed records were left behind.

One should, however, not be misled by the scientific appearance of forensic testimony. Keenan and Weizman write that 'the aesthetic, political, and ethical complications that emerge with the introduction of the object in war crimes trials indicate that this innovation is not simply one in which the solid object provides a stable and fixed alternative to human uncertainties, ambiguities, and anxieties. Rather,' they add, 'the complexities associated with testimony – that of the subject – are echoed in the presentation of the object. Human remains are the kind of objects from which the trace of the subject cannot be fully removed' (2012: 13). Even crime scenes are historical creations. Greg Siegel writes, 'the crime scene is a quintessentially modern invention, a product of the emergence in the nineteenth century of forensic science, with its peculiar logics and discourses, protocols and technologies' (2011: 96). Expert declarations are not science, but are rather only testimony in another human, subjective form. The authors of *Mengele's*

Skull assert that even though we place faith in forensics, and forensic science is vital, it can convey a false impression; it too is subject to narration and interpretation. An expert offers evidence, yet he or she still must make a claim. Keenan and Weizman describe the expert Clyde Snow as 'a Hamlet-like character, rarely photographed without a skull'. They add, 'in court he sometimes poses questions to [the remains] but most often simply speaks on their behalf, or "tells their stories"' (2012: 66). The evidence he provides is only one part of an account of the past. Narratives, based on unearthed evidence, are speculative. The stories cannot be told with absolute precision, and remote pasts are as far removed from us as the distant future.

None of this is to say that to unearth the past is to traffic in fiction. Every bit of historical evidence, every bone that is uncovered, brings historians closer to a fuller account, and anthropologists bring that which has been buried into the light. Forensics has been central in the prosecution of mass murder scenarios, including the 1992–95 Bosnian War. Sarah Wagner describes how the unearthing of unmarked mass graves interacts with the experience of survivors' families and points to the 'dynamic, multivalent aspects of the forensic effort alongside the intimate, powerful instances of recognition experienced by the families of the missing' (2008: 2). Adam Rosenblatt reflects on how the disposal of corpses in mass graves redoubles atrocities, arguing that, where human rights are concerned, 'the violence against the bodies in mass graves reaches across the boundaries of life; it is committed first against living human beings and then against their dead bodies' (2010: 948). In this spirit, work on the Holocaust and the project of archaeological retrieval are important. Keenan and Weizman follow Rosenblatt's argument: 'If the [concentration] camp has been constituted by contemporary theoretical discourse as the paradigmatic space of testimony … then the mass grave, as Adam Rosenblatt has suggested, is the site par excellence of forensics' (2012: 62). The mass grave provides critical information, and expert excavators then tell the victims' stories. How, then, are these stories subsequently enframed?

Cinema is faced with a challenge where it approaches scenes of excavation. Filmmakers have to consider how the pursuit of historical traces can be integrated into a narrative that is always already centred on an absence – what Lanzmann describes as a 'circle of flames', or 'a limit which cannot be crossed because a certain absolute horror cannot be transmitted' (1979/80: 139). His decades-old challenge to Holocaust cinema still resonates, specifically his assertion that archival images, the black and white ones so many of us have seen, mislead. What parts of the past can be reconstructed on film? Lanzmann's objection extends not only to feature films, such as the NBC miniseries *Holocaust* (1978), which he reviled, and to *Schindler's List* (1993), which he felt should never have been made, but also to the large number of documentary films that rely on black and white archival images of the past, those which were either taken by the perpetrators and thus frame the victims in terms of the Nazis' hateful gazes, or those that risk deceiving viewers into believing that they understand what happened.¹ What is to be gained by looking at compilation films and newsreel-type images if the horror was too great to comprehend? Following from Lanzmann's provocation, the Holocaust is neither comprehensible, nor should it be treated as a thing of the past. What function, then, can documentary cinema serve? Can it take a more active role by either allowing survivors to reengage archaeologically with a past that has been covered up, or should it serve as a film-historical corrective, sorting through, undermining, and even excavating the existing archive of widely known images?

What transpired at an Operation Reinhard death camp such as Sobibór is difficult to imagine. As Marek Bem and Wojciech Mazurek point out, the events that took place there can only be given partial life in our imagination, which, together with the assemblage of 'artifacts hidden in the ground' (2012: 11) enable us to construct narratives. We owe it to the victims to unearth the past, but at the same time, many things cannot be properly unearthed. Bem and Mazurek elaborate on the dilemmas involved in understanding and researching Sobibór:

> The constant confrontation with this place of remembrance and the memory of the still living survivors, the expectations of thousands of people for whom this place is a family cemetery, and the need to respect Jewish religious law – all these pose a great challenge for archaeologists. Moreover, the great precision with which the Germans tried to obliterate all trace [sic] of the camp's existence, the post-war destruction of the very few remnants of the camp, the long-term exploitation of the area by the forest industry, easy accessibility, the passing of time, questions of land ownership and the incessant use of the railway platform – these, in turn, have contributed to the deformation and devaluation of everything that could have survived, in the form of traces hidden in the ground, from October 1943 until now. (Ibid.)

The crimes committed at Sobibór were meant to remain hidden; the Nazis suspected they might be prosecuted after the war, and they sought to destroy the evidence. Their actions left behind remarkably few witnesses and virtually no known photographs. The same is true for Bełżec, which was planted over with grass and trees and almost entirely effaced. The historian and archeologist Andrzej Kola states that today there is a 'lack of surface traces of camp architectural structure' (2000: 10). Furthermore, robbers pillaged the ground after the Germans left. If any information exists about the camps today, it can be gathered, according to Kola, 'only by archaeological recognition' (ibid.).

The excavators cannot, of course, even determine how many bodies are in the graves; the numbers are approximations. Robin O'Neil puts the matter concisely, noting that when the Germans tried to get rid of the evidence, to burn the remaining remains, it was found that some bodies burned better than others: the recently gassed burned better than those from the first transports, fat women burned better than thin women, men did not burn well without women, as their fat is better developed than in men. For this reason, the bodies of women were used to build the base of the pyres intermixed with other bodies and combustible material. Blood, too, was found to be a very good combustible material and the young burned even better because of their softer flesh. (2008: 180)

As is documented in Guillaume Moscovitz's documentary *Bełżec* (2005), the archaeologist Kola has, with great effort, located the sites of that camp's mass graves, some of which likely contain tens of thousands of victims. That documentary has no photographic images of the camp in operation; there are none. It instead reconstructs the past based on the work of excavators and their drills, on an interview with the son of a painter who once may have seen the camp from the outside, and on a witness who can offer the filmmaker only a sketch in the sand of the camp's death chamber.[2]

AN EXCAVATOR'S GAZE: *BIRTHPLACE*

The Nazis attempted to destroy the evidence, and time now pushes the human and architectural remains deeper and deeper into the earth. Excavation can act as a counter movement, pressing against that process. It tries to reverse time, and it thus presents cinema with unique challenges. A film such as *Birthplace* [*Miejsce urodzenia*] (1992), like *Shoah*, takes part, from its very beginning, in the practice of excavation. The survivor at the centre of this documentary, in the mode of Lanzmann and akin to a dogged detective, combs through bystanders' and perpetrators' memories of the past in search of the truth. The film ultimately sends its protagonist digging beneath the surface of the wintry Polish earth. In the case of *Holocaust by Bullets* [*La Shoah par balles: l'histoire oubliée*] (2008), the question is different: how does the camera's lens encounter mass graves, and can such an encounter rewrite our understanding of the past by integrating and re-contextualising photographic documents?

Birthplace was filmed in Poland in 1992, seven years after *Shoah* was released, and witness interrogation is an essential part of its cinema-archaeological approach. Marek Haltof writes that the film, directed by Paweł Łoziński, follows Lanzmann's strategy of 'revisiting the places of the Holocaust and letting the eyewitnesses provide their own testimonies'; he adds that Łoziński 'avoids incorporating archival footage or photographs' (2012: 218). Like *Shoah*, the film relies chiefly on testimony, starting with that of its subject and lead interviewer, Henryk Grynberg, who travels back to Poland, where he was born and persecuted, searching for answers. A series of clues leads him beyond interrogation to exhumation, beyond testimony to excavation. The film's production was a tool for investigation and a means for a survivor to research his own background immediately after Poland emerged from the Iron Curtain at the end of the Cold War. From another perspective, it serves as a factual supplement to *The Jewish War*, Grynberg's autobiographical novel, first published in 1965. It supplies filmic images and thus documentary truths where before there had only been poetic narrative and a child's point of view. Grynberg had formerly conjectured about his family members' fates. The reality, he discovers, was even worse. In the company of the film's director, he uncovers the details of the crimes, including the identity of his father's still unpunished Polish murderers.

The film begins with Grynberg's arrival in Poland, and it is thus what Janet Walker would describe as a 'documentary of return' (2012: 270). Walker notes that such films highlight the visit to a location, specifically a site from which the filmic subject was exiled. She highlights 'a corpus of documentary films that are dramatically shaped by the European visits of Jewish refugees of Hitler's Holocaust to places from which they have previously departed, emigrated or fled; places where they survived; or places from which they were unwittingly removed or rescued' (ibid.). Concerning these 'documentaries of return', she argues: 'with this activity, the possibility of a shift opens up: from Holocaust testimony studies as a mentally recursive and diasporic paradigm in which verbal and written testimonies are conducted, filmed, and archived after the fact and far from the catastrophic event itself, to testimony as a matter of the here and now' (ibid.). From this perspective such documentaries are made contemporary: 'the places to which these (auto)biographical travelers return have persisted all the while. They have their own regional histories, practices, physical situations, and, importantly, current inhabitants' (ibid.). Łoziński's film does not, however, document a return to a concentration camp (as had, for example, Peter Morley's *Kitty: Return to Auschwitz* [1979]). It instead documents a return to a rural Polish village, a space where a Jewish community was wiped from the map.[3] One has to start digging, in other words, not through the ground, but through the thin air of history and memory. The architectural traces of the lost community have been almost entirely effaced; the place that was once there has been levelled and does not even register on contemporary maps.

Throughout *Birthplace* there is neither music, nor are there identifying intertitles to orient the viewer. Our frame of reference is tethered entirely to Grynberg. We follow him throughout his process of discovery, moving with him from one setting to the next. He travels along the distinctively un-modernised roads of central Poland, and one has the impression that there has been little new

Fig. 1 Henryk Grynberg encounters Poland through a windshield.

construction there in the last fifty years. The historical stagnation facilitates his journey into memory. We see the roadside through a vehicle's window, and Leslie Morris has written about sequences shot from within a car through a windshield with reference to Thomas Mitscherlich's Holocaust documentary *Journey into Life* [*Reisen ins Leben*] (1996) – a compilation of interviews with the survivors Gerhard Durlacher, Yehuda Bacon and Ruth Klüger – noting that a shot like this has 'an insistence on an arbitrary and filtered view of the past' (2003: 293). The view is, in this case, not arbitrary, so much as enframed. We are travelling with Grynberg, sutured to him, now returning in the relative freedom and mobility of a car – neither limited by what he can cover on foot nor being forcibly transported in a railcar. In voiceover, Grynberg recalls the familiar lanes and farmhouses of his childhood, locations that, at the time, seemed like the limits of the world. We see recurring images of snow, which here takes on a special significance. It recalls the harsh winters that persecuted Jews were forced to endure without proper protection from the cold. The earth, now covered by an additional layer of snow and ice, prevents literal and metaphoric excavators from digging through the past. Grynberg recalls details, specifically how Jews were once integrated into daily life there, and how they used to trade with the local peasants, as well as the fact that he was not raised with a particularly strong emphasis on Jewish traditions. His mother was prescient and did not want her children to stand out from the Poles.

Fig. 2 Henryk Grynberg walking through the ice and snow in Poland

Grynberg did not read the Torah, and he spoke Polish at home. From this perspective, he experienced Poland not only as a Jew but also as a Pole.

With an excavator's gaze, the camera surveys the Polish surfaces and exteriors; Grynberg takes us inside the houses, and he demonstrates that he has a sly approach in posing questions, similar to Lanzmann's. When he meets a woman who was present at his parents' wedding, she recalls the delicious cake. He follows the thread, gently correcting her, 'Wasn't it a challah?' His question is calculated to elicit whether she knows or understands the difference. She likely knows few if any Jews, so the distinction may be lost on her. His mother is described as having been a 'high-spirited Jewess'. Grynberg gracefully and eventually slips in tougher questions, such as whether his mother came there during the time of the occupation, when she was in hiding. The line of questioning leads to the first site, a dugout that Grynberg himself remembers from childhood, where many from his community were murdered. Barely a trace remains. This ill-defined space both is and is not a cemetery; bones remain there, but there are no markers.

The area is untended and unacknowledged. The film depicts its subjects wandering over the grounds. Because there are no boundaries, they do not know where to stand.

There he begins to uncover the story of his brother's murder. Grynberg last saw his brother, Buciek, when the boy was only 18 months old. By one account, a man named Stacho Latosek abandoned the child on the way to the mill, and another witness tells Grynberg that he had been there in Jadów when a policeman shot the boy in front of witnesses.[4] However his brother met his end, he had been left unprotected because of his Polish protectors' fear of being caught with a circumcised boy. In a larger sense, Buciek was a victim of the German occupation, but it is also evident that those Poles, who had been both paid and entrusted to protect the child, did not fulfil their obligation. While one might understand the bystanders' fear at the time, the contemporary lack of remorse is tinged with residual anti-Semitism, and here Grynberg transitions into the film's second half, in which he begins to look seriously into his father's murder. One by one he encounters those who met his father, Abram, and remember turning him away. Grynberg acts the part of the tenacious detective with only one thought in mind: do you know what happened to my father? Standing at a doorstep, he meets a man who knows something but refuses to share. Even today the fear persists. The man's wife, who speaks from inside the darkness of an extremely modest house, chastises him. She tells her husband: 'Why not tell him? ... His heart is bleeding.' The witness still refuses ('I won't tell any more').

The real facts of the murder are horrifying: in March 1944, Grynberg's father, who had at that point survived a full year alone, was killed with an axe blow to the head. He had placed his valuables in the care of different people, and, in 1944, when it was clear that the Russians were coming, the Poles with whom he had left his property were reluctant to return it. His murder was an effort to conceal a robbery. In the film, Grynberg elicits the alleged perpetrators' names: Jan and Stanisław Wojtynski. Abram had been trying to get milk when he was killed, and his body lay naked on the ground for a week, only his private parts covered by a rag. The Wojtynskis were the ones with motive. They later quarrelled and betrayed one another, and the killing was the subject of gossip. When Grynberg, in *Birthplace*, arrives on Jan Wojtynski's doorstep, he proceeds with caution. The scene recalls tense moments in Joshua Oppenheimer's *The Look of Silence* (2014), in which a surviving family member confronts a perpetrator more than forty years after the fact. Both in Poland and in Indonesia, many wounds remain fresh. In the case of Grynberg's investigation, the process of digging through the past mirrors the excavation of bones; secrets and graves are, in this case, one and the same, and he has to tread carefully. He asks whether his father came to this farm, and he is told a story (possibly a false memory, but more likely an outright fabrication), wherein his father had knelt before one of the brothers, requesting, even insisting that he be killed. Grynberg then asks calmly and quietly: 'Do you know what some people are saying? That your brother killed my father ... some people told me that you also took part in it.' At this point, however, the man's young son becomes aware that Grynberg is seeking the facts, and that his enquiries could have legal ramifications. The younger man intervenes and threatens violence. Digging has revealed the astonishing truth that even today the same violence could be repeated, son upon son. Having provoked the threat, Grynberg shows how little has changed, and he nearly succeeds in closing a gap of many decades. The interview is then hastily concluded.

The account provided in *The Jewish War*, written many years earlier, had been more speculative. Grynberg's narrator pictures Abram: 'He was slovenly, unshaven, and thin. He smelled of rain and mud. He must have looked awful. Heaven knows when he had last washed himself. Was he still aware that he was human?' He then imagines the scene: 'Someone was waiting for him on that last night when he dragged himself all alone along one of his usual paths, clutching a loaf of bread under his coat. It was a question of money. […] One can always count on money, he thought. Money proves that one is human. And if you get killed for it, you are not killed like an animal, but like a human being, for money' (2001: 27, 28). The novel leaves the father's murder abstract, framed as an unspeakable atrocity.

Birthplace, by contrast, explores the atrocious act, digging deeper in its willingness to erase the lines between Polish indifference and animosity, in its relentless pursuit of the truth, and in the harsh light with which it is willing to portray routine ignorance. It also takes us into the ground, beneath the surface of the earth. At the film's most poignant moment, Grynberg follows the clues to the location of his father's body, and a team begins to dig.[5] One can only watch in disbelief as the excavators begin. They first unearth Abram's milk bottle. A shot from the pit, at an extremely low angle, depicts the witnesses' gaze, and reminds viewers that some of these same people, or their parents, might have walked by his father's body years ago. Grynberg himself then descends. Onlookers watch and stare as he digs with his hands, first pulling up bones, and producing, finally, his father's skull. At this point, he has uncovered the past, bringing that which was hidden into light. He holds the skull, fractured by an axe or another sharp implement, before the camera. This, the film's penultimate image, is a *memento mori*. Although the bones constitute a kind of evidentiary proof, no traditional forensics is presented; no scientists are called upon to provide expert analysis. Łoziński and Grynberg focus instead on the Poles' suspect behaviour, and on the residual stench of murder.

The image at the film's end is the antithesis of the perpetrators' trophy pictures, the famous photographs in which, as Jan Tomasz Gross and Irena Grudzińska-Gross write, soldiers are posed 'like hunters who photograph themselves with the game they shot' (2012: 71). The documentary, concluding with this stark visual reminder of death, serves as an autobiographical novel's supplement. Images have, of course, a special status, and images of death may have an even more important one. In an essay on the post-war images of Jewish murder victims, Gabriel Finder and Judith Cohen describe a photograph of Jewish survivors in Biała Podlaska, a small town in eastern Poland, in the spring of 1946 standing in an opened mass grave among bodies of the victims of a mass shooting. They write that those assembled, 'pose for the camera, but their collective gaze, with the exception of a couple of individuals, is drawn ineluctably to the mass of skeletal remains. These survivors are quite literally bearing witness. [...] [O]ne function of this photograph is documentation, to set the record straight, to provide incontrovertible proof of what took place in this *shtetl* under Nazi occupation. But it has another function. The living have quite literally descended into the pit' (2008: 66).

Birthplace documents the living witness's descent into the pit, and in that moment it compresses past and present. In the course of this personal, subjective search for answers – conducted not by a forensic expert but by a survivor – Grynberg also becomes 'a Hamlet-like character', photographed in contemplation of a skull. Bones can be evidence, presented at trial by experts such as Clyde Snow, but, as in this potent image, they can also be enframed by documentary narratives, and situated such that they under-score a confrontation with the irrevocability of death. Writing about a different image, but making a comparable point, Gross and Grudzińska-Gross observe that a pile of bones, or an 'orderly row of skulls', can serve 'as a judicial proof, but not as an expression of compassion'; with an eye to that same dark side of Polish history, and inspired by the same *memento mori*, they conclude: 'Only an individual skull invokes an individual fate. One could address a monologue to it, as in *Hamlet*' (2012: 86).

AS IT APPEARS TODAY: *HOLOCAUST BY BULLETS*

The documentary *Holocaust by Bullets* deals with a project headed by Father Patrick Desbois, the president of the organisation Yahad-In Unum. In that film, a team of researchers goes to the Ukraine, and Desbois, the film's central figure, conducts interviews with elderly witnesses, many of whom were bystanders. The film assembles testimony about mass executions in the East, and, in its project of historical recovery, it also takes after *Shoah*. At various points in the film Desbois asks the local witnesses specific questions, such as whether prisoners were kneeling or standing when they were shot, and how precisely the victims fell into the death pits. In a book that documents much of what takes place in the film, Desbois describes what motivates him to undertake this task, specifically, the desire to give dignity to the Jewish dead. He writes about visiting a cemetery at a village named Ougnif, once the site of a Jewish community. He reflects: '[E]very German killed during the war has been reburied and identified by name. The cemeteries are on the scale of the Reich. Magnificent cemeteries for the Germans, including the SS, little graves for the French, while stones covered in brambles for the tens of thousands of anonymous Soviet soldiers, and absolutely nothing for the Jews. Thus, under the ground, everything is still in order according to the hierarchy of the Reich.' He concludes: 'We cannot give a posthumous victory to Nazism. We cannot leave the Jews buried like animals' (2008: 34).

Father Desbois' story starts with a personal perspective: he had lost a cousin in Mauthausen, another cousin had been a survivor of Dachau, and his grandfather had been taken to a camp known as Rawa Ruska in the Ukraine. Crimes committed by the *Einsatzgruppen* in the Ukraine have been the focus of his research, and he sets out to identify as many sites of mass killings as he can. The film begins with what is among the only known footage of such crimes: a famous amateur film taken at a mass execution in Libau in 1941.[6] *Holocaust by Bullets* thus begins with older, archival images of Jews falling into death pits; a film about excavation opens with an image of a burial. The documentary incorporates and presents the footage again and again. Because so few images of these mass executions exist, the film repeatedly presents them, slowing them down, drawing our attention to them, in the hope that we might see them differently each time. Perhaps, it seems to suggest, the process can bring us to revise our gaze, permitting our eyes to land where they had not previously landed, so that we see the victims anew.

Desbois' mission was clear: to prove the existence of the 'Holocaust by bullets', a term that he has propagated in order to draw his Western European audience's attention to the less commonly discussed executions that preceded the industrialised killings at Auschwitz and elsewhere. For those who were not killed in gas chambers, there is no proper form of cultural memory. Desbois is concerned with how these 1.5 million victims died here, and where the bodies were abandoned. In an echo of *Shoah*, his researchers seek out and question people exiting a church service. The crew is looking for elderly witnesses, ones who might have been present at the scene of the crime. In contrast with *Shoah*, however, the people on the steps of the church offer helpful testimony. Desbois' questions are specific: it may not be clear to the viewer why it is important whether the victims were sitting or standing, but he, through his interpreter, carefully notes every detail. His approach is different from Grynberg's; he is less concerned with the witnesses' culpability (an interest of both Grynberg and Lanzmann) than he is with probing the limits of their memory and determining their testimonies' utility. Desbois manages to establish a different chemistry between the interviewer and the eyewitness, giving the interviewee the feeling that it is not about his or her own culpability, but rather about the more abstract enterprise of establishing historical evidence. In Lviv, where the Jewish population of 90,000 was exterminated, Desbois locates a mass grave. Under the eyes of a rabbi, the site is opened. Hundreds of shell casings prove the cause of death. The film reminds us that disturbing the graves would also be a transgression. It is a contradiction: Desbois wants to unearth the victims and get at the truth; yet, out of respect, he has to leave the bodies interred.

The filmmakers then visit a simple, modest house belonging to a man named Timofei Ridzvanouk, who was born in 1928 and has information about mass executions in

Bakhiv. The Germans had been under orders from Himmler to cover evidence of their crimes. This endeavour, known as Special Action 1005 (*Sonderaktion 1005*), began in spring 1942 and was intended to conceal the traces of Operation Reinhard. Under the supervision of SS Colonel Paul Blobel, local workers were forced to exhume the mass graves and burn the bodies. Blobel was known for having developed disposal techniques, which included layering corpses and firewood in an alternating construction atop a frame of iron rails. The film is a reminder that this disposal operation was not restricted to the Reinhard death camps such as Sobibór and Bełżec, but that it included all those sites in the East where Nazis attempted to conceal their crimes. The witness, Ridzvanouk, recalls events, and the filmmakers ask questions, doing their best to mine his memories. He recalls how trains came, the perpetrators drove the Jews forward with whips, the women dug the graves, and all were made to undress. Another witness comes forward to lead the filmmakers to the old gravel pit, the *Kiesgrube*, which many witnesses have described. There, they unearth bones and parts of skulls, they find holes that stem from plunderers and grave robbers, and they search with a metal detector for bullet casings. At yet another point, standing in a forest, witnesses explain how the corpses of the dead were dug out and burned.

Holocaust by Bullets incorporates a German soldier's sketch of an execution as it was carried out in the Ukrainian town of Zhitomir (labelled 'Exekution in Shitomir'). The drawing is oddly architectural, and it seems to present the mass executions and burials as having been part of a methodical programme. It is also another reminder of the overall lack of photographic evidence. A witness, identified as Nikola Kristitch, was eight years old in 1942 when he saw the shootings, and he starts to break down as he recalls children being shot. He speaks about the grave, in which they lay there 'like herrings', and he describes how the ground continued to move for two days; it heaved.[7] The film then presents a series of

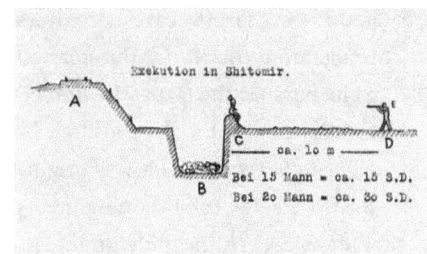

Fig. 3 A German soldier's sketch as depicted in *Holocaust by Bullets*

photos taken during the liquidation of the Mizocz ghetto in October 1942. As Desbois' camera crew reaches the area near Mizocz, these familiar photos, frequently used in Holocaust documentaries, are incorporated into the film.[8] A resident directs the film crew to what he believes to be the ravine where the shootings took place, and the image then dissolves, very convincingly, from a black and white photograph of corpses – one photo from that same collection of photos – to an image of the landscape as it appears today. Desbois, it would seem, has credibly succeeded in locating the hitherto unknown site of the murders amid the woodsy, rural terrain, and the archival photo has, it seems, been confirmed. *Holocaust by Bullets* is thus an archaeological pursuit, yet it also

Fig. 4 A site of mass execution, then and now, in *Holocaust by Bullets*

conducts an imagistic archaeology, communicating with the history of photographs that preceded it. The film suggests that archaeology – specifically, the uncovered forensic evidence including bones and bullet casings – supersedes photography in its evidentiary value. In accord with Desbois' project, we may feel that we know these photographs, but we have now been provided with hard evidence. The assertion that motivates his project is that archaeology is incontrovertible. It is not one narrative among others; as Desbois sees it, these bones *are* the truth.

Most recently, one documentary has engaged directly with excavation, particularly insofar as the word can be connected to its Latin root, *cavus*. Janet Tobias's *No Place on Earth* (2012), a film that takes place largely in caverns, should, strictly speaking, be considered a docudrama, rather than a documentary, because a large percentage of the film consists of reenactments. It is, however, nonfiction cinema in the broadly accepted sense of the term. The film documents the true story of how an adventurous contemporary caver, on a visit to the Ukraine to explore the Verteba and Priest's Grotto caves, discovers grottoes that were once inhabited by Jews seeking refuge from the Nazis. The story strikes him as amazing, and Tobias's film follows him as he pursues the facts. The film couples its interviews with survivors with stylised re-enactments, and with expository information provided by Esther Stermer's memoir *We Fight to Survive*, which was originally published in 1960. As with Grynberg's story in *Birthplace*, the total thoroughness of the Nazi efforts at extermination again seems remarkable. Even the underground grotto and near total darkness – the hiding place of a community that all but buried itself – was hardly sufficient protection.

Perhaps the most unusual moment in the film comes at its conclusion, which involves survivors engaged in spelunking. The film brings several of those who had hidden in the caves, those who were fit enough to make the journey, back to the original site, and it documents their return. I prefer to think that Tobias was not trying to sadistically recreate the conditions of their traumatic confinement, but rather to consider the extent to which her film has, up to that point, been an expedition into dark memories. At its climax, the survivors' gazes, and those of the viewers as well, are enframed by the glow of their headlamps, and we may find ourselves considering cinema's curiously subjective point of access to these caves. The film had aspired to take us, in as much as it is possible and against the admonitions of Lanzmann and others, into the past. Its last gesture, taking us down into the depths, offers insight into the film's predilection for the tools of docudrama. The director struggles, at points, to be 'realistic', as would a feature film rather than a documentary.⁹ It is thus no wonder that the ending, which traces the familial legacies of these survivors, deliberately recalls that of *Schindler's List*, including reproducing that film's highly iconic portrait: a line of survivors, now above ground, crossing an open field.

But documentaries that excavate the past may be less concerned with their realistic imperatives than with their ethical ones. Unearthing can be a means of rewriting. Archaeologists might not unearth the past so that we feel like we are there; that is less a goal of forensic science than it is a goal of cinema. Archaeology can give voice to the dead, and it can recover records where history has, for whatever reasons, been erased. Where the Nazis tried to efface Jewish civilisation entirely, one would have to retrieve it. Although some contemporary documentaries are concerned with making us feel, contra Lanzmann, as though we were actually there, these films' goals occasionally compete and interact with one another. Whether it is in accord with or against their expressed aims, they sometimes include the task of finding remains, digging, interrogating and bringing that which has been buried, covered and recovered into the light.

Notes

1 Lanzmann states his objections to NBC's 1978 television miniseries in 'From the Holocaust to the *Holocaust* (1979/80)'. He writes critically about *Schindler's List* in 'Holocauste, la représentation impossible', published in *Le Monde* (1994).
2 For more on Moscovitz's *Bełżec*, see Prager (2015: 226–9).
3 In this respect the film anticipates works such as Aharon Apelfeld's *Polin, erets yerugah* (2005) as well as the search for the lost *shtetl* at the centre of Jonathan Safran Foer's *Everything Is Illuminated* (2002).
4 In his collection of essays, *Unkünstlerische Wahrheit*, Grynberg says that it was not Latosek, but rather the miller, who abandoned Buciek. The information his interviews elicited was, he acknowledges, not always reliable (2014: 312).
5 The scene recalls the conclusion of Paweł Pawlikowski's Academy Award-winning Polish film *Ida* (2013). Grynberg writes about this similarity between *Birthplace* and *Ida*, noting that even if Pawlikowski's 'strongest scene' – the unearthing of the grave – is not plagiarism, it is 'clearly inspired by the earlier film' (2015).
6 On this footage, see Joshua Hirsch (2004: 1-3). The same footage also appears in Stefan Ruzowitzky's documentary *Radical Evil [Das radikal Böse]* (2013), discussed by Oleksandr Kobrynskyy in this volume. In his effort to understand the perpetrators' mindset, Ruzowitzky attempts to recreate through dramatisation the setting of the original footage. He arguably normalises the horrific scene, integrating it with reenactments and testimony. Patrick Desbois makes an appearance as an expert witness in the film.
7 According to the film's German subtitles, the witness Kristitch says, 'Der Boden quoll auf.'

8   The series includes images numbered 17876 through 17879 of the photo archive collection of the US Holocaust Memorial Museum. Most notably, some of these images were included in Alain Resnais' *Night and Fog* [*Nuit et brouillard*] (1955). For a discussion of these photos see Didi-Huberman (2008: 67).
9   On 'the realistic imperative' in feature films, see Kerner (2011: 15-30).

Filmography

Bełżec. Dir. Guillaume Moscovitz. France, 2005.
Birthplace [*Miejsce urodzenia*]. Dir. Paweł Łoziński. Poland, 1992.
Holocaust. Dir. Marvin J. Chomsky. USA, 1978.
Holocaust by Bullets [*La Shoah par balles: l'histoire oubliée*]. Dir. Romain Icard. France, 2008.
Ida. Dir. Paweł Pawlikowski. Poland/Denmark/France/UK, 2013.
Journey into Life [*Reisen ins Leben*]. Dir. Thomas Mitscherlich. Germany, 1996.
Kitty: Return to Auschwitz. Dir. Peter Morley. UK, 1979.
The Look of Silence. Dir. Joshua Oppenheimer. Denmark/Finlan/Indonesia/Norway/UK, 2014.
Night and Fog [*Nuit et brouillard*]. Dir. Alain Resnais. France, 1955.
No Place on Earth. Dir. Janet Tobias. UK/Germany/USA, 2012.
Radical Evil [*Das radikal Böse*]. Dir. Stefan Ruzowitzky. Germany/Austria, 2013.
Schindler's List. Dir. Steven Spielberg. USA, 1993.
Shoah. Dir. Claude Lanzmann. France, 1985.

Bibliography

Anon. (1992) 'Genetic Testing Closes the Mengele Inquiry', *The New York Times*, 9 April, A7.
Apelfeld, Aharon (2005) *Polin, erets yerugah*. Jerusalem: Keter.
Bem, Marek and Wojciech Mazurek (2012) *Sobibór: Archaeological Research Conducted on the Site of the Former German Extermination Centre in Sobibór 2000-2011*. Warsaw: Foundation for Polish-German Reconciliation.
Blumenthal, Ralph (1985) 'Scientists Decide Brazil Skeleton is Josef Mengele's: Inquiry Rules', *The New York Times*, 22 June, 1, 8.
Cole, Simon A. and Rachel Dioso-Villa (2006/7) '*CSI* and Its Effects: Media, Juries, and the Burden of Proof', *New England Law Review*, 41, 3, 435–69.
Desbois, Patrick (2008) *The Holocaust by Bullets: A Priest's Journey to Uncover the Truth Behind the Murder of 1.5 Million Jews*. New York: Palgrave Macmillan.
Didi-Huberman, Georges (2008) *Images in Spite of All: Four Photographs from Auschwitz*, trans. Shane B. Lellis. Chicago: University of Chicago Press.
Finder, Gabriel N. and Judith R. Cohen (2008) 'Memento Mori: Photographs from the Grave', *Polin: Studies in Polish Jewry*, 20, 55–73.
Foer, Jonathan Safran (2002) *Everything Is Illuminated: A Novel*. Boston: Houghton Mifflin.
Gross, Jan Tomasz and Irena Grudzińska-Gross (2012) *Golden Harvest: Events at the Periphery of the Holocaust*. New York: Oxford University Press.
Grynberg, Henryk (2001) *The Jewish War and the Victory*. Evanston, IL: Northwestern University

Press.

____ (2014) *Unkünstlerische Wahrheit: Ausgewählte Essays*, trans. Lothar Quinkenstein. Berlin: Hentrich & Hentrich.

____ (2015) 'The Aftermath, Ida etcetera', *American Assocation for Polish-Jewish Studies*. Online: http://www.aapjstudies.org/index.php?id=209

Haltof, Marek (2012) *Polish Film and the Holocaust: Politics and Memory*. New York: Berghahn.

Hirsch, Joshua (2004) *Afterimage: Film, Trauma, and the Holocaust*. Philadelphia, PA: Temple University Press.

Keenan, Thomas and Eyal Weizman (2012) *Mengele's Skull: The Advent of a Forensic Aesthetics*. Berlin: Sternberg.

Kerner, Aaron (2011) *Film and the Holocaust: New Perspectives on Dramas, Documentaries, and Experimental Films*. New York: Continuum.

Kola, Andrzej (2000) *Bełżec: The Nazi Camp for Jews in the Light of Archaeological Sources: Excavations 1997-1999*. Warsaw: Council for the Protection of Memory of Combat and Martyrdom/Washington: United States Holocaust Memorial Museum.

Lanzmann, Claude (1979/80) 'From the Holocaust to the *Holocaust*', *Telos*, 42, 137–43.

____ (1994) 'Holocauste, la représentation impossible', *Le Monde*, 3 March, AS1+.

Morris, Leslie (2003) 'Berlin Elegies: Absence, Postmemory, and Art after Auschwitz', in Shelley Hornstein and Florence Jacobowitz (eds) *Image and Remembrance: Representation and the Holocaust*. Bloomington, IN: Indiana University Press, 288–304.

O'Neil, Robin (2008) *Belzec: Stepping Stone to Genocide*. New York: JewishGen Inc.

Prager, Brad (2015) *After the Fact: The Holocaust in Twenty-First Century Documentary Film*. New York: Bloomsbury.

Rosenblatt, Adam (2010) 'International Forensic Investigations and the Human Rights of the Dead', *Human Rights Quarterly*, 32, 4, 921–50.

Schweitzer, N. J. and Michael J. Saks (2007) 'The *CSI* Effect: Popular Fiction about Forensic Science Affects the Public's Expectations about Real Forensic Science', *Jurimetrics*, 47, 3, 357–64.

Siegel, Greg (2011) 'The Similitude of the Wound', *Cabinet*, 43, 95–100.

Stermer, Esther ([1960] 1975) *We Fight to Survive*. Montreal: Jewish Institute of Higher Research.

Wagner, Sarah E. (2008) *To Know Where He Lies: DNA Technology and the Search for Srebrenica's Missing*. Berkeley, CA: University of California Press.

Walker, Janet (2012) 'Moving Testimonies: "Unhomed Geography" and the Holocaust Documentary of Return', in Jakob Lothe, Susan Rubin Suleiman and James Phelan (eds) *After Testimony: The Ethics and Aesthetics of Holocaust Narrative for the Future*. Columbus, OH: Ohio State University Press, 269–88.

CHAPTER FOUR

The Willing Amnesia
THE HOLOCAUST IN POST-SOVIET CINEMA

Olga Gershenson

In November 2013, a ten-part drama series, *Cry of an Owl* [*Krik sovy*], premiered on Russian Channel One. Everything about the series suggested a position of cultural prominence: Channel One is the main state outlet, its content is understood to be endorsed by the regime and it is distributed throughout post-Soviet space. The series had the highest production values, directed by award-winning filmmaker Oleg Pogodin, and starred Sergei Puskepalis, Maria Mironova and other A-list Russian actors. *Cry of an Owl* was an instant popular and critical success, becoming one of the highest-rated TV productions of the time (see Kondrashev 2013).

Genre-wise, the series is a standard-edition police drama, a tightly-wound whodunit; but thematically, it is a historical excursion into early post-Stalin Russia, with the KGB officer Mitin (Puskepalis) as a main character. Such a loaded historic subject invites broader questions of memory, specifically the twin catastrophes of Stalin's and Hitler's regimes. The way *Cry of an Owl* deals with the still explosive legacy of Stalinism aligns with the party line in Putin's Russia: the plot pays only lip-service to the commemoration of Stalin's secret police crimes. The KGB man is not only a leading character, but a charismatic and positive one. Although his love interest has been herself a victim of Stalin's repressions, the punitive apparatus overall comes out well. The film suggests that Stalin's secret police might have gone overboard, but the new cadre, KGB officers and their colleagues in the police forces, are all represented as solid good guys.[1] Instead of grappling with the difficult past, the series is nostalgic about the good old Soviet times, with its supposedly clear moral compass. No wonder the series received an FSB (formerly KGB) film prize.²

The series' approach to war crimes and the Holocaust is equally significant. By digging into the mysterious past of a Russian provincial town, Mitin discovers an entire German spy ring. Several inhabitants are suspected to have been on the German payroll since the Nazi occupation, participating in heinous crimes, including actions against the Jews. In the course of a lengthy investigation, with many false leads and dead ends, Mitin finally arrives at a Nazi archive, where he discovers documents incriminating local Nazi collaborators and informers. It was not just a few people, it turns out, but nearly everyone in town who was implicated in the crimes.

And this is where the plot takes a curious turn: defying our expectation for a trial or a public denunciation, Mitin simply chooses to let the sleeping dogs lie. In making this choice, he is influenced by an old janitor, who serves as a philosopher and a moral compass (and is likely the filmmakers' mouthpiece). The janitor finds the archive in Mitin's room and burns it, explaining to Mitin in an impassioned monologue: 'No need to dig in the past… Who needs the truth? Who would want to know that their father or grandfather was a traitor or an executioner? Do you want such a truth?' This wilful disposal of the past is presented as a moral choice, since in the final scene of the series Mitin, who discovered a copy of an archive on microfilm, still conceals it from everyone. He literally hides it in his closet, and life carries on as if the incriminating documents had never existed. This closeted archive is an apt metaphor for the culture of memory in Russia today. 'Who needs the truth?' the series asks, and emphatically answers: nobody. This call for suppression of all kinds of historic memory is readily extended to crimes perpetuated by the Soviet regime, by Nazi occupation and, importantly, to the various victims of these crimes, including Jews, who were killed with active help of local collaborators and passive acquiescence of bystanders. As Aleida Assmann observes, in contrast to the Western world, Russian attitudes to its traumatic past are characterised by 'a tendency to oblivion … forgetting the history' (2014). The Russian answer to the painful questions of historic responsibility is amnesia. Significantly, it is a willing amnesia.

This culture of amnesia suggested by *Cry of an Owl* might not be the only approach to collective memory in Russia, but it is certainly the dominant one.³ What does this mean for the state of Holocaust memory in Russia? What are the perceptions of the Holocaust in current Russia? Exploring these questions in this essay, I will rely on analyses of recent Russian films.

THE SOVIET HERITAGE

The received wisdom is that the Holocaust simply was not represented on Soviet screens – that there were no Holocaust films in the Soviet Union, just as there were few other ways to commemorate the Jewish loss. To a large degree this assumption is correct. Although the Soviets never denied the Holocaust or formally banned its commemoration, in actuality any attempt to speak of Jewish victims was silenced. The Holocaust was not to be treated as a unique and separate phenomenon.[4] Instead, the Holocaust was universalised or externalised. In the process of universalisation, the Holocaust was subsumed as part of the overall Soviet tragedy, with Jewish victims euphemistically labeled 'peaceful Soviet citizens'.[5] When crimes against Jews were discussed as such, only the events of the Holocaust outside the borders of the Soviet Union were mentioned, a phenomenon I have elsewhere called 'externalisation'.[6] To silence discussion of the Holocaust, these two mechanisms were used in tandem: universalisation allowed the Soviets to cast Slavs and communists as the main target of Hitler's attack and to erase Jewish victimhood; externalisation was used to avoid any implication of local bystanders or Nazi collaborators, and it absolved the Soviet leadership from any historic responsibility for mass Jewish losses on their soil.

As a result, there was no official commemoration of the Holocaust in the Soviet Union. Nevertheless, some cultural producers attempted to acknowledge and commemorate the Holocaust, even in the face of official silencing. Their artistic output includes a number of films, which were produced and distributed (or not) in constant negotiation with Soviet censorship.

Paradoxically, Soviet filmmakers were among the first in the world to portray Jewish persecution. In the late 1930s, several Soviet dramas, including *Professor Mamlock* (1938), directed by Herbert Rappaport and Adolf Minkin, and *The Oppenheim Family* [*Sem'ia Oppengeim*] (1938), directed by Grigorii Roshal, explicitly attacked Nazi anti-Semitism. All were banned in 1939, following the Molotov-Ribbentrop pact. *The Unvanquished* [*Nepokorennye*] (1945), directed by Mark Donskoi, was among the first films ever to portray a Jewish massacre on Soviet soil, but it was taken off screens soon after its premiere, at the time of Stalin's anti-Semitic policies. Most Holocaust-themed films in the Soviet Union were made in the period of post-Stalin liberalisation, including *Ordinary Fascism* [*Obyknovennyi fashizm*] (1966), directed by Mikhail Romm, *Eastern Corridor* [*Vostochnyi koridor*] (1966), directed by Valentin Vinogradov, *Commissar* (1967), directed by Aleksandr Aksol'dov, and *Sons of the Fatherland* [*Syny otechestva*] (1968), directed by Latif Faiziev. However, even during these relatively liberal times, such films faced opposition by the Soviet regime. Banned outright or marked as 'undesirable' by the censors, most remained phantoms, forgotten or entirely unknown. At the end of the liberal era in the late 1960s, Jewish-themed cultural production was terminated altogether. The Holocaust would not openly become a subject of Soviet films again until the Perestroika era, in the late 1980s, when several such films were made, including *Ladies' Tailor* [*Damskii Portnoi*] (1990), directed by Leonid Gorovets, *Our Father* [*Otche Nash*] (1990), directed by Boris Ermolaev, and *Exile* [*Izgoi*] (1991), directed by Vladimir

Savel'ev. Yet even these films were barely seen and the Holocaust remained a phantom on the late Soviet screens (see Gershenson 2013: 206–16).

These Soviet-era films were the products of their time. In Soviet films, the Holocaust rarely assumed a central position in the narrative. The fact of Jewish suffering was used to address something else: the entirety of the Soviet people, the sweeping narrative of the war, or even a critique of Soviet totalitarianism. Representation of the Holocaust in these films was limited by the prevailing Soviet policies of universalisation and externalisation. It was further restricted by the tenets of socialist realism, demanding a lacquered portrayal of reality with positive heroes and clear plots. Finally, due to the erasure of Jewish tradition in the Soviet Union, Christian symbolism was deployed in these films along with, or even instead of, Judaism (see Gershenson 2013: 223–8). This Soviet legacy cast its long shadow on representations of the Holocaust even in post-Soviet cinema.

HOLOCAUST FILMS IN POST-SOVIET RUSSIA

At the end of 1991, the Soviet Union was dissolved. Along with the state, the entire Soviet film industry ceased to exist. By the early 2000s, filmmaking gradually bounced back, and several Holocaust films were made. But this was not necessarily a cause for celebration – the treatment of the Holocaust in these films was heavy-handed, simplistic and sentimentalised. A Belarus/German co-production, *Babi Yar* (2003), directed by Jeff Kanew, set in occupied Kiev, is supposed to be a tragic story of a Jewish family and their non-Jewish neighbours, but its dramaturgy and unconvincing acting turn it into cheap melodrama. Another *Babi Yar*, a TV film, made in Ukraine and directed by Nikolai Zaseev-Rudenko in 2002, tells a story of a Jewish woman, a survivor of Babi Yar, who comes to visit the site of the atrocity many years later. Improbably, there she encounters a former Nazi who also came to visit, and the two share a bizarre vision of Madonna as they partake in bouts of grandiloquence. Another female survivor is featured in a Russian/American co-production, *The Burning Land* [*V Iiune 41*] (2003), directed by Mikhail Ptashuk. This survivor – a young American Jew, who went to visit the old country at the wrong time – not only miraculously escapes, but also manages to return to the United States, where she transforms her adventures into a Broadway musical. Unlike these films, a Lithuanian/German co-production, *Ghetto* (2006), directed by Audrius Juzenas, is based on a solid dramaturgical source, a play by Joshua Sobol set in the Vilnius ghetto, but the resulting film is also simplistic and melodramatic.

The events of the Holocaust are reflected in the subplots of several later films, the best of them being *Daddy* [*Papa*] (2004), directed by Vladimir Mashkov, which features a heartbreaking scene of an execution in the Tulchin ghetto.

In 2008, Russian state-owned Channel One broadcast a state-funded sixteen-part TV series, *Heavy Sand* [*Tiazhelyi Pesok*], directed by Anton Barschevskii, based on Anatolii

Rybakov's novel of the same name. The novel was for years one of the very few works of Soviet literature that gave expression to Jewish history and culture. At the centre of the epic plot is the life story of a Jewish couple, Rakhil and Yakov, set in a *shtetl* of Snovsk (the actual place where Rybakov spent his childhood). The last episodes of the series are dedicated to the horrors of life in the ghetto, where Rakhil loses her beloved husband and two children. At a key moment, when the ghetto is faced with liquidation, Rakhil becomes a resistance leader and organises the escape from the ghetto. This series could have become a seminal representation of Jewish life and the Holocaust, but instead it does not manage to convey the gravity of the situation and the complexity of its characters, representing Jews with idealised simplicity. This idealisation revisits the tenets of socialist realism, only now, instead of workers and revolutionaries, Jews are model citizens and exemplary human beings. In Russia, the series was aptly dubbed 'Very Heavy Sand' (see Gershenson 2013: 220–1).

In a radical departure from Soviet times, the Holocaust in the early twenty-first century becomes a subject of several important documentary films, presenting for the first time testimonies of Russian Holocaust survivors. *David* (2002), directed by Aleksei Fedorchenko, offers a portrait of a Jewish man who survived medical experiments in a Nazi concentration camp only to be thrown into a Gulag after his liberation and return to the Soviet motherland. Naturally, the film reveals painful parallels between the two totalitarian regimes. *Children from the Abyss* [*Deti iz bezdny*] (2002), directed by Pavel Chukhrai as a part of the internationally produced mini-series *Broken Silence*, weaves together testimonies, archival photographs and documents to tell harrowing stories of Russian Jews who survived the Holocaust as children. More recently, a TV documentary *Kiselev List* [*Spisok Kiseleva*] (2008), directed by Iurii Maliugin, paid tribute to a Russian partisan, Nikolai Kiselev, who led to safety over two hundred Jews who had escaped extermination in occupied Belarus. The film's main achievement is its moving interviews with actual survivors saved by Kiselev; but its one-dimensional representation of partisans as heroes glosses over real tensions between Jews and non-Jewish partisans and civilians.

All these films differ radically from the ones made during the Soviet era. With censorship restrictions completely removed, these films no longer universalise: they speak openly about the Jewish identity of their characters and about the persecutions Jews faced. Similarly, instead of externalising the Holocaust, they locate the events in the Soviet territories; some of them even cautiously addressed instances of local anti-Semitism and collaboration with the Nazis. It became more common to encounter minor Jewish characters or Holocaust references in war dramas. The discourse of the Holocaust was no longer taboo. And yet, the Soviet legacy was not completely exorcised. Ironically, the very representation of the Holocaust is also a part of the Soviet legacy of 'issue films', as is the application of a socialist realist method to idealise Jewish characters. Unfortunately, representing the Holocaust openly, without relying on hints and hidden messages, did not result in quality films.

HOLOCAUST FILMS IN 'NEW RUSSIA': RULES AND EXCEPTIONS

Cinematic representation of the Holocaust in the early post-Soviet years was limited both by Soviet legacy and by current realities of film production. Still, the fact that the Holocaust finally became a relatively common subject was itself significant. In the 2010s, new tendencies set in. In 2012, the mini-series *Life and Fate* [Zhizn' i Sud'ba] premiered on Channel One, and became an instant post-Soviet classic. Directed by Sergei Ursuliak, the prominent filmmaker known for his interest in history and memory, the series is a well-done adaptation of Vasilii Grossman's seminal novel of the same name. This novel, seized by the KGB in 1960 and published in Russia only in 1988, is an epic narrative of life in Stalin's Russia, told through the story of a Jewish scientist, Victor Shtrum, and his family. Naturally, the war and the Holocaust play an important role in this story. But in the twelve-part dramatisation, the events of the Holocaust are only referenced in a four-minute scene, when Shtrum (Sergei Makovetskii) receives the last letter from his mother who perished in a death camp. Yet the events of the Holocaust remain off-screen: the camera shows only Shtrum crying as he reads the letter (which is narrated by a male voice). Only for a few brief moments, archival black-and-white footage of deportations and torture of Jews is superimposed on the pages of the letter. But these images are vague and function only as signifiers of the tragic events. As a result, the events of the Holocaust that constitute one of the central themes in the novel are not individualised through characters and are not developed on-screen.[7] The choice to omit almost entirely such an important part of the novel suggests a new turn to the obfuscation of the Holocaust. This scene might have been filmed in Soviet times. In 2013, Channel One followed with *Cry of an Owl*, which gives an even more explicit answer to the question of Holocaust memory: amnesia.

Although the Holocaust has fallen out of fashion in the Russian film industry, there are exceptions. Two recent independent Russian films, the short *Shoes* [*Tufel'ki*] (2013), directed by Costa Fam, and the documentary *Holocaust: Is It Wallpaper Paste?* [*Kholokost – klei dlia oboev*] (2013), directed by Mumin Shakirov, focus on the memory of the Holocaust. Significantly, both caused strong reactions at home and have circulated at film festivals abroad. These two films, and the high profile they achieved (rare for shorts and documentaries), make a fascinating case-study of Holocaust representations in contemporary Russia, and of its successes and failures.

Holocaust: Is It Wallpaper Paste?

The premise of this documentary sounds like a joke: Evgenia and Ksenia Karatygin, twin sisters competing in the *Insanely Beautiful* Russian reality show, get stumped by a question: 'What is the Holocaust?' The sisters grapple for the answer: 'Holocaust, it doesn't ring a bell. Maybe it's something related to office supplies... Or perhaps some household product...' Out of their depth, they start guessing: 'Holocaust is wallpaper paste.'

A clip depicting this debacle went viral on YouTube. In a matter of days, half a million people watched it. Among the viewers captivated by this moment was Mumin Shakirov, a Moscow-based filmmaker, who at that time worked for Radio Svoboda (Radio Liberty), a US-backed broadcaster providing alternative news and information about Eastern Europe. Shakirov sensed an opportunity to raise Holocaust awareness, and immediately invited the twins to his studio for a conversation with Alla Gerber, a Holocaust educator, which was turned into a TV show. The success of this broadcast gave Shakirov the idea to take the girls on a trip to Auschwitz and document it on film. He told me that part of his inspiration was the story of Jade Goody, the late British reality TV star, who became famous for demonstrating incredible gaps in her most basic general knowledge, generating a debate about education and class in the UK. Shakirov saw the Karatygin sisters as Russian Jade Goodies, whose equally shocking gaps in knowledge about world history might start an important conversation.

Shakirov's documentary opens with observational footage that, in its visual quality, resembles reality TV. It culminates in the scene with the sisters' faux pas. Then, the documentary seemingly shifts genres, and from a reality show transforms into a road movie, as the camera documents Evgenia and Ksenia's journey to Auschwitz. The journey is intercut with interviews with the girls and conversations with their mother, which function as flashbacks to their childhood in a provincial Russian town. The girls are conventionally pretty, but unremarkable; as is their desire to be famous. Their upbringing is equally unremarkable, though marred by the loss of their father to illness. After they move to Moscow for college, they start auditioning for reality TV shows, until they become famous for not knowing what the Holocaust is.

It is quite clear that at first they do not see their performance as a problem – they admit to making no attempt after their appearance in the show to find out about the Holocaust, or to understand why their answer provoked controversy. For them, this scandal is, as they put it, another 'moment of fame'. They gladly accept an invitation to go to Auschwitz – a trip abroad – as an opportunity for excellent PR. An observational-style camera captures their bug-eyed enthusiasm and puppy-like innocence. At first, we watch the sisters with disbelief, but they are so warm and good-natured that we, the audience, start sympathising with them. On a train to Poland, they speak excitedly about getting ready for a trip – receiving passports, holding foreign money for the first time. Nothing prepares them for the actual destination.

The most instructive moments of the film are interviews with the girls' mother and their schoolteacher. The mother, an older working-class woman, admits that neither she nor her neighbours have ever heard of 'this Holocaust'. But the history teacher, younger and more educated than the mother, is embarrassed to the point of being defensive. The Holocaust, according to her, was covered at school: 'Perhaps the girls just missed this class or didn't pay attention to the material.' Then she grows more contemplative, even wonders whether her lesson was memorable enough, but at the end she excuses herself – she didn't have appropriate pedagogical materials. 'Perhaps,' she says, 'one day I will get to the point of teaching an entire class session on the Holocaust. But for that I need to be ready myself. I myself first need to see something that will deeply affect me.'

The girls' mother belongs to a generation of people who came of age during the Soviet era, when commemorating the Jewish catastrophe was extremely rare. (The term 'Holocaust' itself only came into usage in Russia in the 1990s.) But the teacher's comments are more thought provoking. She is an educator, a professional historian with a university diploma, who, presumably, should have the knowledge and the tools to teach about major historical events. Her complaint that she does not have access to pedagogical resources to teach about the Holocaust is telling. The teacher even admits indirectly that she herself needs to learn more, to be more motivated before she can embark on teaching an entire class session – that is, 45 minutes – on the subject. Why is this well-meaning teacher feeling so unprepared when such a plethora of material is available online and in print? Even if Holocaust education in Russia still has a long way to go, it seems unlikely that a motivated teacher could not find material that 'deeply affects' her, be it in books, photos, films or virtual exhibits. Perhaps we can read the teacher's position as a commentary on the general absence of motivation and responsibility in Russia to deal with the lessons of the Holocaust as the central genocidal event of the twentieth century, or as a part of a particular local history.

What are the lessons that Evgenia and Ksenia finally learn when they arrive at the Auschwitz-Birkenau museum? Predictably, their naïve excitement transforms into shock as they walk among the barracks and get a guided tour through the abject exhibits. The images on screen, depicting the horrors of the camps, are familiar to Western eyes, but the girls' reaction makes them appear powerfully new. Particularly powerful is an exhibit about Dr. Mengele's experiments on twins, illustrated on screen by grotesque photographs from the museum collection. The camera closes up on the twins, as their sad faces reveal a sudden sense of empathy and identification with the victims.

After the tour, one of the girls is too overwhelmed to speak, but the other feels a new sense of mission: 'Nowadays, many people in Russia don't know about it [the Holocaust], and thanks to you [Shakirov], we are among the minority who do know ... and now it is our responsibility to tell others.' But what would they tell? The short tour is enough to bring tears to their eyes but can scarcely fill the gaps in their understanding of such a complex historical event. Still, empathy is there, which may be more important than a full grasp of history, given the current Russian climate of intolerance and xenophobia.

Fig. 1 Screenshot from *Holocaust: Is it Wallpaper Paste?* Courtesy of Mumin Shakirov

In fact, it is Russia's growing xenophobia that motivated Shakirov to make this documentary. Shakirov and his family are secularised Central Asian Muslims with roots in Dushanbe, in what is now Turkmenistan, members of an ethnic and religious minority who are often harassed and assaulted in Russia. In Moscow, there are riots against people from Central Asia and the Caucasus. The targets of these riots are often migrant workers, perceived as an economic and cultural threat.[8] Shakirov admitted to me that he is seriously concerned not only about career prospects but also about the safety of his dark-skinned sons. This concern led to his interest in the subject of the Holocaust, and his identification with Jews, the paradigmatic persecuted minority.

The increasing racism in Russia is an important context for understanding this film and the position of the filmmaker. Still, why does Shakirov take his protagonists on a tour of Auschwitz? During the war, as many as 2.6 million Jews were murdered on Nazi-occupied Soviet territory.[9] It is true that most victims were killed in Ukraine, Belarus, Moldova and Lithuania, former republics of the Soviet Union (of which Russia is a successor state). But even within contemporary Russian borders, former 'RSFSR' (Russian Soviet Federative Socialist Republic), there were dozens of ghettos and numerous sites of mass executions. Why not start the girls' Holocaust education in their home country?

For Shakirov, the answer was obvious: 'I chose Auschwitz because it's an iconic place, because it immediately signifies the Holocaust,' he told me. This choice is not surprising, given the universally recognised status of Auschwitz as 'a metonym for the Shoah' (Huener 2003: 15). But Shakirov also has a personal connection to Auschwitz: he learned about the camp as a child and always wanted to visit the famous museum. He remembers studying about Auschwitz in school in Dushanbe. In Soviet schools, Jews were not mentioned as a historically specific victim group; instead, Auschwitz was presented as a site of Nazi crimes where people of various nationalities were exterminated. Shakirov pointed out to me that a more important influence was his father's stories. In the 1970s, when it was difficult and rare for Soviet citizens to go abroad, his father went on a tour to Poland, visited Auschwitz, and brought back books, postcards and brochures. Like the Soviet school, the tour did not focus on Jews, but the camp itself left a tremendous impression on Shakirov's father, who talked about it to young Mumin.

Just like such personal memories, cinematic representations of Auschwitz are powerful signifiers of the Shoah. Crematoriums, chimneys, piles of hair and photos of skeletal victims constitute the core Holocaust imagery and provide evidence of the Nazi crimes. And yet, the ready cinematic value of Auschwitz does not provide the full answer to a question: why focus on Auschwitz in a Russian Holocaust documentary? Another part of the answer is the legacy of Soviet externalisation of the Holocaust.

As mentioned above, the policy of externalisation during the Soviet era had significant consequences for Holocaust iconography, which relied predominantly on familiar camp imagery (see Gershenson 2013: 161, 209–10, 224). Such representation combined 'the best of both worlds': it passed the approval of the censors and gave filmmakers an effective visual shortcut for representing the Holocaust. It was politically appropriate – in accordance with the party line, it located the Holocaust outside Soviet borders and omitted the subject of the executions of Jews in Soviet territory during the war, thus conveniently avoiding the difficult questions of local collaboration and historic responsibility.

The process of taking historic responsibility is painful. Such a process of soul-searching not only by the first, but also by the second generation of perpetrators and bystanders took place in Germany and is arguably starting to take place in Poland, but it has not yet begun in Russia.[10] At the moment, nothing indicates that it is likely to happen. Shakirov's sensitive and thoughtful documentary is more evidence of the continual Soviet legacy of externalising the Holocaust. Yes, the film shows the girls' shock and awe at learning about the heinous crimes of Nazism. But these historic crimes lie entirely outside the realm of their experience; they took place in an entirely different era and, according to the logic of the film, in a foreign land. The girls come back to Moscow as shocked travellers, with a mission 'to tell others'. But they are not required to look into their own community's past. The Holocaust is conveniently externalised, even exoticised. It is not clear if the girls come into contact with actual Jews in their everyday lives, or even know what being Jewish means, or if they draw parallels with other religious or cultural 'others' who face xenophobia in contemporary Russia. Through the Karatygin sisters, their mother and their teacher, the film exposes alarming gaps in the historical knowledge of contemporary Russian youth and adults, but Shakirov does not attempt to probe and explore these gaps.

Shakirov's film, then, both disrupts and perpetuates the Soviet legacy. The Holocaust in the film is not universalized – it is a subject of direct conversation. Moreover, the film challenges the current climate of historical amnesia in Russia, exposing and problematising the fact that many people in Russia do not know, or do not care to know, about the Holocaust. At the same time, the Holocaust is still presented in this film as a historic event that took place elsewhere, and that does not concern Russian citizens. One may have a good cry visiting a tragic foreign site, then return home to business as usual, with no reason to ask probing questions about your own society. The Holocaust and other genocidal crimes are separated from everyday life by the safe distance of time and space. Unsurprisingly, Shakirov's film ends, literally, on a happy note: back in Moscow after their gruelling trip, the girls belt out a pop song about a mother's love, as their own mother greets them with flowers.

Shoes

A few months before the Karatygin sisters became a YouTube sensation, Dmitrii Parshkov, a friend of filmmaker Costa (Konstantin) Fam, was visiting Auschwitz. After seeing the museum exhibits – piles of suitcases, glasses, shoes – Parshkov called Fam with an idea: to tell a story of the Holocaust through one pair of shoes, from the storefront to the museum vitrine. 'I was jolted,' recalls Fam, 'to express the tragedy of millions in one sentence!' (2013). Fam grew up in Ukraine as the son of a Vietnamese immigrant father and a Jewish mother; in other words, he is an heir to death and violence on both sides of his family, and he knows first-hand what it means to be a member of an ethnic and religious minority. When he was growing up in the Soviet Union, he experienced harassment as both an Asian and a Jew. Since he was a film student, Fam felt that the Holocaust was 'his' subject. The day after Parshkov's phone call, Fam told me, he wrote the first draft of *Shoes*. The resulting film is a Russian-Belarus-Czech co-production, supported by the Auschwitz museum.

In a span of 18 minutes, the camera follows a young Jewish girl, or rather her feet, as she buys beautiful red shoes, falls in love, gets married, has a child, and then loses all she has when the Nazis invade. Her husband, betrayed by a local collaborator, is taken to the gas chambers at Auschwitz. Presumably, she meets the same fate, as at the end of the film we see the same pretty red pumps, now worn down and wrinkled, among the famous exhibit of a pile of shoes, signifying all that is left from the murder of millions. To drive the point home, the camera only shows us the characters' feet, never their faces, as if their humanity was gone even before they were reduced to piles of objects. The film ends, perhaps not happily, but at least on a redemptive note: the now aged collaborator

Fig. 2 Screenshot from *Shoes*. Courtesy of Costa Fam

comes to pay his tribute to the deceased at the Auschwitz museum. Ironically, he is the only character who is shown in full.

The point of Fam's film is to tell an affecting story. Although the film is premised on a gimmick, as the director himself admits, it succeeds in painting a tragedy in broad strokes: a life of good people destroyed by the brutal force of Nazism. Competent cinematography results in poignant, albeit predictable, and palatable images. The problem is that, in telling this emotional story completely stripped of historical details, the filmmaker inadvertently taps into the Soviet legacy, most significantly that of externalising the Holocaust.

The film is set at an undefined place, presumably somewhere in Europe. Aside from ambient music, the film is silent: there is no dialogue, and hence no language to identify the characters and the location. Nostalgic images on screen depict a kind of a *shtetl*, with markets, horses, wells and a Jewish wedding, complete with breaking the glass and circle dancing. Then, the happy couple goes on a honeymoon to Paris, instantly transformed from barefoot peasants into sophisticated bourgeois tourists. The picture is vague, but one thing is clear: the action does not take place in the Soviet Union. Stalin's regime curtailed foreign travel, and so Soviet Jews did not vacation in Paris, nor did they live in places untouched by the Soviet regime. Instead of an actual historical reality, the film depicts our ideas of pre-war European Jewish life. This historical and geographical abstraction continues to externalise the Holocaust: as in Soviet times, it remains an event that took place elsewhere, or nowhere in particular, but certainly not in occupied Soviet territories.

There is another important way in which the film's depiction of the Holocaust reveals an uncomfortable parallel with the Soviet past. As mentioned above, throughout Soviet history, the Holocaust was largely silenced. Foreign Holocaust films were rarely, if ever, shown there, and Soviet films were too scarce to develop a visual language for representing the Jewish catastrophe. The significant debate about the limits and possibilities of Holocaust representation that has taken place in the US and Europe since the 1970s did not reach the Soviet Union.[11] The parameters of this debate, especially its critical examination of graphic and sentimentalised depictions of violence, remained unknown to most Russian filmmakers and audiences.

The scene in *Shoes* depicting death inside the gas chamber is a case in point. On screen, dozens of bare feet shuffle, advancing, quiet and orderly, in a bluish luminous light. Melancholy instrumental music turns it into a spiritual symbolic scene. Here the abstract approach to history backfires, as the violent, abject deaths of the victims are turned on screen into a sentimentalised symbol. This aestheticisation of suffering dehumanises victims of Nazi violence, even though the film specifically seeks to memorialise them.

Moreover, it is problematic to represent the Holocaust through the perspective of footwear. The red shoes are an easily-recognisable allusion to *Schindler's List*, where a little girl in a red coat stands out in a black-and-white frame. As in Spielberg's highly successful film, the camera's obsessive focus on this red spot, contrasting the monochromatic world of the picture, creates a sensationalist and sentimental image.

In important ways, *Shoes* is out of sync with its time. Today, it is no longer sufficient simply to state that the terrible events occurred and to elicit empathy for the victims. The best international Holocaust cinema now strives to tell a particular story, to find an authentic perspective, to avoid emotional manipulation and, most importantly, to raise issues related to memory and responsibility, especially of second- and even third-generation victims and perpetrators. This is the case, for instance, with the Polish film *Aftermath* [*Pokłosie*] (2012), directed by Władysław Pasikowski. Here, the main characters, two Poles, gradually uncover the extent to which their community was implicated in the murder of local Jews during the Nazi occupation. They find out that nearly everyone was implicated. The great accomplishment of the film is that it shows what kind of resistance, including physical violence, the two protagonists face even today. Probing the past is painful, as the reception of *Aftermath* in Poland confirmed: it provoked criticism from ethno-nationalists for tarnishing the Polish reputation, while others rallied behind the film. *Aftermath* started a national conversation about the role of ordinary Poles during the Holocaust (see Grollmus 2013). By contrast, *Shoes* tells a feel-good Holocaust story: Jews are good, Nazis are bad, and even a collaborator repents: there are no challenging questions and no uncomfortable revelations.

By relying on a gimmick, and by avoiding particular stories grounded in an actual historical and cultural context, the film avoids dealing with uncomfortable subjects of historic responsibility. Even as Soviet censorship ended in the late 1980s, its power seemingly extended into the future: the history of the Holocaust in the Soviet Union continues to be largely unrepresented. For Russians, this is safer, as it allows them to avoid the shocks that may arise from asking difficult questions about elderly neighbours or grandparents. It is easier to locate the Holocaust story in a nostalgic never-neverland, depict brutal death as an ascension into the light, and focus on an unusual angle – literally, a camera angle on the shoes. This allows the film to begin nowhere in particular, and to end in Auschwitz, rather than Kiev, Minsk or Smolensk.

Shoes had already had a triumphant run on Russian and European film festivals, and at several Jewish film festivals in North America. Emboldened by its success, Fam is now working on two sequels to *Shoes*, which, taken together, will form a feature-length trilogy titled *Witnesses* [*Svideteli*]. As Fam explained to me, the second part of the trilogy will present the Holocaust through the perspective of a dog raised by a Jewish owner that is later taken to guard a concentration camp. The final part will trace the history of a violin made in pre-war Nuremberg which finds its way to a concert near the Wailing Wall in present-day Jerusalem. It is unclear whether these short films will overcome the limitations in portraying the Holocaust evident in *Shoes*.

FROM AMNESIA TO REMEMBRANCE?

Post-Soviet films stand in marked contrast to those completed or attempted during the Soviet era. And yet, the Soviet legacy of silencing the Holocaust continues. This is part of a larger problem: memory work is still not done in Russia.

Within memory studies, there is a tradition that theorises three distinct aspects of collective memory: communicative, cultural and political (see Assmann 2006). Communicative memory has a limited time scope – two or three generations – and is based predominantly on everyday communication; cultural memory, on the other hand, extends for a longer period, and can be expressed through formal commemorations (texts, ceremonies and monuments) and practices of observance around them. Cultural memory is carried out by various bearers, such as historians, media and educators. Finally, as Jan Assmann has suggested (2010: 122), an externalised symbolic aspect of cultural memory carried out by top-down institutions becomes identified as political memory. Collective memory in the Soviet Union, and later in Russia, has excluded the memory of the Holocaust on all three levels.

This lack of Holocaust memorialisation in Russia has historic explanations. First, in the immediate post-war years, the events of the Holocaust were largely prohibited from discussion in the Soviet Union (see Gitelman 1993). This prohibition stymied the transmission of personal memory and, unlike in other countries, communicative memory of the Holocaust has never formed.

Second, the Holocaust never became a part of cultural memory. Throughout the Soviet era, any attempts to memorialise the Holocaust through monuments, literary texts, art and media were completely or partially censored. The memory of the Holocaust was subsumed by the memory of the Great Patriotic War. In Putin's Russia, the memory of World War II is still firmly couched in old Soviet terms with a particular emphasis on the victory and heroism of the Russian people (see Konradova and Ryleva 2005). Moreover, today this Soviet-style approach is becoming increasingly nationalistic, playing up the regime's claim for Russia's special historic role and unique path (see Ferretti 2005). In this version of the memory of the war, there is no space for a Jewish catastrophe.

Finally, regarding political memory, the state has failed to acknowledge and memorialise the Holocaust. It is noteworthy that Russia, like Belarus and Ukraine, is not a member of the International Holocaust Remembrance Alliance (IHRA), even though the events of the Holocaust took place on its territory. With few exceptions, there is no official commemoration of the Holocaust through major museums, rites or other practices; the Holocaust is not a part of state-authorised school curricula, and outside of the efforts of the Moscow-based Holocaust Center there is no formalised training of teachers on the subject (see Altman 2005).

Russia's most striking failure is that the Holocaust in that country is still interpreted as an internal Jewish affair, with limited relevance to anyone else. By contrast, in the Western world, the Holocaust is an event of universal history, a paradigmatic genocide, a crisis of modernity with repercussions for all citizens of the world.[12] Some historians go as far as to ask, 'Can countries or civilizations that do not acknowledge the Holocaust develop universalistic political moralities' and affirm 'the uniqueness and sacredness of the Holocaust as a touchstone of universal moral maturity?' (cited in Assmann 2010: 108). Those are the questions that Russia must face.

Russia lives in a state of willing amnesia about the Holocaust, as well as about other aspects of its history. The crimes of Stalin's regime are still neither atoned for nor memorialised on a national level. Writing about a different cultural context, Michael Rothberg points out how memory of traumatic historic events is often perceived as a scarce resource, resulting in a zero-sum competitive approach to memorialisation. He suggests thinking of memory as a multidirectional process and a limitless resource, whereby connecting and honoring seemingly disparate catastrophes can actually result in a better understanding of them, and in a richer form of memory (2009: 1–33). This cannot be more right in the context of Russia, with its interconnected legacies of communist terror, Stalin's repressions, World War II, the Holocaust and other ethnic and religious persecutions. As Tymothy Snyder (2010) has showed, these historic events should be understood in the context of each other. In my opinion, the memories, too, should be connected. However, there is a persistent sense in Russia that memory is a zero-sum game. Not only marginal anti-Semites but even some progressive thinkers believe the Holocaust should not be memorialised in Russia as a distinct and separate event.[13] In their logic, Jewish victims are just a part of the larger losses of the Great Patriotic War, and it is sufficient to focus on the generalised story of the entire event.

The inertia of the Soviet discourse, which universalised and externalised the Holocaust, is still a factor – no one wants to take historic responsibility for the crimes committed on Soviet soil. The Jewish Holocaust remains an uncomfortable subject, easier to push away than to acknowledge. This is why filmmakers like Mumin Shakirov and Costa Fam, who, despite this discomfort and amnesia, dare to deal with the subject, deserve credit. Their films, however different, have a lot in common: they rely on a gimmick in their approach to the Holocaust (the reality-show slippage in one case, the footwear angle in the other). They externalise the Holocaust by avoiding local history and setting the action at Auschwitz. But importantly, these films are both 'labours of love', initiated by the filmmakers themselves and produced on minimal budgets, with the help of private donors, Jewish organisations and crowdfunding. The two filmmakers deserve special credit for seeing their films as educational vehicles. Shakirov conducted over fifty screenings not just at festivals, but also at schools, museums and community organisations across Russia, some in collaboration with the Russian Holocaust Center. Fam is even more ambitious – once his trilogy is complete, he envisions a cross-platform outreach campaign, including curriculum development, with on- and off-line events. In the atmosphere of collective amnesia in Russia today, Shakirov's and Fam's sense of mission around their Holocaust films is cause for hope.

It is noteworthy that these two films, exceptions to the amnesia rule, were created by members of ethnic minorities in Russia, and not necessarily Jews: a Central Asian secularised Muslim in one case and a Ukrainian-born Jewish-Vietnamese in another. Both filmmakers are visibly marked as non-whites, members of persecuted minorities associated in contemporary Russia with illegal guest workers, who face hostility and marginalisation on personal, social and state levels. It is not by chance that these two filmmakers became acutely aware of their otherness in recent years, that they started thinking deeply about Jews as a persecuted minority, and about the Holocaust. The two films show, or rather hint at, the relevance of Holocaust memory in today's Russia and its adaptation to the needs of the new persecuted minorities. Perhaps this is the first indication of interpreting the Holocaust in Russia as a universal event that has a lasting meaning for all citizens in the society, Jews and non-Jews alike.

Although the two films are problematic in the way they continue the Russian tendencies to externalise the Holocaust, they hold the potential to make Russians begin looking at the Holocaust directly. As a first step, this may encourage young Russians (and their parents and teachers) at least to know what happened specifically to Jews, and begin integrating the Holocaust into everyday thought. Perhaps next, Russians may be able to turn the spotlight on themselves.

Notes

1   On the proliferation of positive characters of KGB/NKVD officers on recent Russian TV, see Lipovetsky (2014).

2   In addition to the awards from the Russian Association of Film and TV Producers, *Cry of an Owl* was awarded first prize by the FSB for the best artistic and literary productions representing the work of the organisation.
3   Alternatives to amnesia are evident in the activities of the Russian historical and civil rights society 'Memorial', recording and publicising the Soviet totalitarian past and trying to memorialise its victims, and the 'Holocaust Center and Foundation', a Moscow-based organisation conducting scholarly research and publications and developing Holocaust education in Russia.
4   On Soviet treatment of the Holocaust, see Gitelman (1993, 1997).
5   On universalisation, see Arad (2001), Berkhoff (2009) and Feferman (2009).
6   For a discussion of externalisation, see Gershenson (2013: 2).
7   In contrast, the letter is a basis for a US/French co-production *The Last Letter* (2002) by the renowned filmmaker Frederick Wiseman. Similarly, in an eight-hour BBC radio drama *Life and Fate* (2011) based on the novel, the letter is thematised in an episode, and the character of the mother, played by Janet Suzman, is individualised.
8   For more background on this issue, see Berman (2013).
9   The numbers of the Holocaust victims in the USSR vary, depending on how and in which borders they are calculated. Here, I am relying on Yitzhak Arad's estimate in his *The Holocaust in the Soviet Union* (2009: 525).
10 For background on *Vergangenheitsbewältigung* in Germany, see Niven (2001). On Poland, see Huener (2003: 227–47) and Abrosewicz-Jacobs (2010).
11 For a brief overview of the debate, see Baron (2005: 10–22).
12 On the perception of the Holocaust as a universal event, see Assmann and Conrad (2010: 8). On the perception of the Holocaust in Russia, see Kukulin (forthcoming).
13 See, for instance, an interview with Leonid Katsva (2013), a famous history teacher in Russia.

Filmography

Aftermath [*Pokłosie*]. Dir. Władysław Pasikowski. Poland, 2012.
Babi Yar. Dir. Jeff Kanew. Germany/Belarus, 2003.
Babi Yar. Dir. Nikolai Zaseev-Rudenko. Ukraine, 2002.
The Burning Land [*V Iiune 41*]. Dir. Mikhail Ptashuk. Russia/USA, 2003.
Children from the Abyss [*Deti iz bezdny*]. Dir. Pavel Chukhrai. Russia, 2002.
Commissar. Dir. Aleksandr Askol'dov. Soviet Union, 1967.
Cry of an Owl [*Krik sovy*]. Dir. Oleg Pogodin. Russia, 2013.
David. Dir. Aleksei Fedorchenko. Russia, 2002.
Eastern Corridor [*Vostochnyi koridor*]. Dir. Valentin Vinogradov. Soviet Union, 1966.
Exile [*Izgoi*]. Dir. Vladimir Savel'ev. Soviet Union, 1991.
Ghetto. Dir. Audrius Juzenas. Lithuania/Germany, 2006.
Heavy Sand [*Tiazhelyi Pesok*]. Dir. Anton Barschevskii. Russia, 2008.
Holocaust: Is It Wallpaper Paste? [*Kholokost—klei dlia oboev*]. Dir. Mumin Shakirov. Russia, 2013.
Ladies' Tailor [*Damskii Portnoi*]. Dir. Leonid Gorovets. Soviet Union, 1990.
The Last Letter. Dir. Frederick Wiseman. USA/France, 2002.
The Oppenheim Family [*Sem'ia Oppengeim*]. Dir. Grigorii Roshal. Soviet Union, 1938.
Ordinary Fascism [*Obyknovennyi fashizm*]. Dir. Mikhail Romm. Soviet Union, 1966.

Our Father [*Otche Nash*]. Dir. Boris Ermolaev. Soviet Union, 1990.
Professor Mamlock. Dir. Herbert Rappaport and Adolf Minkin. Soviet Union, 1938.
Shoes [*Tufel'ki*]. Dir. Costa Fam. Russia, 2013.
Sons of the Fatherland [*Syny otechestva*]. Dir. Latif Faiziev. Soviet Union, 1968.
The Unvanquished [*Nepokorennye*]. Dir. Mark Donskoi. Soviet Union, 1945.

Bibliography

Abrosewicz-Jacobs, Jolanta (2010) 'Holocaust Education after 1989 in Polish Schools – and Beyond', in Kate Craddy, Mike Levy and Jakub Nowakowski (eds) *Poland: A Jewish Matter*. Warsaw: Adam Mickiewicz Institute, 77–103.

Altman, Ilya (2005) 'Memorializatsia Kholokosta v Rossii: Istoria, Sovremennost', Perspektivy', in Mikhail Gabovich (ed.) *Pamiat' o Voine 60 Let Spustia: Rossia, Germania, Evropa*. Moscow: Novoe Literaturnoe Obozrenie, 509–31.

Arad, Yitzhak (2001) 'Stalin and the Soviet Leadership: Responses to the Holocaust', in John K. Roth and Elisabeth Maxwell (eds) *Remembering for the Future: The Holocaust in an Age of Genocide. Vol. 1: History*. Houndmills: Palgrave, 355–70.

Arad, Yitzhak (2009) *The Holocaust in the Soviet Union*. Lincoln: University of Nebraska Press/Jerusalem: Yad Vashem.

Assmann, Aleida (2006) 'Memory, Individual and Collective', in Robert E. Goodin and Charles Tilly (eds) *The Oxford Handbook of Contextual Political Analysis*. Oxford: Oxford University Press, 210–24.

____ (2010) 'The Holocaust – A Global Memory? Extensions and Limits of a New Memory Community', in Aleida Assmann and Sebastian Conrad (eds) *Memory in a Global Age: Discourses, Practices and Trajectories*. Houndmills: Palgrave Macmillan, 97–119.

____ (2014) 'Rossiane Staratel'no Pytaiutsia Steret' iz Pamiati Ochen' Mnogoe...' Interview by Egor Vinogradov. *Deutsche Welle*, 23 October. Online: http://www.dw.com/ru/алейда-ассман-россияне-старательно-пытаются-стереть-из-памяти-очень-многое/a-18012698?maca=rus-rss-ru-cul-1054-rdf

Assmann, Aleida and Sebastian Conrad (2010) 'Introduction', in Aleida Assmann and Sebastian Conrad (eds) *Memory in a Global Age: Discourses, Practices and Trajectories*. Houndmills: Palgrave Macmillan, 1–17.

Assmann, Jan (2010) 'Globalization, Universalism, and the Erosion of Cultural Memory', in Aleida Assmann and Sebastian Conrad (eds) *Memory in a Global Age: Discourses, Practices and Trajectories*. Houndmills: Palgrave Macmillan, 121–38.

Baron, Lawrence (2005) *Projecting the Holocaust into the Present: The Changing Focus of Contemporary Holocaust Cinema*. Lanham, MD: Rowman & Littlefield.

Berkhoff, Karel C. (2009) '"Total Annihilation of the Jewish Population": The Holocaust in the Soviet Media, 1941–45', *Kritika: Explorations in Russian and Eurasian History*, 10, 1, 477–504.

Berman, Ilan (2013) 'Why Russia is Growing More Xenophobic', *The Atlantic*. Online: http://www.theatlantic.com/international/archive/2013/10/why-russia-is-growing-more-xenophobic/280766/

Fam, Costa (2013) 'Slova 'Zhidenysh' i 'Churka' Mne Prikhodilos' Slyshat' Odnovremenno', Interview by Maria Shubina. *Booknik. SKCG*, 13 December. Online: http://booknik.ru/today/

faces/slova-jidenysh-i-churka-mne-prihodilos-slyshat-odnovremenno/

____ (2014) Personal interview. 22 May.

Feferman, Kiril (2009) *Soviet Jewish Stepchild: The Holocaust in the Soviet Mindset, 1941–1964*. Saarbrücken: Müller.

Ferretti, Maria (2005) '"Neprimirimaia Pamiat": Rossia i Voina. Zametki na Poliakh Spora na Zhguchuiu Temu', in Mikhail Gabovich (ed.) *Pamiat' o Voine 60 Let Spustia: Rossia, Germania, Evropa*. Moscow: Novoe Literaturnoe Obozrenie, 135–47.

Gershenson, Olga (2013) *The Phantom Holocaust: Soviet Cinema and Jewish Catastrophe*. New Brunswick, NJ: Rutgers University Press.

Gitelman, Zvi (1993) 'Soviet Reactions to the Holocaust, 1945–1991', in Lucian Dobroszycki and Jeffrey S. Gurock (eds) *The Holocaust in the Soviet Union: Studies and Sources on the Destruction of the Jews in the Nazi-Occupied Territories of the USSR, 1941–1945*. Armonk: Sharpe, 3–27.

____ (1997) 'Politics and the Historiography of the Holocaust in the Soviet Union', in Zvi Gitelman (ed.) *Bitter Legacy: Confronting the Holocaust in the USSR*. Bloomington, IN: Indiana University Press, 14–43.

Grollmus, Denise (2013) 'In the Polish Aftermath', *Tablet*. Online: http://www.tabletmag.com/jewish-arts-and-culture/129082/in-the-polish-aftermath

Hansen, Miriam Bratu (1996) '*Schindler's List* Is Not *Shoah*: Second Commandment, Popular Modernism, and Public Memory', *Critical Inquiry*, 22: 292–312.

Hösler, Joachim (2005) 'Chto Znachit 'Prorabotka Proshlogo'? Ob Istoriografii Velikoi Otechestvennoi Voiny v SSSR i Rossii', in Mikhail Gabovich (ed.) *Pamiat' o Voine 60 Let Spustia: Rossia, Germania, Evropa*. Moscow: Novoe Literaturnoe Obozrenie, 156–70.

Huener, Jonathan (2003) *Auschwitz, Poland, and the Politics of Commemoration, 1945–1979*. Athens, OH: Ohio University Press.

Katsva, Leonid (2013) 'My Rabotaem ne s Ogurtsami, a s Det'mi', *Snob. Snob Media*, 19 February. Online: http://snob.ru/selected/entry/57637?v=1437564368

Kondrashev, Aleksandr (2013) 'Ivan Mitin Protiv Vragov Naroda', *Literaturnaia Gazeta*, 13 November.

Konradova, Natalia and Anna Ryleva (2005) 'Geroi i Zhertvy: Memorialy Velikoi Otechestvennoi', in Mikhail Gabovich (ed.) *Pamiat' o Voine 60 Let Spustia: Rossia, Germania, Evropa*. Moscow: Novoe Literaturnoe Obozrenie, 241–62.

Kukulin, Ilya (forthcoming) '"Teni Vsekh Butyrok i Treblinok": Neskol'ko Predpolozhenii o Tom, Pochemu Shoah ne Schitaetsia Samostoiatel'nym Sobytiem v Istroii Rossii', *Fabula: Lecherche en Literature*.

Life and Fate. Dir. Alison Hindell. BBC Radio 4, 18–25 September.

Lipovetsky, Mark (2014) 'Breaking Cover: How the KGB Became Russia's Favourite TV Heroes', *The Calvert Journal*. Online: http://calvertjournal.com/comment/show/2433/the-rise-of-kgb-television-series

Niven, Bill (2001) *Facing the Nazi Past: United Germany and the Legacy of the Third Reich*. New York: Routledge.

Rothberg, Michael (2009) *Multidirectional Memory: Remembering the Holocaust in the Age of Decolonization*. Stanford, CA: Stanford University Press.

Shakirov, Mumin (2014a) Personal interview. 12 July.

____ (2014b) Personal interview. 15 October.

Snyder, Timothy (2010) *Bloodlands: Europe between Hitler and Stalin*. New York: Basic Books.

CHAPTER FIVE

Wilhelm Brasse's Photographs from Auschwitz
TESTIMONY AND PHOTOGRAPHY IN IREK DOBROWOLSKI'S *THE PORTRAITIST*

Tomasz Łysak[1]

Wilhelm Brasse's cinematographic testimony, recorded by Irek Dobrowolski in *The Portraitist* [*Portrecista*] (2005), brings into focus the Auschwitz photographer who persevered in self-imposed anonymity for decades after the end of World War II. Even though his identity was known only to a narrow circle of archivists at the Auschwitz-Birkenau State Museum, the images he produced loom large in the iconography of the Holocaust. Not only do they illustrate the functioning of Auschwitz and the murderous policy implemented there, but they have also come to define the Holocaust in general. This mechanism of decontextualization of photography for symbolic purposes, Janina Struk (2004) has illuminated in reference to a few famous images from the era. Furthermore, the Auschwitz photographer's work has been displayed in the permanent exhibit in the State Museum. *The Portraitist* is an important contribution to the visual commemoration of Auschwitz-Birkenau as the documentary complements archival images with a personal story of the photographer. The film employs staging and presentation of prints of photographs taken or developed by Brasse in order to assist the witness in his testimony. The filmmaker does not stop at the presentation of historical details as he intends to show the personal consequences Brasse suffered because of his incarceration and work for the camp administration.

Wilhelm Brasse (1917–2012) was born in Żywiec to a Polish mother and a father of Austrian descent. At the beginning of the war he refused to claim German identity, and he was eventually arrested during a hike across the Bieszczady Mountains on his way to join the Polish army in France. Sent to Auschwitz, the 22-year-old professional photographer from Katowice was given the prisoner number 3444 on 30 August 1940. Working in the *Erkennungsdienst*, the official photographic unit at Auschwitz, Brasse took the majority of mug shots of prisoners. He was also responsible for photographing medical experiments conducted on humans at Auschwitz. In addition to this, he completed other photographic assignments as requested by the SS officers in charge of the unit and by other Germans from the camp administration. Dobrowolski's documentary was not the first film to feature Brasse; he made a brief appearance in *Liebe Perla* (dir. Shahar Rozen, 1999), a German/Israeli co-production about the plight of a family spared annihilation due to the 'professional' interest of Dr. Joseph Mengele in the medical condition of dwarfism.

Brasse's anonymity was partially due to the publication policy of the Auschwitz-Birkenau State Museum. Even though he was recorded (on audio tape) and transcribed by the archivists in 1959, 1977 and 1984 and again in September 1989, with the most recent interviews conducted on video (in 2000 and 2006), none of these testimonies found their way beyond the walls of the archive. Brasse's photographs have also remained largely disconnected from his name. The archive at the State Museum collects prints in an album with plastic pockets, and in this format the collection provides no information as to the identity of the sitters. Reversing this tradition of anonymity, Dobrowolski's documentary played a pivotal role in bringing Brasse and his role in the proliferation of mug shots and medical images from Auschwitz to public attention. Following the film's premiere, the ex-photographer accepted invitations to screenings of the film and to the promotion of Maria Anna Potocka's book about him. In 2013, Anna Dobrowolska, the executive producer of *The Portraitist*, published a book based on outtakes from the documentary film which stands as the most comprehensive presentation of the photographer's testimony, further enriched with other available sources.

While the interpretation of Dobrowolski's documentary is my point of departure, I am going to widen the scope of the analysis and the range of materials to include various other interviews with the photographer. Thereby, I intend to offer a double contextualisation of the film: shedding light on the practices of photographic identification in the camp and comparing the photographer's self-presentations on various occasions. My study of Auschwitz photographs and their use in *The Portraitist* is guided by a set of research problems including the affinity of images to respective genres – mug shot, studio portrait and medical photography – and the relationship between testimony and photographs. These photographic genres provide the structure for Dobrowolski's documentary as Brasse explains the functioning of the camp in an overview of the visual output of the photo unit. In the final part of this essay I place *The Portraitist* in the context of Polish Holocaust documentaries and more general practices of commemoration.

MUG SHOTS AND STUDIO PORTRAITURE IN AUSCHWITZ-BIRKENAU

The mug shots of the new arrivals (approximately 50,000 people were recorded upon admission to the camp system) constitute the bulk of the photographic record of the camp.[2] Auschwitz identification photographs were a far cry from being a neutral record of faces, as the pictures forced an identity on the new arrivals in a similar manner to the uniforms, camp numbers and shorn hair. Even though the photographs did not serve as a means of practical identification, they nevertheless disciplined the prisoners, i.e. provided a record of their status and place in the camp hierarchy.[3] The disciplining is also discernible in the process of taking the photographs, with prisoners placed in front of a stationary camera in three predetermined positions: three quarters, head on and in profile. Photographing relied on teamwork as, apart from Brasse, another prisoner was charged with swapping film cassettes, and a third one was responsible for changing the prisoner number in the right profile shot (see Brasse 2011). These formal requirements diminished the role of the photographer, whose task was reduced to releasing the shutter since the other parameters were preset. The interviewers collecting testimony from Brasse are typically interested in the technical details of camp photography because they could not elicit this information from other prisoners.

Complementing these official duties, 'deep' psychological portraits of SS officers actively participating in their photographic self-expression provided ample opportunities for Brasse to shine as a master of his craft. The SS-men who partnered with the photographer in shaping their iconic self, trying to communicate their desired character traits, acknowledged his professional expertise. These two types of photographs, that is, mug shots and studio portraits, are indicative of the deployment of the visual in molding racial consciousness in Germany. The studied poses of the SS officers in Auschwitz might have been influenced by popular magazines such as *Volk und Rasse*, which featured portraits of Nazi Party officials intent on appearing 'at once masterful and humane' (Maxwell 2008: 189). These photographs followed the guidelines of traditional studio portraiture (Himmler's portrait reproduced by Anne Maxwell is a paragon of the genre). Therefore, it is justified to argue that instructions given by Brasse's sitters were motivated by both acknowledgment of the generic tradition and popular representations of high-ranking members of the NSDAP. Thus, Brasse reaped the fruits of his formal training, oblivious to the more varied uses of portrait photography at the time. Max Grabner – the head of the camp Gestapo and the single most dreaded officer in the camp – was uneasy before his shoot, so Brasse improvised a solution to reduce the tension, asking the sitter to think about his native Alps. It was only with the benefit of hindsight that Brasse was able to juxtapose the print of the portrait with Grabner's psyche: 'He has a human appearance in the photograph, his eyes express something other than the well-known penetrating gaze of the murderer, who [Grabner] really was' (quoted in Potocka 2011: 107).

Janina Struk's comprehensive study of Holocaust photography devotes considerable space to the *Erkennungsdienst*. The unit was headed by two SS officers and staffed by a group of prisoners. Wilhelm Brasse was one of them. According to Struk, he owed his position not only to his extensive skills but also to his native knowledge of German (2004: 103).[4] Upon admission to Auschwitz he performed a number of jobs, frequently shifting work details. When the need arose to find a photographer he was summoned on the basis of the information provided in his admission form. Brasse was chosen from a group of other prisoners as he passed the practical test with flying colours (see Brasse 2000, 2006). Initially, in 1940 and 1941, Polish political prisoners were photographed, but the later change in the type of new prisoners was not reflected in the photographic records (see Struk 2004: 104). After the practice of cataloging new arrivals had been discontinued due to shortages in photographic materials, Brasse was assigned new tasks – including the documentation of medical experiments. This would typically entail photographing the prisoner pre-mortem, documenting their physical irregularities; the photograph was subsequently attached to the medical record and dispatched with the internal organs to Berlin. Moreover, doctors solicited photographs of inmates with artistic tattoos to preserve both an image of the person and the prepared skin with the inked artwork. Another 'new' photographic topic would be to record nude young women on the orders of Dr. Mengele, who was delighted with the quality of his own portrait shot by Brasse (see Brasse 2011). The photographer was struck by the discrepancy between youthful beauty and the sealed fate of his models: 'I was fully aware that they were going to die. They didn't know. [...] To photograph these women and to know that they were going to die was so highly distressing. They were so full of life and so beautiful' (Brasse quoted in Struk 2004: 109). Struk admits that this confession obtained from Brasse in 2000 constituted a crisis in the photographer's testimony, and she dropped the topic as being too emotionally taxing. It does not mean that Brasse was unable to broach this topic with other interviewers. For the audience interested in the traumatic, his emotional response has equal value to minimalist style testimony prevalent in oral history. On most occasions, however, he has no difficulty incorporating his emotions and moral judgement into a cohesive narrative. Therefore, Brasse embraces the ethics of memory rather than the ethics of silence.

PHOTOGRAPHY AS A MEMORY PROP

Both Struk, in her book, and Dobrowolski, in his film, feature contemplation of the prints of camp photographs to trigger testimony. The photographer is asked to revisit pictures he took himself and those developed in the darkroom of the *Erkennungsdienst*. On most occasions, memories summoned in this manner fuel Brasse's narrative. At times, particularly painful memories cut testimony short due to a conflict between the remembered and the utterable. The uniqueness of the testimonial situation consists in the availability of the visual material. That said, their concrete presence is not tantamount to a fixed meaning but demands interpretation. What catches the eye in Dobrowolski's documentary is the director's preoccupation with visual reenactment: the setting recreates a pre-war photo atelier with Brasse serving as a model. This repositioning of the photographer turns him into a sitter whose soul is to be unveiled. By this token, Dobrowolski is not solely interested in minimalist style testimony but seeks emotional responses. In Philippe Lejeune's theory of autobiography, the protagonist of an autobiographical narrative is referred to as a model, thereby creating a connection to the same word as it is used in photography for the person posing for a shot. In *The Portraitist*, the ex-photographer accordingly occupies a double position: of a photographic topic and of a narrator. His narrative contains elements of a life story as its temporal dimensions extend from before to after the war. The pivotal part devoted to the camp demonstrates Brasse's unique insider knowledge of the functioning of the concentration camp and its internal hierarchy. Dobrowolski divides Brasse's testimony into chunks with their own micronarratives and arranges them to present different aspects of photographic work in the camp: mug shots in general, identification photographs of memorable prisoners, studio portraits of SS officers and unusual requests, for example a wedding photograph showing a prisoner with his wife and child who arrived at the camp for their nuptials. (An Austrian communist and a Spanish forced labourer incarcerated at another German camp were granted permission to marry in Auschwitz on 18 March 1944. The bride and their son left the camp the day after the ceremony, while the groom stayed at Auschwitz and was later executed for attempting to escape.) For the most part, the order of the stories is not chronological. Instead, they are arranged according to thematic criteria, accompanying the visuals. On the other hand, each micronarrative is cohesive, and Brasse comes across as an engaging storyteller.

The film's opening shot presents Brasse in a photographic atelier as he switches the studio lights on and reflects on the qualities of a perfect portrait. Then, the witness revisits the past while recalling what was expected from him in the camp. For him, the natural appearance of a model is a prerequisite for an acceptable image. This professional view of photographic records did not cease after Brasse lost the comfort of his own atelier while working for the *Erkennungsdienst*. He barely influenced the semi-automated process of picture-taking with the immobile camera and set lighting. To some extent he controlled the facial expressions of the prisoners in front of the lens, for whom smiling or showing too much pain was out-of-bounds. The latter was problematic since prisoners frequently had black eyes, bruises or cuts. To exacerbate the situation, the Kapos often resorted to violence in the corridor leading to the photographic room. The appearance of the models was assessed by an SS-man on duty, and in his absence Brasse would decide whether a photograph would pass muster. When the prisoner's condition was deemed substandard, the procedure would be postponed. Such a preoccupation with proper appearance echoes Georg Simmel's argument on the aesthetic qualities of the human face: 'a change that is limited, actually or apparently, to one element of the face – a curl of the lips, an upturning of the nose, a way of looking, a frown – immediately modifies its entire character and expression. Aesthetically, there is no other part of the body whose wholeness can as easily be destroyed by the disfigurement of only one of its elements' (1965: 276). Inasmuch as permanent changes alter the way in which we perceive a person, temporary injuries could hamper later identification. For this reason, as Robert Sobieszek argues, the emphasis placed on acceptable looks in front of the camera stems from the theoretical underpinnings of photographic identification:

> The satisfaction with neutral likeness explains the deadpan looks found in the majority of ordinary portraits, from the slowly exposed daguerreotype to the formally posed salon portrait and to the instantly exposed modern snapshot. [...] And likeness forms the basis of pictorial identity, just as it is at the heart of nearly all systems seeking to visually classify or typify human beings according to predetermined criteria. (1999: 91)

In some cases Brasse forgot these requirements when he photographed prisoners, having learnt that the majority of those sent away would soon be killed (see Brasse 2011). Few stories can be told about the bulk of the photographic record as repetitive actions usually leave few distinct memories. There is no denying that the anonymity of inmates has its roots in their treatment by the administration of Auschwitz-Birkenau. Brasse's explanation of the generic requirements of identification photography seeks to identify the typical qualities of the process.

The majority of mug shots and medical photographs taken by the *Erkennungsdienst* could be seen as an example of a photographic genre described by Susie Linfield as 'pictures of people about to be murdered' (2010: 66). According to her, the violence is yet to hit the photographed with its full force since they are – and here she borrows a phrase by Jean Améry – in the 'waiting room of death' (ibid.). This classification is not just a figure of speech. Brasse recounts the story of three Jewish acquaintances photographed when their life in the camp was drawing to a close. He offered them each a cigarette and a piece of bread and pleaded with their executioner – Wacław Rudzki, a Polish Kapo – 'to kill them without inflicting unnecessary suffering'. The plea never stopped stirring up his conscience (the episode recurs both in *The Portraitist* and in Potocka's interview). To complicate his moral choices even further, Brasse could have

Fig. 1 Brasse's sitter Czesława Kwoka, camp no. 26947. Courtesy of the Archive of the Auschwitz-Birkenau State Museum

terminated his incarceration at any moment if he had decided to sign the *Volksliste* (a list of *Volksdeutsche*, ethnic Germans living outside the Third Reich before the war started; in Brasse's case it would have entailed conscription to the *Wehrmacht*, Germany's armed forces). He did not give in to the pressure upon his arrest and he refused to change his mind afterwards because of his heartfelt Polish patriotism, which he asserts in the film. However, in hindsight he questions his decision: 'Had I known just ten per cent of what happened later maybe I would have signed' (2006).

In the context of Holocaust documentary, a shift to memory has a number of objectives: soliciting survivor testimony, remembering the dead and returning names to people photographed or filmed during the war. Dobrowolski combines these strategies. In *The Portraitist*, Czesława Kwoka, a Polish child inmate (1928–1943), is among a tiny group of sitters recognised by Brasse, who vividly recalls the circumstances of their encounter. Her portrait is one of the most frequently reproduced images, both in publications and in museum exhibitions, and it is a staple element of the permanent exhibition at the Auschwitz-Birkenau State Museum, in the children's block.[5] Kwoka's symbolic status is corroborated by her digital identities: an extensive page on Wikipedia and a Facebook profile (based on information from the former). Let us open the door to speculation as to why she has been chosen to represent the fate of children in the camp.[6] Her regular facial features, delicate charm and innocence all appeal to post-war audiences. Brasse admits in the documentary that 'she looked so young, so disarming in fact ... [she was] good looking and not emaciated'. Traces of having been beaten testify to the brutality of the SS overseers. There is a marked difference between the first photograph in which her gaze is turned upward and the second one with a sheer look of horror in her eyes. The former evokes religious iconography (a headscarf, beauty suggestive of inner virtue, an absent gaze) and the popular photographic genre of First Communion studio photography, while the latter is a reflection of acute pain and immense suffering. Dobrowolski singled out Kwoka beforehand as Brasse is presented in the film with large format individual prints of her portraits in contrast to the smaller contact prints of the other mug shots.

There are two key modes of presenting photography in *The Portraitist*: for illustrative purposes relying on their indexical value and as physical prints held by the witness in his hands. In the first mode the images are typically animated by zooming in, or exaggerated contrast is added in postproduction, while in the second, Brasse is filmed sitting on a chair with prints on his lap, usually in close-up, showing the photographer's hand with the print and allowing him to explain the technical aspects of a given portrait. The relative importance of the photograph is tied to its dimensions, as they appear on the cinema screen: run-of-the-mill mug shots are contact prints while larger ones depict people of whom Brasse has vivid memories (Kwoka, Grabner and unnamed victims of the medical experiments). The photographer complements the images with stories of the shoot, giving equal weight to the behaviour of the sitters and the setup of the studio, including his ingenuity in accommodating unusual requests. Furthermore, Dobrowolski uses creative license in manipulating the photographs in order to illustrate the processes of memory work: when Brasse talks about the number of mug shots taken, the faces flicker in quick succession – a film equivalent of Sir Francis Galton's composite portraits (see Phillips 1997). CGI also serves to fill the gaps in the preserved visual record: there are two digital reconstructions of lost images. The first mode is typical for iconographic film, relying on voiceover to explain the visuals. In the case of *The Portraitist* it is the witness and not an off-screen narrator who contributes the narrative. The second mode, in which the behaviour of the witness in front of the camera is subject to scrutiny as much as the story being told, reveals affinity to cinéma vérité. The presentation of photographs invites questions concerning the agency of the Auschwitz photographer.

Fig. 2 Wilhelm Brasse with a photographic print in Irek Dobrowolski's *The Portraitist*

Is there a possibility to look for traces of resistance in Brasse's work in the *Erkennungsdienst*? The expressionless portraits, linked by Sobieszek to photographic modernism (1999: 80–169), deny the possibility of getting to know the personality of the sitter on the basis of their photographic image. Under the deindividualising conditions of the concentration camp, a quest for prisoners' souls via the medium of photography would be a frivolous waste of time.[7] The sheer fact of being incarcerated cancelled out the uniqueness of the inmates and rendered their 'authentic' inner lives of no value to the camp administration. The photographer had no power to redress this imbalance, being a prisoner himself and having only brief encounters with the photographed inmates.

Thus, he could only reconstruct the prior lives of his pre-war acquaintances. Is Brasse's lack of knowledge about the sitters typical for identification photography? Photographic cataloguing is the core of August Sander's extremely ambitious project called *Face of Our Time* (2008). In Sobieszek's view 'Sander's comment, "Every person's story is written plainly on his face," had more to do with social class and the physical effects of certain occupations than with emotional character' (1999: 25). Contrary to the famous German photographer, Brasse could not rely on external markers of social identity because at their entrance into the camp system, the prisoners were stripped of them. Instead, they presented 'naked faces' to the camera – signs of what Giorgio Agamben (1998) describes as bare life to which prisoners were reduced in the camp. In this respect, Brasse was a tool of the camp administration and cannot be seen as a resister.

However, Dobrowolski sees him as an exemplary and tragic figure who had to witness the concentration camp in operation as a result of his Polish nationalism. It is worth mentioning that interpretations of Auschwitz-Birkenau differ in Poland and abroad. In the former context, until recently, the camp stood as a symbol of Nazi policy against Poles (a testament to the efforts of Communist propaganda); while internationally it has been seen first and foremost as the site of the extermination of Jews. Showing Brasse in a favourable light might be interpreted as part of Polish historical policy: an exemplary Pole who did not lose his moral integrity in the camp. The topic of Brasse's self-identification is repeatedly broached in the film. Brasse belatedly offers an ethical perspective on the photographing in the camp. He took the mug shots without a second thought, but tried to ease the discomfort of the female victims of medical experiments.

MEDICAL PHOTOGRAPHY IN THE CAMP AND GENDERED COMMEMORATION

No aesthetic considerations prohibited the taking of gynecologic photographs of prisoners undergoing Dr. Eduard Wirths's medical experiments (see Kater 1989: 29). The Auschwitz photographer proved the only weak link in this disinterested and detached process. The photographs of medical experiments performed by Dr. Mengele were to haunt Brasse ever after. However, Dobrowolski's characterisation of Brasse in this regard is not as nuanced as it could have been.

Janet Jacobs places photographs of medical experiments in the context of feminist studies, averring that their use in post-war commemoration was a form of 'feminization of the Holocaust in Auschwitz' (2006: 246). In her view the exhibition policy at the current museum is gender biased with an emphasis placed on images of women whose nakedness is a symbol of their inferiority to the clothed perpetrators. Is Brasse in the same category by virtue of his proximity to the perpetrators? He did not photograph out of his own volition, but was full of compassion for the victims, and strove not to aggravate the situation via unnecessary physical contact. The photographer reiterates his unease with photographing the experiments in the majority of interviews in which this topic is brought up: in Dobrowolski's footage for the film, in testimonies for the Auschwitz-Birkenau State Museum and, last but not least, in Potocka's book. As Carol Quinn has stated: 'Although the Nazi victims claim that we should not use the data, perhaps what they are really objecting to is their not having control over whether and how it should be used. Perhaps after getting that control, the victims would choose to use the data to save lives' (2000: 323). The moral issues connected with the use of medical data gathered via unethical experiments are also pertinent to the post-war use of photographs as part of the experimental process. The ethical assessment of this use is further complicated by the ends to which the images are put. What about their presentation beyond the context of medicine? Does placing the images in the context of historical/testimonial narrative cleanse them of the moral stigma attached to the use of medical data? No photographs of pathological changes are used by Dobrowolski. He does not shock the viewer with images of flesh wounds or frostbite such as those filmed by the Red Army film crew in January and February 1945. Instead, the key medical photograph discussed in the documentary shows naked emaciated teenage girls in a group while the other images are only described in Brasse's testimony. In this respect the filmmaker stops short of perpetuating the original damage.

There is a recurring motif in audio and video testimonies given by Brasse, namely, the interaction between the photographer and his naked female models. Dobrowolski does not pick up this topic. However, in the video testimony given for the Auschwitz-Birkenau State Museum Brasse claims: 'In a group, women don't have the same effect on a man' (2006). This interview was conducted by two interviewers, one male and one female. For the most part the interviewee only addresses the man. At this point, he turns to the woman explaining the extent of his embarrassment. Furthermore, as if anticipating the question, he avers that he never looked at girls as 'a sexually starving man'. In another interview he admits to 'being aroused but not sexually' (quoted in Potocka 2011: 79). According to his description, he even took pains to ease the discomfort of his models arranging for them a space behind a photographic screen to get undressed so that they would be seen naked only for the moment of the actual photograph.

The way *The Portraitist* remains silent about sexual exploits of members of the photographic unit shows how the film treats Brasse's testimony as raw material for larger rhetorical goals. Brasse, in his testimony for the Auschwitz-Birkenau State Museum, explains why he avoided romantic relationships in the camp: Jewish nurses working for Dr. Clauberg allegedly teased him by making him rub against their breasts while he was passing. A *Blockälteste*, a female prisoner in charge of a barrack, asked him openly whether he frequented the camp brothel. At this point, the interviewer enquires about the possibility of having affairs with Jewish nurses rather than going to what was called the 'Puff'. Brasse confesses that he consciously reduced his interaction with them to flirting. He got to know the German and Polish girls from the brothel as they had their 6x9cm photographs and not typical mug shots taken in the studio. On this occasion, he was urged to frequent the 'Puff'. By his account in this testimony, prostitution in the camp had two faces: the legal one organised in order to boost the productivity of privileged prisoners and the black market on which German Kapos were 'selling' Jewish inmates for cigarettes. In Brasse's account, the girls in the brothel were far from unhappy. At this point, most probably sensing that he had touched upon an inappropriate topic he asks: 'Are you recording this? I'm telling such heresies'; even if he had never witnessed the black market prostitution, he was of the opinion that it should have remained a camp secret: 'I'm saying this, but it shouldn't even be recorded' (ibid.). His doubts echo the widespread view that 'only criminals went [to the brothel], men in league with the SS and untroubled by the need for solidarity' (Des Pres 1976: 190).

It is in the longer interview (only published by Anna Dobrowolska in 2013), based on the outtakes from *The Portraitist*, that Brasse's admission about the brothel is made public. The photographer does not feel shame that he frequented the camp brothel. This practice was commonplace among the crew of the photo unit and other privileged prisoners from Brasse's circle, as a story about his friend, a graphic artist, demonstrates. Tadeusz Myszkowski promised to draw caricatures of the SS officers at their behest, provided that he would be locked up in the brothel for three days (see Dobrowolska 2013: 213). Afterwards, Myszkowski bragged about his sexual exploits during that period. All this is at odds with the sympathetic portrayal of Brasse in Dobrowolski's film. It must have been impossible for the filmmaker to accommodate Brasse's admission to have used the services of the brothel into an account of his moral integrity. The adoption of the post-war moral compass in order to judge the behaviour of the inmates comes at the risk of distorting the complexity of survival. Dobrowolski's decision to edit out more troubling elements from the testimony proves that the testimonial power of a documentary film is a function of the original footage and its editing.

Medical photographs are given equal weight to mug shots as the filmmaker treats them as a metaphor for inhumanity at Auschwitz-Birkenau. Their presentation portrays the photographer as a moral agent rather than a privileged individual in the hierarchy of prisoners. It is in the unpublished interviews that issues of gender surface, and Brasse admits that his masculinity was a key factor in his interaction with the models. Dobrowolski's presentation of Brasse as a moral hero bypasses the issues of gendered relations in the camp. The male photographer differentiates between various types of female victims (downplaying the gendered suffering of male ones) on the basis of his perception of the abuse they went through. The amicable relations he had with the women from the brothel blind him to their fate. A more compassionate perspective on this camp institution is to be found in the Polish documentary *Girls from Auschwitz* [*Dziewczęta z Auschwitz*] (2010), directed by Kinga Wołoszyn-Świerk, in which female survivors and historical experts talk about violence against women in the camp, including the phenomenon of prostitution.

DOBROWOLSKI'S PORTRAYAL OF BRASSE IN THE LIGHT OF OTHER SOURCES

Dobrowolski has contributed to the commemoration of the camp by crediting Brasse as the author of numerous iconic images. Historically, we can also speak about a concomitant shift in the perception of the victims as being anonymous, endowing them instead with faces and personal stories. In the decades following the liberation, the impression of the de-individualising function of the photographs might have been reinforced by commemorative publications such as photographic albums with reproductions of wartime images of the camp, stills from liberation footage and post-war photographs of the site (see Cegłowska and Dałek 1982; Świebocka and Świebocki 1992).

Polish Holocaust documentaries approached the problem of the victims' anonymity from a number of perspectives: as a fact which cannot be changed, such as *Archeology* [*Archeologia*] (1967), directed by Andrzej Brzozowski, or in the context of photography as a nostalgic meditation on the lives lost, such as *I am Looking at Your Photograph* [*Patrzę na Twoją fotografię*] (1979), directed by Jerzy Ziarnik. The former focuses on the archeological excavations of objects brought by victims to Birkenau (no names are linked to the finds), while the latter shows unattributed pre-war photographs of Polish Jews. It was only recently that the identities of the majority of the photographed were reconstructed thanks to research and a call on the Internet for surviving relatives (see Zawodna 2009). Polish documentary films rarely pick a single witness to narrate the story of the Holocaust. If this is the case, the survivors in question participated in key events or had access to information that cannot be corroborated otherwise. It suffices to mention Marek Edelman and his take on the history of the Warsaw Ghetto Uprising – *Chronicle of the Warsaw Ghetto Uprising According to Marek Edelman* [*Kronika powstania w getcie warszawskim według Marka Edelmana*] (1993) – directed by Jolanta Dylewska, Samuel Willenberg and the revolt in Treblinka – recounted in *The Last Witness* [*Ostatni świadek*] (2002) – directed by Michał Nekanda-Trepka, or Henryk Mandelbaum (the only member of the *Sonderkommando* living in Poland), filmed for a number of documentaries. Dobrowolski's generic choice to pick a biographic form and to abstain from imposing the perspective of a voiceover narrative values a subjective account of the past over a more distanced use of a multi-voiced documentary work.

The Portraitist – via the use of audiovisual testimony – supplements the longstanding practice of employing an uncredited visual quotation of mug shots or medical imagery. Dobrowolski's documentary instead juxtaposes archival material with testimony. At times, such use is meant to counterbalance Brasse's narrative and explain the context in which the photographer took the mug shots/medical photographs. However, on two occasions these visual quotations are directly related to his testimony: first, when the so-called *Sonderkommando* photographs are shown; and second, when towards the end of the film faces edited out from the photographs literally haunt the narrator. In the first case, Brasse recalls the sitter, a German SS telephone operator who insisted on having her nude bust included in the shot and later committed suicide. A photograph most likely taken by a member of the *Sonderkommando*, which captures the incineration of bodies in an open pit, is internally edited providing graphic proof for the atrocities the telephone operator witnessed from her office, whose windows faced the crematorium at Auschwitz I (see Potocka 2011: 92).[8] It needs to be stressed that the *Sonderkommando* photograph depicts Birkenau in the summer of 1944 and there is little possibility that the German girl could have seen the scene photographed due to the distance between the two parts of the camp and the restricted access to the killing installations in Birkenau. Instead, Brasse claims that she observed the crowds entering Crematorium I and the smoke belching from the chimney (see Potocka 2011: 93). On the other hand, the burden of witnessing atrocities structures this episode, so that the two events juxtaposed here – the photo shoot and her suicide – lack a specific temporal attribution and thus can only be linked by association. Thus, this iconic image of atrocity, taken in an act of resistance but consecutively canonised in countless publications on Auschwitz or the Holocaust in general, offers the audience a chance to identify with the sensitive German, whose suicide Brasse attributes to her empathy for the victims (ibid.). And yet, such identification is impossible not only because of the intervention of the medium but also due to experiential excess which is incommunicable. In this respect, Dobrowolski's film is caught in the paradox of testimony illuminated by Robert Eaglestone: testimonial form based on literary conventions invites identification, but simultaneously the genre 'prohibit[s] identification on epistemological grounds … and on ethical grounds' (2003: 118). The epiphanic nature of the events in question, namely the fact that they are 'hardly bearable' (2003: 127), rules out identification even further. Moreover, it may be interpreted as distrust in the power of testimony to communicate the mental states of others. Instead, the audience is asked to fill the void on their own.

In the second instance, editing faces out of the mug shots and animating them 'emerging' from a dark void emulates the 'devil in the box' mechanism of trauma by virtue of which the post-war photographic atelier becomes a 'scene of trauma', and the appearance of the young women unleashes horrors of the past. Trauma can be seen as Dobrowolski's interpretive strategy, which stands in contrast to the predominantly minimalist narrative in which Brasse delivers most of his testimony. There is no denying that the application of filmic techniques evoking trauma provides a climax and tension in the film's narrative structure. Yes, trauma belongs to the past but in the documentary it also legitimises the photographer as an ethical witness. In this capacity Brasse sees the suffering of others, does not seek self-promotion and agrees to participate in public commemoration.

The documentary's pivotal scene, showing Brasse's watery eyes as he confesses with a trembling voice to having cursed God and his mother for giving birth to him, is tied through the film's editing to his photographing of medical experiments. In fact, following the premiere of the film, Brasse expressed grave misgivings about the inclusion of this scene because his mother had been 'very good'. What is more, the heartrending crisis in the testimony was triggered by a recollection of his life-threatening emaciation in the Melk camp, where he was transferred after the evacuation of Auschwitz. After the liberation, photography seemed all too logical a career path. This, however, as Brasse recollects, proved impossible due to 'some sort of psychological whirl, the images sprang forth as if I saw them in front of my eyes. I sometimes thought that I saw these children, these Jewish girls' (2006). Contrary to Dobrowolski's edit of the photographer's testimony, Brasse did not lament abandoning photography. Moreover, his business, producing artificial sausage skins, thrived under 'hideous Communism' (ibid.).

Dobrowolski highlights the role of the photographer in the production of the visual record of the camp, filling in the gaps in the official commemoration of the photographic unit. Furthermore, *The Portraitist* presents Auschwitz photography in a number of ways: as an institutional practice, as a set of images, as artefacts used conventionally for commemoration and, last but not least, as illustrations of the personal story of the key witness. The three photographic genres in question, namely, mug shots, studio portraiture and medical photography, provide a framework for interpreting the site. The mug shots imposed an identity on the new arrivals, criminalising them as part of the process of admission. Studio portraiture offered a proof of status, reserved for those in positions of power. Finally, medical photography turned the models into case studies of various diseases and pathological changes, following the perfidy of the SS doctors' scientific agenda.

The question remains, however, as to what extent the photographer can challenge the meanings given to the photographs taken in the camp. With his apt statement 'Appearance would then become the veiling and unveiling of the soul', Georg Simmel divorced the surface from the inner self (1965: 281). In the sociologist's view making assumptions about somebody's personality on the basis of their appearance risks distorting the truth. In this manner Simmel goes against theories popular in Nazi Germany. On a number of occasions in the documentary Brasse 'bares his soul' and reveals the ordeal of his sitters as his testimony is superimposed on visual documentation.[9] Even though the unveiling of the souls of the majority of sitters was impossible to achieve, the beam of light projected on a chosen few runs counter to the systematic de-individualisation of inmates.

Dobrowolski does not follow in the footsteps of Claude Lanzmann, whose intrusive manner of interviewing at times brought witnesses to tears or caused an emotional crisis. It is to be underlined that a comparison of the edited documentary with the outtakes shows that the French filmmaker at times sought intimacy with his interviewees, such as Filip Müller and Abraham Bomba. In the rushes he seems to be a much more considerate interviewer than in the final edit. Polish filmmakers rarely engage in an aggressive confrontation with witnesses even if the latter crossed the line between bystanders and perpetrators, as is the case with the killers of their Jewish neighbours in the Jedwabne massacre 1941, which appear in Agnieszka Arnold's documentary *Neighbors* [*Sąsiedzi*] (2001).

Witnesses brought to tears are crucial in documentaries that lend equal weight to the emotional aspects of the story and to the factual content. In *The Portraitist*, despite the lack of conspicuous manipulation during shooting, Brasse felt betrayed by the liberties the film took in linking two separate topics – photographing the medical experiments and his existential crisis at the Melk camp – in order to arrive at the emotional truth; namely, the effects that Brasse's incarceration and his photographic duties had on his emotional life in the camp. The valuing of the affective is to show Brasse as an individual forced by circumstances to perform certain duties in the camp.

THE PORTRAITIST AND RECENT TRENDS IN POLISH HOLOCAUST DOCUMENTARY

How typical is Dobrowolski's documentary in comparison to Polish cinema as a whole? Polish Holocaust documentaries in the twenty-first century can be linked to larger trends in commemoration: a historical policy of identifying aspects of the past in line with the agenda of Polish nationalism, elegiac forms of honouring the dead and a critical reinterpretation of Polish war history. In fact, these tendencies already have been discernible in the decades after the fall of Communism in 1989. In the period in question, three documentaries gained international recognition: Dariusz Jabłoński's *Photographer* [*Fotoamator*] (1998), *The Portraitist* and Jolanta Dylewska's *Polin: Scraps of Memory* [*Polin: Okruchy pamięci*] (2008). These productions share a preoccupation with the archival visuals: *Photographer* with Walter Genewein's colour slides of the Łódź Ghetto, *The Portraitist* with Brasse's Auschwitz photographs and *Polin* with pre-war home movies of Jewish immigrants to the United States visiting their relatives in Poland. The meaning of the images in question is communicated via testimony: Arnold Mostowicz, formerly a Jewish doctor in the Łódź Ghetto, debunks images taken by Genewein, the chief accountant of the Jewish district and an amateur photographer, as being false (see Łysak 2013), Brasse points to the institutional context of documenting the camp, while Dylewska carefully selects interviews with Polish neighbours of murdered Jews in order to prove that these two ethnic groups co-existed peacefully before the war. Even though Dylewska's documentary is accused of distorting Polish-Jewish relations (see Janicka and Żukowski 2012), the director seems to invite the symbolic inclusion of Jews into Polish history and evokes nostalgia for their loss.

The past twenty-five years can also be seen as the heyday of testimony with filmmakers rushing to document the accounts of survivors, witnesses and, at times, perpetrators. In this vein, documentaries have contributed to processes of memory work such as 'a return of memory' or even 'the revenge of memory' (see Łysak 2010). In this respect, Polish cinema has fuelled attempts at reevaluating the national past or, conversely, has sought to perpetuate the nationalist narrative of Polish martyrdom and victimhood coupled with downplaying more controversial aspects of wartime history. The former can be exemplified by two groundbreaking films: Agnieszka Arnold's *Neighbors* and Paweł Łoziński's *Birthplace* [*Miejsce urodzenia*] (1992). Łoziński aids Henryk Grynberg – an eminent Polish-Jewish emigré writer – in the process of discovering his father's grave. His father was murdered by a Polish farmer on the eve of the liberation and buried by the side of a country road in an unmarked grave. Arnold in turn proposes an ethnography of memory using the example of Jedwabne, a small town north-east of Warsaw in which local Jews were killed by their Polish neighbours on 10 July 1941 (see Gross 2002; Polonsky and Michlic 2004). The filmmaker discovers that the atrocity was an open secret and that the initial receptiveness of interviewees to the project subsided once the pogrom became a topic of national debate (see Łysak 2010: 124–5). Dobrowolski's contribution to Polish memory culture explores interesting but 'safe' aspects of the past, capitalising on the shift to memory in Holocaust cinema in the past couple of decades.

Dobrowolski uses the convention of historical documentary in its microhistorical guise in order to identify a gap in knowledge about Auschwitz-Birkenau. His approach derives its strength from two sources: the status of Auschwitz photography in commemoration and the personal story of the photographer. By downplaying the moral complexity of Brasse's position in the camp hierarchy, Dobrowolski promotes national historiography. The filmmaker perceives Brasse as a moral agent with his stint at the camp a result of his refusal to renounce his Polishness. From what we know, there is no proof that Brasse combined his official duties with photographing as a sign of resistance (as was the case in the Łódź Ghetto, where Jewish photographers took some photographs clandestinely). And yet, Brasse reportedly sabotaged the order to destroy the visual evidence prior to the liberation of the camp thanks to which the bulk of the record has been preserved. Dobrowolski's reliance on a single witness rules out a dialogical approach, and because of this there is no hint of a critical distance in relation to the witness. Instead, the filmmaker relies on microhistory as a mode of recall. The publication of the book based on the outtakes and archival research at the Auschwitz-Birkenau State Museum has changed the perspective promoted by the film in that certain facts are confirmed by other witnesses (see Dobrowolska 2013: 73, 81). The printed medium allowed for the presentation of a more nuanced story of the *Erkennungsdienst*, which is rich in factual details. The book can also be seen as a homage to commemorative efforts of the Auschwitz-Birkenau State Museum, using oral history in a more traditional manner, and as a contribution to the culture of commemoration in the same vein as Dobrowolski's documentary. Nevertheless, credit should be given to the documentarian for the masterful use of cinematographic conventions in order to bring the reality of the camp back to the witness and, by extension, to show the audience the unknown and forgotten aspects of life and death at Auschwitz.

Notes

1 Research for this project was funded by the National Science Centre granted in decision no. DEC-2012/07/B/HS2/01612. I would like to thank Edyta Chowaniec and Szymon Kowalski from the Auschwitz-Birkenau State Museum for their assistance in archival work.
2 The number of surviving photographs is 38,916; of these 31,969 are images of men and 6,947 are images of women (see Zambon 1995: 6).
3 For a Foucauldian interpretation of mug shots see Finn (2009: 1–30) and Rowlinson (2009: 125–47).
4 On the other hand, Brasse claims that he learned German at school since his mother did not speak the language (2006).
5 The Yad Vashem Insitute, the Imperial War Museum in London and the United States Holocaust Memorial Museum have likewise included mug shots of Kwoka in their permanent exhibitions. The number of photographs displayed varies: from giant spreads of enlarged prints to an arrangement of individually exhibited mug shots illuminated by a strong side light.
6 I owe credit to Roma Sendyka for bringing this question to my attention.
7 On the reluctance to use the notion of dehumanization, see Lang (2010).
8 The image in question comes from a set of four photographs taken clandestinely by a member of the Special Unit; two of them were shot from the inside of the gas chamber, the third shows naked women awaiting their turn to be killed, while the fourth is of an abstract quality, showing branches against the sky. On the circumstances of photographing see Stone (2001); for a critical discussion of these photographs, see Didi-Huberman (2008).
9 Recently, Brasse acknowledged that the prisoners' eyes seen in the prints now are indicative of their destituteness (2011).

Filmography

Archeology [Archeologia]. Dir. Andrzej Brzozowski. Poland, 1967.
Birthplace [Miejsce urodzenia]. Dir. Paweł Łoziński. Poland, 1992.
Chronicle of the Warsaw Ghetto Uprising According to Marek Edelman [Kronika powstania w getcie warszawskim według Marka Edelmana]. Dir. Jolanta Dylewska. Poland, 1993.
Girls from Auschwitz [Dziewczęta z Auschwitz]. Dir. Kinga Wołoszyn-Świerk. Poland, 2010.
I am Looking at Your Photograph [Patrzę na Twoją fotografię]. Dir. Jerzy Ziarnik. Poland, 1979.
The Last Witness [Ostatni świadek]. Dir. Michał Nekanda-Trepka. Poland, 2002.
Liebe Perla. Dir. Shahar Rozen. Germany/Israel, 1999.
Neighbors [Sąsiedzi]. Dir. Agnieszka Arnold. Poland, 2001.

Photographer [*Fotoamator*]. Dir. Dariusz Jabłoński. Poland, 1998.
Polin: Scraps of Memory [*Polin: Okruchy pamięci*]. Dir. Jolanta Dylewska. Poland/Germany, 2008.
The Portraitist [*Portrecista*]. Dir. Irek Dobrowolski. Poland, 2005.

Bibliography

Agamben, Giorgio (1998) *Homo Sacer: Sovereign Power and Bare Life*, trans. Daniel Heller-Roazen. Stanford, CA: Stanford University Press.
Brasse, Wilhelm (1984) Testimony. 6 April. Archiwum Państwowego Muzeum Auschwitz-Birkenau [APMA-B], *Testimonies Collection*. Vol. 114. 220-30. Unpublished transcript.
____ (1989) Testimony. 1 September. APMA-B. *Testimonies Collection*. Vol. 125. 50-52. Unpublished transcript.
____ (2000) Testimony. 14 November, DVD. *Auschwitz Oral History Collection*, PMA-B/V-DVD/K-195. Recorded by Helena Kubica.
____ (2006) Testimony. 21 July, DVD. *Auschwitz Oral History Collection*, PMA-B/HMA/0040. Recorded by Kamila Ziółek, Artur Pałyga.
____ (2011) DVD interview for Maria Anna Potocka. *Wilhelm Brasse, Fotograf 3444, Auschwitz 1940–45*. Kraków: Muzeum Sztuki Współczesnej.
Cegłowska, Teresa and Jerzy Dałek (eds) (1982) *Auschwitz-Birkenau*. Katowice: Państwowe Muzeum Oświęcim-Brzezinka/KAW.
Des Pres, Terrence (1976) *The Survivor: An Anatomy of Life in the Death Camps*. New York: Oxford University Press.
Didi-Huberman, George (2008) *Images in Spite of All: Four Photographs from Auschwitz*, trans. Shane B. Lillis. Chicago: University of Chicago Press.
Dobrowolska, Anna (2013) *Fotograf z Auschwitz*. Warsaw: Rekontrplan.
Eaglestone, Robert (2003) 'Identification and the Genre of Testimony', in Sue Vice (ed.) *Representing the Holocaust*. London: Vallentine Mitchell, 117–40.
Finn, Jonathan (2009) *Capturing the Criminal Image: From Mug Shot to Surveillance Society*. Minneapolis, MN: University of Minnesota Press.
Gross, Jan Tomasz (2002) *Neighbors: The Destruction of the Jewish Community in Jedwabne, Poland*. New York: Penguin.
Jacobs, Janet (2006) 'The Female Body as Atrocity Text: The Feminization of the Holocaust at Auschwitz', *English Language Notes*, 44, 2, 243–51.
Janicka, Elżbieta and Tomasz Żukowski (2012) 'Przemoc filosemicka', *Studia Litteraria Historica*, 1, 1–39.
Kater, Michael H. (1989) *Doctors Under Hitler*. Chapel Hill, NC: University of North Carolina Press.
Lang, Johannes (2010) 'Questioning Dehumanization: Intersubjective Dimensions of Violence in the Nazi Concentration and Death Camps', *Holocaust and Genocide Studies*, 24, 2, 225–46.
Linfield, Susie (2010) *The Cruel Radiance: Photography and Political Violence*. Chicago: University of Chicago Press.
Łysak, Tomasz (2010) 'Strategies of Recall in Post-1989 Polish Documentary and Artistic Films about the Holocaust', in Magdalena Marszałek and Alina Molisak (eds) *Nach dem Vergessen: Rekurse auf den Holocaust in Ostmitteleuropa nach 1989*. Berlin: Kadmos, 115–35.

_____ (2013) 'On the Impossibility of Believing in the Documentary: Dariusz Jabłoński's *Photographer*', *Kwartalnik Filmowy*, special issue, 128–39.

Maxwell, Anne (2008) *Picture Imperfect: Photography and Eugenics 1870–1940*. Eastbourne: Sussex Academic Press.

Phillips, Sandra S (1997) 'Identifying the Criminal', in Sandra S. Phillips, Carol Squiers and Mark Haworth-Booth (eds) *Police Pictures: The Photograph as Evidence*. San Francisco: San Francisco Museum of Modern Art, 29-40.

Polonsky, Antony and Joanna B. Michlic (eds) (2004) *The Neighbors Respond: The Controversy over the Jedwabne Massacre in Poland*. Princeton, NJ: Princeton University Press.

Potocka, Maria Anna (2011) *Wilhelm Brasse, Fotograf 3444, Auschwitz 1940–45*. Krakow: Muzeum Sztuki Współczesnej.

Quinn, Carol (2000) 'Taking Seriously Victims of Unethical Experiments: Susan Brison's Conception of the Self and Its Relevance to Bioethics', *Journal of Social Philosophy*, 31, 3, 316–25.

Rowlinson, Mark (2009) *American Visual Culture*. Oxford: Berg.

Sander, August (2008) *August Sander: Face of Our Time*. Munich: Schirmer/Mosel.

Simmel, Georg (1965) 'The Aesthetic Significance of the Face', trans. Lore Ferguson, in Kurt H. Wolff (ed.) *Essays on Sociology, Philosophy and Aesthetics*. New York: Harper Torchbooks, 276–81.

Sobieszek, Robert A. (1999) *Ghost in the Shell: Photography and the Human Soul, 1850–2000 – Essays on Camera Portraiture*. Cambridge, MA: MIT Press/Los Angeles County Museum of Art.

Stone, Dan (2001) 'The Sonderkommando Photographs', *Jewish Social Studies*, 7, 3, 132–48.

Struk, Janina (2004) *Photographing the Holocaust: Interpretation of Evidence*. New York: IB Tauris.

Świebocka, Teresa and Henryk Świebocki (eds) (1992) *Auschwitz: Voices from the Ground*. Krakow: Państwowe Muzeum Oświęcim/Parol.

Zambon, Giuseppe (ed.) (1995) *Abels Gesichter: I Volti di Abele: Auschwitz*. Frankfurt: Zambon.

Zawodna, Marta (2009) 'Nazwać każdego po imieniu: Kolekcja fotografii z walizki w Auschwitz', *Kultura i Społeczeństwo*, 53, 4, 97–115.

PART TWO

THE ETHICS OF MEMORY

CHAPTER SIX

The Singular Jew
REPRESENTING NATIONAL SOCIALISM'S JEWISH VICTIMS IN RECENT HISTORICAL CINEMA

Jennifer M. Kapczynski

This article explores a troubling pattern in recent German historical films depicting World War II: a tendency to concentrate the story of Germany's persecuted Jewish population in the figure of a lone Jewish character. I dub this figure the 'Singular Jew'. He (the majority of these figures in recent cinema are male) is singular in both senses of the word. The Singular Jew is individual – a stand-alone 'stand-in' representing the fate of German Jewry as such. He is also singular in the sense of 'remarkable or exceptional', both because his fate is the only one of its kind within the story world of the film, and because he can reasonably represent only a tiny fraction of the history for which he serves as a symbol. Crucially, he serves this narrative function in films that grant only limited attention to the Holocaust itself, which is presented as a side story in a larger plot about World War II and its aftermath. As a result, the particular historical context he is tasked with representing appears hazy, strangely specific (insofar as it is reduced to one character) and yet vague (to the extent that the historical particularities of the Holocaust are often skipped over or referenced only obliquely). In what follows, I aim to unpack some of the consequences of deploying such a Singular Jew to tell the story of persecution and genocide and to consider alternative representational strategies that might move away from this sort of reduced figuration. I will concentrate on two recent examples. The first of these, Philipp Kadelbach's *Unsere Mütter, unsere Väter* (2013) (released in the US under the title *Generation War*) is actually a television miniseries, today arguably the dominant entertainment format for popular historical fiction in Germany. The second case I consider is *Lore* (2012), a German/Australian adaptation of Rachel Seiffert's novel *The Dark Room* (2001), directed by Cate Shortland and released on the festival and then art-house cinema circuit. What interests me in particular is how each of these works, in its effort to depict the National Socialist era for the sake of present-day audiences, negotiates the meaning of 'German-Jewish' experience within the context of a larger 'German' wartime and post-war moment.

As I will lay out, both *Unsere Mütter, unsere Väter* and *Lore* rely heavily on the figure of the Singular Jew. That is, each film introduces a solitary principal Jewish character whose task it becomes to represent the fates of the German-Jewish population under National Socialist rule. In both works, this Jewish-German figure is male and a love object, at once desirable and forbidden. This pattern is by no means specific to these two films: indeed, the trope of 'Jewish-gentile' romance has emerged as a key theme in German historical cinema since unification, in works such as *Comedian Harmonists* (1997) and *Aimée & Jaguar* (1999), as well as more recent works like the TV spectacular *Dresden* (2006) (see Koepnick 2002). Indeed, although the premiere of Kadelbach's series was accompanied by extensive media hype proclaiming its novelty and originality, my interest in *Unsere Mütter, unsere Väter* has to do specifically with its paradigmatic qualities. My interest in *Lore*, by contrast, is driven by the manner in which Shortland deploys the Singular Jew in order to turn this representational convention on its head. As I hope to make clear in what follows, the films part ways precisely in how they manage the representational workload of this solitary Jewish figure. As a consequence, they differ critically in how they position their respective audiences vis-à-vis the work of coming to terms with a legacy of perpetration and the task of memorialising the victims of National Socialism.

More specifically, through their young protagonists, both *Unsere Mütter, unsere Väter* and *Lore* implicitly grapple with the question of how today's audiences – born at a significant historical remove from the era of the Third Reich and Holocaust – should relate to the task of remembrance. This question has only grown more urgent as the dying out of living witnesses has compelled subsequent generations to rely ever more upon representation as a means to connect to this history. It is a problem that has come to dominate recent scholarship on Holocaust memory in a wide range of works. These include important studies such as Michael Rothberg's *Multidirectional Memory: Remembering the Holocaust in the Age of Decolonization* (2009) or Daniel Levy and Natan Szaider's *The Holocaust and Memory in the Global Age* (2006), each of which considers the transnational dynamics of Holocaust memory in the contemporary era, as well as numerous scholarly enquiries into the effects of mediation (and particularly, photography and film) on the creation, transmission and shaping of Holocaust memory, among them

Marianne Hirsch's *Family Frames: Photography, Narrative, and Postmemory* (1997) and *The Generation of Postmemory: Writing and Visual Culture After the Holocaust* (2013), Alison Landsberg's *Prosthetic Memory: The Transformation of American Remembrance in the Age of Mass Culture* (2004), Gary Weissman's *Fantasies of Witnessing: Post-war Efforts to Experience the Holocaust* (2004) and Joshua Hirsch's *Afterimage: Film, Trauma, and the Holocaust* (2004), to name just a few.

Strikingly, both films navigate the process of representing the National Socialist past and the Holocaust through the motif of photographic evidence. This, of course, is not a new theme: indeed, it is impossible to conceive of remembering the Holocaust *without* photographs as a mediating force. As Sybil Milton notes, the Nazi regime made 'routine administrative use of photographs' (1999: 303), as did Germany's censored press, and the images captured by Allied forces of the liberation of the camps constituted a 'major photographic record' (1999: 309), later employed in the service of both post-war re-education and war crimes trials. These are complemented by the many illicit snapshots produced both by Nazi perpetrators and, on rare occasion, by their victims. Then there are those photographs taken beyond the narrower confines of the camps – images created in the years of National Socialist persecution and genocide, but recording such subjects as the conditions of ghetto life, exile and even snapshots of daily life as yet not (at least evidently) interrupted. The fact that this rich visual corpus has been subject to frequent recycling in a range of representational forms has raised key critical questions. In particular, scholars have interrogated whether the atrocity images, having been cited to the point of becoming iconic, today aid or rather hinder the process of meaningful historical engagement with the Holocaust itself.[1]

More specifically, both Kadelbach's and Shortland's films accord significant weight to the work of the camera and the photographic album in preserving and mediating history for the present. Although distinct in their application of it, both films share a core preoccupation with the medium as that which most succinctly grants memory an afterlife. In this respect, both films work consciously within a contemporary memorial aesthetic that, as Marianne Hirsch and Leo Spitzer note, privileges 'archival photographs and objects' (2008: 169), presuming (in a paraphrase of novelist W. G. Sebald) 'that [photographs from the past] have a memory of their own that they bring to us from the past' (2008: 187, 188). In similar terms, Ulrich Baer describes the power of certain photographic images to 'deliver, straight up and apparently across the gulf of time between viewer and the photographically mummified past, a potent illusion of the real' (2002: 2). In *Unsere Mütter, unsere Väter* and *Lore*, this 'gulf' divides the moments before and then following the onset of Jewish persecution: both works prominently feature photographs of a Jewish figure taken at a time that *precedes* his victimhood. Crucially, these images capture an elusive 'time before' that serves as a visible marker of all that was/shall/may be lost, prompting a certain mournful perspective vis-à-vis the German-Jewish world invoked – akin to what Hirsch and Spitzer characterise as the intrinsic 'belatedness of photographic looking' (2008: 173).

As the comparison of Kadelbach's and Shortland's films will show, the manner in which each of them treats photographic evidence reveals something deeper about its relationship to the indexical value of the image in and of itself – what Tom Gunning terms a photo's 'truth claim' (2008: 23). This relationship to indexicality – that is, the text's underlying understanding of how the photograph relates to that which it represents – has a bearing not only on how the films, and we as viewers, make sense of these photographic images of the pre-war diegetic world, but also how each film presents the figure of the Singular Jew within the larger framework of the history of the Holocaust. Whereas Shortland problematises the indexical value of the image from the very outset, Kadelbach's work naïvely presumes a perfect correspondence between an image and its meaning or message – part of its particular brand of historicist approach, which treats the past as entirely representable, and at the same time routinely presents fiction in the guise of fact. A clear link emerges: the greater the reliance on the indexical value of images, the greater the dependence on the Singular Jew as a functional representative of German-Jewish experience under conditions of persecution and genocide.

Photographic truth-value is integral to the authenticating strategies of historical cinema – what Tobias Ebbrecht (2007a) dubs 'docudramatizing'. But it also cuts to the core of debates about the representability of the Holocaust and reflects something of the intellectual divide within Holocaust Studies that Michael Rothberg has described as a clash between 'realist' and 'antirealist' approaches to the question of genocide (2000: 3), which alternately insist on the Shoah as the result of representable historical factors able to be rendered knowable through the application of scientific enquiry, or that instead stress the special status of the Holocaust as a fundamentally unknowable, even sublime phenomenon. The 'persistence of the question of realism' – 'one of the central problematics that the Holocaust forces back into view' (Rothberg 2000: 8) – poses a particular challenge for the medium of film, which, as Cathy Gelbin has argued, has a 'potential to close mimetic gaps particularly to the untrained eye' (2011: 28) and hence 'may resemble physical reality so closely that it exacerbates the possibility of mistaking filmic representation for reality' (ibid.). Gelbin goes on in her essay to mount an eloquent defence for those cinematic strategies of self-referentiality that call attention to the medium, and so undercut the danger she describes. My intention here, however, is to explore precisely the sort of mimetic collapse between fiction and fact that Gelbin initially identifies – a collapse in which Kadelbach's film engages, I argue, and that Shortland's film resists. In so doing, I am mindful of Rothberg's insights that just as 'there can be no assumption of a direct access to history' (2000: 9), it is also true that we need not privilege discourse and representation 'at the expense of the real' (2000: 8), and that a middle ground (what Rothberg terms 'traumatic realism') might be found in emphasising 'how the ordinary and extraordinary aspects of genocide intersect and coexist' (2000: 9).

THE SINGULAR JEW AND THE SURVIVAL OF THE ARCHIVE: *UNSERE MÜTTER, UNSERE VÄTER*

When the four-and-a-half-hour teamWorx television miniseries *Unsere Mütter, unsere Väter* aired on German television station ZDF on three consecutive evenings in March 2013, it was accompanied by a wave of media fanfare touting both its novelty and its importance as a contribution to the contemporary discourse regarding the National Socialist past. This is a common strategy for the studio, whose productions, as Paul Cooke notes, 'are – somewhat counter-intuitively perhaps – *regularly* marketed as *exceptional* moments in the German mediascape' (2013: 541). Station publicity for the three-part drama promised 'contemporary history, told for contemporary times' (Anon. 2013). *Spiegel* critic Christian Buß luridly praised the drama's taboo-defying scope: 'Did you shoot someone? Betray a friend? Have sex with a Nazi bigwig? The gruesomely faithful world-war drama *Generation War* is finally breaking the silence of the generations. The ZDF-miniseries marks a turning point for German television' (2013).[2] In an op-ed piece, public intellectual Frank Schirrmacher – the film's biggest booster – stressed the urgency of the matter: 'Don't wait for a high holiday, gather your family together now: the ZDF three-part miniseries ... begins on Sunday and offers the last chance to talk about the history of the war across all generations' (2013).[3] Although reviews were by no means uniformly positive, it is possible to discern a clear thread in much of the publicity and press coverage: a view that the series constituted a timely, relevant and pathbreaking event.

The series' multichannel marketing approach was indeed innovative, designed to facilitate above all else the kinds of viewer identification (suggested by the possessive 'our' embedded in the very title of the film) and viewer participation that Schirrmacher envisioned. ZDF created a free mobile app (in the form of a 'Motion Comic') that offered supplemental background information for each of the series' fictional main characters. The ZDF website further supported a platform entitled 'Memory of the Nation' ('Gedächtnis der Nation') via which viewers could upload their own accounts of German history, and during the actual broadcast of the third installment, viewers were invited to connect to ZDF's blog via live chat or Twitter and offer comments or pose questions to the series' 'team of experts'. Whether the multimedia approach made the difference, or the series was carried by the reputation of the teamWorx studio brand (which, with prior hits *Dresden* [2006] and *Die Flucht* [2007], has firmly established itself as the lead producer of so-called 'event television' in Germany), the viewer numbers for *Unsere Mütter, unsere Väter* were impressive. The premiere episode earned an estimated 7.22 million viewers, or more than 20 per cent of the television audience, falling only just behind Germany's most-beloved crime drama, *Tatort* (see Schroeder 2013).

In terms of its narrative structure and affective appeal, Kadelbach's was less original than its marketing campaign, and a viewer familiar with the conventions of contemporary historical film will be hard pressed to see in *Unsere Mütter, unsere Väter* anything other than a textbook example, with a 'look' that ties it to other teamWorx productions such as *Dresden* or *Die Flucht* as well as other recent theatrical releases such as Oliver Hirschbiegel's *Downfall* [*Der Untergang*] (2004). Consistent with the genre's representational codes, the series places a premium on perfecting its illusion of historical accuracy. It adopts period-appropriate props, costuming, music and sets that look familiar not simply because they resemble actual archival images, but also because they cite the conventions of other contemporary historical films. The series' quest for verisimilitude also extends to the aesthetic plane: its colour palette offers a carefully orchestrated imitation of Nazi-era Agfacolor film stock, characterised by contrasting blue, green-gray and crimson hues. All of these formal details work together to create an 'antiqued' look with a general nostalgic feel. At the same time, *Unsere Mütter, unsere Väter* follows the pattern of the genre in organising itself around the stories of fictional figures – what Ebbrecht dubs the 'personalization and individualization of history' (2007b: 225). These characters occupy the visual and affective foreground, while 'history becomes a replaceable background for schematic storytelling' (2007b: 227). These conventions cross the divide between the large and small screen, moreover. The crossover is particularly evident in the case of teamWorx productions: although created for television, they are recognisable for their exceptionally high production values, which give their series a lush, 'expensive' look that evokes the conventions of quality cinema but that is expanded to fill a running time no longer feasible for mainstream theatre releases.

As Laurel Cohen-Pfister notes, the series also offers a 'programmatic emotionalization of the German war experience that consciously skirts conventional didactic discussions of guilt and shame' (2014: 105) – an approach that was identified by much of the film's German reception as groundbreaking, but that is actually entirely characteristic of the affective structure of post-unification historical cinema, or what Cohen-Pfister refers to as 'docudrama' (ibid.). A key component of that programmatic depiction is the series' constellation of familiar characters and plots: it concentrates on the fates of five youthful main characters, each of whom represents a recognisable type, and whose respective war stories are interwoven to the point of straining belief. First and foremost is Wilhelm (played by Volker Bruch), an up-and-coming Wehrmacht officer and, by the terms of his society, an all-round 'stand up guy'. As the film's voiceover narrator, he also constitutes the principal figure of identification. His younger brother Friedhelm (Tom Schilling) is, by contrast, 'poetic' – a bookworm loathe to join in the bloody business of warfare. Charlotte (Miriam Stein) is a fresh-scrubbed nurse trainee eager to serve the fatherland, but woefully innocent of the brutal realities of field medicine. Greta (Katharina Schüttler) dreams of becoming a professional singer and is as glamorous and sexually adventurous as Charlotte is naïve.

Lastly, there is Viktor Goldstein (Ludwig Trepte). Passionate and a touch rakish, a would-be designer unhappily employed in his father's tailoring business, he is the long-time lover of Greta and the sole Jewish figure in the circle of friends. Viktor is not literally the only Jewish figure in the film: his parents play a side part as a pair of kindly but bewildered souls, who are slow to grasp the danger that threatens them. Father Goldstein (Samuel Finzi) is a convinced patriot, so blindly faithful to the nation persecuting his family that when they are forced from their apartment (whether into a ghetto or deportation, the film leaves open), he packs their copy of *Mein Kampf* just below a stack of family snapshots, referring to it bitterly as *'their* [i.e. the Nazis'] Bible', but stowing it away nonetheless. But Viktor's parents remain marginal figures, eventually disappearing without a trace, and it is Viktor who clearly embodies the film's Singular Jew, charged with representing the Jewish experience of his generation. This is in stark contrast to the series' non-Jewish figures. Although, as already noted, all of them represent identifiable types, the non-Jewish characters together form a (however schematic) composite picture of wartime German youth. In that sense, one could argue that they are never meant to be read individually, but rather as a set of complements. Viktor, by contrast, must function on his own, despite the variety of expressions of Jewish life that existed historically in Germany during the period represented, and which the series could have chosen to highlight. At the same time, Viktor's inclusion in the circle also shapes our reading of his non-Jewish friends. Their willingness to associate freely with him as late as June 1941 (itself implausible, since by that time Germany's Jews were forced to live largely isolated from the non-Jewish population) functions as implicit proof of their immunity to the prevailing anti-Semitic ideology of the time, or what Cohen-Pfister refers to as evidence of their 'inherently moral core' (2014: 107). Historian Ulrich Herbert (2013) found fault with the series on precisely these grounds, noting that the principal characters seem to 'exist outside of history' ('wie aus der Zeit gefallen'), insofar as neither they nor the larger series offers any clear sense just how popular Hitler's regime, including its anti-Semitic policies, really were in 1941.

Viktor's status as the group's Singular Jew is set up early in the film, during a key establishing scene in which we observe the five friends celebrate a final send-off before departing, each to pursue a different strand of the war experience. The moment is framed with nostalgia, as if to recall a final moment of togetherness before the war destroys their idyllic community. The friends share cake and champagne, dance and joke with one another, until the moment when the festivities are brought to a dramatic halt by the intrusion of Gestapo man Dorn (Mark Waschke), future lover to Greta and persecutor to Viktor. Greta manages to fend off Dorn with a bit of flirtation, but once he leaves, the party comes to a quick end. As a parting gesture, though, Viktor suggests commemorating the event with a photograph: 'Let's take a picture!' ('Machen wir ein Foto!'). The short sequence that follows is critical for the larger series: the snapshot created will go on to serve as an organising motif for the larger work, reappearing at regular intervals throughout the series in the hands of each character, seemingly connecting them even when apart while also visually reinforcing their shared point of origin. Charlotte ponders hers when she hears (incorrectly) that her beloved Wilhelm has died; Friedhelm uses his to scrawl a crucial farewell letter home; and even Viktor manages to hang on to his, despite imprisonment in a concentration camp, which would likely have stripped him of such personal possessions. Perhaps most significantly, Greta will cannibalise her own copy, cutting out Viktor's face with the idea that Dorn will procure a fake passport for him and thereby enable his escape. As it turns out, Dorn not only arranges for the passport, but also for Viktor's arrest, setting in motion his deportation rather than exile. The shot of the cropped photograph makes for one of the series' more potent visual metaphors, suggesting that in repurposing the image in this fashion, Greta seeks simultaneously to save and excise Viktor from memory.

Fig. 1 The circle of friends in *Unsere Mütter, unsere Väter*

Tight, handheld camerawork and rapid cuts lend the photography sequence a feel of both intimacy and contingency, as if with the winding camera timer, the countdown for our characters has already begun. This is further reinforced by the maudlin voiceover narration, offered from Wilhelm's position of post-war hindsight. He declares: 'We were five friends' ('wir waren fünf Freunde'), as though the group's members had never had cause to differentiate themselves in the way that Hitler's regime would, and he recalls their naïve former faith in things like the future and their own invincibility. 'We would soon learn otherwise' ('wir sollten es bald besser wissen'), he intones grimly. Viktor, who capers about as his friends pose before the camera, takes on the role of artistic instigator, and, in a larger sense, he provides the figurative 'glue' that will bind together their respective fates. Capturing the moment and their circle, Viktor authors the principal image of pre-war life that will accompany each of the figures throughout their wartime journey. As the creator of this foundational image, Viktor is also established as the group archivist. Yet crucially, although he is central to its preservation, he is also relegated to its edge. Indeed, the photo and the voiceover narrative accompanying it together capture a moment

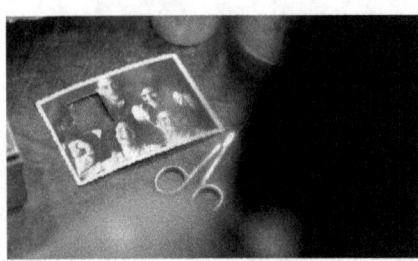

Fig. 2 Excising Viktor's image

imagined from its inception as irretrievably lost – a fleeting picture of shared German-Jewish happiness. The spectacle of symbiosis in *Unsere Mütter, unsere Väter* recalls Eric Santer's concept of 'narrative fetishism' – 'a strategy of undoing, in fantasy, the need for mourning by simulating a condition of intactness' (1990: 144). Yet even as this image of intactness unfolds, it is presented as tinged with the folly of youth. Thus while on one level the film imagines the friends as all inhabiting the same figurative 'family album', Viktor's place in that album appears to be at its margins.

The war experiences that ensue after this celebration will leave all of the friends, with the possible exception of Viktor, fundamentally changed (although it might be said that each really only transforms from one stock character type into another). Charlotte and the Winter brothers encounter a range of frontline horrors, from war crimes to rape. The bright-eyed Charlotte grows jaded, and the once obedient officer Wilhelm goes AWOL. 'Artistic type' Friedhelm becomes a hardened killer, but the film hints that he cannot live with his own transformation, and in the final days of the conflict, he commits suicide by intentionally provoking enemy fire and walking headlong into it (an issue to which I will return). Back at the home front, Greta treads a path of complicity. Although she begins her love affair with Dorn in an attempt to save Viktor, she continues it because he can further her artistic career. She becomes a star, but eventually overplays her hand, and after publicly making seditious remarks she is imprisoned and then executed just days before the war's end. Both deaths are presented in the film as all the more tragic for having been avoidable, and in the case of Greta, there is even a 'tragic twist'. As a woman, as a starlet, and as a non-Jew, she was never 'supposed' to die; as I will explore later, the film by contrast tends to frame the death of German Jews as an anticipated outcome, thereby normalising their victimisation.

In an improbable (albeit not impossible) parallel plot contrivance, Viktor survives the war, breaking out of a cattle car headed to Auschwitz and joining up with a band of fierce – and fiercely anti-Semitic – Polish partisans (a plotline that particularly outraged contemporary Polish audiences). He returns to Berlin to search for survivors, considerably sadder than he once was, but otherwise unchanged in character. In various respects, this 'surprise' ending brings Viktor's singularity to the fore with particular force. As the only main German-Jewish figure in the film, he is tasked implicitly with representing the fate of an entire population, and yet his story can only be described as exceptional, a fact that the film masks quite efficiently through its pretence to historical truth, but one that makes his representative status all the more problematic. His escape, of course, is precisely *not* typical of the experience of German Jews deported to the camps – as a survivor, he numbers among what Primo Levi famously referred to as the 'not only exiguous but also … anomalous minority, who by their prevarications or abilities or good luck did not touch the bottom' (1989: 63). The fact that he narrowly averts incarceration or death in Auschwitz, moreover, adds another layer to his troubling singularity; for

Auschwitz, today commonly taken as a synecdoche for the Holocaust, itself constitutes an imperfect symbol for the larger history of the genocide of European Jews. As historian Timothy Snyder cautions, Auschwitz 'is in fact only the beginning of knowledge, a hint of the true reckoning with the past still to come' (2009).[4] In contrast to the death camps of Operation Reinhard – Bełżec, Sobibór and Treblinka, not to mention the thousands of informal sites of mass murder that characterised the Nazis' genocidal project – Auschwitz was a labour camp as well as a site of genocide, and it had an uncharacteristic number of survivors. While this fact has had a profound impact on the production of Holocaust memory, it has also skewed conventional understandings of the camps and the Holocaust more generally. To cite Snyder's succinct phrasing: 'Auschwitz as symbol of the Holocaust excludes those who were at the center of the historical event' (ibid.). Viktor's tale is in this sense doubly singular – atypical insofar as he escapes the fate the word 'Auschwitz' is meant to invoke, and further anomalous in that Auschwitz itself was never typical to begin with.

The series' treatment of the work of mourning – and embedded within it, notions of the photograph and the archive – returns to the foreground in its conclusion. I will focus on three key scenes from the final moments of the series, which together illuminate the larger memorial project of *Unsere Mütter, unsere Väter* as well as some of its more troubling underlying fictions. The first spans the moment from Friedhelm's death to Viktor's search for his missing parents; the second shows Viktor's quest for evidence concerning Greta's fate; the third depicts the final reunion of the three surviving friends, Viktor, Charlotte and Wilhelm, in a rubble-filled Berlin.

Friedhelm is the only figure in the series to die by choice, and yet his demise is framed entirely in terms of martyrdom. The war has effectively ended, but instead of surrendering he deliberately provokes the Russian soldiers surrounding his tattered unit, discharging his weapon and walking toward them in order to draw their fire. The implication is that he does so for two reasons: to prevent the teenaged conscripts in his care from wasting their own lives in the service of a lost cause, and to end his own pain, born of his transformation from a dreamy reader of Rilke to a callous murderer. The young man that once proclaimed 'the war will only bring out the worst in us' appears to crumble under the weight of his own prophecy. The camerawork and soundtrack work together to create a highly melodramatic tone that further frames his figure as a martyr: a stirring orchestral score overlays a series of medium shots that show his body being torn apart by bullets, rendered in slow-motion so we might linger at the spectacle of his (literal) mortification. Notably, his is the only death granted this sort of attention in the film: of all of the many dead who might be recalled, his receives pride of place, suggesting that the series accords it the greatest symbolic significance.

If the depiction of Friedhelm's death fits the familiar narrative of the tragedy of a wasted German youth (here, understood as non-Jewish), this takes on particularly troubling dimensions when we consider how the sequence ends. Immediately following a close-up that affords an intimate view of Friedhelm's dying face, the series cuts to an extreme close up of a bulletin board densely covered with posted signs seeking lost family members, culminating in a shot of a name registry that prominently features the names Dachau and Auschwitz (the two camps with perhaps the best international name recognition). The juxtaposition places Friedhelm in a constellation of mass casualties of war, but in a manner that emphasises his individual sacrifice while leaving the identity and fate of that mass largely undifferentiated.

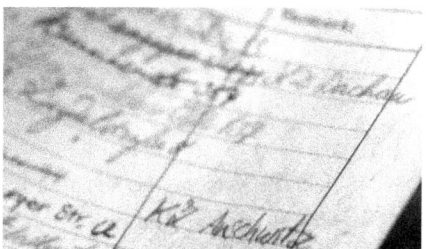

Fig. 3 The registry of the missing

This parallelism takes a cynical turn when a subsequent shot reveals that Viktor is the person thumbing through the name registry, presumably because he is seeking news of his missing parents. While this constitutes a reasonable action, of course, this scene nevertheless once again inscribes Viktor into the role of archivist, as the one who must assume the burden of assembling a record of the past and of honouring the dead. This image is only burnished a short while later, when, in a scene showing his hunt for evidence of Greta's fate, he manages miraculously to locate the one record detailing her death from out of a veritable sea of strewn paperwork. Again, from the point of view of the story that has been constructed throughout the series, his actions appear 'natural' – Viktor loved Greta, and so of course he must search for any trace of her once the war has ended. If one gets outside of this emotional framework that the series encourages, however, and views this character constellation with more distan-

Fig. 4 Viktor searches for signs of Greta

ce as a fictional construction, its problematic nature comes into view as a perfect historical fantasy, in which victim and perpetrator populations are neatly reversed. To wit: the film conjures the spectacle of the living 'Jew' mourning the dead 'German'.

Erin McGlothlin (2014) has identified the plot of the 'wrong victim' in contemporary German Holocaust narratives; that is, stories in which we are prompted to mourn the death of a non-Jewish victim during the Holocaust on the grounds that his or her demise is unintended or even unnatural. This plot not only produces a misplaced mourning, but also, as McGlothlin argues, tends to reassert the inevitability of Jewish victimisation. In conjuring the 'wrong victim', the intended target comes to seem the 'right' one. By extension, escaping death like Viktor comes to seem a kind of accidental or erroneous survival. Thus while audiences might reasonably cheer his escape, this 'surprise twist' has disturbing consequences for the larger commemorative politics at work in the film. Simply put, the film displaces Jewish victimisation and instead foregrounds the tragedy of non-Jewish German losses, mirroring a more general contemporary tendency, as Cohen-Pfister notes, to exclude Jews 'from the national imaginary in discourses on "German" suffering' (2014: 111). As viewers, we are not asked to mourn Viktor or his parents – he survives and they simply disappear. This becomes all the more complicated when we consider how the work of mourning is bound up with Viktor as the series' Singular Jew: in drastic fashion, the film skews its picture of the past to conjure a German world in which 'our mothers and fathers' were never really anti-Semitic, the (Singular) Jew survived and non-Jewish victims lay the greatest claim on us as figures deserving of commemoration.

This is nowhere more obvious than in the final sequence of the series, which shows the three surviving friends as they gather in the ruins of their local pub to toast to the fallen and to remember their last shared celebration and a time when they all still believed the war would 'be over by Christmas'. With a toast 'to Friedhelm and Greta' (with no mention of the film's other dead, for example Viktor's parents), the film cuts to a flashback sequence just over one minute in length: in quick succession, we are treated to a series of miniature vignettes drawn from the friends' original farewell party, when their collective wartime journey first began. The tone of the sequence is overbearingly sentimental. The original dialogue is no longer audible, having been overlaid by a stirring piano score that provides a melancholic musical commentary. The colour of the sequence has also been adjusted, so that in contrast to the dingy blue-grey tone of the post-war setting, the past appears literally golden, its yellow hues heightened to accentuate its nostalgic appeal. The editing, which on the one hand slows certain sequences slightly, and on the other flicks from vignette to vignette with rapid speed, further augments the scene's overall impression as a collage of fleeting, irretrievably beautiful moments. The sequence ends by coming to rest on a close-up of the photograph taken at that primal celebration, as a series of superimposed titles give the birth and death dates of each of the five. This melding of image and text at once closes the narrative loop of the film and transports the film into the contemporary viewing moment – a common trope in historical 'event television', which renders 'history itself ... a contemporary event through its re-enacted representation' (Ebbrecht 2007b: 221). While viewers will already be aware that Greta and Friedhelm lost their lives in 1945, the dates for the surviving three provide some important updates. Viktor, we learn, died in 1997; Charlotte in 2003; and Wilhelm, our guiding narrator, is still alive at the advanced age of 93. While the insertion of these 'facts' serves as a final salvo in a long string of authenticating gestures in the series, it reinforces the picture of Viktor as comparatively unscathed by his experiences of persecution (having lived to the respectable age of 76). Perhaps more crucially, in constructing Viktor as a survivor and informal archivist, the series depicts Viktor – and, suggestively, the German-Jewish population that he, as the film's Singular Jew, comes to represent – as an agent of memory rather than its subject. While we might charitably read this as an attempt by the filmmaker to establish the continued importance of German-Jewish culture in the contemporary nation (since, among other things, Viktor survives to see the post-unification era), the unsavory consequence of this particular fiction is to obscure viewers' awareness of German-Jewish absence – that is, its very lack of presence in the post-war period. That all of this is couched in a narrative that betrays a naïve faith in indexicality only makes this mobilisation of the Singular Jew all the more problematic. Returning almost compulsively to the image of the five friends gathered before the camera, *Unsere Mütter, unsere Väter* seems to insist on the place of the Singular Jew within the frame, without ever acknowledging the inadequacy of this singularity as a means to represent a historically diverse population and set of experiences, and without ever seeming to recognise how much his figure is re-inscribed repeatedly as marginal. By the same token, the nostalgia engendered by the closing return to the photograph is notably indeterminate: this visual reminder of an irretrievable past compels audiences to recall a time before Hitler and the Holocaust, but it is unclear whether they are meant to mourn a German-Jewish community destroyed (historically, never as whole or unproblematic as the image suggests), or whether they instead should long for a time as yet unencumbered by the burdens of German guilt and remembrance.

In its use of the closing image as an incitement to mourn only the series' non-Jewish dead, *Unsere Mütter, unsere Väter* participates in a troubling tendency in contemporary German historical film to engage in a kind of competitive memory politics, in which Jewish stories, and the Holocaust more generally, are either displaced altogether or pushed so far to the margins as to seem insignificant. Although the decision to include Viktor indicates that the series may have hoped to do justice to stories of German-Jewish experience under fascism, in the end the gesture smacks of tokenism. When the film literally steers clear of Auschwitz – as Viktor leaps from the deportation train in the nick of time – it constructs a view of German history that seems at best a wishful fantasy, and at worst, a form of patently dishonest revisionism. In the same vein, the series displaces the problem of anti-Semitism to Polish territory, remains silent about the real appeal of National Socialism for the 'mothers and fathers' invoked in its title, and generally paints the war generation as caught up in a history not of its own making, bystanders rather than engaged participants in the events of the war.

While one cannot perhaps fault a film for the work it is not, it is nevertheless a useful thought experiment to consider alternative endings for the series. Imagine the different tone of the penultimate sequence in rubble-strewn Berlin if both Greta and Friedhelm had survived the war and Viktor had died instead. What would that final gathering look and feel like if, in place of the current constellation, we saw the four non-Jewish characters gather in their former hangout to contemplate the absence of their dead Jewish friend? Even leaving the current plot intact, another option would have been to return *not* to the image of the intact photo, but instead to the sight of Greta's copy, from which Viktor was eliminated through a few deliberate cuts of the scissor. It might have made for a much more apt metaphor for his marginal position within the circle and offered a more effective avenue for viewers to contemplate the violence and loss that were wrought by the persecution of Germany's Jewish population in the course of the Holocaust. At the same time it would have tempered the marginalisation of Jewish victimhood inherent in the manner in which the series deploys the Singular Jew.

UNDOING THE SINGULAR JEW: *LORE*

In Cate Shortland's film *Lore*, photographs register absences, document atrocities and invoke real and figurative family albums interrupted by war and genocide. The film is based on the central episode of Rachel Seiffert's novel *The Dark Room*, which as the title suggests is itself preoccupied with the photographic medium; but in her adaptation Shortland goes even further in exploiting the function and limits of the archival image. Like *Unsere Mütter, unsere Väter*, *Lore* also works with the character convention of the Singular Jew. But while Kadelbach's series employs its central Jewish figure in the service of a narrative privileging non-Jewish suffering, *Lore* pulls the rug out from under any such conceit. Shortland's film sets up the construct of the Singular Jew only to dismantle it, shattering any illusion of post-war German-Jewish wholeness and calling renewed attention to precisely the sort of losses that Kadelbach's series smoothes over. This deconstruction in *Lore* is closely connected to the manner in which the film interrogates the indexical value of the image as such, and in stark contrast to *Unsere Mütter, unsere Väter*, Shortland highlights the inherent partiality of the photograph, the stories it cannot save for posterity or even represent. In *Lore*, we are repeatedly drawn back to the fragility of the image, through photographs that are stolen, torn from their original setting, immolated, buried and generally stripped of their capacity to signify clearly.

Set in the early days of the post-war period, *Lore* tells the story of its eponymous character, a young girl of fourteen (powerfully rendered by Saskia Rosendahl), whose parents are interned by the Americans for their participation in Nazi crimes. Left to fend for herself, Lore must lead her four younger siblings from Bavaria to their grandmother's house on the northern coast. Along the way, the children take up company with the brooding young Thomas (Kai Malina), whose passport and a telltale tattoo identify him as a Jew. Despite an upbringing that has taught her to revile him as a 'parasite', Lore finds herself drawn to Thomas. The two begin a tormented sexual relationship marked alternately by attraction and aggression, until the day that Lore's brother Günter (André Frid) steals Thomas's passport in a ploy to compel him to remain with their ragtag group. The plan backfires. When a group of occupation officers board their train, the now paperless

Thomas slips away, never to be seen again. The film ends as Lore and her siblings finally reach Hamburg and begin to settle uneasily into a new life with their grandmother.

From the outset, *Lore* foregrounds photography's importance as a medium for both private and administrative documentation. When the film opens, Lore's parents are preparing to flee their villa, packing cherished possessions and frantically destroying incriminating material. As part of the purge, Lore's father sets fire to a huge mound of paperwork. Select close-ups allow us a view of the material to be destroyed: file cards for murdered victims of the so-called 'euthanasia' programme. As the fingerprints and mug shots go up in flames, we become aware of the loss of an index in a broader sense. With the destruction of these records, key evidence, perhaps the last trace of those who were murdered, is turned to ash. At the same time, the image of the ravenous fire recalls the spectre of the crematoria, metaphorically linking the images of these once-indexed, now indexless individuals to the larger history of genocide.

Fig. 5 Destroying incriminating evidence in *Lore*

A short while later, as the family hides at a small Bavarian farm, Lore's mother selectively dismantles the family photo album, once so carefully packed for their journey, and again, the images go into the flames. A medium close-up of the stove shows a burning snapshot. The face already consumed, the figure is now only recognizable by its SS uniform, perhaps belonging to Lore's father. Like the earlier records, its indexical value is ruined. While all of this destruction is committed, of course, in recognition of the photograph's potential value as 'proof', Shortland's emphasis on what disappears, rather than what is documented, hints at an inherent fragility in the process by which the photo makes meaning. This can be contrasted fruitfully with the use of the image in Kadelbach's film, where the group snapshot is brought out whenever a character wants to establish a clear link to the past. In *Lore*, we are forced to wonder instead to what extent the image is able to signify at all: its very susceptibility to destruction in Shortland's rendition calls into question the image's reliability as a means to convey meaning, since the routine alteration and elimination of images in the film compels us to ponder the vast number of images that likely have not survived. In this sense, any 'truth' referenced in one of the film's photographs seems intrinsically partial and contingent.

Fig. 6 Burning tell-tale family photos

Subsequent shots and scenes reveal the redacted family album, highlighting the book's obvious holes, and also making clear the close connections between the album as a repository of both personal and political moments. While this suggests the poisonous ideological climate in which Lore was raised, it also expands the album from a collection with a strictly familial significance to one invested with greater socio-cultural meaning. Its glaring gaps evoke the holes in both familial and national narratives, suggestively marking the moment of genesis for a longer post-war trajectory of silence and omission. This comes to the fore most starkly when Lore first encounters documentary evidence of the Holocaust. In a public square, villagers gather around a poster publicising the atrocities, documented during the liberation of the concentration camps. Lore leans in to examine one image in particular, reaching out to touch it – smoothing out a wrinkle in the paper, but with a tenderness that suggests she recognises the person represented. Although as viewers we can only make out the hazy outline of a man in uniform, in the larger context of the film – with our knowledge of her parents' political activities and the suggestive manner in which she touches the image – we are encouraged to believe that she has just encountered a photograph of her father. Pulling away from the poster then, a dab of glue adheres to Lore's finger, its viscosity suggestive both of her budding sexuality and the moral taint conferred by this contact. For the first time, the scene suggests, Lore is forced to confront her father's complicity in the system of genocide referenced by the accusatory poster; at the same time, the stickiness of the glue hints at the difficulties she will face as she tries to disentangle her own relationship to the man and the guilt with which he is associated. Lore returns to the poster that evening and, under cover of darkness, tears away the image. While we might read this as another cover-up (and, in fact, later in the film Lore buries the incriminating image, along with a portrait of her father to which she has been comparing it), the film's larger preoccupation with a photographic record rendered incomplete suggests another reading. As viewers familiar with the gaps in the family album, we are invited to imagine the stolen image as one that might mend the narrative that the album once told – that is, we are prompted to restore the proof of perpetration to its proper place in the book (in the process, making possible a more complete retelling of familial and national history).

At the same time that Lore struggles to reconcile her image of her father with the haunting images of the concentration camp, which reveal (whether literally or by implication) his identity as a perpetrator, she is forced to confront the gulf between her real interactions with Thomas and the propagandistic view of Jews inculcated by her National Socialist family and the larger culture in which she has been raised. Initially wary of him as a stranger, she grows outright hostile when she finally deduces that he is Jewish, a hostility that he in some ways seems to match. The two characters perform a delicate and often contradictory dance, shifting without warning from feelings of mutual dependency to desire and disgust, so that every close encounter becomes a potential act of violence or lust. In far starker terms than the Lore of Seiffert's novel, Shortland's central character fights an internal battle between the pull of lived experience and that of indoctrination.

The extent to which Shortland understands this struggle as a broader cultural renegotiation brought on by the collapse of the Reich and Allied occupation is rendered in symbolic terms in the first sexual encounter that Lore and Thomas share, which takes place immediately after she has torn away the image from the atrocity poster. An obviously inebriated Thomas lurks in the background as Lore purloins the photograph, and when she begins to walk away he staggers toward her, demanding to see it. She refuses, and he responds by grabbing her roughly and shoving her up against the very poster she has just defaced, burying his face in the crook of her neck. She ends the assault with a firm slap, but the anger and violence that infuse this first exchange colour each of their subsequent sexual encounters, making clear that the history of atrocity forms the literal backdrop for their union. Each time the young lovers come together, it is as though the images of the recent past – from the grotesque stereotype of the Jew in Nazi propaganda to the grim skeletal remains of Jewish camp victims depicted in the poster – haunt their interactions. Thomas seems to want to satisfy an urge for vengeance as much as sexual gratification, and Lore can only permit herself to submit to her own desires insofar as she denigrates the object of her longing at the very same moment she embraces him. How we are meant to read the aggression that lurks just beneath his interactions with Lore is unclear. It might be a sign of the brutality induced by his own wartime experiences, but what these were remains unclear as well, and any effort to read his motivations is frustrated by the fact that we can never be certain where his lies begin and end. His anger might stem from the recognition that Lore desires him as a 'Jew', so that he enacts a peculiar kind of racial rivalry with the identity he impersonates. But at one point in the film, Thomas also identifies himself as having been a serial thief – a detail that suggests that, even as a non-Jew, he may have spent time in the concentration camps. If this were true, his aggression might be read as the channeling of a desire for revenge against the German population responsible for his wartime imprisonment, and perhaps even a form of surrogate Jewish revenge fantasy; that is, a wish to seek vengeance on behalf of those who perished in the same setting he once inhabited. At the same time, while Thomas is the only living figure in the film to be identified as Jewish, through the thematisation of the gulf between reality and caricature, the viewer begins early on to discern the ways in which Shortland subjects his singularity to scrutiny: in contrast to Kadelbach's series, we are unable to identify Jewishness here with any single image.

This incommensurability of conflicting representations, the problem of missing and surrogate photographs, and the more general rift that seems to characterise the relationship between index and meaning, all come full circle toward the end of the film, when we finally learn the reason behind Thomas's flight from the train. As Lore and her surviving siblings undertake the final stretch of their journey, bound in a horse-drawn cart across the sand flats near their grandmother's home, Günter timorously admits his crime. 'Promise not to tell?' he asks, as he retrieves Thomas's missing wallet from inside his coat: 'I only did it so he wouldn't go.' As Lore opens the folio, Günter adds the critical clue that at last explains their companion's disappearance, and that finally undoes permanently the 'evidentiary authority of photography' (Hirsch and Spitzer 2008: 174). We hear Günter declare 'das ist er nicht' ('it's not him') as we see a close-up shot of Lore's hands unpacking the wallet's contents: a German passport marked with the ignominious 'J' identifying its holder as Jewish, and yellow cloth Star of David. Lore reads aloud the name on the papers, 'Thomas Weil', and Günter explains: 'He said it didn't matter. The man was a Jew, he was dead anyway ["der war sowieso schon tot"]. The Americans like Jews. So he pretended to be a Jew.' When Lore asks the real name of their companion, Günter cannot help her: 'He never told me,' he explains. We also never learn how the imposter came by the passport, or whether its original bearer really has died. Their conversation ends when Lore comes to a small stack of photographs. 'Das sind Fotos von den toten Juden,' Günter explains – 'those are photos of the dead Jews' – (critically, a plural form that the subtitle in the American release misses). With that, Lore stashes the packet away and the conversation ends, but the story of the stolen passport, and the images contained within it, frame the final moments of Lore's development in the film, as we witness her begin to come to terms more deeply with the horrific realities of the regime her family so ardently supported.

Tellingly, Lore's enquiry is arrested when she finds the snapshots. Facing the stolen wallet, Lore for the first time confronts a new, more personal and intimate proof of the genocide. This scene also marks the moment when Shortland most definitively dismantles the conceit of the Singular Jew. Indeed, a plurality of identities seems to permeate the moment. Their companion's passport, we learn, was stolen from a man both German and Jewish, although the theft is of no consequence, according to Günter, because its owner was always already destined for death. Günter's casual remark that 'those are photos of the dead Jews' further places the passport's former owner, the real Thomas Weil, within a multitude or plurality of victims. In the process, these images provide a counterweight to the other 'photos of the dead Jews' that haunt the film and Lore herself, forcing the viewer to expand his or her perception of the 'dead Jew' as such. This is only further complicated when one considers Günter's initial comment about the passport: when he asserts 'that's not him', the line refers most obviously to the fact that their companion was living under an assumed name. But suggestively his words prompt us to wonder: who was the 'real' Thomas Weil after all? Was he the man in the passport, labelled a pariah by a murderous state? Or was he the man we can discern in the casual family snapshots that accompany it? And how are these two sets of records to be reconciled?

A short while later, Lore retrieves the photographs in order to examine them more carefully, as if bent on solving precisely this puzzle. Turning the snapshots over for the first time, she finds further traces of their former owner: 'Thomas with Lisa, 1936' and

'Lisa Breakfast – Spreewald'. The names jolt us into awareness not only of the very existence of these individuals, but also their names, an acute reminder of the identities that they bore before the National Socialist system systematically deprived Germany's Jewish population of civil rights, names and then lives. In fact, as the director relayed in an interview: 'The photographs in Thomas's wallet are of my husband's family. That's his mother and his grandma and grandpa. So for us the film's very personal' (James 2013). The final image in the pile – showing the joyous arc of a diver suspended in midair – captures a bygone moment of leisure and freedom of movement, made bitter with the awareness that its subject likely met a violent death.

Fig. 7 A stolen image of pre-war Jewish life

With the matter-of-fact phrase 'he was dead anyway' the film transmits a complex series of messages about the post-war German setting it aims to represent. It makes the geno-cide the subject of common knowledge. It reveals a basic callousness toward National Socialism's victims (as if the death of Jews were inevitable, and as if, as a 'dead man', the real Thomas Weil could not be further victimised by something so mundane as identity theft). Lastly, it raises the question: *Is* the real Thomas Weil 'dead anyway', and what is the true identity of his imposter? Importantly, the film leaves us with little clarity regarding the true character of either man. While we can venture a guess as to each of them, we are never given the consolation of a clear answer. That the film raises these questions by means of a photographic figure saturated with signs both of 'Germanness' and 'Jewishness' – from the snapshot of the Spreewald to the yellow star – reinforces just how much these identity markers, once intertwined, have come to be construed as mutually exclusive.

Framed in revealing close ups, the faces in the stolen photos seem to stare out at us, as if challenging the audience to confront both their existence and absence. Gone is any pretence of perfect commensurability between this residual archive and the missing. Instead, the film references the vast scale of Holocaust crimes by subtly reminding us of our inability to correlate bodies and papers, that is, of the indexical limitations presented by any single image or document. And most importantly, with the revelation that the narrative's original Singular Jew is a fake and quite possibly not even Jewish at all, the film here gives the lie to the very figuration it has thus far employed. In so doing, it unravels the very idea of the Singular Jew, rendering the German-Jewish story under National Socialist persecution suddenly plural, irreducible to any one individual. The fissure in knowledge opened up by Lore's discovery, and of the film's open ending more generally, reinforces a sense *not* of narrative and historical closure, but of an open process of remembering that demands an awareness of those gaps – both in individual family histories and in the historical record – that cannot simply be filled again. It invites us to contemplate an expansive version of the past characterised by complicated, overlapping, multiple, even intersectional identities and histories – a past that is not German *or* Jewish, but both, and in which the relationship between margin and centre is not easily mapped.

TOWARD A PLURALISTIC SINGULARITY

In her analysis of the documentary *Anne Frank Remembered* (1995), Griselda Pollock is particularly critical of the film's ending, which concludes with a famous, and often abbreviated, passage from Frank's published diary. The quote expresses her gratitude for the God-given gift of writing; the passage is read aloud by actress Glenn Close, over a still shot focusing on a well-known image of a smiling Anna, 'freezing her open, cheerful, girlish face in time' (2007: 132).[5] In Pollock's view, the film should have ended with another image altogether, that is, at the point at which it inserts a short excerpt of archival footage – the only known filmed evidence of Anna Frank, newly uncovered during the making of the documentary. For Pollock,

> the 'moving footage' becomes an uncanny index of a historical moment in time of the *living* Anna Frank that can resist and transcend our current over-familiarity with her iconic image, frozen in photographs and selective quotations from her *Diary*. [...] The effect of such an affecting moment 'rediscovered' and restored open this documentary (always premised narratively on retelling of a past that has a known endpoint) onto a devastating contemplation of the meaning of her being dead. (2007: 125–6)

To restate Pollock's point, the motion picture footage of the girl suddenly releases her from her iconic status, bringing her perhaps not back to life, but at the very least back to some sort of lived complexity, as a person whose loss can only be appreciated when we become conscious of how much living still lay ahead of her at the time she was murdered. By contrast, the film's *actual* ending works to reassure audiences with the notion that through her published words, Anne Frank has managed to live on – in the process, erasing our consciousness of her actual death. Pollock deems this a 'sentimental refashioning of Holocaust commemoration through the apparently immortal, undefeated image of a young girl's adolescence in hiding [that] perversely makes the victim herself, provide us, the bystanders, with comfort in our distress at encountering her suffering' (2007: 139).

Pollock's argument is closely related to my own analysis of the figure of the Singular Jew in *Unsere Mütter, unsere Väter* and *Lore*. Kadelbach's series engages in precisely the sort of perverse 'sentimental refashioning' she identifies in Blair's documentary, tasking the figure of Viktor with recording and remembering his fallen non-Jewish friends while downplaying his own experiences of suffering, whether as a result of his personal persecution or the unresolved matter of his parents' disappearance and presumable murder. The final image of film reasserts an image of originary wholeness that belies the historical complexities of German-Jewish relationships, and at the same time seems designed to comfort us insofar as we are never compelled to confront the sorts of absences brought about in German-Jewish communities by Nazi persecution and genocide. Shortland's film does something quite different: in suddenly separating the character 'Thomas' we have come to know from the man in the stolen photographs, the notion of loss is magnified. To cite Pollock again, who herself draws on Roland Barthes' theory of photography, Shortland effectively creates a 'punctum', allowing the viewer to 'break through the stadium/tedium of facts and figures which also allow us to avoid understanding something of it for ourselves: what Schiller would name an *aesthetic* knowledge of this traumatic event that must occur on an unprotected affective plane' (2007: 132). Rejecting a simplistic indexical relationship in which a single image or figure can establish a neat and complete link to the past, Shortland points toward the need for complex and pluralistic depictions of the Holocaust – images, in other words, that gesture toward the complexity and plurality of its victims' real stories. At the same time, she denies her viewers the comfort of any platitude about 'living forever in memory'. Over and over again, her film forces us to consider not only what images capture, but also what they do not.

In this light, it is worthwhile to consider Pollock's concluding warning in her essay on Anna/Anne Frank, about the consequences of the wrong kind of singularity. As she writes, 'the purely cultural or aesthetic practices of monuments, memorials, museums, and art works will fail to avoid the fetishism of all commemorative narrative unless we find means of holding *in a single figure* the relational disaster of the fascist or totalitarian act and the human victim' (2007: 139; emphasis added). Following Pollock, the Singular Jew identified in these films does not pose a problem in his singularity as such, but rather insofar as his figure is rendered with or without sufficient nuance. If the Singular Jew is to serve any truly representative function, it will have to be accompanied by an acknowledgement that no figure can alone embody the entirety of Holocaust history or memory.

Notes

1 For a range of approaches, see, among others, Hirsch (2000); Zelizer (2000); Baer (2002); Keilbach (2009).
2 'Hast du einen Menschen erschossen? Einen Freund verraten? Sex mit einem Nazi-Bonzen gehabt? Das grausam genaue Weltkriegsdrama 'Unsere Mütter, unsere Väter' bricht endlich das Schweigen der Generationen. Der ZDF-Dreiteiler markiert eine Zeitenwende für das deutsche Fernsehen.' (Unless otherwise noted, all translations are mine.)

3 'Warten Sie nicht auf einen hohen Feiertag, versammeln Sie jetzt Ihre Familie: Der ZDF-Dreiteiler ... beginnt am Sonntag und ist die letzte Chance, über die Generationen hinweg die Geschichte des Krieges zu erzählen.'
4 Thanks to Erin McGlothlin for making me aware of Snyder's text, as well as for her more general insights on the subject of Auschwitz's singularity and the role that Viktor plays as an informal 'archivist' in Kadelbach's series.
5 I follow Pollock's example in using the spelling of 'Anna' to represent the historical personage, and 'Anne' to refer to the figure as created through literary, theatrical and cinematic representation; see Pollock (2007: 140, n.1).

Filmography

Aimée & Jaguar. Dir. Max Färberbock. Germany, 1999.
Anne Frank Remembered. Dir. Jon Blair. UK/USA/Netherlands, 1995.
Comedian Harmonists. Dir. Joseph Vilsmaier. Germany/Austria, 1997.
Dresden. Dir. Roland Suso Richter. Germany, 2006.
Die Flucht [*March of Millions*]. Dir. Kai Wessel. Germany, 2007.
Lore. Dir. Cate Shortland. Germany/Australia/UK, 2012.
Unsere Mütter, unsere Väter [*Generation War*]. Germany, 2013.

Bibliography

Anon. (2013) 'Zeitgeschichte, zeitgemäß erzählt: Für den Dialog der Generationen – Vorwort der Redaktion.' *ZDF*. Online: http://www.zdf.de/unsere-muetter-unsere-vaeter/zeitgeschichte-zeitgemaess-erzaehlt-26275822.html
Baer, Ulrich (2002) *Spectral Evidence: The Photography of Trauma*. Cambridge, MA: MIT Press.
Buß, Christian (2013) 'ZDF-Weltkriegsepos: Glaube, Liebe, Hitler', *Spiegel*. Online: http://www.spiegel.de/kultur/tv/zdf-weltkriegs-epos-unsere-vaeter-unsere-muetter-a-886932.html
Cohen-Pfister, Laurel (2014) 'Claiming World War II and Its Lost Generation: *Unsere Mütter, unsere Väter* and the Politics of Emotion', *Seminar*, 50, 1, 104–24.
Cooke, Paul (2013) 'Reconfiguring the National Community Transnationally: teamWorx, Television, and the "Eventization" of German History', *Modern Language Review*, 108, 2, 539–58.
Ebbrecht, Tobias (2007a) 'Docudramatizing History on TV: German and British Docudrama and Historical Event Television in the Memorial Year 2005', *European Journal of Cultural Studies*, 10, 1, 35–53.
____ (2007b) 'History, Public Memory and Media Event: Codes and Conventions of Historical Event-Television in Germany', *Media History*, 13, 2/3, 221–34.
Gelbin, Cathy (2011) 'Cinematic Representations of the Holocaust', in Jean-Marc Dreyfus and Daniel Langton (eds) *Writing the Holocaust*. London: Bloomsbury.
Gunning, Tom (2008) 'What's the Point of an Index? Or Faking Photographs', in Karen Beckman and Jean Ma (eds) *Still/Moving: Between Cinema and Photography*. Durham, NC: Duke University Press, 23–40.
Herbert, Ulrich (2013) 'Nazis sind immer die Anderen', *TAZ*, 21 March. Online: http://www.taz.

de/!5070893/

Hirsch, Joshua (2004) *Afterimage: Film, Trauma, and the Holocaust*. Philadelphia, PA: Temple University Press.

Hirsch, Marianne (1997) *Family Frames: Photography, Narrative, and Postmemory*. Cambridge, MA: Harvard University Press.

____ (2000) 'Surviving Images: Holocaust Photographs and the Work of Postmemory', in Barbie Zelizer (ed.) *Visual Culture and the Holocaust*. New Brunswick, NJ: Rutgers University Press. 214–46.

____ (2013) *The Generation of Postmemory: Writing and Visual Culture After the Holocaust*. New York: Columbia University Press.

Hirsch, Marianne and Leo Spitzer (2008) '"What's Wrong with This Picture?": Archival Photographs in Contemporary Narratives', in David Lazar (ed.) *Truth in Nonfiction: Essays*. Iowa City, IA: University of Iowa Press, 163–90.

James, Nick (2013) 'Children of the Damned'; Interview with Cate Shortland, *Sight and Sound*, 23, 3, 44–6.

Keilbach, Judith (2009) 'Photographs, Symbolic Images, and the Holocaust: On the (Im)Possibility of Depicting Historical Truth', *History and Theory*, 48, 2, 54–76.

Koepnick, Lutz (2002) 'Reframing the Past: Heritage Cinema and Holocaust in the 1990s', *New German Critique*, 87, 47–82.

____ (2003) '"Honor Your German Masters": History, Memory and National Identity in Joseph Vilsmaier's *Comedian Harmonists* (1997)', in Randall Halle and Margaret McCarthy (eds) *Light Motives: German Popular Film in Perspective*. Detroit, MI: Wayne State University Press, 349–75.

Landsberg, Alison (2004) *Prosthetic Memory: The Transformation of American Remembrance in the Age of Mass Culture*. New York: Columbia University Press.

Levi, Primo (1989) *The Drowned and the Saved*, trans. Raymond Rosenthal. London: Abacus.

Levy, Daniel and Natan Sznaider (2006) *The Holocaust and Memory in the Global Age*, trans. Assenka Oksiloff. Philadelphia, PA: Temple University Press.

McGlothlin, Erin (2014) 'Rewriting the Fantasy of the "Wrong" Victim in Jochen Alexander Freydank's *Spielzeugland*', *New German Critique*, 123, 113–34.

Milton, Sybil (1999) 'Photography as Evidence of the Holocaust', *History of Photography*, 23, 4, 302–12.

Pollock, Griselda (2007) 'Stilled Life: Traumatic Knowing, Political Violence, and the Dying of Anna Frank', *Mortality*, 12, 2, 124–41.

Rothberg, Michael (2000) *Traumatic Realism: The Demands of Holocaust Representation*. Minneapolis, MN: University of Minnesota Press.

____ (2009) *Multidirectional Memory: Remembering the Holocaust in the Age of Decolonization*. Stanford, CA: Stanford University Press.

Santer, Eric (1990) *Stranded Objects: Mourning, Memory and Film in Post-war Germany*. Ithaca, NY: Cornell University Press.

Schirrmacher, Frank (2013) 'Die Geschichte deutscher Albträume', *Frankfurter Allgemeine Zeitung*, 3 March. Online: http://www.faz.net/aktuell/feuilleton/medien/unsere-muetter-unsere-vaeter/unsere-muetter-unsere-vaeter-im-zdf-die-geschichte-deutscher-albtraeume-12115192.html

Schröder, Jens (2013) '*Tatort* besiegt *Unsere Mütter, unsere Väter*', MEEDIA, 18 March. Online: http://meedia.de/2013/03/18/tatort-besiegt-unsere-mutter-unsere-vater/

Seiffert, Rachel (2001) *The Dark Room*. London: Pantheon.
Snyder, Timothy (2009) 'Holocaust: The Ignored Reality', *New York Review of Books*, 16 July. Online: http://www.nybooks.com/articles/archives/2009/jul/16/holocaust-the-ignored-reality/
Weissman, Gary (2004) *Fantasies of Witnessing: Post-war Efforts to Experience the Holocaust*. Ithaca, NY: Cornell University Press.
Zelizer, Barbie (2000) 'Gender and Atrocity: Women in Holocaust Photographs', in Barbie Zelizer (ed.) *Visual Culture and the Holocaust*. New Brunswick, NJ: Rutgers University Press. 247–71.

CHAPTER SEVEN

Locked Doors and Hidden Graves
SEARCHING THE PAST IN
POKŁOSIE, SARAH'S KEY AND *IDA*

Tobias Ebbrecht-Hartmann[1]

In May 1945, during the liberation of Europe, the US Army entered the German town of Falkenau, the former capital of Bohemia. There, the 1st United States Infantry Division made a shocking discovery. Opening doors to storerooms at a camp on the outskirts of the town, soldiers found piles of dead bodies. One of these young soldiers later became a movie director in Hollywood and restaged the horrifying moment in a film he dedicated to his former army unit. In this film, disrupting the routine of fighting, the soldiers open the door to a room. Fast cut shots focus on the face of one soldier and then show, in a disturbing reverse shot, the gaze of a frightened prisoner.

This sequence from Samuel Fuller's *The Big Red One* (1980) presents a sudden encounter with a shocking but hidden and suppressed secret. Fuller's depiction thus literally visualises the 'return of the past' in the sense that Dominick LaCapra described when discussing a 'disturbance in the symbolic order' caused by 'ghosts of the past': 'If they haunt a house (a nation, a group), they come to disturb all who live – perhaps even pass through – that house' (2001: 215). The disruptive montage of *The Big Red One* signifies the supposed disturbance: it is not only Fuller's attempt to replace his personal memories with images from a countervailing order (the cinematic order of genre cinema) but indicates a particular approach to dealing with disturbing ghosts and reappearing 'skeletons in the closet' in cinema. The sequence from *The Big Red One* also refers to previous footage recorded by Fuller in May 1945 at the actual camp in Falkenau. There he shot, using his private 16mm Bell & Howell camera, twenty minutes of a scene ordered by his battalion commander, Captain Kimble R. Richmond. Richmond had instructed leading citizens of the neighbouring town to retrieve the dead bodies from the camp, dress them, carry them in a procession to the cemetery, and bury them. This moment of 'restoring' the symbolic order (Fuller later described it as a lesson on human dignity) was recorded by Fuller's camera.[2]

This essay will review recent attempts to frame cinematically the act of facing 'ghosts from the past', opening the cupboards of France and Poland's national histories and placing them in the context of contemporary European memory discourses about the Shoah.

A BURIED PAST?

After the war and the immediate post-war period, most of the 'skeletons', the millions of those murdered in the Shoah, remained, at first, in the closets of forgetting.[3] At that time the Cold War delivered the framework for any politics of memory, and re-establishing order and bridging the chasms that were fracturing Europe were the preferred political tasks within a slowly evolving process of European reconciliation. Although not referring to the fate of the Jews and other victims of Nazi politics at all, none other than Winston Churchill, in a speech he gave in 1946, explicitly indicated the need to forget and interrelated the vision of a unified Europe with a demand for oblivion:

> We must all turn our backs upon the horrors of the past and look to the future. We cannot afford to drag forward across the years to come hatreds and revenges which have sprung from the injuries of the past. If Europe is to be saved from infinite misery, and indeed from final doom, there must be this act of faith in the European family, this act of oblivion against all crimes and follies of the past. (2014)

The path for post-war European politics was clear. Mutual trust to build a common future for hostile nations seemed on the one hand to imply a mutual act of oblivion regarding past crimes, which were, on the other, accompanied by the establishment of often conflicting national narratives of heroism and suffering alongside the lines of the Cold War. Such 'myths elaborated by politicians, intellectuals and the media to order and explain those events and to overcome the pain associated with them' also aimed to found stable 'narratives of the past which serve to give an identity to a collectivity such as a nation' (Gildea 2002: 59). Thus 'European memory' at that time was mostly a contradictory and competing mosaic of national narratives built around blind spots and rejected conflicting memories that were not only dividing Europe along the conflicts of the Cold War but also within the competing ideological entities.

Thereby, according to Helmut König, these national myths served to spare all incriminatory aspects of wartime Europe – in all societies that were affected by the experiences of German occupation, anti-Semitism, mass murder and collaboration (2008: 24). As a consequence, disrupted and divided Europe invented itself after the war as an assembly of nations with harmonised national histories built around gaps and voids that excluded everything that could harm national unity and consistent self-perception:

> But only much later would it become clear just how much post-war Europe rested on foundation myths that would fracture and shift with the passage of the years. In the circumstances of 1945, in a continent covered with rubble, there was much to be gained by behaving as though the past was indeed dead and buried and a new age about to begin. The price paid was a certain amount of selective, collective forgetting, notably in Germany. But then, in Germany above all, there was much to forget. (Judt 2010: 62)

This was in fact true for both newborn German states, although both extensively used references to the past in order to legitimate their respective post-war constitutions. While both were projecting continuities with the past on the other state, they tried to avoid engaging into conflicting memories shaping their own society. West Germany tried to integrate both Nazi supporters as well as the German resistance, which led to certain controversies during the debates on compensation payments to the State of Israel and the rearmament of the Federal Republic. The GDR, on the other hand, offered their citizens the chance of collective guiltlessness while projecting all responsibility for the Nazi crimes on West Germany and rejecting, due to its loyalty within the Eastern Bloc, any claims for particular compensation of Jewish victims. Other European countries also developed selective national memories of wartime. While the Soviet Union was cultivating its self-image of being a victim and a liberator, it was suppressing the memories of the Hitler-Stalin Agreement as well as the fate of numerous Soviet prisoners in Nazi camps that were falsely accused of collaboration. Similarly the Polish communist leadership was preserving Poland's collective experience of victimhood as well as the commemoration of Communist resistance. But Polish collaboration with Nazi occupiers as well as anti-Semitic murders in the immediate aftermath of the war were kept in oblivion. The same was true regarding the resistance struggle of the (non-Communist) Polish Home Army.

Nonetheless, the buried and often carefully locked past repeatedly re-emerged. European cinema was always situated at the boundaries between historical imaginary and the return of the repressed. It assisted in building national narratives of heroism and suffering, but it also catalysed those moments that would reveal the seemingly buried but always persisting past. Such an incident was, for example, the controversy surrounding Alain Resnais' film *Night and Fog* [*Nuit et brouillard*] (1955), in which he used a photograph that clearly showed French policemen guarding detention camps for Jews waiting for deportation. In Germany, Wolfgang Staudte's films depicted stories in which the skeletons quite literally escaped from their German closets, although he hardly mentioned Jewish suffering during the Shoah at all. That was true for *Murderers Among Us* [*Die Mörder sind unter uns*] (1946) but in an even more controversial way for *The Fair* [*Kirmes*] (1960), which is set in a post-war German town in which the residents suddenly discover the remains of a German deserter who had killed himself. The discovery reminds the inhabitants of their guilt at not having assisted the young man hiding from the Nazi military police. A year before, Staudte had made *Roses for the Prosecutor* [*Rosen für den Staatsanwalt*] (1959), a film about a state prosecutor who effectively hid his Nazi past until a box of chocolates uncovers the truth. And in his *Destination Death* [*Herrenpartie*] (1964) a group of German tourists to Yugoslavia transform back into the Nazi soldiers they were when committing massacres against civilians in the course of so-called anti-partisan activities. Even more confrontational, but within a surrealist framework, directors of the Czech New Wave of the 1960s also addressed suppressed elements of their nation's past. Films like Ján Káder and Elmar Klos's *The Shop on Main Street* [*Obchod na korze*] (1965) and Juraj Herz's *The Cremator* [*Spalovač mrtvol*] (1969) broached tabooed subjects, such as collaboration with the Nazi occupiers.

But despite the impact of such powerful cultural examples – and in a global context one has to mention of course also the fundamental impact of the *Holocaust* television series (1978), directed by Marvin J. Chomsky, on the recognition of the Shoah – it was not until the decline of Communism in the early 1990s that the buried past reemerged on the political surface of Europe.[4] This eruption shattered the continent in the form of unsettled political issues, such as compensation and restitution.[5] And it revealed the gaps between national narratives, personal experiences and conflicting transnational memories. Two incidents in particular shaped this transformation. One catalysing moment was the International Forum on the Holocaust held in 2000 in the Swedish capital of Stockholm (see Radonic 2010: 58). Subsequently, the Shoah (besides important cultural and historiographical exceptions publicly recognised only during the course of the 1980s and, mainly, the 1990s) transformed again. It now turned from a traumatic rupture of modern civilisation – as it was described by scholars in psychology as well as by historians after a closer encounter with the specific experiences of survivors, i.e. in context of documentary films such as *Shoah* (1985) or initiatives such as the Yale Fortunoff Archive or the Steven Spielberg Shoah Foundation and its Visual History Archive – into a constitutive point and fundament of European identity. Political concepts, such as Europe's dedication to human rights and minority rights, were now closely related to the lessons from Europe's past. Furthermore, European intellectuals such as German sociologist Ulrich Beck based their visionary concepts of a 'cosmopolitan Europe' particularly on the commemoration of the Shoah, in which 'the break with the past draws to the power of the future' (2006: 171). But in such political and theoretical conceptions, the heterogeneous layers and perspectives tend to be more universalised. It seems like the conflicting memories resulting from differing national and personal experiences of Europe's twentieth century are harmonised instead of recognised as a necessary interplay of particular experiences with universal impact.

EUROPE'S CONFLICTING MEMORIES

But the tension between particular (national) perceptions of the past and its universal shaping became particularly obvious regarding the second incident that fundamentally catalysed Europe's struggle over its ambiguous past. The expansion of the European Union in 2004 added Eastern European experiences of the twentieth century to the mélange of competing and conflicting pasts (see Radonic 2010: 74–5). The memory of the Shoah shaped and challenged the ideal of a unified Europe because the horrors of that past were still vivid in the various national and personal memories that fundamentally divided Europe, including those countries that were attacked, robbed and enslaved by the Nazis, as well as those who welcomed the Nazi invaders as liberators or, as a result of the occupation, collaborated with them and participated in their criminal project of extermination. It is therefore not surprising that the European project in its ambiguity openly refers to the past, in particular to the Shoah, in order to construct a 'negative' but harmonised European memory of the event that transgresses its inherent antagonism. World War II and the Shoah thus play a crucial role as a 'negative founding myth' (Leggewie 2011: 123) of a new, interdependent Europe. Following Europe's attempts of reconciliation through integration, it became obvious that the dividing memories of this negative past had to be reconciled within the new supranational entity, including its paradoxical interrelation of national identities and historical narratives with transnational interlacement (see Radonic 2010: 53). Thereby, oblivion was successively replaced by extensive commemoration, and the divided past transformed into a universalised European experience while conflicting memories with different perspectives were put aside in favour of a single fixed point of remembrance (see König 2008: 25).

Conflicting national memories of defeat versus liberation, conflicting transnational memories, the Jewish experience of suffering from discrimination and extermination versus the non-Jewish experience of occupation and war and suppressed interior memories such as collaboration and the committing of criminal acts encouraged by German authorities still indicate a challenging and persisting past. Politically, these conflicting memories were mediated in acts of public commitment and apology. Already in 1985, the then president of the Federal Republic of Germany, Richard von Weizsäcker, described the conflicting memories of the end of the war in Germany, admitting that a majority of Germans still recalled 8 May 1945 as a day of national shame and defeat. But in his speech, Germany's highest representative encouraged his fellow citizens to understand the date in fact also as liberation of all Germany from the inhumanity and tyranny of the National Socialist regime, an admission that was repeated in the course of public commemorations ten years later (see Weizsäcker 1985: 2).

In this context, then president Jacques Chirac of France gave a remarkable speech in July 1995 at the commemoration of the events of July 1942, when 12,000 Jews were rounded up and herded in preparation for their forthcoming deportation into the Vel d'Hiver winter cycling stadium in Paris (see Rozett and Spector 2000: 353). The roundup, as well as the guarding of the stadium and other transit camps in France, were not carried out by German soldiers, but by French officials and police on their behalf (see Turan 2011). In an act of fully acknowledging French collaboration, previously removed from the country's national memory, President Chirac apologised for French assistance in the deportation of Jews.[6] He also critically addressed French 'amnesia or denial' and thus retrieved those suppressed memories that were hidden under the surface of public commemoration (see Michalczyk 2013: 145).[7] After Chirac's acknowledging of French collaboration during the Vichy regime, this part of the nation's history will then, according to Richard J. Golsan, 'continue to form part of the timeless "negative [founding] myth" at the heart of postmodern European identity: the Shoah itself' (2006: 74).

Similarly, in 2001, then president Aleksander Kwasniewski of Poland addressed a taboo subject relating to Polish national memory in his speech on the sixtieth anniversary of an anti-Jewish pogrom in Jedwabne. On 10 July 1941, following the invasion of German troops, the small Polish town exemplified 'perhaps the most horrific case of Polish anti-Semitism' (Mayurczak 2013). At the order of the Germans, Poles gathered 340 Jews into a barn and burned them alive. Sixty years later, President Kwasniewski apologised for the crime and challenged his fellow countrymen: by 'paying homage to the memory of the murdered and most deeply deploring the despicable perpetrators of the crime, [we] give expression to our pain and shame, we manifest our determination to learn the truth'. Furthermore, this act of acknowledging what was hidden and falsified for six decades pointed towards the future in order 'to overcome the evil past, [with] firm will of understanding and agreement'. Therefore, the Poles' willingness to face the black marks on their national past has also to be seen in the context of the process of European expansion to the east, as well as of the Stockholm forum: 'Thanks to a great nation-wide debate regarding this crime committed in 1941, much has changed in our lives in 2001, the first year of the new millennium. Today's Poland has courage to look into the eyes of the truth about a nightmare which gloomed one of the chapters in its history' (Kwasniewski 2001). This reorientation (and according revision) of the Polish nation's approach towards its own past was on the one hand a result of the increasing Europeanisation in some Eastern European countries prior to the expansion of the European Union in 2004. On the other, such challenging of national myths were and are often initiated by public debates and controversies that induce conflicting memories into the national narratives of the past.

NEW JOURNEYS TO THE PAST

This was clearly the case regarding the challenging of the Polish self-perception as sole victim during wartime. The 'great nation-wide' debate mentioned by Kwasniewski followed the publication of a book on the 'Case of Jedwabne' by historian Jan T. Gross (2002: 69). His study, *Neighbors,* carefully reconstructs the events of July 1941 on the basis of testimonies, eye witness accounts and court files. But what caused the book's powerful impact was that Gross exceeded the limits of historical reconstruction in not only presenting historical research and evidence but documenting a personal as well as collective journey into a troubling and yet largely unknown past. His account was based on 'lonely voices reaching us from the abyss' (2002: 78), voices of survivors that had been ignored, suppressed or disregarded. The case of Jedwabne thus not only illustrates the concealment of the past which lead to a situation where, in the words of Adam Michnik, the burned and butchered Jews from Jedwabne 'were murdered again, denied a decent burial, denied tears, denied truth about this hideous crime' (2001); it also indicates the disturbing persistence of an absent but nevertheless close past described by Eva Plonowska Ziarek, who – like most second-generation Poles – 'grew up without knowing any Jewish people or learning about the Jewish history of my town' (2007: 303). But it was exactly this absence that, in a confusing way, was the impulse behind digging up the past, exemplified by the case of Zbigniew Romaniuk, an amateur historian who collected gravestones from a local Jewish cemetery that were being used as paving stones or for sharpening knifes and scythes in farm buildings (see Hoffman 1997: 24). Such random but sustaining encounters led to the uncanny 'discovery of a layer of the past so close to the surface and yet so perplexing', the discovery being made possible by digging up information 'that had been part of the familiar world, and yet it was thoroughly unknown' (Hoffman 1997: 25).

Cinema in a particular way encourages such expeditions that metaphorically or literally lead towards the past. German films from the early 1990s such as Michael Verhoeven's *The Nasty Girl* [*Das schreckliche Mädchen*] (1990) or Jörg Graser's *Abraham's Gold* (1990) adapted the narrative of the investigative journey in order to prove the persisting presence of the past in recently unified Germany. Dani Levy's *The Giraffe* [*Meschugge*] (1998) then transgressed the national framework in order to tell of the dead-ly return of a hidden family secret within the parameters of German-Jewish-American encounters. It thus resonated with debates about German perpetrators and demands for compensation that Germany faced in the mid-1990s.

Such transnational texture of journeys was effectively applied to cinematic commemoration of the Shoah in Liev Schreiber's *Everything Is Illuminated* (2005). The film is based on the bestselling novel of the same name by Jonathan Safran Foer, which described his own journey to Eastern Europe to find traces of his grandparents' vanished hometown. It is structured through a series of encounters with the landscape and the local population that strikingly tie past and present.

Like *Everything Is Illuminated*, many contemporary European films commemorating the Shoah engage the past from the perspective of an unsettled present. Much more than about uncovering the historic truth, these films are about the difficult challenge of coming to terms with a hidden, suppressed and vanished past and with the conflicting memories that are still rising from it. We will now turn to a close analysis of three recent examples, two from Poland and one from France, that illustrate the different ways contemporary European cinema encounters the ghosts from the past within the framework of conflicting European memories.

HIDDEN GRAVES

In 2012, controversy about Polish collaboration during the German occupation recurred again with the release of Władysław Pasikowski's film *Aftermath* [*Pokłosie*], which was loosely based on and inspired by Gross's book *Neighbors*, discussed above. 'This is one of our last historical taboos,' stated the film's producer, Dariuz Jabłonski, 'and I have a feeling that it's a topic we've been avoiding' (quoted in Anon. 2012). Accordingly, the film's story is set in a near present and told as a 'modern-day story' (Pasikowski quoted in Quart 2013: 24). After having lived and worked for twenty years as a construction worker in Chicago, Franciszek Kalina, an emigrant from Poland, returns to his rural hometown. There his brother Jozek had turned into something of a loner after he had begun collecting misused Jewish tombstones from before the war and assembled them on his family's cornfield into a 'makeshift cemetery' (Hoffman 2013), a reference to Zbigniew Romaniuk, the amateur historian who did something similar in his own hometown.

More and more, the two brothers are drawn into the secrets of the past and transform into outcasts, viewed by their neighbours with suspicion. The film frames this through an intensification of uncanny tension, most importantly experienced by Franciszek, who is presented as an ambivalent character transforming from an ordinary anti-Semite into a dedicated searcher for historical truth. In its centre, the film uncovers a collectively buried secret, the fate of the town's Jewish population, who were brutally killed by the locals who then expropriated their lands and property. 'What's central to the film is its courageous illumination of a dark moment in Polish history, and preserving the memory of Jewish suffering at the hands of Poles' (Quart 2013: 23). Therefore *Pokłosie* does not only succeed Gross's *Neighbors* but also provides an increased emotional and therefore additionally challenging re-encounter with the troubling past for the Polish audience. The audience witnesses the post-1990 events as a disturbing 're-enactment' of the anti-Jewish hatred from the past, which now turns against the two brothers. Gradually, the local population unites against the 'investigation' of Franciszek and Jozek, and as the objection against their search turns more and more aggressive and violent the two Polish bothers are increasingly labeled as 'Jews'. Thus the uncanny moments of 'repetition' turn them into the revenants of those who were once murdered by the ancestors of the villagers. We perceive this increasing conflict through the eyes of Franciszek, who also discovers his own family's involvement in the murderous events and 'finds himself reluctantly drawn into uncovering what happened there during Nazi occupation' (Anon. 2012). He plays the role of a 'detective and digs through old property records' (Holden 2013) in the local archive, while his brother continues to excavate the Jewish heritage of the town's past in the form of the heir-less tombstones. Finally, 'Franciszek and Joze[k] exhume everything from land records to bodies' (Grollmus 2013).

Thus, the past is only evoked through acts of discovery and excavation in the present. At no point does the film try to reconstruct visually the troubling and disturbing past horrors, because, as director Pasikowski emphasises, 'flashbacks can't provide the same kind of "presence"' (quoted in Quart 2013: 24); it is from this presence of the past in the present that the film's compelling approach evolves. *Pokłosie* is intended as a 'confrontation' (ibid.). The film therefore functions as a medium that triggers such a confrontational encounter and affects the audience, especially through the tensions unfolded by the conflicts of the storyline and with the help of stylistic devices and genre patterns. Through this emotional dimension, walls constructed around an unpleasant and disturbing past are gradually ruptured and therefore it may be no coincidence that *Pokłosie* evokes spatial metaphors in different contexts such as the ruins of the brothers' family's former house, in which the Jewish neighbours once were killed. Besides providing an image for the ruptured walls built around unpleasant memories, this image also evokes references to the ruin as a symbol for material remnants of the past, to the house as an enclosed space and, in regard to the horror genre, also as a haunted place.

This genre reference is intensified through additional elements from the thriller and horror film genres. *Pokłosie*'s '[u]nlocking the past is akin to opening a crypt and releasing the undead' (Holden 2013); therefore, the evoked 'mysteriousness of the dark woods surrounding the farm is well used to build tension' (Quart 2013: 23). The core scene of the film, which literally adopts the motif of digging in the past, evokes all of these horror moments and at the same time activates the imagination of the audience. The incriminatory silence of the locals is confronted by the remaining material remnants of the past. 'What can the house tell us?' Jozek asks his brother when he suggests reinvestigating the ruins of their father's old farmhouse. But, in fact, the house becomes the last remaining witness in a network of lies and secrets. When the brothers start digging, the ruins reveal the horrifying truth. Lost in rain and mud, Franciszek and Jozek exhume bones and sculls from those who were burned alive there. In an act of physical exertion paired with spiritual repentance, through the recitation of the Catholic rosary two contradictory moments – revelation of guilt and purification – are combined in this highly allegorical scene. Finally, the brothers sit exhausted next to the pile of mortal remains when, ghost-like, an old woman appears from the woods. She suggests burying the 'poor souls' in the graveyard made by Jozek. It turns out that the woman is the only one to speak about the crimes committed by the local population. Like a ghost from the past, she reveals the historic truth to the brothers and the remaining skeletons from the town's closet. Finally, Jozek himself falls victim to the persisting and repeating dark past. Following the ambivalent religious overtones of the film, his brother finds him hanging at the farm's barn door, crucified by angry neighbours.[8] The last images show a Jewish youth group visiting the new Jewish 'graveyard' and reciting *kaddish*, the Jewish prayer for the dead, mirroring the earlier excavation scene.

Pokłosie's confrontational approach towards the past and its 'unblinking representation of the brutality directed at the Kalina brothers' immediately 'provoked a storm of criticism' (Hoberman 2013). In some smaller cities, screenings of the film were even cancelled due to protests by nationalist politicians and organisations (see Grollmus 2013). On the other hand, more than 300,000 Poles saw the film after its release and around 100,000 bought the DVD (see Hoffman 2013).

Despite the final scene, in which the Jewish mourners significantly 'stand entirely apart from the film's action, unaware and untouched by what has just transpired in this little town' (Grollmus 2013), *Pokłosie* exclusively and consciously focuses on the Polish perspective and its struggle with the past. In contrast to accusations of being anti-Polish, the film aims to initiate a therapeutic process of facing the nation's past and historical truth. 'The truth is dangerous for those who are guilty, but inconvenient for everyone,' says Pasikowski, explaining his approach. 'Moreover, the post-war generations have a duty to face the truth, regardless of the consequences. Not just philosophically, because truth is beautiful, but also for practical reasons, since you can't build a positive image if you haven't confessed your sins and been forgiven' (quoted in Hoffman 2013). Thus, historical recognition and religiously connoted reconciliation are combined, similar to Europe's ongoing attempts to come to terms with the continent's past. 'The truth had to be repeated as many millions of times as there were Holocaust victims, until that terrible, basic truth got into the heads of even those most immune to knowledge, even the biggest simpletons living somewhere in the antipodes of Europe' (Pasikowski quoted in Quart 2013: 23–4). Facing conflicting memories and unearthing suppressed acts of local collaboration become vital parts in this process of historical recognition. Films like

Pokłosie, in a manner different from acts of political acknowledgment and historical debates, confront this formerly suppressed and still persisting history in a more emotional and appealing but also sometimes shockingly disturbing way.

LOCKED DOORS

Similar to *Pokłosie*, Gilles Paquet-Brenner's *Sarah's Key* [*Elle s'appelait Sarah*] (2010) adopts elements from an 'emotional detective story' (Turan 2011) and combines them with patterns from the horror genre and revelation of family secrets. Its storyline also departs from the present and refers to a controversial historical event in French history. Its main protagonist is Julia Jarmond, an American journalist living in Paris who is married to a French architect. Explicitly referring to President Chirac's speech from 1995, in which he apologised for French complicity with Nazi Germany, *Sarah's Key* depicts the tragic events of July 1942, when Parisian Jews were arrested, gathered and then deported with the help of French police and civil servants, as an unsettled part of French history. The film alternately depicts events of 1942 and 2009. On the historical level, it reenacts the mass arrests of July 1942 through the eyes of Sarah Starzynski, a Jewish girl who is brought to the extremely overcrowded Vélodrome d'Hiver with her parents. The latter are deported shortly after, while Sarah is detained in another camp from which she finally escapes. She survives the war hidden by a French family, but leaves France after the war for the US, where she abandons her Jewish origins. The historical narrative's stirring tension arises from the fact that before her deportation Sarah had locked her little brother in their apartment's closet in order to protect him.

> Thus Sarah's story grips you like a horror movie, complete with certain fictional contrivances. She tries desperately to return home to free her brother but at almost every turn is met by terror. The first scenes – of the arrest and at the velodrome – are the most indelible. You may want to hide your eyes. (Saltz 2013)

In fact, the scenes shot in the reconstructed Vélodrome (the historic site was demolished and vanished from French historical consciousness, together with the events) offer a 'powerful reconstruction of the Dante-esque interior of the Vel d'Hiv' (Flitterman-Lewis 2011: 51) and provide a 'microcosm of the roundup' (Michalczyk 2013: 152). But this microcosm is mainly supposed to trigger, illustrate and mirror the conflicts of Julia's connection to a disgraceful family secret. Thus, like *Pokłosie* and despite its re-enactments, *Sarah's Key* is not mainly about the historic events, in contrast to Roselyn Bosch's *The Roundup* [*La Rafle*] (2010), another French film from the same year.

Julia finally realises that the fate of Sarah's locked-up bother is closely linked with that of her husband's family, which had moved into the Starzynski family's apartment in 1942, after their deportation. The intertwined storylines thus evoke, on the one hand, an investigative mode, which unfolds the past events piece-by-piece and is constantly interrupted by sequences from the present. The film therefore does not provide a consistent and linear historical narrative, but shows the past as an ensemble of scars and traces that still shape the present. Furthermore, this narrative structure allows the conflict to rise slowly. On the other hand, the entangled time levels are connected through parallel structures and reappearing motifs through which both characters, Julia and Sarah, are also bound together and even mirror each other (see Michalczyk 2013: 151).

This results in a complex entanglement in which identity, memory and historical consciousness are negotiated. Julia's journalistic and historical quest, for example at the *Memorial de la Shoah*, and constant references to current French politics of memory, such as Chirac's public apology, transgress personal destiny and transcend the numerous historic and present conflicts.

The particular point of this entanglement between past and present and between Julia's and Sarah's lives is similar to the plot of *Pokłosie*, a place bearing witness. Her husband's family's apartment literally hosts the hidden room, which transforms into Sarah's brother's grave. But while in *Pokłosie* the past returns as shocking revelation and reappears in the aggressive hostility of the local population, *Sarah's Key* successively replaces Sarah's disturbing fate with Julia's own story, or as Rachel Saltz critically emphasises: 'The film looks away for you, by cutting to the present-day story and going limp, as life-and-death drama is replaced by life as we know it. Julia is pregnant and wants to keep the baby, but her husband doesn't' (2011).

Because of such simplified analogies between past and present – Julia's husband pressuring her to agree to an abortion, and his family's benefitting from the Starzynski family's fate – the double storyline tends towards a closure of differences between both time frames and the experiences connected to them. In the end, Julia's newborn daughter, also named Sarah, symbolically takes the place of the Jewish protagonist, thus harmonising two contradictory memories and conflicting family stories. Julia, the American journalist and transnational actor, therein symbolises a third place beyond victims and collaborators with which the audience can identify in order to ease the conflicting tensions that are evolving from a still persistent past.

At the end, the 'physical key which locks the hiding place where Sarah Starzynski's four-year-old brother was told to remain until the situation became safe' (Michalczyk 2013: 151) transforms into a metaphorical key that opens the closed doors of the French and European past in order finally to ban the 'ghosts of history' (Flitterman-Lewis 2011: 51). Thereby the disturbing past slowly vanishes. While the use of re-enactments, on the one hand, makes the horrors bearable, the present storyline eliminates their disturbing presence:

> The motivation of *Sarah's Key*, according to the director, is less about instruction than about making this history inclusive and accessible to people with no particular connection to the events. Yet while the high emotional impact of the film comes from Paquet-Brenner's desire to make his audience empathize with the events, irrespective of their opinions or origins, the price of universalizing the tale seems to be in de-Judaicizing its content. (Flitterman-Lewis 2011: 51)

Thereby *Sarah's Key* participates in a culture of memory that tends to universalise the past in order to make it accessible and therefore usable for the present. Such a universalising understanding of history, as shown paradigmatically in Gilles Paquet-Brenner's demand, 'should not be a burden. It should be taken as an opportunity to improve ourselves' (quoted in Michalczyk 2013: 151). But what is lost in this universalised memory is the tension evoked by the conflicting memories of the past and by the inadequate mourning for the dead who are still not laid to rest.

BURYING THE DEAD

Paweł Pawlikowski's *Ida* (2013) offers an encounter with the past of a different kind. Although set in the past and shot in a 'hard-focus black and white' (Denby 2014), the film evokes the Holocaust only in retrospect, as haunting personal memories, through the quest for origin and identity, and via ghosts that were never laid to rest from a persisting and painful past. The film is set in 1961 and tells the story of Anna, an orphan and novice in a Catholic convent. Anna learns that she has an aunt and is ordered by her Mother Superior to visit her. In Łodz she meets Wanda Gruz, a local magistrate and a Communist Party member. Wanda confronts Anna with her previously unknown family heritage. Born as Ida Lebenstein, she is in fact Jewish and was hidden in the convent to be saved from deportation. The two, quite different, women depart on a journey to the village where Wanda grew up and later left her sister and her family in order to fight the Germans; and where Ida was separated from her parents, who were hidden by a Christian family and then betrayed.

Similar to *Pokłosie*, the film touches on the conflicting memories of Polish society, but in contrast to that film, *Ida* merges the Polish perspective with a Jewish experience. While Anna/Ida is situated at a threshold between Polish-Catholic and Jewish identity, Wanda represents not only the experience of the Holocaust (and Polish resistance) but also the memories of the post-war Communist era. Because it is set in 1961, a time shaped by the agony of Stalinism, the film introduces an additional layer of conflicting memories. Thus it combines Polish memories of the Nazi occupation, resistance and collaboration with the Communist post-war years and the experience of disillusionment, as well as ambiguous and traumatic Jewish memories from the war and the post-war period such as the experience of anti-Semitic massacres in the immediate aftermath of the war in places like Kielce and others, until the new wave of state-sponsored anti-Semitism at the end of the 1960s brought Polish-Jewish history to nearly a final end. Wanda's frustration about the reality of her utopian belief and her demotion, which seems to be related to her Jewish background, anticipates these later developments.

The main narrative structure for this unfolding of conflicting memories and opposing identity positions is provided by the motif of the journey and the patterns of the investigative detective story: '*Ida* becomes both an investigation of sorts and an intermittent road movie, featuring a dialectically opposed odd couple – Catholic and Communist, innocent girl and hard-living political intellectual, lover (of Christ) and hater (of the Polish past)' (Denby 2014). In this entanglement of characters, memories, identity positions and ideologies, the film intertwines 'both an individual's fate and a Polish fate' (ibid.) and thus enables a cinematic negotiation of the complex Polish-Jewish past.

This negotiation is not only narrated through the characters and their shifting subject-positions, but additionally intensified through the visual style and genre patterns of the film. The static framing of the camera in combination with the black and white images highlight the isolation and devastation in Poland of the 1960s. But this visual style also creates a notion of unease that implicitly evokes the scars and traces of the present as well as the return of suppressed memories. The heaviness of the unsolved past 'takes the form of the spartan interiors and vast blank skies that frequently push Anna to the bottom of the frame' (Fuller 2014: 71). Within this framed cinematic space 'the two women are equal in their isolation and their need to pull together the shards of identity in a country that has been almost entirely broken' (Denby 2014). David Denby broadens this relation between the characters and Polish history even further by stating: 'Wanda, we can't help thinking, *is* Polish history, both grieved over and unredeemed' (ibid.).

Space and characters seem to merge. The travellers to the past are 'dwarfed by the godless landscape, which inevitably evokes some of the woods and fields in Claude Lanzmann's *Shoah* and Władysław Pasikowski's *Aftermath*' (Fuller 2014: 71). And Tim Robey (2014) even compares the character of Wanda to Lanzmann, 'who prowled the unyielding turf of rural Poland in *Shoah*, asking all the difficult questions, swatting off evasion with deadly insinuation'. Finally, the two women arrive at the place that keeps the secret of their family's destiny. In the woods they make a shocking discovery. Similar to *Pokłosie*, an act of excavation marks the centre of the journey to the past. In contrast to the anger and sorrow during the very same situation in *Pokłosie*, *Ida* frames the exhumation as a dark but quiet moment: 'The wind drops in a forest when Poland's secrets are literally unearthed, and the film's most haunting effect is audible for a microsecond – it's the soft, hollow and tenderly muffled rattling of bones' (ibid.).

Ida is a 'horror film without ghouls' (Denby 2014). Even the failures of the past, the betrayal of Anna/Ida's family by their Christian neighbours, are not singled out but become part of the overall dominant atmosphere of anxiety, grief and disillusion that shapes the film. The most intensive moment is filmed as a reverse-shot of the exhumation. Wanda and Anna/Ida drive to a Jewish cemetery. In early daylight they wander between the graves and then bury the bones and sculls of their relatives. Recalling the burial ceremony in Sam Fuller's 16mm film from Falkenau, *Ida* offers a moment of establishing a new order and an adequate form of mourning, a way of laying to rest the dead without burying the past: 'Acknowledgment, not revenge, is the movie's driving force' (ibid.). The following drive through an alley of trees opens a window of light at the horizon, thus symbolising the possibility of a future. But this future is inaccessible, at least for Wanda, the representative of the war generation and her disappointed trust in the new post-war Communist leadership of Poland. Her subsequent suicide – she throws herself from a window – signifies the repetitive moment of a persisting and still unsolved past.

CONCLUSION

While political acts of commemoration and acknowledgment often tend towards perpetuating rituals of remembrance in favour of political efforts, films are able to negotiate and mediate conflicting memories without necessarily limiting them to narrow narratives. They are able to align a multitude of perspectives and thus create an interplay of opposing positions. Because cinematic narratives are basically built on tension, films can openly address conflicting perceptions of the past and furthermore apply genre patterns that might favour certain approaches towards the past. The three films discussed in this essay combine elements from the horror genre with the motif of journeys and searching. They can thereby affect the viewers but also present shifting subject positions within the narrative that are affected by the past. The films illustrate attempts to release the ghosts of the past and confront the skeletons in the closets of European memory. Thereby they also demonstrate the persisting presence of the past, especially the scars and traces of wartime occupation and the Shoah within European societies, at times even contextualising them through explicit references to current debates on European politics relating to the past and the persistence of conflicting memories.

Nevertheless, all three films make differing attempts at dealing with this disturbing presence, although they all depart from the present instead of reconstructing the past. *Pokłosie* depicts the past as recurring in a present that is still fundamentally shaped by the misdeeds of history. The narrow setting, a small town in rural Poland, intensifies tensions evolving from the 'reappearance' of past ghosts. But the film consciously abstains from including a Jewish perspective. The audience is instead drawn into the conflict through the returning brother who is situated both in and outside the rural drama. Thus in *Pokłosie*, closeness (to the fate of the murdered) develops through distance (from the local community).

In contrast, *Sarah's Key* develops distance (from the Jewish experience) through closeness (an act of absolute identification). The main character, Julia, makes it possible to transgress the binary opposition of perpetrators (or collaborators) and victims. The film thereby adopts the 'third position of the witness' that was described by Daniel Levy and Natan Sznaider as 'historically an American one, but it is possible for victims and oppressors to adopt it, as well' (2006: 155). This position is closely related to an attempt at universalisation: 'The third role of the observer has enabled this group to dislodge the Holocaust from the context of the nation-state and to humanize it' (2006: 156). But a crucial effect of this de-territorialised and humanised approach is also a loss of distinction. *Sarah's Key* illustrates the result of universalising memory in a significant act of replacement that follows the stages of revelation and recognition. Finally, Julia's own child, rejected by her father, replaces the Jewish protagonist and thereby 'heals' the wounds of the persisting traumatic past.

Although remaining within a very specific territorial frame, *Pokłosie* also performs an act of replacement that finally makes recognition possible. At the end, Jozek becomes a sacrifice in an attempt to Christianise the Shoah. The film then adopts the narrative of a passion play and emphasises that Jozek's death is a precondition of redemption. Nevertheless, the final sequence, combining the Jewish mourning ceremony with Franciszek watching from the side, also indicates the persistence of different, and sometimes conflicting, perceptions of the past.

Ida merely seems to succeed in transforming the fragmented past into a new subject position. In this film as well, such transformation follows an act of replacement. At the end, Anna/Ida takes the place of her Aunt Wanda. But in this act of replacing Wanda, who personifies the persisting destructiveness of the past(s), the ambiguity of a present affected by the past does not vanish. Instead, the film creates a cinematic state of tentativeness:

> In the film's key sequence, Pawilkowski cuts from Wanda's tatty state funeral, where the assembled mucky-mucks begin to play a tape of 'The Internationale,' to a jazz club, where Coltrane's 'Equinox' is being tooted out by a sax player with a thing for Anna/Ida, who is sitting at a nearby table wearing Wanda's period-precise cocktail dress. [...] The final image of the young, liberated former nun seems to suggest a dialectically ordained synthesis of two women: Anna/Ida has, in essence, cast off the chains of both Church and State, no longer constrained by either the aesthetic demands of Catholicism or the cold autocracy of Iron Curtain Poland. (White 2014: 45)

In confronting the 'disturbance in the symbolic order' (LaCapra 2001: 215), in laying to rest the dead without finally being able to silence the ghosts from the past, the film ends with a multilayered prospect. Although it adheres to the impossibility of finally solving and burying the past, the film creates a cinematic interspace between different historical time layers, conflicting memories and cultural expressions. Thus the film emphasises a 'future-orientated' memory (Levy and Sznaider 2006: 197) that still bemoans the traumatic past and recognises the ruptured present. Thereby *Ida*, more than *Pokłosie* and *Sarah's Key*, which are still bound to a particular or mere universal perspective, creates a cinematic mode of negotiating conflicting memories that also takes into account that 'the problem of response and the difficulty of attempts to come to terms with unsettling after effects and haunting presences are not clearly circumscribed or "properly" the preserve of anyone' (LaCapra 2001: 215). Current European films such as those discussed in this essay offer a response to the unsettled past(s) in an ongoing cinematic process of coming to terms with the persisting after-effects of the Holocaust.

Notes

1. Research for this essay was kindly funded by the Smart Family Institute of Communications.
2. Fuller's footage was publicly shown for the first time in the documentary film *Falkenau, The Impossible* (1988), directed by Emil Weiss, in which Fuller introduces and comments on the material (see Ebbrecht 2011: 111).
3. In these immediate post-war years, of course, the victims of the Shoah, although hardly mentioned as Jews, were quite visibly addressed in education films about the Nazi concentration camps as well as in newspaper reports and in the context of the Nuremberg trials.
4. Obviously, during the 1980s some important political debates and incidents on the national as well as international arena had paved this path. Especially West Germany was shuttered by controversies, such as the Historian's debate. Internationally, the visit by German Chancellor Helmut Kohl and US President Ronald Reagan at a military cemetery in Bitburg that also has graves of SS officers, caused political tensions.
5. Although on the political agenda since the early 1950s (I already mentioned the West German consultations with Israel in compensation during the 1950s that lead to the Luxemburg Agreement) the new situation after German reunification brought the issue back into the international political arena. The German government as well as German business companies got under increasing attack due to several open questions on compensation and reparation. The fact that a final agreement on these questions was postponed until the unification of both German states as well as new documents – for example proving the manifold ways ordinary Germans benefitted from stolen Jewish property, the controversy on Swiss usage of financial savings by Jews murdered during the Shoah as well as the still open issue of Forced Labor (Zwangsarbeit) – caused several law suits and public campaigns as well as international commissions and conferences trying to settle these still unsettled demands.
6. The persistence of the French's avoiding of engaging the history of collaboration was significantly proved by the critical reaction in France to Marcel Ophuls' *The Sorrow and the Pity* [*Le chagrin et la pitié*] (1972) and the 'censorship through inertia' (Golsan 2006: 87) that Ophuls had to face.

7   Referring to Henry Rousso's classic study from 1987 on France during the 1940s, Richard J. Golsan emphasises that, of course, the 'history and memory of this period have produced a seemingly endless stream of political and judicial scandals and generated a long series of controversial films and books', but also states that 'it is clear that the history and memory of the period have not been – and may never be – completely integrated into the continuum of the nation's past' (2006: 73, 74).

8   This, of course, is a highly symbolical image referring not only to a universal motif of suffering and sacrifice from Christian origin but also repeating (while in the context of the film's thwarted narrative also subverting) a cultural symbol for Poland as the 'Christ among the Nations'. This symbol for Catholic Poland as victim of Nazism also appeared in Agnieszka Holland's *Europa Europa* [*Hitlerjunge Salomon*] (1990). But in the case of *Pokłosie*, it is the Poles who slaughter other Poles.

Filmography

Abraham's Gold. Dir. Jörg Graser. West Germany, 1990.
Aftermath [*Pokłosie*]. Dir. Władysław Pasikowski. Poland, 2012.
The Big Red One. Dir. Samuel Fuller. USA, 1980.
The Cremator [*Spalovač mrtvol*]. Dir. Juraj Herz. Czechoslovakia, 1969.
Destination Death [*Herrenpartie*]. Dir. Wolfgang Staudte. West Germany/Yugoslavia, 1964.
Europa Europa [*Hitlerjunge* Salomon]. Dir. Agnieszka Holland. Germany/France/Poland, 1990.
The Fair [*Kirmes*]. Dir. Wolfgang Staudte. West Germany, 1960.
The Giraffe [*Meschugge*]. Dir. Dani Levy. Germany, 1998.
Holocaust. Dir. Marvin J. Chomsky. USA, 1978.
Ida. Dir. Paweł Pawlikowski. Poland, 2013.
Murderers Among Us [*Die Mörder sind unter uns*]. Dir. Wolfgang Staudte. Germany, Soviet Occupation Zone, 1946.
Nasty Girl [*Das schreckliche Mädchen*]. Dir. Michael Verhoeven, Germany, 1990.
Night and Fog [*Nuit et brouillard*]. Dir. Alain Resnais. France, 1955.
Roses for the Prosecutor [*Rosen für den Staatsanwalt*]. Dir. Wolfgang Staudte. West Germany, 1959.
The Roundup [*La Rafle*]. Dir. Roselyn Bosch. France/Germany/Hungary, 2010.
Sarah's Key [*Elle s'appelait Sarah*]. Dir. Gilles Paquet-Brenner. France, 2010.
The Shop on Main Street [*Obchod na korze*]. Dir. Ján Káder and Elmar Klos. Czechoslovakia, 1965.
The Sorrow and the Pity [*Le chagrin et la pitié*]. Dir. Marcel Ophuls. France/Switzerland/West Germany, 1972.

Bibliography

Anon. (2012) 'Film about Massacre of Jews Touches Nerve in Poland', *Haaretz*, 13 December. Online: http://www.haaretz.com/jewish-world/jewish-world-news/film-about-massacre-of-jews-touches-nerve-in-poland-1.484737
Beck, Ulrich (2006) *The Cosmopolitan Vision*. Malden: Polity Press.

Churchill, Winston (2014) 'Speech delivered at the University of Zurich, 19 September 1946', *Council of Europe*. Online: http://www.coe.int/t/dgal/dit/ilcd/archives/selection/churchill/ZurichSpeech_en.asp

Denby, David (2015) '*Ida*: A Film Masterpiece', *The New Yorker*, 27 May. Online: http://www.newyorker.com/culture/culture-desk/ida-a-film-masterpiece

Ebbrecht, Tobias (2011) *Geschichtsbilder im medialen Gedächtnis: Filmische Narrationen des Holocaust*. Bielefeld: transcript.

Flitterman-Lewis, Sandy (2011) 'Sarah's Key – La Rafle', *Cineaste*, 36, 4, 51–4.

Fuller, Graham (2014) '*Ida*', *Film Comment*, May-June, 71.

Gildea, Robert (2002) 'Myth, Memory and Policy in France since 1945,' in Jan-Werner Müller (ed.) *Memory and Power in Post-war Europe: Studies in the Presence of the Past*. Cambridge: Cambridge University Press, 59–75.

Golsan, Richard J. (2006) 'The Legacy of World War II in France: Mapping the Discourses of Memory', in Richard Ned Lebow, Wulf Kantsteiner and Claudio Fogu (eds) *The Politics of Memory in Post-war Europe*. Durham, NC: Duke University Press, 73–101.

Grollmus, Denise (2013) 'In the Polish Aftermath', *Tablet*, 17 April. Online: http://www.tabletmag.com/jewish-arts-and-culture/129082/in-the-polish-aftermath

Gross, Jan Tomasz (2002) *Neighbors: The Destruction of the Jewish Community in Jedwabne, Poland*. New York: Penguin.

____ (2003) 'Jews and their Polish Neigbors: The Case of Jedwabne in the Summer of 1941', in Joshua D. Zimmerman (ed.) *Contested Memories: Poles and Jews During the Holocaust and Its Aftermath*. New Brunswick, NJ: Rutgers University Press, 69–82.

Hoberman, James Lewis (2013) 'The Past Can Hold a Horrible Power', *The New York Times*, 25 October. Online: http://www.nytimes.com/2013/10/27/movies/aftermath-a-thriller-directed-by-wladyslaw-pasikowski.html?pagewanted=all

Hoffman, Eva (1997) *Shtetl: The Life and Death of a Small Town and the World of Polish Jews*. Boston, MA: Houghton Mifflin.

Hoffman, Jordan (2013) 'The Film Poles Don't Want You to Watch Debuts in the US', *The Times of Israel*, 31 October. Online: http://www.nytimes.com/2013/10/27/movies/aftermath-a-thriller-directed-by-wladyslaw-pasikowski.html?pagewanted=all

Holden, Stephen (2013) 'Old Hatreds Just Won't Stay Buried', *The New York Times*, 31 October. Online: http://www.nytimes.com/2013/11/01/movies/aftermath-directed-by-wladyslaw-pasikowski.html?_r=0

Judt, Tony (2010) *Post-war: A History of Europe since 1945*. London: Vintage.

König, Helmut (2008) 'Europas Gedächtnis: Sondierungen in einem unübersichtlichen Gelände', in Helmut König, Julia Schmidt and Manfred Sicking (eds) *Europas Gedächtnis: Das neue Europa zwischen nationalen Erinnerungen und gemeinsamer Identität*. Bielefeld: transcript. 9–37.

Kwasniewski, Aleksander (2001) 'The Official Address Delivered by the President of the Republic of Poland on July 10, 2001, in Jedwabne, Poland.' Online: http://www.dialog.org/hist/kwasniewski.html

LaCapra, Dominick (2001) *Writing History, Writing Trauma*. Baltimore, MD: Johns Hopkins University Press.

Leggewie, Claus (2011) 'Seven Circles of European Memory', in Peter Meusburger, Michael Heffernan and Edgar Wunder (eds) *Cultural Memories: The Geographical Point of View*. Heidelberg: Springer, 123–43.

Levy, Daniel and Natan Sznaider (2006) *The Holocaust and Memory in the Global Age*. Philadelphia, PA: Temple University Press.

Mazurczak, Filip (2013) 'The Consequences of Being "Anti-Polish"', *New Eastern Europe*, 17 January. Online: http://www.neweasterneurope.eu/interviews/548-the-consequences-of-being-anti-polish

Michalczyk, John J. (2013) 'The Complicity of the French in *The Roundup* (*La rafle*, 2010) and *Sarah's Key* (2010)', in John J. Michalczyk and Raymond G. Helmick (eds) *Through a Lens Darkly: Films of Genocide, Ethnic Cleansing, and Atrocities*. New York: Peter Lang, 145–54.

Michnik, Adam (2001) 'Poles and the Jews: How Deep the Guilt?', *The New York Times*, 17 March. Online: http://www.nytimes.com/2001/03/17/arts/poles-and-the-jews-how-deep-the-guilt.html

Quart, Leonard (2013) 'Breaking National Taboos: An Interview with Władysław Pasikowski and Dariusz Jabołonski', *Cineaste*, 39, 1, 22–5.

Radonic, Ljiljana (2010) *Krieg um die Erinnerung: Kroatische Vergangenheitspolitik zwischen Revisionismus und europäischen Standards*. Frankfurt: Campus.

Robey, Tim (2104) '*Ida*' *The Telegraph*, 26 September. Online: http://www.telegraph.co.uk/culture/film/filmreviews/11120570/Ida-review-perfect.html

Rozett, Robert and Shmuel Spector (2000) *Encyclopedia of the Holocaust*. New York: Facts On File.

Saltz, Rachel (2011) 'The Horror of Yesterday and the Everyday of Today', *The New York Times*, 21 July. Online: http://www.nytimes.com/2011/07/22/movies/sarahs-key-directed-by-gilles-paquet-brenner-review.html

Turan, Kenneth (2011) 'Movie Review: *Sara's Key*', *The Los Angeles Times*, 22 July. Online: http://articles.latimes.com/2011/jul/22/entertainment/la-et-sarahs-key-20110722

Weizsäcker, Richard von (1985) 'Gedenkveranstaltung im Plenarsaal des Deutschen Bundestages zum 40. Jahrestag des Endes des Zweiten Weltkrieges in Europa am 8. Mai 1985 in Bonn.' Online: http://www.bundespraesident.de/SharedDocs/Reden/DE/Richard-von-Weizsaecker/Reden/1985/05/19850508_Rede.html

White, Jerry (2014) '*Ida*', *Cinemascope*, 57, 44–5.

Ziarek, Ewa Plonowska (2007) 'Melancholic Nationalism and the Pathologies of Commemorating the Holocaust in Poland', in Dorota Glowacka and Joanna Zylinska (eds) *Imaginary Neighbors: Mediating Polish-Jewish Relations after the Holocaust*. Lincoln, NE: University of Nebraska Press, 301–26.

CHAPTER EIGHT

The Ethics of Perspective and the Holocaust Archive
SPIELBERG'S LIST, THE BOY IN THE STRIPED PYJAMAS AND FATELESS

Martin Modlinger

> History reproducing itself becomes farce. Farce reproducing itself becomes history.
> – Jean Baudrillard (2002: 69)

Baudrillard's observation above of course refers to Marx, who had criticised Hegel for failing to realise the qualitative change in history's repetitions (Marx and Engels 1968: 96).[1] But Baudrillard's statement is not merely about the quality of historical events or persons and their relationship to their predecessors, as Marx's had been. In fact, he overturns Marx's inversion of Hegel (see Mazlish 1972: 336); Hegel, after all, had seen repetition as ratification of existence: 'By repetition that which at first appeared merely a matter of chance and contingency, becomes a real and ratified existence' (Hegel 2011: 286). Baudrillard now sees a similar process towards 'real and ratified existence' in the repetition of farce, that is, in the creation of history from the non-real. Of course, his observation on the relationship between history and farce is a mere detail in what he theorised as an effacement of reality in a globalised world. It is, however, quite pertinent to the question of memory and imagination discussed in the context of Holocaust cinema, as it provides an idea as to how history, memory and the farcical or the hyperreal might be thought of as entities that continually bring forth and ratify each other, indeed without clear indication of what might constitute the true origin of this process of reproduction and ratification.

This essay, however, will neither attempt to give a full overview of twenty-first-century Holocaust cinema as reproduction of itself, nor will it provide in-depth studies of some prominent examples. The much smaller aim here is rather to suggest a mode of analysing contemporary Holocaust cinema that hopefully accounts for some key developments in Holocaust memory, reproduction and representation over the last few decades. In order to do this, I will first trace some important shifts in the relationship between Holocaust history, memory and 'the public', then seek to contextualise this in the constantly growing visual archive of the Holocaust and, in a final section, provide three short examples (*Spielberg's List* [2003]; *The Boy in the Striped Pyjamas* [2007]; and *Fateless* [2005]) of what this focus on the engagement with the visual archive of the Holocaust might be able to achieve.

DEVELOPMENTS IN HOLOCAUST HISTORY AND MEMORY

Despite ongoing and important research into the history of the Holocaust and related genocides – Timothy Snyder's groundbreaking study *Bloodlands* (2010) comes to mind, for example – engagement with this part of human history is less and less at home in the disciplines of history or sociology. It has been taken over, and not just recently, by a focus on memory and memorialisation (see, for example, Assmann 2006) and questions of ethics and aesthetics brought forward by the processes of selection, interpretation and reproduction that are necessarily involved. Still, after close to forty years of memory and imagination's rivalry with history – if we consider Marvin J. Chomsky's 1978 TV series *Holocaust* and Elie Wiesel's criticising it as trivialised 'semi-fact' and 'semi-fiction' as a starting point – the debates are still very much interlinked.[2]

There is clearly something different about Holocaust cinema in the twenty-first century. The reason for this, however, might actually lie not so much in a changing relationship between Holocaust history and memory but in a changing role of memory and imagination itself. This is not to say that the historical event of the Holocaust has lost (or gained) interest in the public; it is to say that what constitutes this 'public' has changed, as well as the ways in which this public is offered and consumes images of events such as the Holocaust.

Of course there is the obvious generational shift: we now live in times where the few (child) survivors left are vastly outnumbered by the so-called second-generation, which is in turn vastly outnumbered by the one or even two following generations. In a way, however, speaking of generations already means losing sight of potentially the most important development in Holocaust memory: the adoption of Holocaust memory by individuals and groups whose relation to the event of the Holocaust is nothing more and nothing less than a construction; and that it is this very status as constructed relationship that determines Holocaust memory. This is just a slightly stronger claim than the one Marianne Hirsch makes in *The Generation of Postmemory*:

> 'Postmemory' describes the relationship that the 'generation after' bears to the personal, collective, and cultural trauma of those who came before – to experiences they 'remember' only by means of the stories, images, and behaviors among which they grew up. But these experiences were transmitted to them so deeply and affectively as to *seem* to constitute memories in their own right. Postmemory's connection to the past is thus actually mediated not by recall but by imaginative investment, projection, and creation. (2012: 5; emphasis in original)

Hirsch's idea of postmemory is necessarily still transgenerational – but it is, essentially, not a relationship based solely on family ties or even societal or cultural commonalities. She explicitly speaks of 'familial' (based on the 'literal second generation') as well as 'affiliative' transmissions of postmemory (2012: 36), the latter essentially opening 'imaginative investment' to just about anyone *wanting* to partake in postmemory. 'Imaginative investment, projection, and creation' are no longer processes limited by biological or biographical connection; on the contrary, they are the means of connecting with a history replete with the most basic human questions. They are the means of becoming part of, and shaping, a master narrative.

Similarly, as Andreas Huyssen writes, *trauma* more generally has achieved the status of a 'master signifier', having become 'an ideal paradigm in which personal, national, cultural, and possibly also global memory could be negotiated and its elements written and erased with and against each other' (2003b: 16). And the Holocaust – being the starting point of a vastly grown interest in trauma – has taken exactly the same path. The well-researched and wide-ranging studies undertaken on the matter in recent years, among them Aleida Assmann and Sebastian Conrad's edited anthology, *Memory in a Global Age* (2010), Astrid Erll's article 'Travelling Memory' (2011), Michael Rothberg's monograph, *Multidirectional Memory* (2009), or Kendall R. Phillips and G. Mitchell Reyes' collection, *Global Memoryscapes* (2011), can be summarised in a rather simple, but immensely important point: the Holocaust, decades after it had been called 'un-speakable', and wrongly so, is now a means of mass communication.[3] The images and narratives wrested from the Holocaust have developed from the early, mostly Yiddish texts and plays – which scholarship has neglected or not taken seriously for more than half a century now – and the later, mostly US-American novels and films – which until today surpass in influence those from other cultural spheres – into transnationally shared icons and memes. Spreading with the speed of broadband internet, they are now part of a possibly global cultural memory.

The 'central truth of our time,' as Terrence Des Pres has called it, is that 'at some unconscious level, the image of the Holocaust is *with us* – a memory which haunts, a sounding board for all subsequent evil – in the back of the mind ... for all of us now living: we, the inheritors' (1994: viii; emphasis in original). This central truth now lies just as much in the inescapable presence of the image as it does in the 'we': 'all of us now living'. Michael Rothberg's useful figuration of memory as being 'multidirectional' and no longer strictly 'competitive' proposes exactly this:

> Far from blocking other historical memories from view in a competitive struggle for recognition, the emergence of Holocaust memory on a global scale has contributed to the articulation of other histories – some of them predating the Nazi genocide, such as slavery, and others taking place later, such as the Algerian War of Independence (1954–62) or the genocide in Bosnia during the 1990s. (2009: 6)

What remains to be seen, however, is the extent to which a globalisation of Holocaust memory – that is, both its international integration and its local adaptation, as much as it may have helped articulate other histories – has gone hand in hand with a loss of specificity or a trivialisation of historic circumstances, actions and behaviours. This is not an argument about the perceived or actual uniqueness of the Holocaust; certainly, the globalisation of Holocaust memory has led to a growing number of comparative approaches simply because the number of potent discourses about atrocities such as the American-Indian genocide or the Rwandan genocide has increased – and the studies mentioned above are prime examples for this – but this does not necessarily lead to Holocaust relativisation or denial.

The problem of trivialisation of Holocaust memory, although intensified by the presence of similar traumatic memories, is predominantly an internal one. According to Natan Sznaider, the Holocaust discourse was already dominated by (mainly) European paradigms of interpreting the Holocaust in which 'the concept of Nazis as perpetrators is abandoned in favour of metaphors, according to which those truly guilty are not palpable human beings, but rather "modernity", "bureaucracy" or even "humanity"' (2008: 81; my translation). Whether the replacement of the perpetrator with metaphors or grand narratives obscures or indeed enlightens our understanding of (Holocaust) history is not easily determined. The emphasis on the metaphorical and universally human, however, has contributed to the Holocaust's communicability, that is, both to its gradual move away from the 'unsayable' and to its status as universal language of trauma and loss.

Indeed, the very idea of such a development amounting to trivialisation is debatable. One would be safe to argue that there remains a 'core' of Holocaust memory clearly dedicated to historical facts, witness accounts and the explanations and contextualisations put forward by the historical, sociological and philosophical professions. Around this core, however, partly nurtured by it and partly independent from it, a rhizomatic structure has grown, and this Deleuzian interconnected entity is what truly enables the multidirectionality of Holocaust memory.[4] This is also what connects processes of identity-construction through Holocaust memory to the Deleuzian ideas of difference and multiple belonging. As Rothberg writes,

> pursuing memory's multidirectionality encourages us to think of the public sphere as a malleable discursive space in which groups do not simply articulate established positions but actually come into being through their dialogical interactions with others; both the subjects and spaces of the public are open to continual reconstruction. (2009: 5)

Such a 'cosmopolitisation of memory', to use Daniel Levy and Natan Sznaider's term (2006: 12), especially of Holocaust and trauma memory, is not least determined by similar experiences of flight and expulsion around the world, as Huyssen has argued: 'In an era of ethnic cleansings and refugee crises, mass migrations and global mobility for ever more people, the experience of displacement and relocation, migration and exile seems no longer the exception but the rule' (2003b: 24). Jeffrey C. Alexander (2004) similarly notes that collective traumata no longer adhere to geographic or cultural boundaries, and that the Holocaust, due to its emblematic status, no longer primarily points to specific events in specific locations at specific points in time but has become a symbol for suffering itself. And Geoffrey Hartman, in his monograph *Scars of the Spirit* (2002), discovers parallel developments within Holocaust literature and Holocaust theatre: here as well, historic specificity recedes while more generalised figurations of suffering take centre stage. According to Hartman, the Holocaust takes on the role of a 'framing legend [which] is so well known that it does not have to be emphasized' (2002: 81). Maybe it is therefore better to speak of an expansion and reconstruction of Holocaust memory, or of its 'globalization paradox', as Huyssen has called it, than of mere trivialisation. In this sense, the Holocaust 'has become a cipher for the twentieth century as a whole and for the failure of the project of enlightenment' (Huyssen 2003a: 13, 14), while simultaneously bringing forth a tendency of particularisation and localisation.

At any rate, the continual construction and reconstruction of both the 'public' in general and its memory in particular still need building blocks, or communally shared and interchanged fragments of history and memory; in other words, an archive to draw from.[5] If any ethical judgement is deemed necessary, it might best be placed in the examination of the engagement with the archive, that is, with the practices of anamnesis in visual representation.

THE VISUAL ARCHIVE OF THE HOLOCAUST

The visual archive of the Holocaust consists of innumerable photographs, films and film fragments of varying length, pieces of visual art and visual historical documents such as maps and drawings. This archive is constantly growing, and especially in the twenty-first century it is becoming ever more accessible globally through the world-wide web. However, not all constituent elements of this archive enjoy a similar rise in number or popularity. While, for example, Yale's Fortunoff Video Archives or indeed Steven Spielberg's Shoah Foundation have collected tens of thousands of eyewitness accounts, the number of images to have come to any prominence from there or other archives is negligible. Yael Hersonski's *A Film Unfinished* (2010), dealing with the making of a 1942 German propaganda film about the Warsaw Ghetto, and Andre Singer's *Night Will Fall* (2014), taking up Sidney Bernstein's and Alfred Hitchcock's 1945 documentary on Nazi concentration camps, are perhaps the only exceptions of note in recent years. While Marianne Hirsch thus rightfully speaks of an 'archival turn' in postmemory, referring to the growing number of archival projects and postmemorial practices in the world-wide web (2012: 227–49), this archival turn is clearly accompanied by a fictional turn as well, a movement towards images and narratives no longer strictly (or even remotely) connected to historical events.

In essence, the amount of 'real' images, bar the few still newly found or rediscovered historical images, especially of 'real' images that have become iconic, is mostly fixed, while fiction offers ever-new imaginations of the past. Just as our memory of Greek and Roman times is now at least just as much defined by contemporary TV shows and blockbuster movies as it is by the writings of, for example, Herodotus and Cicero, so is Holocaust memory unavoidably moving further and further towards fiction. Meryl Streep's Academy Award-winning role as Sophie in *Sophie's Choice* (1982), Willem Dafoe's boxing champion Salamo Arouch in *Triumph of the Spirit* (1989) (and its images of Auschwitz-Birkenau, partly shot at the historical site), the girl in red in *Schindler's List* (1993) or Adrian Brody's emaciated hands in *The Pianist* (2002) have all become iconic parts of Holocaust memory. Thus, the collective memory of the Holocaust refers to an increasingly fictional archive, an archive not least determined by a market for powerful, disturbing, evocative images. 'Truth', however one may want to define it, is only one of many forces in this discourse, and certainly no longer the strongest.

Within this archive, one development is especially noteworthy: the dominant image to represent the Holocaust is now clearly that of the concentration camp (see Köppen 1997: 146; Ebbrecht 2011: 202–3), specifically that of the extermination camp. It dominates over images of, for example, labour camps or death marches. There may be good reasons for this: after all, this is where millions of victims were murdered. However, the visual attention to camps and crematoria goes hand in hand with, maybe even causes, a lack of attention to other stages and forms of the implementation of this genocide, among them: the persecution of the Jewish population in Southern Europe and North Africa; the Nazi-led or spontaneous pogroms, for example in Romania (for example, the Iași pogrom of 27 June 1941); the mass killings carried out by the *Einsatzgruppen* in the East, such as the Babi Yar massacre of September 1941; and also 'smaller', yet daily and partly public executions. 'The Holocaust' consisted of all these crimes and more. Concentrating on 'the camp' unfortunately excludes much of this from view.

Furthermore, where depictions of mass shootings such as the Babi Yar massacre by necessity also offer images of the perpetrators, holding or firing their guns, images of the concentration camp seldom present single perpetrators. These instead offer images of the system and the mechanics of the Holocaust (railway lines, electrified fences, barracks, crematoria) and thus rather place questions of responsibility and guilt with 'the system' of Nazism, not the individual (see Ebbrecht 2011: 202–3). The camp, as 'super-signifier' of the Holocaust, is of course also representative of the industrial scale of the genocide, but it nevertheless rather supports a reading of the Holocaust as a bureaucratic event, devoid of individual choices on part of the perpetrators, and maybe even a result of human nature more generally.[6]

This has direct consequences for approaches to the question of evil. Mainly examining Holocaust literature, but also referring to Holocaust film, Robert Eaglestone has noted how contemporary 'perpetrator fiction, constantly and seemingly unconsciously, appears to avoid precisely an engagement with the "why" behind the fundamental question of evil' (2012: 15). Citing Gillian Rose's thought experiment of a film that leads the audience to empathise with an SS officer even up to the point of murder (1996: 50), he outlines how unthinkable such an undertaking would have seemed just a decade ago, and how exactly this idea, minutely described and illustrated, has manifested itself in controversial yet also successful novels such as Jonathan Littell's *The Kindly Ones* (2006) or Steve Sem-Sandberg's *The Emperor of Lies* (2011). More as a side-note, Eaglestone also lists the 'basically not very good' example of the last scene in Mark Herman's film *The Boy in the Striped Pyjamas*, where 'a terrible and possibly unjust sympathy is evoked for the commandant of a death camp ... crying out in realization that his son has been murdered by his own genocidal machinery' (2012: 14).[7] My aim here, however, is not to offer ethical judgement, as Eaglestone does. Jumping to questions of decency and adequacy right away misses the very important aspects of why and how such controversial depictions come into being, and how they relate not only to the history of the Holocaust but also to its history of representation. I should therefore rather like to take a step back and examine how films like *The Boy in the Striped Pyjamas* engage with the visual archive of the Holocaust.

ANSWERING THE CALL OF THE ARCHIVE: HOLOCAUST SIMULACRA

Within this archive and increasingly beyond it, as we have seen, the images offered to us by *Schindler's List*, for example, have become iconic; they determine to a large degree our visual repertoire of the Holocaust in general and of the camp in particular. Even though these images may be regarded as 'fabrications', as Claude Lanzmann does in his critique of the film (1995: 175–6), they are of course not entirely fictitious. Spielberg went to great lengths to replicate historical photographs in his film, including, but not limited to, details from the Płaszów camp or pictures of Amon Göth, and, most prominently, Margret Bourke-White's famous photographs from Buchenwald – which, to name another example of canonisation in Holocaust memory, also feature in Art Spiegelman's *Maus*, and whose relationship to *Maus* and memory is also part of Marianne Hirsch's discussion of postmemory (2001, 2012).

Spielberg is by no means alone in such undertakings, leading to an unintentional, yet powerful shift in Holocaust iconography: in aiming to reproduce faithfully the historical images of the Holocaust, these very images are being replaced by their fictitious twins. While the 'original' images (which, of course, also offer no direct access to history) are only swept aside, not eliminated in Holocaust memory, a case could still very well be made for the presence of a simulacrum. At the very least, Baudrillard would have found ample material for such a claim in Israeli artist Omer Fast's *Spielberg's List*.

Fast's film, a brilliant example of the hyperreal, is a one-hour-long art project on the role of images and witnesses in constructions of narrative, memory and reality. Fast interviewed Polish residents who had worked as extras – both as Nazis and victims – in Spielberg's film (hence the title), and juxtaposes the interviews with scenes from *Schindler's List* and images of today's Krakow taken along a tour presenting anecdotes about the filming to tourists. Some of the extras interviewed are also Holocaust survivors, and this becomes the main issue in Fast's montage of the different levels of memory, representation and imagination.

For the most part, it remains largely (and deliberately) unclear whether the interviewees are talking about other people's or even their own historical experience in Nazi-occupied Poland, or their role on the set of Spielberg's film (for example, 'They were looking for Semitic types' [05:58]). Fast also regularly employs two versions of subtitles for the two parallel channels of his installation as a means of challenging the viewer's notion of testimony and what is 'truly' being said. Minute differences between the two screens of this installation sometimes offer hints as to whether the interviewees recount their experience as extras or historical fact, but often enough the original Polish voice track remains ambiguous as well ('Well, I don't have a good memory' vs. 'Well, I don't have good memories' [18:30]). Boundaries are blurred even further when an older man

Fig. 1 *Spielberg's List*: Amon Goeth's house, part of a Schindler's List history tour

reports how tourists today prefer visiting Spielberg's set instead of the remains of the real Płaszów camp (they 'see Krakow through the eyes of Mr. Spielberg' [47:40]). Spielberg's replica of the camp, built in a quarry near Krakow, is indeed still in good condition, complete with inner and outer fences, barbed wire and a tombstone road (the real camp was built on the site of a Jewish cemetery), and thus, according to the interviewee, affords visitors a more realistic experience. To complicate matters further, the Liban & Ehrenpreis quarry had indeed served as a labour camp, but for roughly eight hundred non-Jewish Poles, as a 'Straflager des Baudienstes im Generalgouvernement' between 1942 and 1944. Here, too, many prisoners died, and a small memorial commemorates the dead. The copy is preferred over the real version – just as Spielberg's film, at least for many, has become a 'better' point of access to the history of the Holocaust than the innumerable books and documentaries offered by historians.

CHANGING PERSPECTIVES: THE ROLE OF THE CHILD

Such processes of visual exchange and interchange between history and memory can also be found quite prominently in representations of a specific group within Holocaust victims and survivors: children. Children play a very significant role in the formation and proliferation of Holocaust memory. For example, the photograph of 'the girl with the headdress', nine-year-old Sintisa Settela Steinbach from the Westerbork Camp – until 1994 erroneously identified as a Dutch Jewess – has become, as Thomas Elsaesser notes, 'like Anne Frank, a symbol of the Holocaust most generally' (2009: 83; my translation), being used also in Alain Resnais' *Night and Fog* [*Nuit et brouillard*] or Konrad Wolf's *Stars* [*Sterne*] (1959).[8] Writing on the overall role of children in the representation of the Holocaust, Mark Anderson also notes how 'from the famous picture of the boy with upraised arms in the Warsaw ghetto to the artwork and poetry of young prisoners in Theresienstadt – children have consistently proved to be the most moving and believable witnesses' (2007: 2). While Anderson's example of the picture of the boy with upraised arms might be better categorised as 'symbol' rather than 'witness', his general point holds true: children are perceived as being uniquely qualified to offer factual as well as emotional testimony.

This most likely also led to the prominence of children or children's perspectives in fictional representations of the Holocaust, ranging from the various takes on Anne Frank's life to the girl in red in *Schindler's List* – apart from the opening scene and the epilogue the only touch of colour in Spielberg's otherwise black-and-white emulation of historical images – and from the autofictional boy in Elie Wiesel's *Night* to Bruno and Shmuel in Herman's *The Boy in the Striped Pyjamas*.[9] For Anderson 'virtually all breakthrough moments in non-Jewish American awareness of the Holocaust ... have highlighted the role of children, whose defenselessness serves as a metaphor for the general plight of Holocaust victims' (ibid.). This is certainly also true in regard to the global awareness of the Holocaust.

It is, however, not only the presumed defenselessness that accounts for the prominence of children and children's perspectives in Holocaust history and memory. According to Andrea Reiter, 'it is the gaze of the child that allows us to see in a new way that which we think we already know. [...] Unlike the authoritarian gaze of the parent, the child's gaze is naïve but accurate' (2000: 84). It may be innocent, but it is not deliberately ignorant, as adult perspectives can be. Furthermore, the child's naïve gaze emulates the distance between most of 'the public' and the experience of those who lived through or perished in the Holocaust. Charting the Brechtian strategies of *Verfremdung* common to many constructions of the child's perspective in contemporary Holocaust fiction, Debbie Pinfold notes: 'The child may be born into a specific social and cultural context, but it takes some time before the values of that society become its own; ... its perspective, however provisionally, is that of an outsider' (2001: 4). If one were to construe the ideal witness, part of yet not fully determined by the social and cultural context at the time, immensely curious yet not in a position to influence matters, reporting also what is not or not yet fully understood about the times, actions and behaviours around them – the figure of the child would come very close indeed.

EMOTIONAL TRUTH: *THE BOY IN THE STRIPED PYJAMAS*

It is this outside perspective of the ideal child witness that is at the very heart of Mark Herman's *The Boy in the Striped Pyjamas*. Plotwise, the film, based on John Boyne's novel of the same title (2006), has little to offer in terms of historical accuracy or even probability. Bruno is the eight-year-old child of a concentration camp commandant, yet completely oblivious even of the concept of Jewishness or what fate might await the people 'in striped pyjamas'. He is forced to leave Berlin and live with his family in a house right next to the camp. One day, walking along the fence, he meets Shmuel, a boy sharing his exact birthday, who happens to 'live' on the other side of the fence. After many days of talking and playing games together (always sitting on either side of the fence), Bruno decides to help Shmuel find his father. After putting on 'striped pyjamas' and crawling under the fence into the camp, Bruno and Shmuel together with others are quickly picked up by the guards and marched to the gas chamber. Bruno's sister and parents, realising where Bruno must have gone, fail to find him in time.

From Bruno's ignorance to his and Shmuel's undisturbed hours at the concentration camp fence – and it is this image of the two children divided by the fence that was used for all advertisement material for this Miramax/Walt Disney production – not much, if anything at all, would stand up to historical scrutiny. One must concede, however, that Herman is very aware of this. The film's goal is not to reproduce historical truth; indeed, it problematises the very idea of finding truth even in documentary films when, in a very prominent scene, a recently completed propaganda film (actually consisting of scenes based on the infamous Theresienstadt propaganda film known as 'Der Führer schenkt den Juden eine Stadt') is screened in the commandant's office. *The Boy in the Striped Pyjamas*, just like the book on which it is based and to which it is very faithful, seeks to offer, in Boyne's words, an 'emotional truth'. To convey this emotional truth, the film uses elements of Holocaust memory and its visual archive, without being, in a strict sense, a movie about the genocide. It is, like the book, a Holocaust fable offering a simple moral lesson: divisions between humans are arbitrary and lead only to inhumanity.

Drawing from the visual archive, the film redeploys the most prominent images of the Holocaust: the fence, the (guard and prisoner) uniform, whose function Bruno does not quite understand, the gas chamber and smoke rising from the chimney. Of course this has been called a disrespectful appropriation of suffering by many critics, especially

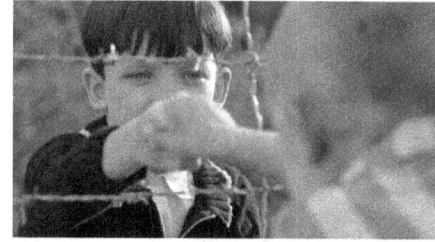

Figs 2, 3, 4, 5 *The Boy in the Striped Pyjamas*: the propaganda film (top left) and Bruno and Shmuel at the fence

by those at home in Holocaust Studies proper; one reviewer called it a 'Hollywood version of the Holocaust' and 'literally a Disneyfication (you wonder whether The Gas Chamber ride is being installed outside Paris)' (Grant 2008: n.p.). However, it has also been welcomed by teachers all around the world as a simple yet powerful introduction to the questions raised by the Holocaust. The novel and film's place in many school and university curricula also speak for their usability as pedagogic material.[10]

In this regard as well, *The Boy in the Striped Pyjamas* is just one example of a broader trend. As Anderson notes, 'in school curricula, documentary films, memorials, and museum exhibitions, "objective" history often gives way to gripping, visually enhanced "stories", while a careful contextualization of German antisemitism and European Jews is replaced by an ethics lesson on religious tolerance and respect for "otherness"' (2007: 12). And yet even this is not entirely new in (visual) Holocaust discourse. Already, more than a quarter of a century ago, Elie Wiesel lamented that 'an authentic documentary like "The Final Solution," by the four-time Oscar winner Arthur Cohn' could not find a distributor, while 'cheap and simplistic melodramas' were very much in demand; audiences 'get a little history, a heavy dose of sentimentality and suspense, a little eroticism, a few daring sex scenes, a dash of theological rumination about the silence of God and there it is: let kitsch rule in the land of kitsch, where at the expense of truth, what counts is ratings and facile success' (1989: n.p.).

However, reducing films like *The Boy in the Striped Pyjamas* to nothing more than kitsch, geared at a mass market for the only reason of financial profit, would mean losing sight of what and how these movies perform in terms of Holocaust remembrance and (re-)imagination. To reduce everything but the most faithful documentary to 'kitsch' is also to miss the immense importance of Holocaust (or rather Nazi) narratives and aesthetics for popular and counter-culture. 'Nazi-Chic' and 'Nazi-Trash', as Marcus Stiglegger (2011) notes, especially the Sadiconazista movies from the 1960s onwards, have to a great extent shaped the stereotypisation of NS- and Holocaust imagery, and thus influenced even films like *Schindler's List*.

At any rate, Boyne's book and Herman's film have embraced (and are carried by) the recent developments in Holocaust memory detailed above: a shift towards fiction and globally translatable and consumable narratives and images, the redefinition of trauma as a means of communication between cultures and times, and the figure of the child as outside perspective on seemingly all too familiar events. *The Boy in the Striped Pyjamas* does not attempt to 'understand' the Holocaust historically, sociologically or philosophically;[11] it seeks, through Bruno's naivety, to represent visually the madness of the fence, and it is uncompromising in this goal. As critic Stephen Applebaum has noted: 'Survivors' stories, or the stories of so-called righteous gentiles such as Oskar Schindler, may be uplifting and life-affirming, but they do not reflect the truth of the Holocaust: that most people perished. [The] novella did not duck this truth, and neither does Herman's adaptation' (2008: n.p.). And Herman, very well aware of how other movies have made their way into the canon of Holocaust film and thus formed part of the visual archive of the Holocaust, states quite boldly: 'In a way, the ending is sort of payback to the ending of *Life is Beautiful*' (quoted in ibid.).

This does not mean that this film has to be regarded as a 'good' or 'bad' movie, as Eaglestone sought to categorise it, or as a successful or failed attempt at bringing images of the Holocaust into the twenty-first century. It does mean, however, that it is through films like this and their engagement with the visual archive of the Holocaust that we might be best able to trace the development of Holocaust memory in times of globalisation and cosmopolitisation.

SUBVERTING THE ARCHIVE: *FATELESS*

One last, and quite different example may help elucidate this further: Lajos Koltai's *Fateless* [*Sorstalanság*], adapted from the novel of the same title by Imre Kertész. Again very faithful to the book – Kertész himself wrote the screenplay – it follows child protagonist György Köves, a fourteen-year-old boy with no understanding of what it means to be Jewish, from his father's last days in Budapest before he is sent to a labour camp to his own experience of life in the Auschwitz, Buchenwald and Zeitz camps. Through all this and up to the liberation of the camp, György remains eerily calm and composed; he takes the events unfolding around him, including all inhumane and barbaric treatment, to be 'quite natural', not requiring any explanation, only description. To understand this rather unusual position, we need to examine how *Fateless* engages with the archive of the Holocaust, specifically with movies (and other narratives) that have had great impact on Holocaust memory. Kertész for example clearly took issue with *Schindler's List*. For Kertész, Spielberg's film was kitsch:

> I know that many will not agree with me when I apply the term 'kitsch' to Spielberg's *Schindler's List*. It is said that Spielberg has in fact done a great service, considering that his film lured millions into movie theaters, including many who otherwise would never have been interested in the subject of the Holocaust. That might be true. But why should I, as a Holocaust survivor and as one in possession of a broader experience of terror, be pleased when more and more people see these experiences reproduced on the big screen – and falsified at that? (2001: 269)

For Kertész, a falsification, and therefore kitsch, is anything and everything that does not account for the ethical implications of Auschwitz, namely that nothing, especially not a human being and the very idea of humanity, can emerge untouched by Auschwitz. Furthermore, he insists that Auschwitz and the Holocaust are not something alien to

Fig. 6 *Fateless*: György and Bandi Citrom running and dancing

human beings and their experience, but organically linked to our way of life, and part of what is euphemistically called 'civilisation'. For the same reason, Kertész, in the very same article, lauds Roberto Benigni's *La vita è bella* [*Life Is Beautiful*] (1997), because it unmasks civilisation, humanity and everything else that seems to be of value, as a mere game, played by Guido and his son Joshua as well as by everyone else in order to survive.

Koltai's *Fateless* constantly frustrates the viewers' demand for György to react to the situation into which he is forced, a 'situation, which he has to experience and live as if it were a completely logical series of events, despite the fact that nothing is logical' (Kertész 2004). But this absurd situation 'has to be interpreted as being logical ... because this is the only way [people in a totalitarian regime] can survive' (ibid.). In his book, as Kertész goes on to explain, 'language had to reflect this absurdity' (ibid.); in Koltai's film, the images are burdened with the same task. This is not easily achieved, especially because the images as part of the visual archive of the Holocaust come charged with the meanings attributed to them over decades. It is rather difficult to depict a concentration camp as a place that can offer moments of happiness when the iconic images suggest the very opposite; and yet this is exactly what Kertész and Koltai attempt to do, to point to moments of normality, even joy, in *l'univers concentrationnaire*. Of course there is no reason to accuse either of any form of denial; on the contrary – pointing to moments of joy (such as a short break from forced labour or a group of prisoners singing for the others) highlights even stronger the everyday normality of suffering and ever-present death. Very early on in his journey through the camps, György comes to understand this: 'I was beginning to grasp the simple secret of my universe. I could be killed anywhere, any time' (36:30).

In most scenes where the film thus attempts to depict the absurd, almost farcical, co-presence of inhumane logic, death and joy, the images themselves take on the quality of the absurd, being, as they are, projected against their long history of exemplifying nothing but suffering. A striking example of this is György's and his friend Bandi Citrom's running and dancing along the camp's fence at sunset during a short break: 'That certain hour between returning from the factory and the night-time call. A particular hour, bustling and liberated, which I waited for and loved the most in the camp' (1:06:00). This scene, replete with the iconic images of the Holocaust (prisoner uniforms, emaciated bodies, barracks and mud everywhere on the ground), is set in an almost peaceful light, mirroring perfectly the disturbing calm György displays in his acceptance of his present situation; but it also concludes with the reason why this particular hour could indeed be one to be loved: 'Incidentally, it was also supper time.'

Again, it is the child's perspective that enables this shift in meaning. 'In their unprejudiced and uninformed attitude,' as Andrea Reiter writes about such focalisations, 'children not only notice details which escape the adult but interpret them in a way which makes them seem even more horrific' (2000: 85). The figure of another prisoner, a well-situated engineer, well-versed in matters of how things used to be 'among civilised people', is a suitable example of this difference in perspective. In contrast to György, he is utterly

Fig. 7 *Fateless*: The crematorium's smoking chimney, upside down

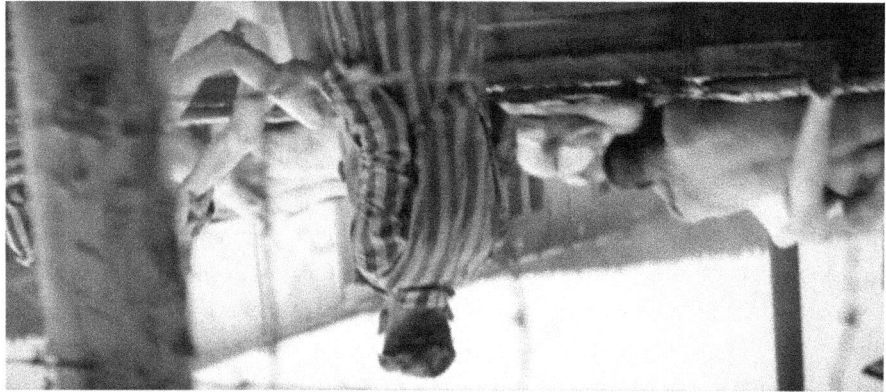

Fig. 8 *Fateless*: Prisoners loading bodies onto a cart, seen from György's perspective

unable to grasp and adapt to life in the camp; he cannot accept the absurd and illogical as the new state of things, and, holding on to his idea of humanity during a selection on arrival in the camp, he perishes.

Lastly, there is one more prominent example of how György's perspective quite literally overturns Holocaust iconography. When György is being carried to the *Krankenbarracke* (1:40:00), the camera replicates his point of view, showing the camp and all its iconic images turned upside-down: the crematorium's chimney, the barbed wire fence, a number of barracks, piles of dead bodies on the ground or on carts. As Tobias Ebbrecht has already noted, this way the film 'subverts the familiar images and creates an awareness of them in a process of alienating repetition' (2011: 228-9). For Kertész and Koltai, history has to be unmasked as farce, and the 'alienating repetition' of familiar images, coming back to Hegel and Baudrillard, is how this is to be achieved in a process of ratification.

CONCLUSION

This, then, may be the main difference between *The Boy in the Striped Pyjamas* and *Fateless*: while the former draws on the visual archive of the Holocaust in order to establish a transnational and transgenerational narrative of trauma under an 'emotional truth', the latter seeks to question and subvert iconic representations of the Holocaust in an ethical project of re-defining the meaning of Auschwitz for the history of civilisation. Yet both, for better or worse, cannot escape the archive of the Holocaust and the meanings it has produced, ascribed to and retaken from its images. Together with Omer Fast's *Spielberg's List* and countless other films, they are bound by and to the intertextual framework of the cultural archive, both part of the construction and the unmasking of the visual Holocaust archive as hyperreal Holocaust memory.

'Imaginative investment, projection, and creation' (Hirsch 2012: 5), the means of participating in a postmemory of rhizomatic structure and global proportions, indeed cannot be seen as agents of mere trivialisation or even Holocaust denial. The international integration and local adaptation of Holocaust memory, together with a fictional turn in the composition of the visual Holocaust archive, have brought forward new ways, even necessities, of engaging with the archival image, history and memory of the Holocaust. Holocaust cinema in the twenty-first century not only deals with, and at times subverts, the inescapable presence of the archive; it has also, through its prominence, iconic imagery and language of trauma, developed into a global means of communication about other atrocities. Both developments are cases of repetition in a sense – a repetition of imagery and a repetition of history – but neither can be accused of reducing truth or history to farce in Marx's sense; and judging them only in terms of adequacy or decency would be to miss the importance of their engagement with the history of Holocaust representation. Most importantly, much of twenty-first-century Holocaust cinema is well aware of the creation of history from the non-real (Baudrillard) through decades of Holocaust representation and especially the replacement of historical images with their fictitious twins. Pointing us to the possible origins and complications of these ratifications of history through repetition of images, as for example *Spielberg's List* and *Fateless* do, is no small achievement indeed.

Notes

1. Marx may actually have taken the idea from Engels; see Mazlish (1972).
2. 'The story is gripping, the acting competent, the message compelling [...] [T]his TV series will show what some survivors have been trying to say for years and years. And yet something is wrong with it. Something? No: everything' (Wiesel 1978: n.p.).
3. David Cesarani (2012) highlights how especially Yiddish and Polish literature, theatre and historiography took up the Holocaust immediately after 1945. These works did not find their way into influential archives, however, or were neglected for other reasons. Hasia R. Diner similarly stresses the numerous forms through which the Holocaust was written about even early in the 1960s (2009: 365).
4. Roughly the same idea is behind Andrew Hoskins' (2009) paradigm of a 'Network Memory', in which and through which a highly medialised and mediatised memory actualises itself.
5. There is a case to be made for the nature of these building blocks as mere memes in a double sense, that is, as fragments of memory, and as transmissible cultural unit in the sense of Dawkins (1989) and Blackmore (1999).
6. Raul Hilberg, in his *The Destruction of the European Jews*, was probably the first to put forward the vision of the Holocaust as gigantic 'machine' or administrative process (1985: 55), an idea popularised further through Hannah Arendt's description of 'the banality of evil' (1963).
7. This, by the way, was exactly what director Mark Herman intended: 'I love the fact that people are confused about their emotions [about the adult Nazi characters] and their feelings towards them' (cited in Applebaum 2008).
8. To be exact, Rudolf Breslauer's photograph is now a symbol of the Porajmos, thus part of the ongoing effort to draw the Romani genocide from out of the shadow of the Holocaust.
9. Black and white images and films (with very few notable exceptions) determine the cultural memory of World War II and the Holocaust, and thus their perceived authenticity (reality, after all, was in colour) determines our idea of how this period in time 'really looked like'. Spielberg chose black-and-white over colour for this very reason (see Davis and Womack 2001: 154).
10. The German Bundespresseamt even sent 15,000 copies of the film to German schools, as part of the 'Israel-Jahr', 2008.
11. In his afterword, Boyne writes that 'only the victims and survivors can truly comprehend the awfulness of that time and place; the rest of us live on the other side of the fence, staring through from our own comfortable place, trying in our own clumsy ways to make sense of it all' (2006: n.p.).

Filmography

The Boy in the Striped Pyjamas. Dir. Mark Herman. UK/USA, 2008.
A Film Unfinished. Dir. Yael Hersonski. Germany/Israel, 2010.
Fateless. Dir. Lajos Koltai. Hungary/Germany/UK/Israel, 2005.
Night Will Fall. Dir. Andre Singer. UK, 2014.
Nuit et brouillard [*Night and Fog*]. Dir. Alain Resnais. France, 1955.
Shoah. Dir. Claude Lanzmann. France, 1985.
Spielberg's List. Dir. Omer Fast. Israel, 2003. Two-channel video installation.
Sterne [*Stars*]. Dir. Konrad Wolf. East Germany/Bulgaria, 1959.
La vita è bella [*Life Is Beautiful*]. Dir. Roberto Benigni. Italy, 1997.

Bibliography

Alexander, Jeffrey C. (2004) 'Toward a Cultural Theory of Trauma', in Jeffrey C. Alexander, Ron Eyerman, Bernhard Giesen, Neil J. Smelser and Piotr Sztompka (eds) *Cultural Trauma and Collective Identity*. Berkeley, CA: University of California Press, 1–30.

Anderson, Mark M. (2007) 'The Child Victim as Witness to the Holocaust: An American Story?', *Jewish Social Studies: History, Culture, Society*, 14, 1, 1–22.

Applebaum, Stephen (2008) 'Disney's *The Boy in the Striped Pyjamas* – The Stuff of Nightmares', *The Scotsman*, 10 September.

Arendt, Hannah (1963) *Eichmann in Jerusalem: A Report on the Banality of Evil*. New York: Viking Press.

Assmann, Aleida (2006) 'History, Memory and the Genre of Testimony', *Poetics Today*, 27, 2, 261–73.

Assmann, Aleida and Sebastian Conrad (eds) (2010) *Memory in a Global Age: Discourses, Practices and Trajectories*. New York: Palgrave Macmillan.

Baudrillard, Jean (2002) 'When the West Takes the Dead Man's Place', trans. Chris Turner, in *Screened Out*. London: Verso, 66–9.

Blackmore, Susan J. (1999) *The Meme Machine*. Oxford: Oxford University Press.

Boyne, John (2006) *The Boy in the Striped Pyjamas*. Oxford: Fickling.

Cesarani, David (2012) 'Introduction', in David Cesarani and Eric J. Sundquist (eds) *After the Holocaust: Challenging the Myth of Silence*. New York: Routledge, 1–18.

Davis, Todd and Kenneth Womack (2001) 'The List is Life: *Schindler's List* as Ethical Construct', in Todd Davis and Kenneth Womack (ed.) *Mapping the Ethical Turn: A Reader in Ethics, Culture, and Literary Theory*. Charlottesville, VA: University Press of Virginia, 151–64.

Dawkins, Richard (1989) *The Selfish Gene*. Oxford: Oxford University Press.

Des Pres, Terrence (1994) 'Introduction', in Jean-Francois Steiner, *Treblinka*. New York: Plume, vii–xviii.

Diner, Hasia R. (2009) *We Remember with Reverence and Love: American Jews and the Myth of Silence after the Holocaust, 1945–1962*. New York: New York University Press.

Eaglestone, Robert (2012) 'Avoiding Evil in Perpetrator Fiction', in Jenni Adams and Sue Vice (eds) *Representing Perpetrators in Holocaust Literature and Film*. London: Vallentine Mitchell, 13–24.

Ebbrecht, Tobias (2011) *Geschichtsbilder im medialen Gedächtnis: Filmische Narrationen des Holocaust*. Bielefeld: transcript.

Elsaesser, Thomas (2009) 'Vergebliche Rettung: Geschichte als Palimpsest in *Sterne*', in Michael Wedel and Elke Schieber (eds) *Konrad Wolf – Werk und Wirkung*. Berlin: Vistas, 73–92.

Erll, Astrid (2011) 'Travelling Memory', *Parallax*, 17, 4, 4–18.

Grant, Linda (2008) 'How Can They Understand?', *The Guardian*, 29 August.

Hartman, Geoffrey (2002) *Scars of the Spirit: The Struggle against Inauthenticity*. New York: Palgrave Macmillan.

Hegel, Georg W. F. (2011) *Lectures on the Philosophy of History*, trans. Ruben Alvarado. Aalten: WordBridge.

Hilberg, Raul (1985) *The Destruction of the European Jews*. Rev. and expanded ed. New York: Holmes & Meier.

Hirsch, Marianne (2001) 'Surviving Images: Holocaust Photographs and the Work of Postmemory', *Yale Journal of Criticism*, 14, 1, 5–37.

____ (2012) *The Generation of Postmemory: Writing and Visual Culture after the Holocaust*. New York: Columbia University Press.

Hoskins, Andrew (2009) 'Digital Network Memory', in Astrid Erll and Ann Rigney (eds) *Mediation, Remediation, and the Dynamics of Cultural Memory*. Berlin: deGruyter, 91–108.

Huyssen, Andreas (2003a) *Present Pasts: Urban Palimpsests and the Politics of Memory*. Stanford, CA: Stanford University Press.

___ (2003b) 'Trauma and Memory: A New Imaginary of Temporality', in Jill Bennett and Rosanne Kennedy (eds) *World Memory: Personal Trajectories in Global Time*. New York: Palgrave Macmillan, 16–29.

Kertész, Imre (2001) 'Who Owns Auschwitz?', trans. John MacKay, *Yale Journal of Criticism*, 14, 267–72.

___ (2004) 'Excerpts from the Harriman Lecture', 21 October. Online: http://harriman.columbia.edu/files/harriman/00220_11.pdf

Köppen, Manuel (1997) 'Von Effekten des Authentischen – Schindlers Liste: Film und Holocaust', in Manuel Köppen and Klaus R. Scherpe (eds) *Bilder des Holocaust: Literatur – Film – Bildende Kunst*. Cologne: Böhlau, 145–70.

Lanzmann, Claude (1995) 'Ihr sollt nicht weinen: Einspruch gegen *Schindlers Liste*', in Christoph Weiss (ed.) *'Der gute Deutsche': Dokumente zur Diskussion um Steven Spielbergs Schindlers Liste in Deutschland*. St. Imbert: Rohrig, 173–8.

Levy, Daniel and Natan Sznaider (2006) *The Holocaust and Memory in the Global Age*. Philadelphia, PA: Temple University Press.

Marx, Karl and Frederick Engels (1968) *Selected Works in One Volume*. New York: International Publishers.

Mazlish, Bruce (1972) 'The Tragic Farce of Marx, Hegel, and Engels: A Note', *History and Theory*, 11, 3, 335–7.

Phillips, Kendall R. and G. Mitchell Reyes (eds) (2011) *Global Memoryscapes: Contesting Remembrance in a Transnational Age*. Tuscaloosa, AL: University of Alabama Press.

Pinfold, Debbie (2001) *The Child's View of the Third Reich in German Literature: The Eye Among the Blind*. Oxford: Clarendon.

Reiter, Andrea (2000) 'The Holocaust as Seen through the Eyes of Children', in Andrew Leak and George Paizis (eds) *The Holocaust and the Text: Speaking the Unspeakable*. London: Macmillan,

83–96.
Rose, Gillian (1996) 'Beginnings of the Day: Fascism and Representation', in *Mourning Becomes the Law: Philosophy and Representation*. Cambridge: Cambridge University Press, 41–62.
Rothberg, Michael (2009) *Multidirectional Memory: Remembering the Holocaust in the Age of Decolonization*. Stanford, CA: Stanford University Press.
Snyder, Timothy (2010) *Bloodlands: Europe between Hitler and Stalin*. New York: Basic Books.
Stiglegger, Marcus (2011) *Nazi-Chic und Nazi-Trash: Faschistische Ästhetik in der populären Kultur*. Berlin: Bertz + Fischer.
Sznaider, Natan (2008) *Gedächtnisraum Europa: Die Visionen des europäischen Kosmopolitismus. Eine jüdische Perspektive*. Bielefeld: transcript.
Wiesel, Elie (1978) 'Trivializing the Holocaust: Semi-Fact and Semi-Fiction', *The New York Times* 16 April.
___ (1989) 'Art and the Holocaust: Trivializing Memory', *The New York Times*, 11 June.

PART THREE

THE LEGACY OF EVIL

CHAPTER NINE

'The Doctor is Different'
AMBIVALENT ETHICS, CINEMATIC HEROICS AND THE FIGURE OF THE JEWISH DOCTOR IN TIM BLAKE NELSON'S *THE GREY ZONE*

Erin McGlothlin

MEDICAL ETHICS IN 'THE GRAY ZONE'

At the centre of Primo Levi's essay 'The Gray Zone' (1986), which thoughtfully examines the varying degrees to which some victims of the Holocaust were coerced with either violence or with privilege to assist in the oppression and murder of other victims, stands an exceptional group that Levi calls 'the crematorium ravens'; namely the Jewish *Sonderkommando* workers of Auschwitz-Birkenau, who provided the heavy and horrific labour in the mechanised murder system of the gas chambers and crematoria.[1] For Levi, the *Sonderkommandos* represent the limit case in a methodical regime of imposed complicity, whereby National Socialism deliberately and cynically attempted to 'shift onto others – specifically, the victims – the burden of guilt, so that they were deprived of even the solace of innocence' (1986: 53). Levi emphatically insists that the *Sonderkommandos* cannot be evaluated by rigid, conventional measures of complicity and collaboration, for existing juridical and ethical categories founder in the face of the radical extremity of their situation as assistants to genocide. He concludes in his meditation on their ethical status: 'Therefore I ask that we meditate on the story of "the crematorium ravens" with pity and rigor, but that judgement of them be suspended' (1986: 60).

For his knowledge of the circumstances of the Auschwitz *Sonderkommandos*, Levi relies in part on the 1946 memoir of Miklós Nyiszli, a Hungarian-Jewish physician who, along with his wife and daughter, was deported to Auschwitz in June 1944, at the height of the notorious genocide of Hungarian Jews at the camp. Upon arrival, Nyiszli was sent to work in the heart of the industrial murder apparatus, Crematorium II at Birkenau. There he had a threefold function: to minister to the health of the SS attached to the crematorium, to treat the members of the *Sonderkommando* and to assist Josef Mengele in his brutal research by performing autopsies of twins and dwarves on whom Mengele had carried out experiments. In his analysis of the limit situation of the *Sonderkommando* labourers, Levi cites several events described in Nyiszli's memoir, including a soccer game between *Sonderkommando* members and SS guards, an episode in which a young girl was discovered by *Sonderkommando* workers to have survived gassing, and the famous revolt by the 12th *Sonderkommando* in October 1944. Curiously, Levi follows Nyiszli's own self-identification when he terms him 'one of the few survivors of the Special Squad of Auschwitz' (1986: 54), an assessment that implies that Nyiszli's work should share some of the conceptual challenges posed by the *Sonderkommandos* (ibid.), even as it to a certain extent elides the unparalleled nature of Nyiszli's privileged position in the camp. However, Levi does not appear to consider Nyiszli's own ethical positioning in the taxonomy of moral ambiguity he terms 'the gray zone', except to mention briefly, with regard to Nyiszli's pathological work on Mengele's twins, that it was a task 'to which, it should be said in passing, it does not appear he strenuously objected' (ibid.). Levi's comment here can be disputed by several passages in Nyiszli's memoir. While it is true that Nyiszli took pride in his performance as a pathologist and seemed to enjoy the challenges that his work with Mengele presented to him, and while the few affective passages in his memoirs relate more to fear than ethical concern about the work he was asked to perform, he clearly did not condone Mengele's methods. At the same time, however, Levi's cutting remark gestures to the significant ethical tensions present in Nyiszli's account. Levi shows himself to be willing to pass judgement on what he sees as Nyiszli's complicity in Mengele's research, a condemnation that directly contradicts his frequent admonishments against adjudicating the status of the *Sonderkommandos*. Levi's censure of Nyiszli thus performatively demonstrates his own conclusion about the dilemma that inherently rises when one attempts to make an ethical evaluation of the activities of those who were forced to serve as what Levi calls the 'vectors and instruments' (1986: 49) of genocide (a predicament to which even Levi is not immune): 'This gray zone possesses an incredibly complicated internal structure and contains within itself enough to confuse our need to judge' (1986: 42).

Levi's ambivalence about Nyiszli – he relies on his account for information about the *Sonderkommandos* but at the same time is clearly disturbed by the ethical status of Nyiszli's testimony – within the context of his discussion of the gray zone of prisoner complicity suggests that the requirements for addressing Nyiszli's case exceed even Levi's capacity for empathetic understanding and forbearance. Moreover, it reflects a broader discomfort in post-war culture regarding Mengele's privileged prisoner assistant, who owed his survival to his participation in ethically compromised activities. Nyiszli's memoir was available relatively early after the war (it was published in 1946 in Hungarian, appeared in excerpted form in English in the early 1950s and was made fully available in 1960 as a mass market paperback under the title *Auschwitz: A Doctor's Eyewitness Account* [see Turda 2014: 45–6]). It has since been widely cited as a critical source in both the scholarship on Mengele and that on the *Sonderkommandos*. However, as Marius Turda has recently argued, his account has been overwhelmingly neglected by both historians looking to reconstruct the Jewish experience of the Holocaust and literary scholars who examine survivor testimony.[2] Even Robert Jay Lifton, in his groundbreaking assessment of Nazi medicine and the behaviour of both SS doctors and Jewish prisoner-doctors in Auschwitz in *The Nazi Doctors: Medical Killing and the Psychology of Genocide*, which was published the same year as Levi's essay, mentions Nyiszli only in his capacity as eyewitness to Mengele's activity, although he does acknowledge that 'the extent of his work with Mengele made him a controversial figure in the eyes of some other prisoner doctors' (1986: 364). Curiously, Lifton does not explore the ways in which Nyiszli, perhaps to a greater degree than the Jewish prisoner-doctors to whom Lifton devotes two chapters (including Jewish doctors who can be considered collaborators), concretely embodied in his work as both pathologist and attending physician what Lifton terms the 'healing-killing paradox' of medicine in Auschwitz. In this inverted medical paradigm (1986: 231), whereby Jewish doctors were unwillingly co-opted in the Nazis' implementation of 'Auschwitz's institutional program of medicalized genocide' (1986: 147), the conventional ethical protocols of Western medical practice, not least of which included the Hippocratic oath, were radically reversed. Jewish doctors, who struggled to right these overturned ethics even as they plainly were forced to abandon them in particular moments and given situations, were thus placed in an untenable position; according to Lifton, they 'had to connect with, even as they struggled to attenuate, the Auschwitz medical reversal of healing and killing' (1986: 216; see also Brown 2011: 102–3).

Nyiszli's work in particular characterises the inverted medical logic of Auschwitz. Not only was the pathological research he carried out for Mengele compromised by his recognition that the corpses had been murdered, he was also required to heal the ailments of the members of the *Sonderkommando* so that they could return to working in the machinery of death only themselves to be devoured by it a short while later. Moreover, by virtue of his forced involvement in Mengele's sadistic medical experiments, Nyiszli enjoyed privileges unavailable to Jewish doctors in the camps proper, a critical advantage in survival that he frankly acknowledges in his testimony. As an unparalleled account of the anomalous experience of a singularly privileged Jewish doctor in Auschwitz – a prisoner who, it must be stressed, was not there of his own will; who, when volunteering his skills as a doctor, was unaware of the nature of the work he would be asked to perform; and who lived in daily fear of being executed along with the workers of the *Sonderkommando* to which he was attached – Nyiszli's memoir exerts pressure on the ethical frameworks we have developed for evaluating prisoners' actions during the Holocaust, including Levi's concept of the gray zone. As a text that produces in its reader a high degree of discomfort and ambivalence, it has been sidestepped as the proverbial hot potato of Holocaust testimony, simply too scorching for the scholarship to touch.

FROM 'THE GRAY ZONE' TO *THE GREY ZONE*

In spite or perhaps even because of its problematic ethical status, Nyiszli's memoir, along with Levi's essay, serves as the primary source for Tim Blake Nelson's feature film *The Grey Zone* (2001), which in a graphic and mostly hard-boiled realist style depicts the inner workings of the Auschwitz crematoria and the last days of the workers of the 12th *Sonderkommando*, ending with their execution immediately after the uprising is suppressed. The film is based on Nelson's 1996 play of the same name and can be seen as part of the wave of popular cinematic representations of the Holocaust that appeared in the 1990s and early 2000s in the wake of Spielberg's *Schindler's List* (1993). However, *The Grey Zone* distinguishes itself decidedly from many other contemporaneous films both in its framing of the Holocaust and the ostensible meaning it ascribes to it. As Matthew Boswell argues, '*The Grey Zone* eschews the redemptory narratives that characterize Hollywood films in general and Hollywood films about the Holocaust in particular, with the result that it lacks the eventual spiritual uplift of films such as *Schindler's List, Life Is Beautiful* [1997] and *The Pianist* [2002]' (2012: 164). Adam Brown locates Nelson's film's departure from the representational conventions of *Schindler's List* in its repudiation of cinematic definitions of heroism so central to Spielberg's film and associates it with a more general move away from Hollywood narratives of recuperation and rescue: 'Implicitly rejecting Spielberg's sentimental depiction of survival as resulting from heroic acts of defiance, some filmmakers have helped establish a new trend – what I term a 'third wave' – in Holocaust film, which focuses on issues of trauma, "guilt" and "compromise"' (2011: 111). Responding to *The Grey Zone* with both praise and scathing criticism, critics have further focused on the film's violation of cinematic taboos with its stark depiction of both the operation of the gas chambers and crematoria and the *Sonderkommando* workers' casually brutal treatment of freshly murdered naked corpses;[3] its deployment of rapid-fire, self-consciously realist and shockingly amoral dialogue in the style of David Mamet and Quentin Tarantino;[4] and its willingness, despite its overall realist ethos, to bend historical fact for dramatic purposes, as, for example, with its conflation of what in Nyiszli's account constitutes two unrelated episodes, namely the *Sonderkommando*'s discovery of a young girl who survived the gassing with their revolt of 7 October 1944.⁵ Critics and scholars note Nelson's reliance on Nyiszli's memoir as source text for the film but, perhaps following Levi, whose essay provides the conceptual framework for the film's representation of complicity, they (with the exception of Adam Brown in *Judging 'Privileged' Jews: Holocaust Ethics, Representation and the 'Grey Zone'* [2013]) tend to focus on the *Sonderkommando* workers as the film's ethically charged figures and to downplay the ways in which it depicts the doctor's precarious ethical status. The film does indeed create a moral nucleus, however dubious, contradictory and unstable, in the *Sonderkommando*'s failed attempt to rescue the young girl and in the doomed heroics of their uprising; an event that, as Brown argues, is presented in the film 'with unsentimental detachment, making clear that the revolt was ultimately futile' (2013: 172). However, while the film clearly endorses Levi's assessment of the *Sonderkommando* prisoners in its depiction of their extremity (Axel Bangert writes that it highlights 'the more ambiguous aspects of the space which separated the victims of the Holocaust from its perpetrators, thus challenging demonic stylisations of National Socialist and the hagiographic transfigurations of Jews alike' [2008: 20]), it also departs from Levi's use of Nyiszli's testimony as simply a lens through which to view what, in 'The Gray Zone', he calls their 'permanent state of complete debasement and prostration' (1986: 53) to create a complex and ambivalent portrait of Nyiszli, erecting thereby a network of ethical tensions particularly around medical questions.

With *The Grey Zone*, which he wrote, directed and co-produced, Nelson anticipates Turda's call over a decade later for scholars to turn at long last to Nyiszli's ambivalent testimony and to recognise its status as 'a multilayered rather than monolithic text' (2014: 44), one that, with its unsettling complicities, can illuminate the tricky practice of medical ethics in the grey zone. In his director's notes, Nelson confesses that his depiction of Nyiszli departs significantly from the portrait that emerges in Nyiszli's memoirs: 'This person, while arguably worthy of Bruno Bettelheim's lacerating introduction to Nyiszli's book, is less interesting to me for the film we'll shoot, and so I've chosen to make Doctor Nyiszli more aware of the compromises he's making, and therefore more sympathetic than I believe he comes off in his own book' (2003: 156). I disagree with Nelson partially on this point. While it is true that the film creates a figure who is much more obviously troubled by the ethical dimensions of his complicity, the film also downplays the feelings of constant fear and vulnerability that the historical Nyiszli describes in his memoir. Nelson's film explores Nyiszli's disquieting role both narratively, in the way that it constructs its dramatic conflict as a battle between compromised ethical positions, and film-aesthetically, through its adept deployment and disfigurement of a common convention of popular film and television, namely the figure of the heroic doctor who, through his act of dramatic rescue, becomes a model for ethical action. As

I will demonstrate with brief readings of two central scenes in the film that dramatise the healing-killing paradox of Auschwitz, *The Grey Zone* invokes formulaic notions of medical heroism in its representation of Nyiszli, exploiting thereby the viewers' expectation of and desire for redemptive rescue attendant to that formula, only to subvert this masterplot of the heroic doctor and reveal its radical incompatibility with the world of the death camp as depicted in the film.

NYISZLI AND THE TROPE OF THE DOCTOR-HERO

In its portrayal of Nyiszli (played in the film by Allan Corduner) and his ethical ambivalence, *The Grey Zone* for the most part closely follows the memoir, emphasising Nyiszli's precarious situation as a prisoner of privilege who lives simultaneously in almost decadent opulence (at least by Auschwitz standards) and in an environment of constant fear, death and necessary obsequiousness. Nelson's film also gestures toward Nyiszli's obvious pride in his professional identity and accomplishments, his attempts to leverage his special status as a doctor in interactions with both *Sonderkommando* prisoners and his SS overseers and his at times frankly deficient moral compass. However, as with his dramatisation of the historical situation of the *Sonderkommandos*, Nelson also embellishes both the extent of Nyiszli's privilege and the ethical dilemmas that arise from it. He then is able to draw a sharper contrast between the tragic situation of the *Sonderkommando* prisoners, who know they are soon to be liquidated and whose not insignificant moral failings, which include murder,[6] are portrayed as a shameful but perhaps inevitable response to their utter abjection in an environment of pure death, and the position of Nyiszli, who is depicted as separate from the *Sonderkommandos* and thus does not expect to share their fate – a portrayal that departs significantly from the memoirs, in which Nyiszli describes cordial relations with the *Sonderkommandos*, with whom he identifies.[7] Indeed, as the SS guard Muhsfeldt (known historically as 'Mußfeldt' and in Nyiszli's memoir as 'Mussfeld' and played in the film by Harvey Keitel) states early in the film, responding to Rosenthal and Hoffman (played by David Chandler and David Arquette), two of the *Sonderkommando* prisoners who emerge as central characters in the film and who question Nyiszli's authorisation to move between crematoria (a privilege not available to them): 'The doctor is different' (Nelson 2003: 14). Moreover, the film implies that Nyiszli, whom Mengele (played by Henry Stram) calls 'an astonishing pathologist' (Nelson 2003: 26), goes beyond the call of duty in his participation in Mengele's research. This further estranges him from the *Sonderkommando* workers, who believe that he volunteered for his post and thus willingly assists with Mengele's sadistic experiments; as Schlermer, a *Sonderkommando* leader played by Daniel Benzali, says to Nyiszli, apparently unaware of the irony of his statement, 'You knew the sort of work you'd be doing, and you continue to do it. [...] You give killing purpose' (Nelson 2003: 78).

The film makes clear that Nyiszli's excellent pathological work for Mengele gains him additional favours from his SS overseers, such as the authorisation to visit his wife and daughter in Birkenau Camp C, for whom he is then able to secure transit from Auschwitz to a labour camp by reluctantly promising Muhsfeldt that he will spy on the *Sonderkommandos* (a dramatic intrigue that is also fabricated by Nelson). The *Sonderkommando* workers in turn resent Nyiszli's ability to save his wife and child and distrust his apparent intimacy with the SS (a familiarity that, as Nelson's finely crafted, sometimes elliptical dialogue in the scenes between Nyiszli and Mengele and Nyiszli and Muhsfeldt demonstrates, belies Nyiszli's position of extreme vulnerability). Nelson thus takes pains to pit the *Sonderkommando* prisoners, who themselves enjoy privileges unimaginable to the common Auschwitz inmate due to their intimate assistance with the killing operations, against Nyiszli, a tension underscored formally in the exchanges between them with the rhythm and pace of the violent dialogue and with the frequent employment of two shots that emphasise the oppositional nature of their relationship (as in the scene in the storeroom between Nyiszli and Schlermer mentioned above, in which the two men are divided vertically in the frame by bunches of long metal hooks and other tools used in the gas chamber and crematorium). In this way, the film constructs a fundamental conflict between the fragile, contradictory and corrupted ethical frameworks both parties manipulate to justify their sphere of activity in the murder process; as Janet Ward puts it, 'There are, in short, plural interpretations battling for dominant positions in this film of nonvictorious resistance' (2004: 33). At the same time, however, as I will demonstrate, it also momentarily aligns them in their common desire to reclaim an ethical self in an atmosphere of radical complicity.

Muhsfeldt's words about Nyiszli's distinctiveness not only describe Nyiszli's special status in the crematorium complex, they also indicate the singular structural and dramatic functions his character plays in the film, at least initially. Although Nelson consciously eschews the cinematic principle of heroic individuality in its representation of the *Sonderkommando* prisoners, who, even though given names, are barely distinguishable from one another, as they are not endowed with backstories and possess minimal recognisable character traits, Brown reminds us that, while the characters of Nyiszli, Muhsfeldt and Mengele are all based on historical counterparts, the four *Sonderkommando* characters (Schlermer, Rosenthal, Hoffman and Abramowics) are invented composites based on *Sonderkommando* testimony (2013: 173). Rather than creating fully fleshed-out figures endowed with individual personalities and idiosyncrasies, Nelson constructs the *Sonderkommando* characters in such a way that they chiefly embody specific ethical or argumentative positions. Nyiszli, on the other hand, is depicted in the film in three distinctive ways: visually, functionally and narratively. First, he is depicted as the one prisoner character whose appearance most aligns with the notion of a conventional protagonist; unlike the *Sonderkommando* workers, whose filthy clothing

– a combination of prison uniform and civilian garb – clearly displays the abject nature of their work, Nyiszli is clad in a crisp white doctor's coat, tailored shirts and fine suits, lending him an aura of authority and credibility, both in the world of the film and for the viewer. Second, he differs from the other prisoners functionally in that he moves easily between the world of the guards and that of the prisoners, possessing a measure of autonomy in both. Third, of all of the prisoners, he has the most narrative impact in the film; his actions – especially his medical resuscitation of the young girl and his attempt to barter with Muhsfeldt for her life by offering intelligence about the *Sonderkommando*'s planned revolt – affect the development of the story. Nelson's careful construction of Nyiszli's distinctiveness as a character and as a doctor appears to contradict the aesthetic and dramatic principles that he developed for the film. As Nelson writes in his director's notes:

> I would normally begin with a bare-bones description of what *The Grey Zone* is; that is, a one- or two-sentence account of its plot following a single protagonist's journey. On this project, however, I don't think that's appropriate. Several people who've read the script have confessed to skipping ahead out of frustration in not being able to figure out 'whom to follow,' as one person put it, confounded as we can all be when a narrative doesn't provide a clear 'hero.' One *shouldn't* be able to find such a person in *The Grey Zone*. Surely Doctor Nyiszli remains alive at the end, but I consider him no more unique as a character vehicle than any of the four *Sonderkommando* members whom we get to know, or even the Girl for that matter, whom many audience members will try and latch onto as a sort of raft on our sea of fire. While there are these in this story who act heroically at given points, this is not a film about heroes. (2003: 139–40)

Nelson's claim that he considers Nyiszli no more a conventional character than any of the other figures in the *The Grey Zone* is a bit disingenuous, given the film's overt structuring of him as a clear protagonist, at least at its beginning, but at the same time his comment is not incompatible with the film's approach to Nyiszli.[8] At its outset, the film appears to satisfy the viewer's expectation (which Nelson clearly characterises above) that she will encounter a type of hero in Nyiszli, only to dash that expectation on the rocks of the ethical realities in which he is forced to operate. By emphasising both his special status as a doctor and his provisional position as the film's protagonist who is charged to step forward and lead the film, *The Grey Zone* utilises conventional notions of the individual hero, in this case the figure of the heroic doctor, a trope common in representations of medicine in American television and film.[9] As Joseph Turow and Rachel Gans-Boriskin argue with regard to the popular depiction of medical dramas from the post-war period to the present:

Television's doctor show formula evolved from a combination of storytelling approaches that had existed in popular films, radio, and literature, as well as the general optimism about the medical institution in the years following World War II. [...] The science and technology of modern medicine seemed to be the new frontier, and the doctor was its hero as surely as the cowboy had once dominated the West. (2007: 265)

Like the hero of the classic western, the 'doctor-hero' in the genre of the televised medical drama, as Elena C. Strauman and Bethany C. Goodier argue, is above all an individual; rather than functioning as a part of a larger medical team, he (and, as Strauman and Goodier remind us, 'the doctor-hero is predominantly constructed as male' [2010: 35]) often acts as a 'maverick' who bucks the system to save his patients and is frequently portrayed as a sort of knightly figure who rushes in to rescue those in medical distress, even if this requires him to 'go against orders or even compromise ethics' (ibid.). The doctor as heroic agent of rescue is thus a common trope in the American cultural imagination that viewers can instantly recognise. Whenever he appears, we know from our experience with this convention that he will expertly and confidently mobilise to rescue and repair injured, gravely ill and dying characters. Like all conventional heroes, he is charged with reversing chaotic decline and with restoring order and health to the character and thus to the world of the story. As viewers, we thus come to rely on him as a stabilising figure of authority who reestablishes normality, reaffirms human life and reinforces prevailing cultural standards. However, in the world of Nelson's film, the death camp Auschwitz, the cultural norm is not the avowal of life, which can be effected by heroic medical rescue, but the practice of mass murder, which operates directly at odds with the aims of the doctor-hero. As I will demonstrate, by deliberately evoking the conventions of medical heroics with his representation of Nyiszli, Nelson creates a fundamental conflict between the doctor's mission and the *raison d'être* of the death camp, working paradoxically *against*, not *toward* conventional cinematic notions of the individual hero. He does this by engaging complex ethical dilemmas that not only belie the assumptions of individual agency presupposed in classical definitions of the hero but also actively corrode the supposed heroism of medical rescue.

AMBIVALENT MEDICAL RESCUE

The opening sequence of the film immediately depicts an ethical situation that foregrounds both Lifton's thesis regarding the radical reversal of the healing paradigm in Auschwitz and Nyiszli's potentially heroic role of medical rescuer. In this scene, an older member of the *Sonderkommando* attempts to commit suicide with the assistance of some of his co-prisoners. Hoffman forecloses the suicide attempt by summoning Nyiszli, who is able to revive the prisoner despite the protests of Rosenthal and Schlermer, both of whom emerge over the course of the film as central figures in the *Sonderkommando*'s planned revolt. After the old man is resuscitated, Rosenthal orders Schlermer to restrain Nyiszli physically while he suffocates the prisoner with a pillow.

In these first few minutes of *The Grey Zone*, the viewer is poised to identify with Nyiszli, whom the film deliberately structures in this initial scene as a potential hero. Lawrence Baron argues that the camera focalises Nyiszli's perspective for the audience: '*The Grey Zone* plunges its audience into the netherworld of amoral choices facing the members of the *Sonderkommando*. A handheld camera glides through dimly lit corridors, tracing the steps of Nyiszli rushing to save a comatose man who had overdosed on sedatives to kill himself' (2005: 287).[10] The velocity with which Nyiszli enters the *Sonderkommando*'s living quarters, which contrasts with the static poses of Schlermer and Rosenthal, allows us to further identify Nyiszli as the active force in the scene, the embodiment of the cavalry to the rescue. His heroic dedication to halting the attempted suicide is recognisable to us as a part of the ethical framework of the physician. He sees his mission as preserving life at all costs, even though, as we later learn in the film, not only is he associated with Mengele's deadly research, but his expertise allows Mengele to increase substantially the scope of the research and thus the body count that results from it. In this scene, Nyiszli asserts his professional persona as a doctor and takes charge accordingly; as he confidently states upon entering the scene, 'If he's alive, I'm treating him' (Nelson 2003: 3). His acute need to fulfil his duty as a doctor and revive the prisoner seems astounding, however, when the viewer becomes cognisant of the environment in which Nyiszli operates: the very house of death in Auschwitz, in the quarters of the *Sonderkommando*, two floors above the gas chamber and directly above the ovens, where thousands are murdered and burned daily. His proximity to the genocide being committed around him is made manifest on a visual level at the end of the scene, when Hoffman, followed by a handheld camera, is depicted in an uninterrupted shot carrying the old man's corpse from the living quarters, down the stairs, and into the oven room of the crematorium.[11] The next shot, an outdoor crane shot of the smoking chimneys, indicates synecdochically what happens to the man's body, which, along with the corpses of Hungarian transports that are 'processed' by the *Sonderkommando*, is transformed into fire, smoke and ash.[12]

Nyiszli's zeal to revive the prisoner in this opening scene, while admirable, seems at best inconsistent with the logic of his environment. To the other prisoners of the *Sonderkommando*, such an attempt at conventional ethical behaviour in the inverted atmosphere of Auschwitz is downright contemptible, an attitude that is evident in their disrespectful treatment of him. Compared to Nyiszli's medical efforts, which are viewed by the *Sonderkommando* prisoners as ineffectual at best and misguided at worst, Rosenthal's brutal act of murder is seen by the other prisoners as a kind of mercy killing that respects the wishes of the deceased; according to Rosenthal, '[That's] what he wanted. That's all' (Nelson 2003: 4). As we learn later in the film from Hoffman's voiceover monologue to the recently revived girl, on the day of his arrival in Auschwitz two weeks earlier, the old man had been forced to burn the corpses of the convoy with which he was deported, including his wife, daughter and two grandchildren. In this context, his suicide attempt is thus depicted as both a radical assertion of selfhood in an atmosphere of total annihilation and a resistance against the Nazi machinery of death. In Auschwitz, in which medical ethics in particular are overturned, Nyiszli's rescue of the prisoner, which in another context would seem both ethically necessary and heroic, and his professional code of medical ethics, which is ineffectual in the environment in which the *Sonderkommando* is forced to function daily, are viewed by the *Sonderkommando* prisoners as a ludicrous remnant of an irrelevant moral realm.[13] In this way, the scene, which begins by summoning Nyiszli in the common cinematic role of active heroic rescuer (a sort of medical Oskar Schindler, if you will), concludes with his heroic power incapacitated, an impotence underscored visually with Schlermer's pinioning of him. By the end of the scene, which lasts for less than two minutes, the film has quickly disarmed the trope of the doctor-hero and called into question the simplistic ethical precepts on which it is based. Later in the film, as the viewer learns of Nyiszli's actual work as a doctor in the camp and the complicated web of complicity it entails, his rescue attempt is cast in another light; in retrospection, it appears that Nyiszli endeavours here not only to right the healing-killing inversion of the Auschwitz environment but also to correct his own ethical failures, especially in the realm of medicine, through his performance as heroic healer in this scene.

HEROIC MEDICAL RESCUE

Although Nyiszli, angered by Rosenthal's murder of the *Sonderkommando* member, states at the end of the opening scene that, moving forward, he will refuse to come if summoned again by the *Sonderkommando* workers, he does respond when called a second time, after Hoffman discovers a young girl (played by Kamelia Grigorova) who has survived the gassing and reveals the fact to Rosenthal. Rather than opposing Hoffman's desire to save the girl (as he did in the case of the old man), Rosenthal helps him retrieve her from a load of corpses about to have their hair shorn without revealing that she is alive, explaining to the men who perform this work, 'We need this body for the doctor' (Nelson 2003: 59). In this second scene of resuscitation, as in the scene with the elderly prisoner, Nyiszli the doctor-hero immediately jumps into action and revives the girl without questioning how his rescue of a singular person in the context of the prevalent atmosphere of death might appear absurd. With this second act of rescue, however, Nyiszli functions not as an individual hero, but as part of a collective, for Rosenthal and Hoffman assist him in his efforts to save her by fetching broth, tea and blankets, while Schlermer reluctantly looks on but does not prevent the rescue.¹⁴ Their interests momentarily aligned, Nyiszli, Rosenthal and Hoffman work together as a team, becoming increasingly invested in her survival despite or perhaps even because of the inversion of healing and killing by which they all have been so desperately compromised.¹⁵ As Brown reminds us:

> Rosenthal, who suffocated the old man in the first scene, pleads with Nyiszli to 'save her ... you've got to fucking save her!' Similarly, the quiet-spoken Hoffman, whose constantly nervous disposition makes him seem the youngest and most emotionally vulnerable of the crematorium workers, tells the girl, 'I pray to God we save you.' (2013: 182)

Like the *Sonderkommando* workers, who, by discovering and retrieving the young girl from the assembly line of death, produce a life out of the mounds of corpses they must daily 'process', Nyiszli, with his revival of the girl and his fierce attempt to protect her, is able to occupy once again his professional role as healer, a vocation continually denied him in the death factory, and momentarily to right the killing-healing inversion of Auschwitz. The film further highlights the lengths to which Nyiszli identifies with Rosenthal's and Hoffman's overwhelming desire to save the girl in a subsequent scene in which he attempts to barter with Muhsfeldt for the girl's life (who, despite the prisoners' attempt to hide her, is discovered by Muhsfeldt). He informs Muhsfeldt about the *Sonderkommando*'s planned uprising, which he has just learned is slated for later that day. Brown argues that both Nyiszli's willingness to collect information on the *Sonderkommando* for Muhsfeldt and his attempt to use his knowledge in order to save the girl's life demonstrate the ambivalent status of his behaviour, which 'is clearly motivated by a turbid combination of self-interest, self-preservation, and mortal terror' (2013: 179):

> As revealed in many other instances throughout the film, the extreme circumstances of 'privileged' Jews such as Nyiszli expose the seemingly antithetical concepts of 'resistance' and 'cooperation' as being intrinsically connected. The complexity of the situation represented in the film is further reinforced through Nyiszli's later attempt to enlist Mühsfeldt [sic] in the efforts to save the girl who survived the gas. (ibid.)

Although Nyiszli does not tell Muhsfeldt when the uprising will take place, he clearly endangers the *Sonderkommando*'s lives with his ruse, which displays a rather perverted ethical calculus in which he privileges the life of the one girl – whom, it must be stressed, he himself resuscitated – over that of the hundreds of *Sonderkommando* labourers and additionally over their planned uprising, which could potentially save additional thousands of lives, were they successful in disabling the gas chambers and crematoria. At the same time, however, his decision to trade intelligence of the *Sonderkommando*'s plans for the life of the girl, however ethically questionable, is not immediately or obviously self-serving. He, like Rosenthal and Hoffman, does not stand to benefit materially from her continued existence and is somewhat in danger as a result of it. And indeed, when Muhsfeldt retracts his offer to save the girl, complaining that the intelligence Nyiszli provides him is not adequate, Nyiszli goes one step further, putting himself in additional danger:

Muhsfeldt:	There's nothing more to discuss.
Nyiszli:	What about your headaches and your drinking?
	This stops Muhsfeldt.
Muhsfeldt:	Excuse me?
Nyiszli:	I'll tell him you're unfit.
Muhsfeldt:	You fucking bastard.
Nyiszli:	And they won't move you somewhere else. I'll want to see her, not a hair on her head, and on the other side. Through the fence if you like, but numbered, shaved, and alive.
	Nyiszli moves closer.
Nyiszli (cont'd):	And to live isn't to kill, Herr Oberschaarfuhrer [sic], because we're not doing the killing. (Nelson 2003: 104–5)

Nyiszli blackmails Muhsfeldt with his own medical knowledge of Muhsfeldt's weaknesses, showing himself willing to violate the ethical code of doctor-patient confidentiality, to exploit his relationship with Mengele (whom Nyiszli threatens to tell about Muhsfeldt's problems), and to risk his own privileged position in order to assure the survival of the young girl.

Axel Bangert argues that the prisoners' revival of the girl 'constitutes an attempt at moral self-assertion … in which the inmates … rediscover their humanity' (2008: 21); similarly, Adam Brown maintains that the rescue 'ignites a glimmer of hope in some of the film's crematorium workers, not in terms of survival, but in terms of finding some means of dealing with their self-loathing and perhaps regaining a semblance of the "humanity" they feel they have lost' (2013: 182). I go even further in my assessment of the meaning of this event for both Rosenthal and Hoffman and for Nyiszli. I argue that their resuscitation of her represents a fleeting but critical moment in which they are able collectively to intervene in the machinery of death and protect and preserve life in the face of its radical negation, meaning that their actions in this scene result not just from their own self-interest in 'rediscovering' or 'regaining' a sense of humanity, but also from a measure of altruistic avowal of life, to which they themselves, by nature of their work in the gas chambers, crematoria and dissection room, are barred from being directly involved. They thus perform the ultimate act of heroism, committing themselves to a dangerous act of salvation and deliverance to which they can contribute but from whose effects they are necessarily excluded. When Rosenthal, not without pride, claims shortly after the rescue, 'WE did this' (Nelson 2003: 111), Schlermer replies: 'Listen to me. Listen. What's going to happen to her will happen, no matter what you do or see. The best thing you can do for her now is finish the day quietly, do as you're told, and wait for later. That's it. That's it for you. It's the Goddamn end' (ibid.). Janet Ward argues that the prisoners' uprising depicted later in the film 'temporarily reaches the level of a conventional heroic narrative' (2004: 33), but it is actually the rescue of the young girl by Nyiszli, Hoffman and Rosenthal, not the uprising that shortly follows it, that appears to conform most with the cinematic conventions of heroic action, especially with regard to the object of their rescue. Lawrence Baron (2005: 289) and Matthew Boswell (2012: 167) argue that Nelson deliberately chose an actress for the role of the young girl who strikingly resembles the paradigmatically tragic young victim of the Holocaust in the public imagination, Anne Frank. In a similar vein, Alex Bangert (2008: 21) and Adam Brown (2013: 182) compare the girl in *The Grey Zone* with the figure of the little girl in the red coat in Spielberg's *Schindler's List*, which has become a prominent example of 'the child as a symbol for moral purity and its murder as a symbol for a life not lived' (Bangert 2008: 24) in depictions of the Holocaust. Nelson's evocation of these two icons of innocence – one historical, one fictional – not only indicates the extent to which he consciously engages with the representational history of the Holocaust (especially the cinematic history), it also allows him to stage an imaginative act of collective rescue. By having Nyiszli and the *Sonderkommando* labourers resuscitate a filmic surrogate for Anne Frank and the little girl in the red coat, he allows them to perform on a symbolic level the heroic rescue and restitution of these tragic icons, an act that transforms the men, at least fleetingly, into paradigms of Holocaust heroism. In this way, Nelson gestures with his self-conscious staging of the collective rescue of the young girl to a possible rewriting – or even redemption – of the cinematic history of the Holocaust. Such a moment of deliverance and atonement engages with, responds to and takes advantage of viewers' desire for redemptive Holocaust narratives, which, following from their experience with *Schindler's List* and *Life Is Beautiful*, they have come to expect from Holocaust film. Such narratives belie both the brutal historical fate of the *Sonderkommandos* in Auschwitz and the extremely low odds of survival for the great majority of people deported there.

THE FAILED ETHICS OF RESCUE AND REDEMPTION

Given the overall character of what Brown terms Nelson's 'anti-redemptory aesthetic' (2013: 174) and the ways in which the film continually undermines conventional notions of heroism, however, the viewer is right to be sceptical of the lasting value or unequivocal meaning of the men's rescue of the young girl and thus also the cinematic heroism that it represents. Like the rescue in the first scene, which begins by mobilising the conventions of the doctor-hero only to dismantle them at the end, undercutting thereby the very idea of medical heroism in Auschwitz, the collective heroism of the men's rescue of the young girl is also carefully disassembled and exposed as futile at the end of the film, both in terms of the fate of the characters and as an aesthetic strategy. Neither the *Sonderkommando* prisoners' inordinate concern for the girl, which contrasts sharply with their rough treatment of both the people whom they escort to the gas chamber and the corpses they drag out of it, nor Dr. Nyiszli's exemplary medical care, is able to secure the girl's survival and thus to reverse their collective ethical decline, even when the episode is accompanied, as it is anachronistically in the film, by the *Sonderkommando's* brave revolt. In the uprising, Rosenthal does not engage in fighting but tries the entire time to locate the young girl (whom Muhsfeldt has entrusted with another guard), essentially confirming Schlermer's earlier objections to him regarding her resuscitation: 'This will foul everything. [...] It's a Goddamn distraction' (Nelson 2003: 62, 63). Schlermer, on the other hand, who objected to the revival of the girl, does fight heroically (in fact, he is the first to spray the SS with machine-gun fire), sacrificing himself to blow up the furnace room. And Nyiszli, our doctor-hero, who engaged in substantial risk to save the girl, hides for the duration of the uprising, cowering under a table in his dissection room while a record player in his study plays Johannes Brahms' *Rhapsodie für eine Altstimme, Männerchor und Orchester*, Opus 53 (*Alto Rhapsody*, Opus 53) from 1869.[16] The diegetic music of this scene transitions to the extradiegetic soundtrack for the rest of the uprising, providing ironic accompaniment for the revolt. Brahms' work is a setting of three stanzas from Johann Wolfgang von Goethe's poem 'Winter Journey in the Harz' ('Harzreise im Winter'), written in 1777, and features a figure who 'has lost his path' ('verliert sich sein Pfad') and suffers from 'hatred of mankind' ('Menschenhaß'), a 'despiser' ('Verächter') who 'secretly devours his own worth in insatiable self-love' ('Zehrt er heimlich auf / Seinen eignen Wert / In ungnügender [sic] Selbstsucht'). The rhapsody concludes with an appeal to the 'father of love' ('Vater der Liebe') to reveal a sound ('Ton') that can 'quicken his heart' and 'open his clouded gaze to the thousand springs around the thirsty one in the desert' ('So erquicke sein Herz! / Öffne den umwölkten Blick / Über die tausend Quellen / Neben dem Durstenden / In der Wüste!') (Goethe 1981: 51). As Aubrey S. Garlington writes of the rhapsody's resolution, 'What better cure for incipient misanthropy than a heart restored by the fullness of love?' (1983: 538). Brahms' work thus performs a resounding call to humanity, in which the misanthrope gone astray can, by listening to the tone of love, find his way back to the human community.

The hopeful – and heroic – call to humanity that promises redemption in Goethe's poem and Brahms' rhapsody, however, does not achieve the same effect in Nelson's film;

embodied in the young girl, whom Nyiszli, Rosenthal and Hoffman rescue out of a defiance of the 'hatred of mankind' around them and an avowal of life (which is of course a kind of love), this sound ultimately falls on deaf ears. The redemptive promise of heroic medical rescue of both the young girl and the icons of innocence for which she is a cinematic surrogate shatters in the merciless ethical atmosphere of Auschwitz. By carefully invoking and then ruthlessly destroying paradigmatic conventions of heroism in the two key scenes of medical resuscitation, Nelson mobilises the notion of a transcendent, stable ethical model made possible by such genre conventions and then repudiates it as contingent, irrelevant and dangerously illusory in the world in which Nyiszli and the *Sonderkommando* workers are held prisoner. Moreover, in refusing in the end to provide the expected redemptive resolution that it evoked with the emotionally and ethically satisfying rescue of the girl, the film makes its viewers aware of the ambivalent ethics of their own desire for a happy conclusion to the situation, at least for the characters they have come to know, even as the historical framework in which this anomalous rescue is imbedded makes clear that such positive examples of deliverance and atonement were extremely anomalous in Auschwitz. In the end, in *The Grey Zone* as in the historical incident, the girl is shot by an SS guard, while Hoffman, Rosenthal and the remaining *Sonderkommando* labourers are brutally liquidated in keeping with the logic of the camp. Apart from the SS guards, of the characters in the film only Nyiszli survives, although his existence at the end is anything but the triumphal avowal of life and heroic virtue represented by survivors in films such as *Schindler's List*. Indeed, we as viewers are to understand that, in surviving the atrocious deaths of both the *Sonderkommando* members and the young girl, Nyiszli has forfeited his ethical claim to any kind of heroic action. As Muhsfeldt tells him shortly after the uprising, 'That's right, Doctor. We will both continue with our work, because that's what the living do. We've saved each other, then. We needn't save anyone else' (Nelson 2003: 126). Nyiszli 'retches' (ibid.) in response to Muhsfeldt's words, but at the end of *The Grey Zone* he is depicted standing among a group of SS guards, dispassionately smoking a cigarette as he watches them commit murder.

Notes

1. Levi mentions only those prisoners who supported the operations of the gas chambers and crematoria at Auschwitz, neglecting to mention the squads of prisoners of the *Einsatz Reinhard* death camps (Treblinka, Sobibór and Bełżec) and other sites of killing (such as Majdanek and Chełmno) who were compelled to perform similar duties.
2. Adam Brown comes to a similar conclusion: 'Nyiszli is simply (and simplistically) described as a "collaborator of Mengele" in one historical text, while his testimony is used elsewhere to stand in for the perspective of the Nazi doctor, implying a problematic parallel between persecutor and persecuted' (2011: 106).

3   For a good discussion of the film's violation of the taboos of representing murder inside the gas chamber, see Bangert 2008: 29–30. As Nelson writes in his director's notes, 'If this was killing on an industrial scale, we're going to be the film that shows it' (2003: 162).
4   Nelson makes clear that the delivery of the dialogue is designed to work against the conventions he associates with Holocaust film: 'The audience should never find refuge in the conventions of Holocaust film dialects that to me seem to distance more than they engage. We'll hear German accents for conversations in German, that's all' (2003: 158). Nelson's latter instruction points to what in my opinion is the film's most unfortunate shortcoming, namely the fact that only those actors portraying German guards, most notably Harvey Keitel in his depiction of Muhsfeldt, employ 'accents' (i.e. an accent other than a recognisably standard American one) in *The Grey Zone*. By emphasising the more naturalistic (if simultaneously stylised) speaking manner of the prisoners and at the same time highlighting the stilted German accents of the SS guards, Nelson employs a widely-used representational strategy for depicting perpetrators that, as I argue elsewhere, constructs them as 'abstract, recondite and one-dimensional' figures that function more as mythical Others than as complex human agents (McGlothin 2009: 213).
5   As Nelson describes the film's departure from its otherwise 'ruthless' (2003: 141) historical accuracy with its conflation of the two separate events, 'Part of what *The Grey Zone* does is to imagine ... the story these two events ... might have create if they *had* coincided. If we do our work honestly, the result will be no less "true" than a film pedantically obsessed with historical chronology' (2003: 155–6). Axel Bangert (2008: 20) has discussed the film's inaccurate timeline, particularly its temporal designation of the uprising. Although lax with 'historical chronology', Nelson's film is nevertheless obsessed with other aspects of historical accuracy (his construction of a scaled replica of the Number 2 Crematorium building being one [see Nelson 2003: 152]).
6   In the most graphically violent scene in a film that, as Adam Brown argues, contains sequences that 'are deliberately made to be hard to watch' (2013: 174), the character of Hoffman beats to death in the undressing room of the gas chamber a man who both challenges him about the lie of the shower room and refuses to hand over to him his gold watch.
7   Nelson writes, 'I've also fabricated somewhat the antipathy the *Sonderkommando* members have for Nyiszli. I don't know that it didn't exist, but it's certainly nothing Nyiszli writes of in his book, nor would he' (2003: 156). Nyiszli writes in his memoir that he himself saw in his relationship with the *Sonderkommando* workers 'a certain intimacy' (1960: 117). Nyiszli emphasises that he assumed that he was a part of the *Sonderkommando*, not separate from it, and fully expected to share its eventual fate (1960: 123).
8   Axel Bangert writes: 'Hoffman, whose character is loosely based on the *Sonderkommando* member Salmen Lewental, represents the guiding figure of *The Grey Zone*', one who 'is designed to undermine heroic convention' (2008: 22).
9   I include here reference to television as well as film because popular representations of doctors in the US have overwhelmingly occurred in the medium of television with the extremely popular genre of the medical drama, beginning in the 1960s with *Dr. Kildare* and televised soap operas, moving through the 1970s and 1980s with *Marcus Welby, Quincy, ME, M*A*S*H* and *St. Elsewhere*, and culminating in the immensely popular, fast-paced medical drama of the 1990s, *ER*, and more recent ironic depictions, such as *House*.
10 Matthew Boswell and Alex Bangert both note that Nelson frequently employs subjective shots throughout the film, 'especially for the events from which an audience member might most

want to distance themselves, such as the death of the girl who survived the gas' (Boswell 2012: 170).

11 Nelson mentions this shot in particular in his director's notes as his conscious attempt to evoke the ways in which the *Sonderkommando* prisoners lived and moved in a total environment of death: 'Whenever I can, I'll block scenes so they traverse several environments. This means, for instance, that when Hoffman shoulders the carcass of the Old Man (in the film's first sequence), we'll follow him through a portion of the *Sonderkommando* barracks, down stairs separating them from the building's ground floor, and directly to the door of the furnace room without cutting' (2003: 146).

12 Nelson's use of the chimney as synecdoche for murder is reminiscent of a similar strategy in Art Spiegelman's *Maus II*, whereby an image of the smoking chimney is used to indicate deaths that the text does not represent visually (1991: 27, 55, 58, 69). Cathy S. Gelbin, working from Hanno Loewy's observation that Holocaust film uses 'metonymies and synecdoches to circumvent the direct representation of the gas-chamber atrocities' (2011: 29), sees *The Grey Zone* as making important modifications to this representational strategy. She argues that the film moves from a heavy reliance on synecdoche at its beginning to a more explicit representation of mass murder (2011: 34). Bangert finds a similar synechdochic strategy at work in the film's innovative use of ambient sound, which 'functions as a surrogate stimulus for the non-represented' (2008: 23).

13 The historical Nyiszli describes a similar scene of suicide in his memoir, which likely serves as the model for Nelson's representation. However, the scene Nyiszli depicts exhibits somewhat less conflict: 'The men of the Sonderkommando grouped around his bed asked me softly, with resignation, "to let the captain go"' (1960: 108). Moreover, Nyiszli recalls feeling ambivalent about his rescue afterward (1960: 109). In the film, Nyiszli, in conversation with Rosenthal immediately prior to the revival of the young girl, confesses to not having fully understood at the time the implications of his resuscitation of the old man (see Nelson 2003: 65).

14 Schlermer does not share Hoffman's and Rosenthal's desire to revive the girl because he believes the endeavour is futile and puts the *Sonderkommando* and their planned uprising in danger. Schlermer's opposition to the rescue, along with the objections voiced by Abramowics (played by Steve Buscemi) later in the film, demonstrate the conflicting ethical positions among the *Sonderkommando* prisoners.

15 Brown suggests that Hoffman and Rosenthal in particular are interested in saving the girl as a means of redeeming themselves for the murders they commit earlier in the film (2013: 182).

16 Nelson had specific plans for the sound design of the film, which includes on the one hand constant and threatening diegetic noise that designates aspects of the industrial killing process (see Nelson 2003: 165), and on the other, a conscious eschewal of a dramatic or emotive musical soundtrack. Aside from the music that accompanies the opening and closing credits and the Brahms piece, which segues from diegetic to extradiegetic during the uprising, there is no extradiegetic soundtrack in the film. Notable is a second instance of diegetic music in the film, the Johann Strauss waltz 'Rosen aus dem Süden' ('Roses from the South'), which is played by an orchestra of prisoners and accompanies deportees en route to the gas chamber (a fictional invention by Nelson). By choosing two well-known works from German musical culture, Nelson not only draws a stark contrast between the greatest achievements of German culture and the depravity and barbarism of Auschwitz, he also demonstrates how the former is used to facilitate the latter.

Filmography

The Grey Zone. Dir. Tim Blake Nelson. USA, 2001.
Schindler's List. Dir. Steven Spielberg. USA, 1993.
Life Is Beautiful [*La vita è bella*]. Dir. Roberto Benigni. Italy, 1997.
The Pianist. Dir. Roman Polanski. France/Poland/Germany/UK, 2002.

Bibliography

Bangert, Axel (2008) 'Changing Narratives and Images [of] the Holocaust: Tim Blake Nelson's Film *The Grey Zone* (2001)', *New Cinemas: Journal of Contemporary Film*, 6, 1, 17–32.

Baron, Lawrence (2005) '*The Grey Zone*: Cinema of Choiceless Choices', in Jonathan Petropoulos and John K. Roth (eds) *Gray Zones: Ambiguity and Compromise in the Holocaust and Its Aftermath*. New York: Berghahn, 286–92.

Boswell, Matthew (2012) *Holocaust Impiety in Literature, Popular Music and Film*. New York: Palgrave MacMillan.

Brown, Adam (2011) '"No One Will Ever Know": The Holocaust, "Privileged" Jews and the "Grey Zone"', *History Australia*, 8, 3, 95–116.

____ (2013) *Judging 'Privileged' Jews: Holocaust Ethics, Representation and the 'Grey Zone.'* New York: Berghahn.

Garlington, Jr., Aubrey S. (1983) '*Harzreise als Herzreise*: Brahms' Alto Rhapsody', *The Musical Quarterly*, 69, 4, 527–42.

Gelbin, Cathy S. (2011) 'Cinematic Representations of the Holocaust', in Jean-Marc Dreyfus and Daniel Langton (eds) *Writing the Holocaust*. London: Bloomsbury Academic, 26–40.

von Goethe, Johann Wolfgang (1981) *Gedichte*, ed. Erich Trunz. Munich: Beck.

Levi, Primo (1986) 'The Gray Zone,' trans. Raymond Rosenthal, in *The Drowned and the Saved*. New York: Summit Books, 36–69.

Lifton, Robert Jay (1986) *The Nazi Doctors: Medical Killing and the Psychology of Genocide*. New York: Basic Books.

Loewy, Hanno (2003) 'Fiktion und Mimesis: Holocaust und Genre im Film', in Margit Fröhlich, Hanno Loewy and Heinz Steinert (eds) *Lachen über Hitler: Auschwitz-Gelächter*. Frankfurt: Edition Text + Kritik, 37–64.

McGlothlin, Erin (2009) 'Theorizing the Perpetrator in Bernhard Schlink's *The Reader* and Martin Amis's *Time's Arrow*', in R. Clifton Spargo and Robert Ehrenreich (eds) *After Representation?: The Holocaust, Literature, and Culture*. New Brunswick, NJ: Rutgers University Press, 210–30.

Nelson, Tim Blake (2003) *'The Grey Zone': Director's Notes and Screenplay*. New York: Newmarket.

Nyiszli, Miklos ([1960] 2011) *Auschwitz: A Doctor's Eyewitness Account*, trans. Tibère Kramer and Richard Seaver. New York: Arcade.

Spiegelman, Art (1991) *Maus II: A Survivor's Tale: And Here My Troubles Began*. New York: Pantheon.

Strauman, Elena C. and Bethany C. Goodier (2010) 'The Doctor(s) in House: An Analysis of the Evolution of the Television Doctor-Hero', *Journal of Medical Humanities*, 32, 31–46.

Turda, Marius (2014) 'The Ambiguous Victim: Miklós Nyiszli's Narrative of Medical Experimentation in Auschwitz', *Historein*, 14, 1, 43–58.

Turow, Joseph and Rachel Gans-Boriskin (2007) 'From Expert in Action to Existential Angst: A Half Century of Television Doctors', in Leslie J. Reagan, Nancy Tomes and Paula A. Treichler (eds) *Medicine's Moving Pictures: Medicine, Health, and Bodies in American Film and Television*. Rochester, NY: University of Rochester Press, 263–81.

Ward, Janet (2004) 'Holocaust Film in the Post-9/11 Era: New Directions in Staging and Emplotment', *Pacific Coast Philology*, 39, 29–41.

CHAPTER TEN

On the Cinematic Nazi

Aaron Kerner

The Nazi monster – is there anything more tawdry? Stone cold killers, characters evil to the core, sexual deviants, deranged scientists with maniacal schemes, the Nazi has been figured in all these fetishistic guises, but what about the Nazi with whom we might identify? And not simply the Nazi who might possess a certain charisma, or smarmy charm such as we find with the Hans Landa character in Quentin Tarantino's *Inglourious Basterds* (2009), or the buffoon Colonel Klink in *Hogan's Heroes*. Seductively malevolent, or clown, these figures are equally as hollow. The Nazi monster is too easy (see Friedlander 1993: 101). Not only is the Nazi monster tawdry, the conventional character-type is deeply dangerous. It is dangerous precisely because it is too easy to dispense with – neutralising history, and foreclosing any possibility for the contemporary spectator to consider the possible affinities with the Nazi character.

Both dramatic and documentary film has received significant critical and scholarly attention, particularly with respect to how to represent the victims of the Holocaust; the ethical quandary of potentially 're-victimising' Holocaust victims through representations, the ethics governing how the gas chambers are to be represented, whether Jewish characters are represented as passive victims, or are seen actively resisting. While there has been quite a lot said about the ethics of representing victims,[1] the same degree of scrutiny has not been applied to the cinematic representation of perpetrators (or for that matter bystanders, or collaborators).[2] In cinema typically the Nazi, the SS-men in the camps, the characters on the 'wrong side', so to speak, are simply presented as evil and so there is nothing left to be said about them, from the historical figure of Amon Goeth in

Spielberg's *Schindler's List* (1993), through Nazi zombies in Tommy Wirkola's *Dead Snow* [*Død snø*] (2009). If motivations are assigned to these characters they are deranged, 'sick' – usually manifesting in some sort of sexual aberration (see Barta 1998: 137–8; Foucault 2000: 165). The issue is *not* whether there are films that host 'good' perpetrators at heart (perhaps Oskar Schindler in *Schindler's List*?), but rather, as a matter of dramaturgy, whether there are films that feature complex perpetrators with whom we may identify. And this is not to say that we agree with a character's actions or moral choices. There are very few films that even attempt to position identification with a Nazi character. Alain Resnais' poetic documentary *Night and Fog* [*Nuit et brouillard*] (1955), which has been criticised for universalising the victim (see Michael 1984), also entertains the idea that perpetrators are no different from us – universalising the perpetrators. More recently, Vicente Armorim's dramatic narrative *Good* (2008) similarly features a 'perpetrator-protagonist' (McGlothlin 2009: 214) who is quite ordinary. The point is not to present how *different* these characters are from us, but how *uncomfortably close* they might be.

Although governed by different conventions and disciplinary principles, historical discourse, just like film or literature, is a constructed narrative; so it comes as no surprise that historical narratives also tend to elide human-depth from characters on the 'wrong side' of history. For instance, Hannah Arendt's Eichmann is no monster, but he is flat as a character – and here I am speaking less to the historical figure, and more to the character that she fashions for us in her reports collected in *Eichmann in Jerusalem*. Arendt paints the portrait of a man either unable or incapable of seeing his own contradictions; a liar, endowed with an incredibly selective memory, a man with a penchant for self-pity in one instance, and unabashed self-aggrandising in the next. Even despite the most strident efforts of the prosecution, Arendt reports, 'everybody could see that this man was not a "monster", but it was difficult indeed not to suspect that he was a clown' (1994: 54).

It is possible to read her volume as a documentary, or historical drama, detailing the atmosphere and the character dynamics in the Jerusalem courtroom, while 'cutting away' to the historical record to offer ample insights into internal SS political struggles and other matters that pertain to the deeply contradictory central character: Eichmann. In the end we are never made to identify with Eichmann, though, and this (in narrative terms) does not appear to be Arendt's intention. We never see the world through his eyes, nor does his character undergo any transformation, or arrive at any epiphany. This is not meant to disparage Arendt, or her text, but rather to call attention to the fact that the *form* of her narrative all but precludes identification with the central character. The narrative devices that conventionally elicit identification – first-person perspective, character transformation – are absent from Arendt's text.

The lack of identification has less to do with Arendt than it does with the form, as Friedlander observes, 'The historian cannot work in any other way [i.e., employing the clinical gaze], and historical studies have to be pursued along the accepted lines' (1993: 92). If there is to be any appreciation that the Nazi-disposition is not wholly alien to us, then, in all likelihood we *need* Nazis with whom we can identify. Arendt's Eichmann does not serve this function. What is at stake here, at the end of the day, is how the Holocaust is narrativised, and ultimately, remembered. And this invites, as Brett Ashley Kaplan suggests in a similar context, a 'pedagogical question' regarding Holocaust memories, namely which strategies are going to 'enliven Holocaust memory' (2007: 148). Let us then begin our search for a Nazi with whom the spectator might identify.

THE TAWDRY PARADIGM

> Nazism has become one of the supreme metaphors, that of Evil.
> – Saul Friedlander (1993: 119)

Juraj Herz's film *The Cremator* [*Spalovač mrtvol*] (1969) features a primary character who runs, as the title infers, a funeral home in Czechoslovakia. On the surface of things Kopfrkingl is ordinary, if a bit odd. A family man, he keeps a modest home and supports his wife and children. Uninterested in politics, at least to begin with, he is indifferent to the fact that his doctor, some of his co-workers and his son's friend are Jewish. The stakes, though, are raised all the more when we discover that his wife is half-Jewish, making his son and daughter quarter-Jewish (a racialised conception of Jewish identity promoted by Nazi ideology). It seems that Kopfrkingl has given none of this a second thought until he is propositioned to join the Nazi Party, and a Party recruiter points out these facts. Dramaturgically we witness Kopfrkingl's character change over the course of the film as he becomes 'enlightened' by Nazi ideology – but in the end he is not really a 'believer' in the ideology, rather he enjoys reaping the benefits by contributing to the cause.

Kopfrkingl conforms to the tawdry Nazi character-type that populates cinematic narratives. At the heart Kopfrkingl is corrupt, a bald-faced liar. In the social arena he exhibits no vice, he characterises himself as an abstainer, refusing drink and tobacco (perhaps finding affinities with Hitler?). But while Kopfrkingl refuses these vices, he routinely visits a brothel. The turning point for Kopfrkingl's character does not rest upon the inculcation of ideological rhetoric, but rather his carnal desire for women. His Nazi minder finally 'convinces' Kopfrkingl to join the cause with an invitation to an exclusive club that features only fit young blonde women. The invitation to this club is, of course, predicated on the submission of his application to the Party. Along with the application Kopfrkingl's minder slips a stack of erotic photographs of the Aryan women that await him. At the club all manner of debauchery unfolds, and set in relation to this orgiastic backdrop, Kopfrkingl undergoes a dramatic change as a character and wilfully allows himself to be seduced into the Nazi programme.

Fig. 1 Kopfrkingl and his Nazi handler at an exclusive club

To assuage guilt the perpetrators might reposition themselves as the victims, knowingly transgressing the taboo against murder, sacrificing their moral-selves, for a 'higher' purpose (see Friedlander 1993: 102–5; Agamben 2002: 23; Bialas 2013: 9). Kopfrkingl adopts this perverse logic when dealing with the 'Jewish problem' within the ranks of his own family. Kopfrkingl, apparently without much pause, and in an effort to climb the social-ladder, kills his wife and children. He stages his wife's death as a suicide by hanging her in the bathroom, and he bludgeons his children to death and places their bodies in coffins waiting to be burned. Killing his own family is the cross that he must bear for the advancement of his own career and the Party's objectives.

It is not the character's transformation from ordinary Czechoslovak citizen to Nazi Party member as such that makes the character tawdry, but rather that the film is loaded with cheap tropes that effectively explain the character's change. From the start the character is a bit 'off', captivated, for instance, by a carnival freak show. And while Kopfrkingl's morbid curiosity initially is read as a particular character quirk, morbid curiosity returns later as evidence of his mental instability, suggesting that the seeds of Nazism are found in mental 'sickness'. Kopfrkingl's fascination with the macabre is also coupled with signifiers of debauchery, particularly drunkenness and lascivious behaviour. The overwrought bacchanal character of the Aryan brothel similarly implies that Nazism is associated with sexual deviance. Kopfrkingl is, in this respect, far from normal; he is mentally unhinged and a pervert, and therefore the cinematic tropes 'explain' his embrace of Nazism.

AN ORDINARY NAZI AND HIS LADY MACBETH

Set in Berlin at the dawning of the Nazi era, Vicente Amorim's *Good* is the story of an accidental Nazi. The primary character, Professor John Halder, writes a novel about a doting husband who euthanises his terminally ill wife. As much as we know about the fictional work, John apparently couches the narrative as an expression of genuine love, insinuating that the husband's deed, though heart-wrenching and undeniably tragic, is in the end the ultimate act of humanity and compassion. John's novel catches the attention of the Nazi hierarchy, and they commission the modest academic to write a non-fiction academic paper on euthanasia. He demonstrates no strong political inclinations, and even a degree of distaste for Nazism – he assumes, like many others, that the regime will not last – but in the end he accepts the commission with some reservations.

The narrative is clearly John's, and we do identify with him. His choices are morally reprehensible, but one might appreciate the trajectory of the character. The dramaturgical chain of cause and effect begins with John accepting the commission, and this choice unleashes (unintended) consequences: he is compelled to join the Party; in his position he forges relationships with Nazi officials; he serves as an honorary member of the SS; and as a representative of the SS he tours asylums for the mentally ill (which will become a blueprint for the genocidal programme). He has to justify his choices (with visible unease) to his analyst and friend, Maurice – both men served together in World War I, and it just so happens that Maurice is Jewish. His chronically ill and senile mother attempts suicide (overdosing on pills), but despite his romantic vision of compassionate killing as detailed in his fictional novel and his academic paper, he intervenes and saves her life. When she finally dies of natural causes he wonders whether he merely prolonged her suffering. With small incremental steps we witness a man faced with certain choices (regarding his career, his family and his emotional investments), which in and of themselves might not amount to much, but collectively they inch him further into the Nazi morass. John is not affable so much as he is pathetic, but nonetheless this is perhaps one of the most 'identifiable' Nazi characters that I am aware of;[3] and the fact that the spectator is compelled to identify with him – through narrative conventions and cinematic syntax (subjective shots) – might also account for the film's incredibly limited distribution and its poor critical reception.[4]

Indicative of this poor critical response is Stephen Holden's *New York Times* review, which lambasts *Good*, claiming that John is a 'moral vacuum' (2008), naïve or stupid, and blind to the impending Holocaust. What Holden fails to acknowledge is that tragedies are largely orchestrated through a character's poor choices, and that is precisely what *Good* is: a tragedy. John is not a (morally) *good* character; he is a tragic one. In tragedies, as in melodrama, characters tend to arrive at a revelation too late (see Neale 1986: 8; Moretti 1988: 162; Burian 1999: 181–2). Oskar Schindler in *Schindler's List*, for instance, realises in overwrought gestures that he could have saved more people if he had not so thoughtlessly squandered his wealth, but makes this revelation only after it is too late. With John, revelations also come too late. Tragic dramas are populated with either naïve or half-witted characters – Hamlet, Othello, Macbeth, Oedipus. Holden, too, is clearly framing his critique through the privileged lens of a historically aware spectator. Cloaked behind Holden's vociferous moral indignation is a near hysterical refusal to identify with the abject other. And this speaks to a wider problem in locating a Nazi character with whom the spectator can identify, because cinematic identification usually invites the spectator to associate with, or in a sense inhabit, the perpetrator-protagonist. And inhabiting the perpetrator-protagonist position threatens the integrity of the clean and proper subject, communing with the abject figure of the Nazi (see Friedlander 1993: 11–12). John's character complicates the standard positioning of good/bad paradigms;

he is by no means good, he is deeply flawed and has 'sold his soul to the Devil', so to speak; but we cannot easily dismiss him as clearly evil either.

Good counters the prevailing conventions of the Holocaust genre breaking free from the stale cinematic tradition that privileges the dangerous fantasy of a Manichean order. Where *Good* falls short, though, is in its unfortunate application of tawdry tropes. Anne, the sultry Aryan Siren, seduces John. She is a bright-eyed student at John's university, and the amorous relationship that develops between the professor and student prompts John to divorce his wife, Helen, eventually leaving her and their two children. John subsequently marries Anne. Rather than establishing a love triangle between Helen, John and Anne, *Good* sets up a triangulated relationship between Maurice, John and Anne.

Fig. 2 The triangulated relationship between Maurice, John and Anne

If any character is monstrous it is the cookie-cutter 'house-wrecker' Anne. She is a quiet Lady Macbeth; she never explicitly pushes John in his career, but she makes implicit gestures and off-screen dealings that manifest in John's ascension. She is the sexual aggressor. She pursues John, attentively sitting at the centre of his class, visiting him in his university office, arriving at his home late one rainy evening soaking wet. The gender dynamics already suggests (within the conventional patriarchal paradigm) the monstrous. Interestingly, the first sexual encounter between the adulterous couple is never consummated – John falls impotent. However, after he is propositioned by the regime to write a paper, his sexual fortunes change. During a conversation between Maurice and John, confiding with his analyst friend about the adulterous sexual affair, Maurice comments, 'I didn't think you had it in you.' The tawdry cinematic trope of coupling Nazism with sexuality is located here, because it is Nazism that fuels John's newfound sexual fortitude.

The Lady Macbeth motif is also filtered through the lens of sex. When John is suddenly commanded to report to duty late one evening he begins to put on his SS uniform. He hesitates and second-guesses his choices up to that point. Anne encourages her husband saying, 'Look at yourself.' As she coaxes John to inspect himself dressed in his SS uniform in the mirror she is on her knees as she finishes buttoning his jacket and appears to fellate the conflicted character. Interestingly, the paper that John is commissioned to write is conceived in the adulterous bed. John, revitalised, light in step, cheerfully drafts his paper in his bachelor-pad, while Anne, in some state of undress, seductively swoons from the bed at the centre of the room. The characters in *Good* are not on par with the highly embellished paedophilic cross-dressing Martin von Essenbeck that we find in Luchino Visconti's *The Damned* [*La caduta degli dei*] (1969). The Essenbecks are an industrialist family, and the SS forge a Faustian bargain with Martin, who, by way of incest and murder claims the familial throne. *Good* is hardly as blatant as *The Damned*. Nonetheless the adulterous origin of John's relationship with Anne – further tinged with her dubious cunning, fellating John at the height of Nazi violence – associates Nazism with sexual deviance. The tawdry character tropes associated with the cinematic Nazi are pervasive, but is there an alternative?

ALL IN THE FAMILY

While the cinema appears devoid of nuanced perpetrator-protagonists, other mediums have been willing to explore the possibilities of rendering this position. To my mind the artist Christian Boltanski has dealt with the Nazi in the most productive manner. In his series *Sans Souci* (1991) – published as a 'family album', many of the images from the series also being used in exhibitions such as *Menschlich* (1996) – the French artist amasses a collection of found photographs that feature Nazis (or some Nazi signifier). However, the images counter the tawdry character-type. In Boltanski's series we find Nazis on dates, clowning-it-up for the camera, German soldiers with their families posing for snap-shots, perfectly ordinary-looking women posed in the family parlour but with a mounted photograph of Hitler in the background. The first plate is a large group photo, perhaps a family reunion, set in front of the palace of Frederick the Great – Sans Souci. The title of Boltanski's series undoubtedly derives from this first plate. Furthermore in the context of Boltanski's collection of photographs the title, which means 'without sorrows', has a rather ironic meaning.[5]

It is not simply the collection of images that counter the historically constructed tawdry Nazi monster, but the manner in which Boltanski presents the series. In the exhibition mode – in vitrines, as photographic albums, organised and catalogued as if at an archive, as Ernst van Alphen (1999) observes – these images strike us as familiar. And more accurately, it is not simply the content of the images that make them familiar, but rather the form in which they are presented. It is Boltanski's representational mode that renders the content 'legible', but smuggling Nazism into the familiar, into normality, prompts an encounter with the uncanny. In its more 'official' mode, Boltanski's work might replicate the discourses of the natural history museum – the exhibition of anthropological artifacts, presented in glass cases in orderly fashion. In Boltanski's more 'private' mode, though no less orderly, he assembles images so that they resemble a family photo album.[6] In the first instance, we witness the disciplinary regimes that feed public historical narratives; in the latter we locate the fodder for family lore – private histories. In either case, but most especially when appropriating the methods of the sober social sciences, Boltanski calls attention to the construction of historical knowledge, and our inheritance of particular imaginaries, including the tawdry Nazi monster. In an installation setting, as well as in the published version of *Sans Souci*, Boltanski reconstructs and calls attention to the 'constructed-ness' of histories, and he implicitly acknowledges the omissions inherent to any emplotment of historical narratives.

Like history, which is erroneously presumed to be a transparent window onto the past, (portraiture) photography is not denotatively neutral. Van Alphen takes issue with German philosopher Hans-Georg Gadamer's conception of portraiture, which the philosopher views as an 'intensified' version of the subject, an 'increase of being' (1999: 35). Van Alphen observes that Gadamer 'presumes *a unity* between signifier and signified, between increase in being and the essential qualities of the sitter' (1999: 36). Boltanski, though, unsettles our preconceived understanding of an image, demonstrating the historical and cultural contingency of (visual) signifiers. The affable Nazi – doting fathers, the eroticism of exuberant youth posing with their dates – does not correspond to the historically constructed image of the monstrous Nazi: 'The intriguing and disturbing effect of *Sans Souci* is caused by the fact that traditional meanings of the family photo album overrule the subjectivities that we expect to be represented *in* the snapshots' (1999: 43). In this guise the Nazi is more 'recognisable', more akin to our own personal experiences, more like us. This is not van Alphen's argument though; rather he argues that Boltanski's images are horribly relative. In the realm of visual signifiers and their presumed corresponding signifiers nothing is certain, there is no inherent unity between them, but instead they are frighteningly slippery.

I view it somewhat differently, as does Boltanski himself, who speaks about these images in the British TV arts programme, *The South Bank Show* (1994): 'What I wanted to say with this piece is that the Nazis were not different from us. They were us, because – it would be much more easy to think that they were only devils. [...] And it is possible for a man to love his own baby in the morning time, and to kill babies in the afternoon.' Boltanski continues to comment on how normal, sweet and loveable the figures are, and yet the implications of Nazi paraphernalia and regalia run counter to what we conceive as normal: 'What frightened me is that I think a little part of us can become a Nazi tomorrow.' Van Alphen wants to preserve the sanctimonious space of 'normality', which insists upon on a Manichean order: that there *are* bad people who are characteristically different from the rest of us (good people). Clearly, Boltanski has no intention of preserving the sanctity of normality. Boltanski's *Sans Souci* destroys the Manichean worldview that van Alphen strives to preserve. Where we might agree, though, is that Boltanski enacts the 'cultural codes' that make the images legible, even *despite* their content, in the familial gaze. We recognise or, in more familiar cinematic terms, 'identify' with the characters in the *Sans Souci* series, regardless of who they might be, because of Boltanski's mode of address, which activates 'the cultural codes of the family album' (van Alphen 1999: 48).

It is worth taking a moment to consider the tactile qualities of the *Sans Souci* catalogue. It is slim, measuring approximately 8.5 inches by 11. The cover is a hard cardboard stock, its surface grayish tan, its outer edge running along the spine of the volume appears faded as if sun-bleached over the course of many years of exposure to sunlight. The reprinted photographs are set on the page as if they are mounted in a family photo album. In between the pages a thin piece of translucent velum 'protects' the 'photographs'. The thin sheet of velum is embossed with a spider-web design; the connotations of the motif suggest any number of things – age, family relations (akin to the webbed branches of a family tree), carnival haunted house and, finally, death (black widow). Holding the catalogue in your hands, there is a slight fuzziness to the cardboard stock, offering a haptic signifier of age. Everything in Boltanski's design is intended to encourage us to read the images in a very specific way that counters our 'natural' inclinations. He places Nazis within the recognisable contours of a familial narrative. It might be interesting to think of Chanoch Zeevi's documentary *Hitler's Children* (2011) in these terms – to view it through the Boltanski-lens. Zeevi's documentary features a handful of descendants of the Nazi regime: Bettina Göring, Katrin Himmler, Monika Göth and Rainer Höß. Many of these individuals negotiate their heritage through family (or archival) photographs. As a spectator we might be predisposed to hate these characters, but what we find are affable individuals espousing progressive values.

PÉTER FORGÁCS: CINEMA'S BOLTANSKI

Hungarian experimental filmmaker Péter Forgács shares affinities with Boltanski's work. Although highly stylised, Forgács's work enacts the familiar cultural codes of the home-movie and the documentary. He collects home-movies, personal photographs and artifacts, and he assembles them into beautifully lush films – 'documentaries' exhumed from family chests, or attics. His 'Private Hungary', a twelve-film series (1988–1997), reworks amateur film and home-movies from the era prior, during and following World War II. As many of Forgács's films, his 'Private Hungary' series treats the material (raw home-movies) in a personal diaristic mode, which offers 'readers and viewers not indisputable facts, but instead a specifically configured relationship to time and history' (Fisher 2008: 241). Boltanski and Forgács share this more private, or personal approach to historical memory.

The Diary of Mr. N (1990), part of the 'Private Hungary' series, is interesting because the protagonists of the film, Mr. N's family, are ostensibly on the 'wrong side'. Although the family's politics are never disclosed, Mr. N and Ilona, his wife, work at the Hungarian Merkuc munitions factory that will eventually supply the German war effort. Prior to and during the war (and presumably even after the war) Ilona worked at Merkuc as a secretary, while Mr. N was employed as an engineer, and one has to assume that he was involved in the production and design of munitions. Mr. N actually documents one of the state-sponsored visits by German officials that come to inspect the facility to identify its production capacity. Together the couple has eight children, four boys and four girls. Whatever their politics might have been, the protagonists come across as likable. They are doting parents, in their younger years charmingly playful, and lovers of the outdoors (we see the couple on a number of rural excursions). Ordinary in just about every respect, this Gentile family is just getting on with life as history swirls all around them.

The film encourages the spectator to identify with the protagonists of the film, Mr. N and Ilona. We see the couple in the spring of their relationship (late 1930s) – playfully courting one another. During the summer months we see the couple frolicking in their swimming attire, in the wintery months strolling through the city. They play peek-a-boo with the camera, or ham-it-up – walking through the snow, in one instance, Ilona right before passing out of frame sticks her tongue out at the camera (and whoever is holding the camera, presumably Mr. N). The film ends in the autumn of their relationship (late 1960s). Mr. N and Ilona show signs of age, but still exhibit geniality lounging in the sun, enjoying the outdoors. Our identification with the Ns comes as little surprise given that the source footage for the film is shot from their perspective, the N family's home-movies. There are nevertheless details in *The Diary of Mr. N* that remind us of the impending doom awaiting the Ns' fellow citizens. On one of the couple's excursions to Kárpátalján, in the summer of 1939, Mr. N documents orthodox Jews living in a small town, the Hungarian-Polish border just weeks before the Germans and Soviets invade, the exterior of a Ukrainian concentration camp (or so it is called in the film) and a graveyard for the victims of World War I. All of these referents are invested with an uncanny charge, given what we know is about to happen and has already happened. On more than one occasion Forgács uses stormy weather in *The Diary of Mr. N* to signify the blowing winds of history that are going to shape Hungary's course during the second half of the twentieth century.

Fig. 3 Mr. N enjoying summer activities

Like Boltanski, Forgács in his appropriation of home-movies elicits a familiar homely narrative. And it is not just the content that elicits the familiar, but the texture of 8mm film – its scratchy wear (the patina of age), its sudden jerks, its framing. It is this texture and the form of the film that lend it the hallmarks of 'hominess'. Of course, content matters, and the plot points of normative heterosexual coupling, which generally governs cinematic narratives – such as marriage, the birth of children, family outings – stand as signposts of a familiar domestic narrative. The home-movie, like the family photo album, situates our characters in an immediately recognisable constellation, and perhaps by virtue of form alone we are already inclined to identify with them, regardless of what their politics might have been, or what role they might have played during World War

II. And, in fact, the family's politics is never addressed in the film. Would we identify less with the N family if their politics were disclosed? My suspicion is that even if the N family subscribed to fascist politics, dramaturgically – that is, simply in storytelling terms – we might be willing to identify with them based on the form of the narrative that places our characters into a customary familial plot.

CONCLUSION: COMING UP SHORT

The imagining of Nazis as monstrous, as Wolfgang Bialas observes, 'creates a radical difference between them and us. The ethical dualism of good and evil assumes that decent, good people have nothing in common with such monsters. Taking a different approach while considering them ordinary people not fundamentally different from us, is much more threatening to our own identity' (2013: 12). And given this threat, I am not in the least bit optimistic that a Nazi with whom we can identify will ever be found on the screen. To reiterate here, I am in no way suggesting that we identify with Nazi politics, or even unwittingly condone Nazism when we identify with a cinematic perpetrator-protagonist. Identification with a cinematic character does *not* inherently amount to a forfeiture of our own moral values. Rather, what I am arguing for is a paradigm shift in dramaturgy, where we very well might be disgusted by a character's ideological views, but with whom as a cinematic character we can identify. Is it possible to situate a Nazi character within standard narrative conventions and cinematic syntax that invites spectator identification, without filtering that character through tawdry tropes? If such a character were to materialise, I suspect that film critics in a knee-jerk chorus will harangue the film and its coercing of our identification; scholars will dismiss the Nazi character as sadistic (or locate some other unconsidered pejorative).[7] The rabid insistence upon clearly evil Nazi characters lulls the spectator into a narcissistic stupor, reassured that the West defeated and purged the fascist taint, that good ultimately vanquished evil. Similarly, Jean Baudrillard, in his response to the 9/11 terrorist attack, 'The Spirit of Terrorism', observes that Western philosophy operates according to a complete misunderstanding, 'on the part of the Enlightenment, or the relation between Good and Evil. [...] We believe naively that the progress of Good, its advance in all fields (the sciences, technology, democracy, human rights), corresponds to a defeat of Evil. No one seems to have understood that Good and Evil advance together, as part of the same movement. The triumph of the one does not eclipse the other – far from it' (2003: 13). Locating an identifiable Nazi is important precisely because it bears the potential to confront this co-presence of good and evil: to see ourselves in the Nazi.[8]

For the most part, the implicit rhetoric of films that host Nazi characters, or engage with the Holocaust, is the sentiment 'never again', or 'never forget' (refrains often heard in the American, German and Israeli context). Although well-intended, such mantras ring painfully hollow because when woefully inadequate efforts have been made in negotiating the motivations of the perpetrator – particularly in the realm of cinematic representations – one is left to wonder just exactly how these ambitions might be met. I am inclined to agree with Susan Sontag, who, reflecting on the Abu Ghraib photographs, posited, 'Perhaps too much value is assigned to memory, not enough to thinking' (2003: 115). There is too much 'evidence of what humans are capable of inflicting' upon one another, Sontag observes, and in the face of the evidence no ethical human being can cling to a thoughtless 'innocence' or 'amnesia' (2003: 114). It would behoove us, in this case, to do more thinking on how we represent Nazis. The resistance to entertaining the possibility of representing an identifiable Nazi is perfectly understandable; the idea of it is stomach-turning, abject. But this is not a reason for us – scholars, critics and filmmakers – to throw-up our hands in defeat.[9]

In the end, though, my endeavour here to locate a Nazi character with whom we might identify has come up short. The Nazi might simply be too cathetic, too much of a lightning rod. Rather than searching for a Nazi character, then, what we might do instead is survey the cinematic landscape for perpetrator-protagonists. In other words, it might be productive to locate characters in a wholly different setting that are dramaturgically on the 'wrong side' and yet invite our identification. Perhaps we might consider a documentary like *The Kill Team* (Dan Krauss, 2013), which features a likeable American protagonist caught-up within a group of American soldiers who killed innocent Afghans for sport. Perpetrator-protagonists are present in contemporary (American) horror. In the *Saw* franchise, for instance, we identify not so much with the perpetrator, Jigsaw, but rather we identify with the system that he enacts (see Kerner 2015). Dexter Morgan in the Showtime series *Dexter* might be another example. Walter White in AMC's television series *Breaking Bad* is perhaps the most striking example. The spectator is fully invested in White's character despite the fact that he sets aside his ethical obligations to manufacture methamphetamine at an industrial scale. He is abject – he is a liar, a manipulator and a murderer – and yet we are still invited to identify with his character. Signifiers of Nazi Germany are actually peppered throughout the series: White takes the alias 'Heisenberg',

Fig. 4 White cuts a deal with the Aryan Brotherhood to conduct a coordinated hit.

is referred to as 'Adolf' (season 3, episode 10) and he contracts with members of the Aryan Brotherhood to conduct a coordinated hit of witnesses being held in three different prisons across the South West (season 5, episode 8), echoing the Night of the Long Knives. Himmler was well aware that the Final Solution levied a heavy toll upon the men and women enrolled in the genocidal programme, but he understood that they were making a 'moral sacrifice' for the German nation. White too sacrifices himself morally for the 'better good' of his family.

In Holocaust research, the incessant demand for 'authenticity' and the debates over the poetic or allegorical mode have retarded our thinking in this area. Other genres, in fact, because of their 'detachment' from history, might be better equipped to negotiate the possibilities of an identifiable perpetrator. The science fiction series *Battlestar Galactica*, for instance, features some interesting examples in constructing perpetrator-protagonists. The central characters, with whom we clearly identify, contemplate genocide ('A Measure of Salvation', Season 3), routinely torture, and turn a blind-eye to a campaign to eradicate 'less desirable' people (clearly coded as Jewish) ('The Woman King', Season 3). There is indeed much more work to be done in locating perpetrator-protagonists, within and beyond the context of Holocaust cinema.

Michael Haneke's work might serve as a possible example of how to approach Holocaust violence obliquely. Haneke's films typically negotiate the uncanny spectre of violence that haunts (Western) culture. In an interview speaking about his film *Caché* (2005) (on the DVD extra), Haneke says that the film is about guilt, 'how one lives with guilt'. Although the film deals with the post-colonial experience in France he insists that this theme could be situated in any country, or time, because as he says, 'In any country, one can find a secret hidden by the "common sense" of that country.' In the context of Holocaust films, the 'common sense' positioning of characters – Nazis are quintessentially evil – belies the possibility that unspeakable violence very well might lurk within us. The primary male character in *Caché*, Georges, for instance, abdicates his responsibility for colonial violence: 'I was only six, how am I supposed to remember?' Max Silverman argues that this denial of guilt, as expressed by Georges, consciously or not allows Haneke to incorporate the 'iconography of the Holocaust to invade a narrative ostensibly about colonial and postcolonial relations between France and Algeria. The abduction of children, disappearance, and denials of guilt have become central elements in our cultural vocabulary of racialized violence and trauma and oblige us, even unconsciously, to view one event (colonialism) in the light of another (the Holocaust)' (2008: 427, n.29).[10]

Haneke does not speak *about* the Holocaust; he speaks *next to* it, to borrow a phrase from Trinh T. Minh-ha (1992: 96). In his discussion with Anthony Lane, Haneke does not want to situate *The White Ribbon* [*Das weiße Band: Eine deutsche Kindergeschichte*] (2009) as a Nazi film *per se*: 'I will not be happy if the film is seen as a film about a German problem, about the Nazi time.' Rather, he says, 'It's a film about the roots of evil' (2009: 66). Haneke embraces, rather than runs from the darker side of the human psyche, saying that, 'There is no crime I couldn't have committed. [...] It is so easy to say, "Oh no, I would never do that", but that's dishonest. We are capable of everything' (ibid.). As Lane correctly observes, Haneke does not want *The White Ribbon*, 'or any of his other works, to be construed as a parable of Nazism. Nonetheless, it seems fair to say that without so drastic a template of savagery and amnesia his films would not be as ruthless as they are' (2009: 67).

The fear, of course, is that if we – scholars, critics and the viewing public – make allowances for an identifiable Nazi, or perpetrator-protagonist, this might in some fashion 'humanise' or in some sense 'justify' a reprehensible history. Or that 'humanising' characters on the 'wrong side' of history will threaten the integrity of our Manichean fantasy. It seems that we have yet to heed Arendt's frightening lesson: 'The trouble with Eichmann was precisely that so many were like him, and that the many were neither perverted nor sadistic, that they were, and still are, terribly and terrifyingly normal' (1994: 276). The cinema has very few of these 'terrifyingly normal' characters. Because if 'never again' *really* is the objective, then we are ethically obligated to construct, or as critics and scholars to engage with, narratives that would allow us to identify with 'terrifyingly normal' characters.

Notes

1 In addition to Judith Doneson's work regarding character tropes in Holocaust films (1978, 1997), there is a long list of significant research dealing with the question of how to represent the Holocaust (or Holocaust victims); to name just three examples: Dominick LaCapra's monograph *Representing the Holocaust* (1994); the cataloguing of a lively debate on the representation of the Holocaust in Saul Friedlander's collection *Probing the Limits of Representation* (1992); and Stuart Liebman's edited volume *Claude Lanzmann's Shoah: Key Essays* (1997).
2 Erin McGlothlin deals with this subject in literature, noting that, 'the perspective of the perpetrators [i.e., Nazis] – in particular, the *narrative* perspective of the perpetrators, meaning their subjectivity, motivations, thoughts, and desires – has been all but ignored' (2009: 213).
3 This pathetic sensibility might also be ascribed to Arendt's Eichmann; she concludes in her postscript that Eichmann 'was not stupid. It was sheer thoughtlessness – something by no means identical with stupidity – that predisposed him to become one of the greatest criminals of that period. And if this is "banal" and even funny, if with the best will in the world one cannot extract any diabolical or demonic profundity from Eichmann, that is still far from calling it commonplace' (1994: 287–8).
4 According to IMDb.com *Good* was made for an estimated $15 million and did not even break $10,000 on its American opening. In total it apparently only made $23,000 in the US. By any measure this is a certifiable financial disaster.
5 Some might argue that the de-contextualisation of Nazi (or Holocaust) images runs the risk of abstracting and obliterating historical reality. I do not subscribe to this position. Brett Ashley Kaplan makes a similar observation regarding Lee Miller's photographs (2011: 84). Also see her chapter 'Collier Schorr: Reenacting Nazis', in the same volume (2011: 122–37). Kaplan discusses the photographer Collier Schorr and her faux tableaux of Nazis in beautiful forest settings, and these images speak to 'a repressed portion of history. [...] We are surrounded by images of Nazis whether in films, newspapers, porn, high art, low art, everywhere'; she concludes that Schorr's recontextualisation of Nazis 'encourages us to meditate on how the landscape of Holocaust

postmemory morphs' (2011: 136, 137).

6   In her landmark book *Family Frames* Marianne Hirsch finds Boltanski's tactic suspicious. Hirsch addresses *Menschlich* (*Human*), an exhibition and catalogue that similar to *Sans Souci* includes images of Nazis, but in this case also included 'images of victims ... Jews and Nazis, French and Swiss, children and adults, guilty and innocent, all together, undifferentiated, represented singly and in groups'. Hirsch views *Menschlich* as a parody of the universal approach to the human experience in Edward Steichen's *The Family of Man*, but in the end she asserts that, 'In Boltanski's representation, the human family is a trap'. Hirsch finds universalising perilous and argues that Boltanski 'duplicates the very universalization he critiques. [...] In their free-floating invocation of the notion of 'Menschlich' – even in its inverted form effected by the grainy prints – they still fall into the seductive snare of the familial look. As viewers peruse the faces, they will find, willy-nilly and perhaps against their better judgment, some areas of commonality, of affiliation and projection. And they will not find any tools of discrimination or differentiation' (1997: 70, 71).

7   Oliver Hirschbiegel's *Der Untergang* [*Downfall*] (2004) sparked a storm of controversy in German critical circles for humanising Hitler. Amongst American critics it favoured somewhat better, but predictably some lambasted it. David Denby in his review, 'Back in the Bunker', for the *New Yorker* magazine, notes with frustration that the cinema has visited Hitler's bunker many times before. 'Why is Hitler so often shown at the end, rather than at an earlier, victorious moment? Obviously, his defeat is an emotional release: every decade or so, as in some primitive ritual, the dictator has to be hauled out of the grave, propped up, and slain again, just to make sure he's dead. It's an understandable impulse, but what new insights into Hitler are gained during this purgation of fear?' (2005). This actually speaks to my present thesis — that the cinematic Nazi is nothing more than a narcissistic foil — and rehearses the tired and erroneous theme that Good triumphs Evil. Regarding the haranguing chorus of film critics, see for instance, the reviews of *Good* collected on the Rotten Tomatoes website <http://www.rottentomatoes.com>.

8   We might find affinities with Julia Kristeva's discussion of the foreigner, where a confrontation with the other might elicit the uncanny (1991: 183). Also see Christopher Browning's chilling account of ordinary men that turn murderous; he ends his book noting that, 'If the men of Reserve Police Battalion 101 could become murderers ... what group of men cannot?' (2001: 189).

9   Matthew Boswell's *Holocaust Impiety* echoes many of the issues that I have raised here regarding an identifiable perpetrator (2012: 15–18). Late in the drafting of this essay some other research has come to my attention: Jenni Adams and Sue Vice's co-edited volume *Representing Perpetrators in Holocaust Literature and Film* (2013); and Gillian Rose's chapter 'Beginnings of the Day: Fascism and Representation' (1996).

10 In *Multidirectional Memory*, Michael Rothberg also makes connections between the postcolonial themes in Haneke's work (specifically in *Caché*) and the Holocaust (2009: 289).

Filmography

Breaking Bad. TV series. USA, 2008-2013.
Caché. Dir. Michael Haneke. France/Austria/Germany/Italy/USA, 2005.

The Cremator [*Spalovač mrtvol*]. Dir. Juraj Herz. Czechoslovakia, 1969.
The Damned [*La caduta degli dei*]. Dir. Luchino Visconti. Italy/West Germany, 1969.
Dead Snow [*Død snø*]. Dir. Tommy Wirkola. Norway, 2009.
Dexter. TV series. USA, 2006-2013.
The Diary of Mr. N. Dir. Péter Forgács. Hungary, 1990.
Good. Dir. Vicente Armorim. UK/Germany, 2008.
Hitler's Children. Dir. Chanoch Zeevi. Israel/Germany, 2011.
Hogan's Heroes. TV series. USA, 1965–1971.
Inglourious Basterds. Dir. Quentin Tarantino. USA, 2007.
The Kill Team. Dir. Dan Krauss. USA, 2013.
'A Measure of Salvation.' *Battlestar Galactica*, Season 3. Dir. Bill Eagles. USA, 2006.
Mephisto. Dir. István Szabó. Germany, 1981.
Night and Fog [*Nuit et brouillard*]. Dir. Alain Resnais. France, 1955.
Raiders of the Lost Ark. Dir. Steven Spielberg. USA, 1981.
Saw. Dir. James Wan. USA/Australia, 2004.
Schindler's List. Dir. Steven Spielberg. USA, 1993.
The White Ribbon [*Das weiße Band: Eine deutsche Kindergeschichte*]. Dir. Michael Haneke. Germany/Austria/France/Italy, 2009.
'The Woman King.' *Battlestar Galactica*, Season 3. Dir. Michael Rymer. USA, 2007.

Bibliography

Adams, Jenni, and Sue Vice (eds) (2013) *Representing Perpetrators in Holocaust Literature and Film*. London: Vallentine Mitchell.

Agamben, Giorgio (2002) *Remnants of Auschwitz: The Witness and the Archive*, trans. Daniel Heller-Roazen. New York: Zone Books.

Arendt, Hannah ([1963] 1994) *Eichmann in Jerusalem: A Report on the Banality of Evil*. New York: Penguin.

Barta, Tony (1998) *Screening the Past: Film and the Representation of History*. Westport, CO: Greenwood.

Baudrillard, Jean (2003) *The Spirit of Terrorism and Other Essays*, trans. Chris Turner. New York: Verso.

Bialas, Wolfgang (2013) 'Nazi Ethics: Perpetrators with a Clear Conscience', *Dapim: Studies on the Holocaust*, 27, 1, 3–25.

Boltanski, Christian (1994) Interviewed by Melvyn Bragg, *The South Bank Show*. BBC, 15 May.

Boswell, Matthew (2012) *Holocaust Impiety: In Literature, Popular Music, and Film*. New York: Palgrave.

Browning, Christopher R. (2001) *Ordinary Men: Reserve Police Battalion 101 and the Final Solution in Poland*. London: Penguin.

Burian, Peter (1999) 'Myth Into Mythos: The Shaping of Tragic Plot', in P. E. Easterling (ed.) *The Cambridge Companion to Greek Tragedy*. Cambridge: Cambridge University Press, 178–210.

Denby, David (2005) 'Back in the Bunker', *The New Yorker*, 14 February. Online: http://www.newyorker.com/magazine/2005/02/14/back-in-the-bunker

Doneson, Judith (1978) 'The Jew as a Female Figure in the Holocaust Film', *Shoah: A Review of*

Holocaust Studies and Commemorations, 1, 1, 11–13; 18.

____ (1997) 'The Image Lingers: The Feminization of the Jew in *Schindler's List*', in Yosefa Loshitzky (ed.) *Spielberg's Holocaust: Critical Perspectives on Schindler's List*. Bloomington, IN: Indiana University Press. 140–52.

Fisher, Jaimey (2008) 'Home-Movies, Film-Diaries, and Mass Bodies: Péter Forgács's *Free Fall* into the Holocaust' in David Bathrick, Brad Prager and Michael D. Richardson (eds) *Visualizing the Holocaust: Documents, Aesthetics, Memory*. Rochester, NY: Camden House, 239–60.

Forgács, Péter (2003) 'The Memory of Loss: Péter Forgás's Saga of Family Life and Social Hell', Interviewed by Bill Nichols, *Film Quarterly*, 56, 4, 2–12.

Foucault, Michel (2000) 'Anti-Retro'; interview by Pascal Bonitzer and Serge Toubiana, ed. David Wilson, trans. Annwyl Williams. *Cahiers du cinema Volume 4 1973–1978: History, Ideology, Cultural Struggle*. New York: Routledge, 159–72.

Friedlander, Saul (ed.) (1992) *Probing the Limits of Representation: Nazism and the 'Final Solution'*. Cambridge, MA: Harvard University Press.

____ (1993) *Reflections of Nazism: An Essay on Kitsch and Death*, trans. Thomas Weyr. Bloomington, IN: Indiana University Press.

Haneke, Michael (2003) 'Darkness Falls', Interview by Nick James, *Sight & Sound*, 13, 10, 17–18.

Hirsch, Marianne (1997) *Family Frames: Photography, Narrative, and Postmemory*. Cambridge, MA: Harvard University Press.

Holden, Stephen (2008) 'Aligning With the Nazis, Blindfold Tightly in Place', *The New York Times*. 30 December. Online: http://www.nytimes.com/2008/12/31/movies/31good.html?_r=0

Kaplan, Brett Ashley (2007) *Unwanted Beauty: Aesthetic Pleasure in Holocaust Representation*. Urbana, IL: University of Illinois Press.

____ (2011) *Landscapes of Holocaust Postmemory*. New York: Routledge.

Kerner, Aaron (2015) *Torture Porn in the Wake of 9/11: Horror, Exploitation, and the Cinema of Sensations*. New Brunswick, NJ: Rutgers University Press.

Kristeva, Julia (1991) *Strangers to Ourselves*, trans. Leon S. Roudiez. New York: Columbia University Press.

LaCapra, Dominick (1994) *Representing the Holocaust: History, Theory, Trauma*. Ithaca, NY: Cornell University Press.

Lane, Anthony (2009) 'Happy Haneke', *The New Yorker*, 5 October, 60–7.

Liebman, Stuart (ed.) (2007) *Claude Lanzmann's Shoah: Key Essays*. New York: Oxford University Press.

McGlothlin, Erin (2009) 'Theorizing the Perpetrator in Bernhard Schlink's *The Reader* and Martin Amis's *Time's Arrow*', in R. Clifton Spargo and Robert Ehrenreich (eds) *After Representation?: The Holocaust, Literature, and Culture*. New Brunswick, NJ: Rutgers University Press, 210–30.

Michael, Robert (1984) 'A Second Look: *Night and Fog*', *Cineaste*, 13, 4, 36–7.

Moretti, Franco (1988) *Signs Taken for Wonder: Essays in the Sociology of Literary Forms*. New York: Verso.

Neale, Steve (1986) 'Melodrama and Tears', *Screen*, 27, 6, 6–23.

Rose, Gillian (1996) 'Beginnings of the Day: Fascism and Representation' in *Mourning Becomes the Law: Philosophy and Representation*. Cambridge: Cambridge University Press, 41–62.

Rothberg, Michael (2009) *Multidirectional Memory: Remembering the Holocaust in the Age of Decolonization*. Stanford, CA: Stanford University Press.

Silverman, Max (2008) 'Interconnected Histories: Holocaust and Empire in the Cultural Imaginary', *French Studies*, 62, 4, 417–28. Online: http://fs.oxfordjournals.org/content/62/4/417.full.pdf+html

Sontag, Susan (2003) *Regarding the Pain of Others*. New York: Picador.

Trinh, T. Minh-Ha (1992) *Framer Framed*. New York: Routledge.

van Alphen, Ernst (1999) 'Nazism in the Family Album: Christian Boltanski's *Sans Souci*', in Marianne Hirsch (ed.) *The Familial Gaze*. Hanover, NE: University Press of New England, 32–50.

CHAPTER ELEVEN

The Holocaust as Case Study
UNIVERSALIST RHETORIC AND NATIONAL MEMORY IN STEFAN RUZOWITZKY'S *RADICAL EVIL*

Oleksandr Kobrynskyy[1]

Radical Evil [*Das radikal Böse*] (2013) is a contemporary documentary that illustrates both the aesthetic potential and the ethical pitfalls of using re-enactment in the cultural framework of Holocaust representations.[2] Stefan Ruzowitzky's film gives a profound account of socio-psychological and historical factors that contributed to turning men serving in German paramilitary mobile squads into mass murderers. Thematically, *Radical Evil* grapples with the harrowing history of mass shootings in the East, an arguably underrepresented aspect of Nazi Germany's attempt to exterminate the Jews of Europe. The film's main preoccupation, however, is to make a point about the continuing genocidal potential in contemporary societies. In this essay, I discuss Ruzowitzky's film in the context of the cultural memory of the Nazi past in post-unification Germany, arguing that *Radical Evil* represents a paradigm shift towards an embedding of the Holocaust into a broader framework of human rights education. Pursuing an agenda of raising ethical awareness, the film forgoes issues of national memory; rather, the film's thematic and aesthetic choices are strongly informed by the political sensibilities of the third generation.

In the first three minutes, the film provides an exposition of both its aesthetic principles and its universalist trajectory. The opening scene, glazed in bright sunlight seen from the inside of what looks like a dark barn, shows from a distance a group of men in uniforms positioning themselves in front of the barn. Off-screen male voices read what sounds like short excerpts from soldiers' diaries and letters, capturing attention by its air of historical authenticity. A gun is charged and extradiegetic rhythmic dubstep music sets in. The scene quickly cuts to a black screen with white letters that provide the viewers with some context, giving factual information that between 1941 and 1943 Jewish civilians were systematically murdered by bullets, and introducing the film's conceptual design: 'This film is based on original quotations from the perpetrators' (English subtitles). Subsequently, the film quickly proceeds from archival footage of reports on the Nuremberg Trials to an interview sequence (in English, with German subtitles) with Benjamin Ferencz, the American chief prosecutor in Nuremberg. Resorting to a split-screen technique, the interview shot is supplemented with footage showing the young Ferencz in the solicitor's stand in the Nuremberg courtroom. Again, historical authenticity is evoked through a reference to original testimony and the employment of archival footage. As a key participant of the Nuremberg Trials and as an expert in international law, Ferencz epitomises credibility. After that, through a minimalist visualisation of the set-up of a psychological test, the film provides an embedding in a scientific context of the history that has so far been represented. The camera angle switches to a bird's-eye perspective, and viewers are acquainted with the Rorschach test, to which defendants at Nuremberg were subjected.[3] The short episode is used to introduce the information that the high-ranking Nazis who were tried by the International Military Tribunal were psychologically healthy men, a finding subsequently corroborated by Ferencz. It is through his words that the film's main hypothesis is formulated: evil is perpetrated by normal people like you and me.

Adopting its title from Hannah Arendt, the film appears in the discursive strand of Western thought that interprets evil as an integral part of the human condition, which can and must be understood.[4] What makes 'radical evil', genocidal behaviour encouraged by totalitarian political systems, most unsettling is that it is perpetrated not by otherworldly monsters but by normal human beings.[5] The film tries to develop this point through an essayistic structure. It consists in fairly equal shares of expert interviews and re-enactment episodes; these are supplemented with re-enactments of psychological experiments, as well as with re-visualisations of archival material, such as film footage, photographs, diaries and *Einsatzgruppen* reports. A short segment of the film consists of rather unremarkable eyewitness interviews, attempting little more than a dutiful fulfilment of what is expected from a Holocaust documentary. The re-enactment episodes, on the other hand, offer the viewer a remarkable face-to-face encounter with the perpetrators. The aesthetics of these episodes hover between the smooth look of a mainstream history documentary and an ambitious, abstracting texture of experimental cinema.

Arguably, this hybridity does not quite succeed aesthetically. In a review for a major German national daily Simon Rothöhler argues that Ruzowitzky 'has inadvertently created a fairly complete anthology of doubtful devices used by the genre of historical documentary' (2014).[6] This critique is not entirely unwarranted. The filmmaker attempts too much when, in a double move, he tries to convey scientific insights and historical knowledge to a broad audience and, at the same time, to create by what looks like breaks and discontinuities a self-reflexive, critical distance to the very act of representation. Like many other recent films dealing with the legacy of the Holocaust, *Radical Evil* responds to a call for self-reflexivity, as was formulated by Gillian Rose when she demanded a film aesthetic 'in which representation of Fascism would engage with the fascism of representation' (1996: 50). However, the film does not achieve the quasi-postmodern edge it ostensibly strives for. While displaying cinematic craft, the film's episodic structure remains entirely subjected to the argumentative progression of the film's rhetoric. In short, Ruzowitzky's compilation of visually gripping episodes does not work in a self-reflexive manner.

According to the director, decisions concerning the film's visual design had to a large part been informed by considerations of historical timeliness. In a 2014 television interview, Ruzowitzky described the conceptual choices he made: 'It was necessary at this point in time to find a new way of dealing with these topics because there has been a generational change.'[7] Thus the director suggests that the film was tailored to the needs of a new generation of viewers. Supposedly, this new generation both expects a visual language in keeping with their socialisation in highly medialised environments and has a perspective on German history that differs from the preceding generations.

How does Ruzowitzky's claim to alleged timeliness relate to the recent proliferation of German productions like *Downfall* [*Der Untergang*] (2004) or *Sophie Scholl: The Final Days* [*Sophie Scholl: Die letzten* Tage] (2005) that deal with the role of individuals and collectives in the Third Reich? In the conclusion to his insightful book, Axel Bangert stresses that recent German films about Nazi Germany and its aftermath provide a highly differentiated view of the collective past through the means of personal encounters:

> They have granted access to the private lives of those figures that have come to symbolize this period of history and exposed viewers to the chaos of war. They have unlocked the doors to personal struggles with Nazism and its legacy, and show a homeland both complicit in persecution and transfigured in memory. In reunified Germany, such images of the Nazi past remain contested. The private is under suspicion of neglecting circumstance; the collective is measured by how it balances 'us' and 'them.' Such scrutiny is necessary and justified. Yet close readings help us to see that intimacy and immersion are not necessarily an escape from the political choices and ethical dilemmas of the past. Instead, they can also serve as a point of contact with them. At its most challenging, this kind of contact puts the viewer in an insecure position. What would I have become? (2014a: 169)

Bangert suggests that German films about the Nazi past produced in the first decade of the twenty-first century, in their aspiration to transmit memory of a troubled past, largely rely upon a kind of critical empathy with previous generations. The personal, he claims, opens a door to the re-negotiation of the collective. A carefully measured distance to historical subjects both allows for a better understanding of the spatio-temporal environments which set limits to individual agents, and it allows for enough historical detachment to invite ethical questioning and critical self-inquiry.

Radical Evil employs this distance in its own, idiosyncratic way. Here, the aspiration of the filmmaker to raise a new generation's ethical awareness by transmission of Holocaust memory is not achieved by evoking empathy with individual life stories. The members of the mobile death squad are embodied by unknown extras acting out the daily activities of a German Police Battalion: talking, eating, smoking, laughing, getting ready for gruesome acts of mass murder.[8] Rothöhler, in his polemical critique of the film, insinuates its discursive closeness to the successful TV miniseries *Generation War* [*Unsere Mütter, unsere Väter*] (2013) when he writes that, again, a German film on the Nazi past delivers 'close shots of "our fathers" (this time without the mother), choosing to see involuntary entanglement everywhere, but hardly showing any perpetrators' (2014).[9] Rothöhler is right in diagnosing the film's tendency to emphasise situational aspects at the cost of a more thorough questioning of individual guilt. However, as becomes evident, the aesthetic programme of *Radical Evil* is more complex than Rothöhler's criticism suggests. Unlike in *Generation War*, the cinematic modelling of the Nazi past is not cast in a melodramatic mode.[10] The extras' restrained acting and average-looking faces are employed to signify familiarity, quickly making clear the filmmaker's agenda to show that nobody is immune from becoming a mass murderer. Yet the representations of this uncanny normality do not remain intact. Vertical lines sharply divide the screen into a gallery of constantly oscillating pictures, whose at times flickering edges signify instability.

Fig. 1 Triptych: receiving orders

Tearing apart the visual surface, the dividing lines structuring the triptych create black in-between spaces, which lend themselves to be read as allusions to something missing – skillfully designed invitations directed at the audience to fill the gaps left over by cinematic representation. The private strangely seems so near and yet so far away: simultaneously, it is both brought close to the viewers by means of close-up shots and it is distanced from them by disrupting the integrity of representation. Ruzowitzky aims at provoking the audience's self-enquiry without employing techniques of immersion. Subtly, the film pays a compliment to its viewers by inviting them to watch it as critical subjects rather than as passive consumers. The distance *Radical Evil* establishes between the audience and the Nazi past allows the viewer to ask the question 'What would I have become?' from the safe position of a detached observer.

THE *EINSATZGRUPPEN*: OLD WINE IN NEW BOTTLES?

In *Radical Evil*, representation of perpetrators focuses on a very specific group employed by the Third Reich in what Peter Longerich calls its 'war of racial annihilation' (2010: 179). This war, according to Longerich's account, proceeded from 'the planned liquidation of ideologically hostile groups' (2010: 183) to shootings of Jewish men, and, in a final escalation, towards an extension of the annihilation mandate to the entire Jewish population. When Nazi Germany invaded Poland, units of the SS and police forces were sent to the East to accompany the *Wehrmacht*, Germany's regular military forces. Among these police forces was the so-called *Sicherheitsdienst* (SD), an intelligence unit of the SS. In hindsight, this name sounds like another cynical euphemism used by the Nazis to lend an air of legitimacy to the crimes committed by state organs. The 'security' service performed for the German homeland by various paramilitary units was the ruthless implementation of imperialist policies by means of purposefully under-regulated use of violence against those who were declared enemies of the Reich. The *Einsatzgruppen*, special armed units composed of various paramilitary divisions, numbering approximately three thousand men by autumn 1941, systematically combed through occupied territories, rounding up and shooting Jews. Along with hardcore National Socialists, the shooters included men whose nationalism was only partly or insignificantly informed by Nazi ideology. It is these 'ordinary men' who take centre stage in Ruzowitzky's universalist exploration of evil.

Radical Evil closes a perceived gap between the existence of substantial research on the one hand and insufficient popular awareness of the *Einsatzgruppen* crimes on the other. In an attempt at educating his viewers about this history, Ruzowitzky constructs his film around the idea of making accessible to general audiences facts that had long been established knowledge in the academic sphere but, arguably, remained underrepresented in popular renderings of the Holocaust.[11] But does Ruzowitzky succeed in making a significant contribution to filling a void in cultural memory of the *Einsatzgruppen*?

Far from being a blind spot in the academic sphere, the atrocious crimes of mobile death squads have been the subject of substantial research. Systematic documentation efforts about these crimes date back to the *Einsatzgruppen* Trials in 1947/48, when a number of SS officers were charged in Nuremberg by US military courts with crimes against humanity, war crimes and membership of criminal organisations. Notwithstanding the potentially exculpating chain of command, Chief Prosecutor Benjamin Ferencz held liable individuals personally accountable. For decades, historians have been establishing the broader picture of how these mass shootings were embedded in the larger context of the so-called 'Final Solution'. Research into the extent of personal involvement showed that there was a considerable scope for individual decisions taken by members of the *Einsatzgruppen*, their local henchmen and German military personnel. Whereas different tasks were assigned in Hitler's war of imperial conquest to the Wehrmacht on the one hand and various paramilitary units under the parent agency of the SS on the other, it has been established beyond doubt that the regular armed forces played a decisive role in enabling the planned extermination of Jewish civilians.[12]

One can argue that in the imagination of American and Western European audiences of the twenty-first century, 'Holocaust images' of the mass shootings in the East have not acquired the same evocative power as representations of ghettos or concentration camps. Jeff Kanew's feature film *Babi Yar: The Forgotten Crime* [*Babij Jar: Das vergessene Verbrechen*] (2003), with its speaking second title and a distressingly radical visual aesthetic, strives to fill what was apparently perceived by its makers as an absence of the *Einsatzgruppen* crimes from collective memories. Naturalistic scenes create drastic images of the mass shootings in a ravine close to Kiev, representing abuse that naked victims suffer in deep anguish, with human beings turning into a mass of piled-up bodies. A noteworthy attempt at making transparent the geographical and historical dimensions of these crimes has also been made by the Catholic priest Patrick Desbois and the Yahad-In Unum research team. Tracking down shooting sites, Desbois and his collaborators conducted a large number of interviews with local residents who had witnessed round-ups of local Jews and the ensuing bloodbaths. The French filmmaker Romain Icard documented this exceptional endeavour in *Holocaust by Bullets* [*Shoah par balles*] (2008).[13] Notably, the film's second title *The Forgotten History* [*l'histoire oubliée*] again makes the claim, five years after Kanew, that a forgotten aspect of the Holocaust needs to be brought to public attention. A similar claim to novelty appears in the *Einsatzgruppen* documentary *Hitler's Hidden Holocaust*, shown on the National Geographic channel in 2009, which also features Patrick Desbois.

The rhetoric of overdue revelation that is employed by recent films blinds out the multiple manifestations of the *Einsatzgruppen* massacres in popular culture. Certainly in the case of late Soviet and post-Soviet audiences, the mass shootings remained vividly present in the consciousness of audiences.[14] On a global scale, the *Einsatzgruppen* have entered public imagination through Marvin J. Chomsky's 1978 TV mini-series *Holocaust* (1978), which features a Babi Yar scene, and D. M. Thomas's novel *The White Hotel* (1981), which uses material from Anatoly Kuznetsov's documentary novel *Babi Yar*, an uncensored version of which was published in the West in 1970 under the pseudonym A. Anatoli. More recently, the crimes became widely known through representations in bestselling fiction, such as Jonathan Safran Foer's magical realist novel *Everything Is Illuminated* (2002) and Jonathan Littell's disconcerting exploration of a perpetrator's mind in *The*

Kindly Ones (2006).¹⁵ There are indeed multiple entry points into this history, and on typing '*Einsatzgruppen*' into an internet search engine, one quickly finds both documentaries produced for television and distressing black-and-white footage showing shootings of civilians. Thus, rather than being 'forgotten', this aspect of Nazi Germany's war of racial annihilation can be considered to have partially but steadily trickled down into the cultural archive of the Western hemisphere. The *Einsatzgruppen* massacres may rank low in the public awareness of the Holocaust; but they hardly constitute a complete lacuna.

The mere fact that Ruzowitzky produced another, albeit in its aesthetic qualities doubtlessly unprecedented, representation of the *Einsatzgruppen* is hardly remarkable. Collective memory depends on ever-renewed representations of the historic past, and the film succeeds in up-dating his viewers about this particular history. The questions rather are why Ruzowitzky chooses the *Einsatzgruppen* for his broader argument, and how the representation of this historical theme is modified by the film's rhetoric. As a public project, the film pursues a double task: both passing on knowledge about the *Einsatzgruppen* and using the *Einsatzgruppen* as a case study on the genocidal potential of the human psyche. The film is more than a documentary about the Nazi massacres in the East. It is an essay on the ethical questions of evil, for which the historical facts about the *Einsatzgruppen* serve as argumentative material.

THE RHETORIC OF RE-ENACTMENT

The historical in *Radical Evil* is subordinated to the rhetorical. Events shown in the re-enactment episodes are not tied to a specific time or place, and the personal documents read out loud by off-screen voices are not presented as life stories of particular individuals. Rather, they are assembled according to the logic of argumentative progression. The short narratives represent the life and functioning of a mobile death squad: how the policemen are ideologically schooled, sent off to their first shooting and allowed to consume alcohol afterwards; the way the men get used to the atrocious acts they commit; and how some of them become keen murderers.

James Phelan suggests that narrative can fruitfully be understood 'as a rhetorical act: Somebody telling somebody else on some occasion and for some purpose(s) that something happened' (2007: 3). The best way to understand the short narratives presented in *Radical Evil*'s re-enactment episodes is to see them as constituents of a larger narrative about typical socio-psychological dynamics in a shooting squad. This narrative is a rhetorical act aimed at convincing the viewers that, given certain settings and circumstances, it is possible to turn morally stable individuals into perpetrators in genocides. Phelan's suggestion for a definition of narrative entails four elements: a communicating agent (somebody), a receiver (somebody else), a particular spatio-temporal setting (on some occasion) and an objective of the rhetorical act (for some purpose). I shall first turn to the question of how the transmission of the rhetorical act between the communicating agent (the filmmaker) and the receiver (film audiences) is structured in the re-enactment episodes.

Like all of its subsequent chapters, the film's first chapter, dubbed 'Mission', begins with a re-enactment episode. Men in uniforms, recognisable only as silhouettes in the opening scene, are now captured in close-up shots. The camera moves through rows of mostly young men, standing still and exchanging timid glances. The rather unconvincing acting is part of the intended film aesthetic. Embodying the off-screen voices are mostly amateur extras, cast to represent an average sample of German society as it would be found among the *Einsatzgruppen*: fierce-looking Nazis mix with ordinary citizens; pimpled youths and middle-aged family fathers look perturbingly out-of-place in their greenish-grey uniforms and polished black boots. In close-up shots mute tableaux are created with a characteristically economical use of body language, what Ruzowitzky in the DVD interview describes as acting inspired by Robert Bresson's aesthetic, which significantly influenced the French New Wave.

This first film chapter is closely modelled on the account of social dynamics within a German police battalion provided by Christopher Browning in his well-researched and highly influential book *Ordinary Men: Reserve Police Battalion 101 and the Final Solution in Poland*. Informed by Major Wilhelm Trapp about the 'unpleasant task' the battalion is ordered to undertake, the men are told details about the existing option of refusing to participate in the shootings. Browning's résumé about the diverging choices made by the troops is as follows:

> Different groups within the battalion behaved in different ways. The 'eager killers' – whose numbers increased over time – sought the opportunity to kill, and celebrated their murderous deeds. The smallest group within the battalion comprised the nonshooters. With the exception of Lieutenant Bachmann, they did not make principled objections against the regime and its murderous policies; they did not reproach their comrades. They took advantage of Trapp's policy within the battalion of exempting from shooting those who 'didn't feel up to it' by saying that they were too weak or that they had children.
>
> The largest group within the battalion did whatever they were asked to do, without ever risking the onus of confronting authority or appearing weak, but they did not volunteer for or celebrate the killing. Increasingly numb and brutalized, they felt more pity for themselves because of the 'unpleasant work' they had been assigned than they did for their dehumanized victims. (2005: 215)

In his account, Browning stresses the role of individual agency in particular historical circumstances, and he tentatively explores the scope of choices that presented themselves to men in paramilitary units. Browning's study was one of the main influences for Daniel J. Goldhagen's controversial book *Hitler's Willing Executioners: Ordinary Germans and the Holocaust* (1996), which caused a heated press polemic in Germany even before it was published in German and contributed to a broader discourse on the role of German society in the Holocaust and the resulting moral, political and financial accountability on the part of post-war generations. Goldhagen, whose argument was later criticised by a number of historians for severe methodological flaws, maintains that not only did the vast majority of Germans not resist the Nazi regime but that most of them enthusiastically supported its anti-Jewish politics, including mass extermination.[16] In spite of what may seem similar foci, the two studies significantly differ in their basic assumptions. Browning discusses a complex array of reasons why these 'ordinary men' became involved in the process of mass killing, including historical, ideological, situational and psychological factors. Goldhagen's more reductive approach focuses on a long tradition of German anti-Semitism, which, in the Holocaust, realised its eliminatory potential. In contrast to Goldhagen, Browning claims he has offered 'a portrayal of the battalion that was multilayered' (ibid.).

If Browning and Goldhagen provide two different interpretational models for the involvement of 'ordinary men' in the Holocaust, *Radical Evil* clearly heeds to the former. Not only is the film zealous to avoid generalisations about German sensibilities, but it almost literally follows Browning's account, transforming it visually into re-enactment scenes and, on the auditory channel, into a juxtaposition of testimony excerpts. While the men in the re-enactment episodes are not given any individual names, Ruzowitzky's film attempts to differentiate between exemplary individual responses that diverged significantly. The off-screen reading of original documents reveals to viewers different patterns of behaviour, ranging from thoughtless conformism to repugnant fulfilment of the assigned duties. Close-up camera shots focusing on the extras' faces show some policemen's visceral reactions to the abject task they are assigned. These images are supplemented by testimonial evidence: letters, in which the men complain about their unpleasant duties. Driven by conformity pressure, as the psychologists interviewed for the film suggest, most men continued to participate in the shootings even after having recognised their ethical unacceptability. Well-chosen extracts from testimonies illustrate to what length shooters went to find justifications for what they were doing on a daily basis.

The exploration of mechanisms of complicity is, thus, at the film's centre of attention, and the representation of these mechanisms is strongly supported by references to psychological experiments as well as by statements of experts. However, the film also dedicates a great deal of consideration to cases of outright refusal, suggesting that the individual decision *not* to participate in non-ethical acts remains possible even in settings structured by extreme conformity pressure. This constitutes the film's sense of hope and its future orientation: ethical choices, the film suggests, are possible even under most adverse historical circumstances.

In its use of re-enactment, *Radical Evil* is closely affiliated to two recent filmic representations of violence. Harun Farocki's *Immersion* (2009) and Joshua Oppenheimer's *The Act of Killing* (2012) present powerful evidence about two very different instances of suffering inflicted by state policies: the individual traumas of Iraq veterans, and the repercussions of the Indonesian killings of 1965/66, respectively. Like Farocki and Oppenheimer, Ruzowitzky uses violence as a point of departure for a more wide-reaching case study about the social psychology of mass killing.

Farocki's two-channel video projection explores the use of exposure therapy by means of augmented reality. Immersed in a kind of video game environment, Iraq veterans suffering from PTSD are made to re-experience the traumatic event. In his multilayered metafictional questioning of the potential of visual media, Farocki problematises the way images are put to use by this therapy method in order both to treat trauma and, paradoxically, to enable soldiers, after recovery, to return physically to battlefields in order to inflict further violence upon others. Both re-enactment and split screen techniques are productively employed in Farocki's installation to reflect upon how politically-induced violence is inflicted and perpetuated.

Radical Evil contains references to Farocki's work in its use of partitioning of the visual surface and in the way the possibilities of visual media are explored for a representation of how soldiers are prepared to inflict trauma. Conceptually, the split screens are employed to cut through layers of time, memory and representation. The synchronic apposition of images in Ruzowitzky's film is used both to illustrate information conveyed by the off-screen voices and, at the same time, to create productive tension in the reception process. Representations of the policemen's cheerful leisure time activities, such as swimming, are juxtaposed with excerpts from *Einsatzgruppen* reports on the numbers of Jews killed and images of piles of naked corpses. *Radical Evil* also contains a cross-medial reference to the technique of double exposure in photography. In a scene depicting ideological preparation for the massacres, a straightforward visual metaphor is used to represent the superimposition of inhumane thought models on the moral compass of psychologically stable individuals with no particular political inclinations. The policemen's faces become part of the projection surface for moving images of the anti-Semitic propaganda of the Nazis. Thus, in *Radical Evil*, the images shown on screen directly call on the viewer to engage intellectually with the contrasting visual prompts. These images are assembled in a particular manner in order to trigger ethically informed responses.

Oppenheimer's groundbreaking *The Act of Killing* grapples with the legacy of Indonesian massacres of 1965/66 by documenting re-enactments of the killings that, in an exceptionally disturbing manner, are performed by the killers themselves. This brilliant ethical tightrope walk puts the very concept of re-enactment on an entirely new footing, adding new facets to the discussion of the place of fiction in the documentary genre. Not only does his film make visible gruesome details of the bloody massacres, but it addresses the more unsettling matter of genocidal potential that perseveres in every human individual.[17]

The uncanny proximity of the perpetrator in *Radical Evil* can be read as an echo of Oppenheimer's film. Ruzowitzky's employment of re-enactment has, however, a function different from the one found in *The Act of Killing*. Oppenheimer stages personal encounters with historically real perpetrators, whose desire to return to the settings of their crimes and the Freudian urge to repeat provide the backdrop for a disconcerting exploration of the human genocidal potential. In *Radical Evil*, on the other hand, re-enactment is modelled in a way that moves atrocities of the past further away rather than bringing them closer. Fictionality, here, operates on a level different from Oppenheimer's film. Close-up shots of the perpetrators' faces are structured in a way that reveals the deliberate constructedness of the cinematic situation. The split screens implement internally a self-distancing of the film from the very objects it represents, thereby projecting the need to make ethical choices towards the film audience. The cinematic technique in both films has metaphoric qualities: the repetition on screen of violent acts in fictionalised settings serves as a metaphor for the potential return of genocidal crimes, suggesting that it is up to the viewers to make ethical choices in their own lives and to oppose actively tendencies that may facilitate the repetition of such crimes in the future.

Fig. 2 Double exposure: 'ordinary men' indoctrinated

Having established the medium (film), the narrative content (different kinds of behaviour shown by men serving in the *Einsatzgruppen*) and the purpose of the rhetorical act (to raise awareness for the genocidal potential of the human psyche and political culture), I now turn to what Phelan calls its 'occasion' (2007: 3). What is the historical circumstance for an Austrian-German filmmaker to make an *Einsatzgruppen* film whose argumentative scope extends far beyond a documentation of the massacres? In the remainder of this essay I accordingly establish how the universalist rhetoric of the film's exploration of complicity relates to contemporary cultural memories of the Holocaust in Germany.

RADICAL EVIL AND THE STRUCTURES OF GERMAN SUBJECTIVITIES IN THE TWENTY-FIRST CENTURY

The film's aesthetic of rational detachment operates in the complex discursive setting of collective identities. In his insightful essay 'The Non-German German and the German

German: Dilemmas of Identity after the Holocaust', A. Dirk Moses analyses 'the structure of German subjectivities' (2007: 51) of the second and third post-war generations. Moses distinguishes between two different identity models, both developed in the postwar intellectual sphere of the political left, the 'German German' and the 'non-German German'. The 'German German', exemplified by the novelist Martin Walser, seeks to find identity in a national community that emphatically embraces a long history not limited to the twelve years of Nazi rule. 'German Germans' conceptualise the majority of their parents' and grandparents' generations as victims of a criminal regime, stressing the totalitarian structures of Hitler's state. They embrace a form of 'progressive patriotism', which refuses to be ashamed of what is seen as a forcefully imposed implication of the German population in the crimes of the regime. Group identity of 'German Germans' is structured by projecting their resentments against the imperative of collective shame allegedly imposed upon the Germans by distant powers, and perpetuated in internal discourses by 'non-German Germans'. This other group, whose intellectual father is Jürgen Habermas, chooses a 'negative identity', which distances itself from its genealogical implication in the national community and expresses rage 'against parents and grandparents for the pollution and stigmatisation of the collective self that they had bequeathed the younger generation' (2007: 57). The 'non-German Germans' understand themselves as 'European citizens of a republic cut off from the national traditions that led to Auschwitz' (2007: 58). While the 'anti-Germans', a third, smaller and less influential group in the leftist sphere, belligerently negates the very project of re-establishing any kind of German national identity, the 'non-German Germans' profess a national community built upon the principles of democracy and human rights. The 'non-German Germans' tend to conceptualise the Nazi past 'as secular metaphor for evil in the West', after which, they argue, a clear historical caesura must be established, accusing the 'German German' of insufficient self-distancing from this past. Both identity models, of which the 'non-German German' proved more influential, reflect the rather similar ambition to reconstruct national selves by relying upon 'projective identification' (ibid.). However, Moses suggests that, recently, there has been a paradigm change: 'With the development of basic trust [in the country's institutions and political culture], the underlying structure that has marked German memory for sixty years is gradually coming to an end' (2007: 94). The fourth generation, according to Moses, has developed 'a new national feeling [...] based not on continuities with the generations that experienced World War II but on the achievements and culture of the Federal Republic' (2007: 93, 94).

First screened in October 2013, *Radical Evil* appeared in Germany after roughly two decades of post-unification discourses about the role average German citizens played in the crimes perpetrated during the existence of the 'Third Reich'. The time between the anniversary year 1995, when a central Holocaust memorial again became a subject of public discussion, and its final opening in Berlin in 2005, was shaped by controversial debates. These debates addressed the involvement of ordinary Germans in the functioning of the Nazi state, and they also brought forth a new victim discourse, in which the suffering of the German population during the last phase of World War II became a central concern.[18] The Holocaust, whose commemoration in the two German states in the years 1949–90 can be tentatively described as volatile, indelibly became part of public discourses of post-unification Germany in 1995, the year of the 50th anniversary of the end of World War II, and after Steven Spielberg's *Schindler's List* (1993) re-instated the Holocaust in the popular awareness. Representations of the Nazi past in films and television productions in the two ensuing decades (1995–2015) are structured by a negotiation of cultural memory between the 'German German' and the 'non-German German' perspectives.

In the 1990s, there occurred what Tobias Ebbrecht describes as a turn in German television from 'explanatory television' to 'visually narrative television' (2007: 36). Films produced by the journalist Guido Knopp moved documentaries on the topic of National Socialism from marginal positions in local stations to prime time on the nationwide state broadcaster ZDF. The documentary series *Hitler's Helpers* (1996, 1998) turned Knopp's name into a brand label, with which German audiences have since then been identifying the topic of National Socialism on television screens. Knopp's docudrama aesthetics of combining historical footage with re-enactment made event television a 'popular history lesson' (2007: 37) for the German audiences. Ebbrecht even suggests that at some point the two modes became indistinguishable for the average viewer (2007: 38). Often accused by high- and middle-brow critics of trivialisation and popularisation, Knopp's documentaries focus on the higher cadres of the Nazi party, largely eclipsing the involvement of rank and file citizens in the criminal actions of the state apparatus. One reason for the popular success of Knopp's 'histotainment' documentaries is that they proved compatible with both 'German German' apologia of the ordinary citizens and the 'non-German German' distance from the historical past.

A different trajectory was chosen by the curators of a controversial exhibition, 'War of Annihilation: Crimes of the Wehrmacht, 1941–1944'. Known as *Wehrmachtsausstellung*, the exhibition featured private correspondence by German soldiers and hundreds of photographs documenting the involvement of the military in genocidal actions. Initiated by the Hamburg Institute for Social Research, the exhibition toured 33 German cities from 1995 to 1999. The exhibition spaces themselves were used as documentary film-settings for Ruth Beckermann's *East of War* [*Jenseits des Krieges*] (1996) and Michael Verhoeven's *The Unknown Soldier* [*Der unbekannte Soldat*], a long-term project completed in 2006. As Axel Bangert points out, both films deal with various 'reactions of shame' (2014b: 165), which the exhibition had prompted among its visitors. The painful public reminder that a large portion of German soldiers, who used to be remembered as having fought a more or less 'clean' war on the Eastern front, actively participated in genocidal practices, supported the 'non-German German' critical position, triggered passionate responses with 'German Germans' and instilled a renewed public process of working through an inconvenient past.

The *Wehrmachtsausstellung* was what Lena Knäpple describes as a transgression by visual means of a dividing line firmly inscribed in the German collective memory between the Wehrmacht as a morally intact institution, on the one hand, and the Nazi criminals, on the other (2007: 288). The dissolution of this distinction in public perception, shocking and scandalous for 'German Germans', coincided with the heated reception of Goldhagen's thesis about the widespread participation of ordinary citizens in the Holocaust. These debates brought forth, dialectically, a situation where the experience of ordinary Germans assumed a critical mass in public discourses. More attention was then paid to the plight of Germans in the last years of World War II, including bombardments of German cities and the mass escape of ethnic Germans from Eastern territories. As Robert G. Moeller writes in his article on the German victim discourse, in 2000, German chancellor Gerhard Schröder suggested a broad comparative framework for a 'century of expulsions' (2005: 174), of which the German experience should become an integral part. Publications like *The Fire [Der Brand]* (2002), Jörg Friedrich's accusatory portrayal of the Allied bombings, provided graphic narratives for the 'German German' woes about the nation's historical suffering.

Heavily influenced by the 'German German' standpoint, representations of the Nazi past in the decade between 2005 and 2015 gradually accepted a more differentiating take on what is still considered as the darkest chapter of German history. The 'German German' perspective is dominant in the event television productions *Dresden* (2006), *March of Millions [Die Flucht]* (2007), *Die Gustloff* (2008) and *Generation War* (2013), all of which address different aspects of German suffering in the twentieth century. A melodramatic mode prevails in these films, what Ebbrecht calls the 're-dramatization of history' (2007: 35). While not excusing crimes of the past, the melodramatisation of the German historical experience assumed a substantial discursive counterweight to the 'non-German German' focus on historical responsibility. It has also contributed to what is perceived as a need to look more closely at individual experiences, and differentiating between individual cases: ordinary Germans are depicted as acting within the boundaries set to them by the historical situation. Within these boundaries, Germans are represented as capable of making ethically informed decisions. Jo Baier's *Not All Were Murderers [Nicht alle waren Mörder]* (2005) narrates the odyssey of fugitive Jews, whose survival is possible only because ordinary Germans hide them along the way. Differentiating representations of non-conformism have shown the potential to reconcile the 'German German' desire to exempt ordinary citizens from general suspicion with the 'non-German German' promotion of engaged citizenship.

While firmly embedded in the tradition of documentary filmmaking on the Holocaust, *Radical Evil* is a far cry from an emotionalised working through of traumatic pasts. Ruzowitzky's film largely refrains from explorations of national memory discourses, emphasising instead more general questions of history and social psychology, and placing its focus on the investigation of individual and collective factors that make genocides possible. *Radical Evil* takes up the attitude of educational documentary, which was dominant before the mode of docudrama became popular (see Ebbrecht 2007: 36). The film's entire conceptualisation can be considered as a result of a shift away from dramatisation of the past towards a cinematic mediation of insights gained by scholarship. Since the historical fact that ordinary Germans actively contributed to the implementation of the 'Final Solution' has by now been accepted in public discourses, attention moves towards explorations of the question why they did so.

Radical Evil, by means of its universalist rhetoric, situates itself within the project of establishing an identity that transcends the two diverging poles described by A. Dirk Moses. The film's trajectory towards abstraction factors out national memory, but, at the same time, it causes ethical problems. While the film uses rational discourse about the circumstances of the genocide, creating an aura of credibility by employment of scientific discourse, individual experience remains strangely distant. This is particularly problematic in the light of the fact that the film fails to deal with the experience of the victims, whose plight is not shown in a manner that evokes empathy.

THE UNIVERSALIST PRINCIPLE AND ITS ETHICAL PROBLEMS

In the introduction to *Becoming Evil: How Ordinary People Commit Genocide and Mass Killing*, James Waller points out that 'questions of motive and the social environment in which evil is practiced must be addressed if we hope to shed additional light on the actions of ordinary citizens doing their "jobs" in extraordinary situations' (2007: 9–10). *Radical Evil* can be read as the filmic correlate to Waller's book: it takes the question of extraordinary evil out of its immediate embedding in Holocaust and Genocide Studies into the broader cultural discourse. Yet the way this universalist principle reduces the Holocaust to the status of a case study entails a number of ethical problems.

By means of the dilettantish acting and alienating techniques of representation perpetrators remain anonymous faces and anonymous voices. There are moments of short melodramatic encounters, and viewers briefly plunge into short contrasting narratives of both blind obedience and brave non-compliance. However, the quick progression of these episodes does not permit sustained narrativisation of individual experiences. As a result, the perpetrators appear as abstract collective entities. The victims are even more distant, existing only as traces of an image seen on the surface of archival film or photography. Problematically, victims are either objectified by the perpetrator gaze or reduced to objects of ethnological interest. While renderings of the crimes remain in the sphere of denotative description, the film hardly ever gives a sense of the radicality of evil the victims were forced to experience; and it rarely provides opportunity to feel empathy. The extremity of the violence the victims went through remains emotionally distant and elusive.

In the episodes filmed in the sleepy Ukrainian town of Bibrka, the film misses its chance of creating critical distance to the bystanders. While neither survivors nor perpetrators are interviewed, the film shows conversations with a handful of eyewitnesses. Senior dwellers of Bibrka, who as young men witnessed the murder of their Jewish neighbours, are asked innocuous questions by a Ukrainian-speaking young woman, whose identity is only revealed in the closing credits. The men take her to shooting sites, but their at times awkward comments, hinting at a distinction between children who did not deserve to die and adults who could not be saved anyway, are never put under critical scrutiny. The long takes of idyllic rural landscapes and the on-screen presence of the interviewer amount to a thinly concealed homage to Claude Lanzmann's grand oeuvre, *Shoah* (1985).[19] However, Ruzowitzky's film never comes close to Lanzmann's subversive investigations of the bystanders' personal role as observers of the Nazi crimes. One may argue that the tranquil Bibrka episodes, which are set right in between the first and the second half of the film, create an effective visual counterpoint to the otherwise panting rhythmic progression of short episodes. Yet the rather sluggish interview sequences come across as byproducts of what must initially have been a broad scope of creative ideas for the film. *Radical Evil* creates a sense of a decreasing cinematic significance of the eyewitness interview and thereby, implicitly, testifies to the gradual disappearance of the eyewitness from cinema screens.

The expert, also increasingly replacing the eyewitness in recent Guido Knopp television productions like *The Germans* [*Die Deutschen*] (2008), gradually substitutes the historical individual as a figure of trust. Following this tendency, expert interviews are the main element supporting the universalist rhetoric in *Radical Evil*. Browning, himself a key agent in German memorial debates, appears as an expert in the film, and he is kept prominent company by the psychologist Robert J. Lifton and the priest Patrick Desbois, as well as the psychologists Dave Grossmann and Roy Baumeister. The way the statements of experts are cut and arranged in post-production creates, rather uncritically, the picture of a sweeping consensus in the academic sphere about historical and socio-psychological factors which cause genocides. The film's self-distancing from its objects of representation, perfunctorily created through visual aesthetics, is now entirely abandoned in favour of persuading its viewers.

Stefan Ruzowitzky has designed a film for a generation of filmgoers that puts trust in the emancipatory power of visual media. *Radical Evil* suggests that creating further representations of past and present evil is a way to prevent future evil. However, the expression of this hope appears over-stated; for instance, when Patrick Desbois' appeal to viewers to activate the attention of mass media for violations of human rights is given the discursive weight of the film's last scene. While films may play a significant role in generating public pressure on political agents, the trust put by the film in the potential of the media to prevent genocides is rather questionable.

TOWARD A POST-NATIONAL MEMORY

Radical Evil is by no means the first cultural product to tackle the topic of the involvement of 'ordinary men' in the Holocaust. What makes this film noteworthy is how the political unconscious of German national memory – and therein I include Austria – structures its universalist rhetoric. Cicero's phrase about history as life's teacher has become a principle shaping Holocaust discourses from the end of World War II to the present day. This can be seen, for instance, at the Holocaust Memorial Museum in Washington, D.C., and in its political activism concerning present-day issues of racism and genocide. Ruzowitzky's pedagogical ambition, in particular, is strongly informed by the desire to remove the German crimes of the past from a national context and to use them as argumentative material in the broader project of exploring the human condition in general.

Focusing on the *Einsatzgruppen* turns out to have been a good choice for Ruzowitzky not so much because this allowed him to make a point by identifying a topic which had been, arguably, too rarely picked up by filmmakers. Rather, the choice was well taken because the historical case of the mobile death squads – men acting within specific circumstances of war, displacement and peer pressure – works well in socio-psychological frameworks of explaining how regimes make 'radical evil' happen. These frameworks in turn assist the film's universalist rhetoric, which allows German viewers to watch it without feeling pressed down by the overwhelming weight of the national past.

Radical Evil's decontextualisation of the historical specificity of the Holocaust turns the *Einsatzgruppen* massacres into a case study contributing to the broader enterprise of human rights education. Ruzowitzky's collage of visual prompts, defying empathic narrativisation of exemplary experiences of the viewers' (great)grandfathers' generation may become a discernible representative of a new strand in German and Austrian Holocaust cinema, a strategy of dealing with the legacy of Nazism and World War II beyond the confines of national memory discourses. The way the film sets about issues of representation may be prototypical for future cinematic engagements with the history and cultural reverberations of the Holocaust in an era after witnessing. While not excusing past crimes, the concomitant universalisation of their significance supports a new conceptualisation of ethical self, moving beyond the divide between the 'German Germans' and the 'non-German Germans' toward a post-German collective identity.

Notes

1. I wish to thank Philipp Sonntag for lively lunchtime discussions and for his critical reading of drafts of this essay.
2. For discussion of re-enactment in documentary films dealing with genocidal violence, see Ten Brink (2012).
3. Social psychologists' interest in the fact of participation of psychologically healthy individuals in large-scale atrocities resulted in much-noted studies on human behaviour in authoritarian structures. Along with the Rorschach test, the film familiarises the viewers with the Asch conformity experiment, the Milgram experiment, the case of Kitty Genovese and the Stanford experiment, using minimalistic mise-en-scène and bird's-eye perspective. For discussion of the Stanford Prison experiment, see Zimbardo (2007).
4. Susan Neiman distinguishes between two standpoints guided by ethical concerns: 'The one, from Rousseau to Arendt, insists that morality demands that we make evil intelligible. The other, from Voltaire to Jean Améry, insists that morality demands that we don't' (2004: 8).
5. For discussion of Arendt's terminology, see Formosa (2007).
6. 'unfreiwillig eine recht vollständige Anthologie zweifelhafter Verfahren des Geschichtsdokugenres erstellt' (all translations from German are mine).
7. 'Es war notwendig, dass man heutzutage eine neue Form findet mit diesen Themen umzugehen, weil es einen Generationswechsel gab' (Ruzowitzky 2004: 3sat).
8. The off-screen voices belong to well-known actors: David Striesow played the part of an SS officer in Ruzowitzky's Academy Award-winning Holocaust drama *The Counterfeiters* [*Die Fälscher*] (2007); Alexander Fehling is known for his role as a drunken German soldier in a key scene in Quentin Tarantino's *Inglourious Basterds* (2009); Benno Fürmann appeared on screen as a Jewish fugitive in Agnieszka Holland's *In Darkness* (2011).
9. 'Schon wieder faszinierte Nahaufnahmen "unserer Väter" (diesmal ohne die Mutter), die überall unfreiwillige Verstrickung, aber kaum noch Täter sehen? Den Eindruck kann man haben.'
10. For the aesthetic of *Generation War*, see Cohen-Pfister (2014), and Jennifer M. Kapczynski's essay in this volume.
11. Ruzowitzky hints at this intention in an interview included with the DVD version of the film.
12. One may go even further back to the *Black Book* project initiated by Ilya Ehrenburg and Vassily Grossman, who as early as 1943 began to collect documents about atrocities committed on Soviet territories. The crimes of the *Einsatzgruppen* are discussed by Raul Hilberg in his seminal history of the Holocaust; and also by Christopher Browning, Wendy Lower, Karel Berkhoff, Yitzhak Arad, Ilya Altman, Dieter Pohl and Jürgen Matthäus. The much-noticed work of Timothy Snyder on the 'bloodlands' of Eastern Europe addresses these crimes by situating them in the broader context of genocidal policies of totalitarian regimes in the twentieth century.
13. Romain Icard's documentary is discussed by Brad Prager in this volume.
14. For Holocaust awareness in the post-Soviet states, see Olga Gershenson's essay in this volume.
15. Liev Schreiber's film version (2005) does not address the circumstances of the mass shootings to the same extent as Foer's novel.
16. For more on the Goldhagen debate, see Shandley (1998).
17. For a discussion of Farocki's and Oppenheimer's work, see the volume edited by Joram ten Brink and Joshua Oppenheimer (2012).

18 Unless indicated otherwise, the sources for the dates are from *Lexikon der Vergangenheitsbewältigung* edited by Torben Fischer and Matthias N. Lorenz (2007: 288–97 and 341–44).
19 Lanzmann was able to conduct secretly recorded interviews with two former members of the *Einsatzgruppen*. Sue Vice (2011) discusses aesthetic and ethical reasons why Lanzmann did not include these interviews in *Shoah*.

Filmography

The Act of Killing. Dir. Joshua Oppenheimer. Denmark/Norway/UK, 2012.
Babi Yar: The Forgotten Crime [Babij Jar: Das vergessene Verbrechen]. Dir. Jeff Kanew. Germany/Belarus, 2003.
The Counterfeiters [Die Fälscher] Dir. Stefan Ruzowitzky. Germany, 2007.
Downfall [Der Untergang]. Dir. Oliver Hirschbiegel. Germany/Austria/Italy, 2004.
Dresden [Dresden: Das Inferno]. Dir. Roland Suso Richter. Germany, 2006.
East of War [Jenseits des Krieges]. Dir. Ruth Beckermann. Germany, 1996.
Everything Is Illuminated. Dir. Liev Schreiber. USA, 2005.
Generation War [Unsere Mütter, unsere Väter]. Dir. Philipp Kadelbach. Germany, 2013.
The Germans [Die Deutschen]. Produced by Guido Knopp. Germany, 2008, 2010.
Die Gustloff. Dir. Joseph Vilsmaier. Germany, 2008.
Hitler's Helpers [Hitlers Helfer]. Produced by Guido Knopp. Germany, 1996, 1997.
Hitler's Hidden Holocaust. Produced by Erik Nelson. USA, 2009.
Holocaust. Dir. Marvin J. Chomsky. USA, 1978.
Holocaust by Bullets [La Shoah par balles: l'histoire oubliée]. Dir. Romain Icard. France, 2008.
In Darkness. Dir. Agnieszka Holland. Poland/Germany/Canada, 2011.
Inglourious Basterds. Dir. Quentin Tarantino. USA, 2009.
March of Millions [Die Flucht]. Dir. Kai Wessel. Germany, 2007.
Not All Were Murderers [Nicht alle waren Mörder]. Dir. Jo Baier. Germany, 2005.
Radical Evil [Das radikal Böse]. Dir. Stefan Ruzowitzky. Germany/Austria, 2013.
Schindler's List. Dir. Steven Spielberg. USA, 1993.
Shoah. Dir. Claude Lanzmann. France, 1985.
Sophie Scholl: The Final Days [Sophie Scholl: Die letzten Tage]. Dir. Marc Rothemund. Germany, 2005.
The Unknown Soldier [Der unbekannte Soldat]. Dir. Michael Verhoeven. Germany, 2006.

Bibliography

Anatoli, A. (1967) *Babi Yar: A Documentary Novel*. New York: Dial Press.
Bangert, Axel (2014a) *The Nazi Past in Contemporary German Film: Viewing Experiences of Intimacy and Immersion*. New York: Camden House.
____ (2014b) 'Shameful Exposures: Ordinary Germans and the Nazi Past in Contemporary German Documentary Film', *New German Critique*, 41, 3, 159–78.
Browning, Christopher R. (2005) *Ordinary Men: Reserve Police Battalion 101 and the Final Solution in Poland*. London: Penguin.

Cohen-Pfister, Laurel (2014) 'Claiming World War II and Its Lost Generation: *Unsere Mütter, unsere Väter* and the Politics of Emotion', *Seminar*, 50, 1, 104–24.

Ebbrecht, Tobias (2007) 'Docudramatizing History on TV: German and British Docudrama and Historical Event Television in the Memorial Year 2005', *European Journal of Cultural Studies*, 10, 1, 35–53.

Farocki, Harun (2009) *Ernste Spiele III: Immersion*. Installation.

Fischer, Torben and Matthias N. Lorenz (2007) *Lexikon der Vergangenheitsbewältigung in Deutschland: Debatten- und Diskursgeschichte des Nationalsozialismus nach 1945*. Bielefeld: transcript.

Foer, Jonathan S. (2003) *Everything Is Illuminated*. London: Penguin.

Formosa, Paul (2007) 'Is Radical Evil Banal? Is Banal Evil Radical?', *Philosophy & Social Criticism*, 33, 6, 717–35.

Friedrich, Jörg (2006) *The Fire: The Bombing of Germany, 1940–1945*. New York: Columbia University Press.

Goldhagen, Daniel J. (1996) *Hitler's Willing Executioners: Ordinary Germans and the Holocaust*. New York: Knopf.

Knäpple, Lena (2007) 'Erinnerungsbrüche und Identitätsentwürfe. VI.A1 Wehrmachtsausstellung', in Torben Fischer and Matthias N. Lorenz (eds) *Lexikon der Vergangenheitsbewältigung: Debatten- und Diskursgeschichte des Nationalsozialismus nach 1945*. Bielefeld: transcript, 288–90.

Littell, Jonathan (2006) *The Kindly Ones: A Novel*. Toronto: McClelland & Stewart.

Longerich, Peter (2010) *Holocaust: The Nazi Persecution and Murder of the Jews*. Oxford: Oxford University Press.

Moeller, Robert G. (2005) 'Germans as Victims?: Thoughts on a Post-Cold War History of World War II's Legacies', *History and Memory*, 17, 1/2, 145–94.

Moses, A. Dirk (2007) 'The Non-German German and the German German: Dilemmas of Identity after the Holocaust', *New German Critique*, 101, 45–94.

Neiman, Susan (2004) *Evil in Modern Thought: An Alternative History of Philosophy*. Princeton, NJ: Princeton University Press.

Phelan, James (2007) *Experiencing Fiction: Judgments, Progressions, and the Rhetorical Theory of Narrative*. Columbus, OH: Ohio State University Press.

Rose, Gillian (1996) *Mourning Becomes the Law: Philosophy and Representation*. Cambridge: Cambridge University Press.

Rothöhler, Simon (2014) 'Doku über NS-Täter: Alles was man falsch machen kann', *tageszeitung*. 20 January. Online: http://www.taz.de/!5050495/

Ruzowitzky, Stefan (2013) 'Fragen an Stefan Ruzowitzky zu seinem Film *Das radikal Böse*', interview. *Das radikal Böse* DVD. W-film Distribution.

____ (2014) 'Lust am Töten: Gespräch mit Stefan Ruzowitzky'. *Kulturzeit*. 3sat, 7 January.

Shandley, Robert R. (1998) *Unwilling Germans?: The Goldhagen Debate*. Minneapolis, MN: University of Minnesota Press.

Ten Brink, Joram (2012) 'Re-enactment, the History of Violence and Documentary Film,' in Joram Ten Brink and Joshua Oppenheimer (eds) *Killer Images: Documentary Film, Memory and the Performance of Violence*. London and New York: Wallflower Press, 176–89.

Ten Brink, Joram and Joshua Oppenheimer (eds) (2012) *Killer Images: Documentary Film, Memory and the Performance of Violence*. London and New York: Wallflower Press.

Thomas, D. M. (1981) *The White Hotel*. New York: Viking Press.
Vice, Sue (2011) 'Claude Lanzmann's Einsatzgruppen Interviews', *Holocaust Studies: A Journal of Culture and History*, 17, 2, 51–74.
Waller, James (2007) *Becoming Evil: How Ordinary People Commit Genocide and Mass Killing*. Oxford: Oxford University Press.
Zimbardo, Philip G. (2007) *The Lucifer Effect: Understanding How Good People Turn Evil*. New York: Random House.

CHAPTER TWELVE

TV as a Historical Archive?
HOW EPIC FAMILY SERIES MEMORIALISE THE HOLOCAUST

Marcus Stiglegger

TOWARDS A NEW ARCHIVE

To reflect on historical, social and political events could be considered a possible 'duty' of the audiovisual media, in particular narrative television and cinema. The great success of programmes and films such as *Holocaust* (1978) by Marvin J. Chomsky and *Schindler's List* (1993) by Steven Spielberg and their influence on public opinion about historical events suggests that the worldwide audience is more open for fictionalised history than for more challenging documentary work, like Claude Lanzmann's extensive interview-film *Shoah* (1985). This poses the question of whether cinema and serial TV have finally reached the status of a historical archive for some audiences. If this is so the goal of Film Studies should be to analyse the specific value of such representations, especially in the case of a significant phenomenon like the Holocaust, which according to Lanzmann is 'un-filmable' (1988: 270). The outcome of such an analysis may well be that such programmes resort to trivialisation and fail to represent history appropriately. In this essay I shall attempt to break down the history of Holocaust cinema into several phases and take a closer look at a number of narrative TV series that effectively challenge many of the rules set by earlier forms of 'Holocaust cinema' and thereby offer a new perspective on a topic that usually only regenerates established images (see Jackob and Stiglegger 2005).

Significantly it was by no means the historians who made the most decisive contribution to the long-term establishment of the problematic term 'Holocaust' – and the crimes connected to it – in both the European and the North American collective consciousness and memory. They may have critically researched sources, documented their findings, published textbooks and produced documentaries on and around the topic, but when compared with the effect by one television melodrama, a family saga, staged in the midst of vicious Nazi war-crimes, suddenly their efforts seem to have little value other than that of confirming the historical accuracy of the scenes of persecution and extermination of 'imaginary' figures. The four-part television show *Holocaust*, whose 1978 broadcast in the USA was followed by around 100 million, was seen in West Germany one year later by an audience of 16 million. From a media-historic perspective, the television event *Holocaust* can be described as a decisive point in the social role of television as a medium of mass communication. The German film and television historian Knut Hickethier comments on the effects the series had on the formatting of public television as follows:

> The defining television event at the end of the 70s was the transmission of the American series *Holocaust* ... which showed the murder of European Jews by the Germans. In setting its focus not on social criticism and resolving the past but rather on fictionalisation and entertainment, this film marks a turning point. [...] Its success was considerable and uncontested. The series was accused of emotionalising, trivialising and falsifying history. (1998: 355; my translation)

In Germany, *Holocaust* made a lasting – one could almost say the first – deep impression, especially on the sons and daughters of the perpetrators. The fact that this impression can be traced back to the transmission of a commercial television mini-series, which intentionally slipped under the customary ductus of distanced impartiality, has to be seen as an important indication of a strong change in the social and medial handling of history in general, and of the history of the genocide of the Third Reich in particular. From then on, the mass-extermination practised under the Nazi regime had a name which everyone knew and could relate to – and which was represented in iconic images.

The lasting effect of this phenomenon can still be seen today, especially in the many films of the 1980s, which attempted to cash in on the success of *Holocaust* on TV. Parallel to the change in the televisual handling of this sensitive topic it is also possible to trace a general change in attitude towards the subject: many US films of the post-New Hollywood-era – coined by the success of blockbusters – were designed on the basis of the new commercial and aesthetic considerations of the entertainment industry, influencing their dramaturgy, imagery and casting in accordance with Hollywood's star system. The fact that among these were also productions which, by means of complex

Fig. 1 *Holocaust*

narrative and more ambitious forms of expression, left television far behind can be seen in films such as Alan J. Pakula's *Sophie's Choice* (1982). However, these more demanding films also fuelled a debate that today still questions the legitimacy of aesthetic representations of the Nazi genocide. According to Matías Martínez, art cannot possibly ignore the largest crime of the twentieth century, yet at the same time such art is essentially impossible, 'because in the opinion of many, the Holocaust defies aesthetic portrayal in a special, perhaps even unique way' (1997: 36; my translation). In this respect, *Schindler's List* marks a turning point since, in its case, the questionable symbioses between commercial and ethical productions is widely acknowledged, by both the public and critics, to have been successful (see Martínez 1997: 37). This film can also be seen as a turning point in another respect. If one looks at the film as a social phenomenon (which it unquestionably was and is), at least two modes of interpretation present themselves.

Firstly, one can speculate whether a trend that had started in the 1970s with the mini-series *Holocaust* came to a provisional end in the 1990s with *Schindler's List*. Little by little a culture of remembrance, which attempted to gain access to the events and environment of Nazi terror by way of fictional film and which always searched for new methods of staging, established itself next to that of the immediate witnesses of the concentration camp terror, the victims and the perpetrators. However, because the witnesses are now increasingly withdrawing from public life, both new and old films need to be critically analysed regarding their intentions and aesthetic principles.

Secondly the arrival of *Schindler's List* made clear the importance of the medium of film as an archive, whose influence on the processes of identity formation in contemporary culture is ever growing. If we accept that film, as an archive, exists as a threshold between the cultural and the communicative/collective consciousness, and does so only by way of critical reflection about old and new films by viewers, then this essay can be understood as a proposal for the critical handling of film as cultural archive.

While the representation of Nazi genocide in the form of feature films is a subject which has already been widely discussed and documented, TV series on the Holocaust have been widely ignored (see Stiglegger 2014). As one can imagine, the filmic representation of events under the Nazi occupation developed slowly at first, then went through several 'experimental' phases until, by the end of the 1970s, it had developed into a form of filmic mediation which could be compared to 'Auschwitz literature', in which a unique iconography of genocide and the concentration camps developed. This development ended, in effect, with the television series *Holocaust*, and even here it is necessary to look at the influence of cinema on television formats in order to be able to take all relevant inter-mediated interaction into account. The following overview covers key films and TV programmes since 1945 that explicitly address the events of the Holocaust, avoiding films that merely draw on the Nazi regime.

FICTIONALISING THE HOLOCAUST DURING THE POST-WAR YEARS

Film theorist Béla Balázs remarked in a 1948 review, which was only made available by editor Hanno Loewy after Balázs's death, that the Polish film *The Last Stage* [*Ostatni etap*] (1947) by Wanda Jakubowska had founded its own genre, and in so doing he almost prophetically lent the 'Holocaust film' an emblematic character similar to that of 'Auschwitz literature'. Jakubowska's film reconstructs the fate of a group of female prisoners, relying on both professional and lay actors, the latter survivors from Auschwitz who returned to the camp's barracks two years after the end of the war. Numerous standard situations in filmic Holocaust representation are to be seen in the film: the roll-call, informing on ones' fellow inmates, torture and, in particular, the nightly arrival of the prison trains, to swirling flakes of snow or ash and sludgy muddy ground. Alain Resnais quoted this scene in *Nuit et brouillard* [*Night and Fog*] (1955), George Stevens integrated it completely into a nightmare sequence in *The Diary of Anne Frank* (1959) and, lastly, Steven Spielberg reconstructed the scene in *Schindler's List*. In his essay 'Fiktion und Mimesis' Loewy stresses that this film, which reconstructed these events soon after the historic horror of their passing, is regarded as a historical document (2003: 37).

With regard to the concentration camp system, one of the most important filmic documents of the 1950s is not a feature film but rather an essay film. In *Nuit et brouillard*,

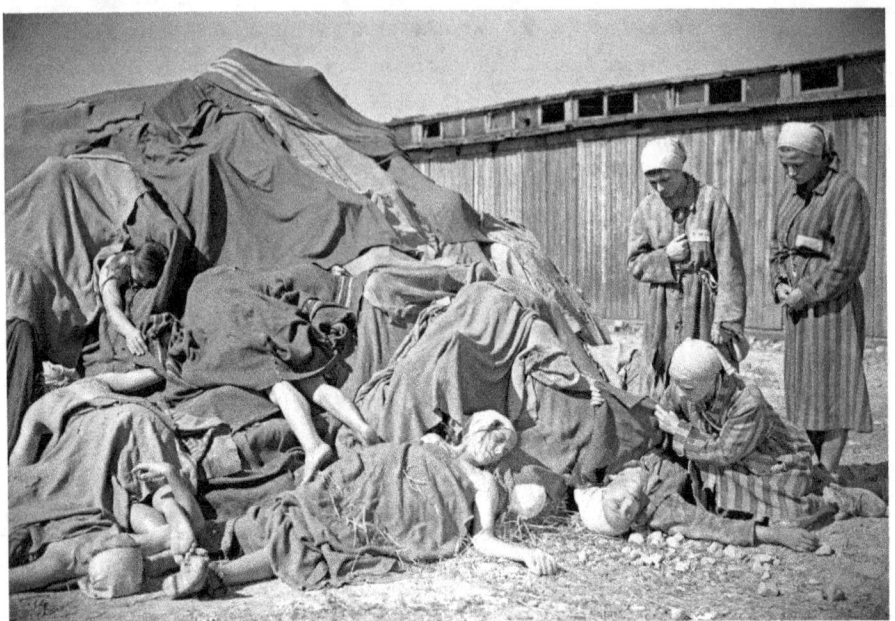

Fig. 2 *Kapo*

Alain Resnais intercuts material that he produced himself with scenes filmed by allied troops during the liberation of the death camps showing masses of dead bodies. In his very subjective, poetic film Resnais established a technique that is also of importance for later Holocaust film. It relies on what Annette Insdorf terms 'meaningful montage' (1983: 29), describing an approach that reflects on the connections between history and memory, between the past and the present. In this respect the influence of this widely screened non-fiction film upon later fictional cinema films is not to be underestimated.

An early foray into the realm of a TV reflection of the Nazi genocide was significantly presented by the first episode of the German mini-series *Am grünen Strand der Spree*

Figs. 3, 4 *Am grünen Strand der Spree, Das Haus in der Karpfengasse*

(1960), which showed executions of Jewish prisoners at the seashore after they had been forced to dig their own graves. This episode refers to subjective war memories of one particular witness, a German soldier. Never before had the mechanics of genocide been shown so precisely and explicitly. The TV programme placed a finger directly into the still open wound of disturbing war memories. Three years later another series called *Das Haus in der Karpfengasse* (1963) told of the everyday life of several inhabitants of an urban city quarter during the reign of the Nazis. Subtle tyranny is present here as well as the deportation of Jews, and that series created a blueprint for later dramatic re-staging of that era.

A VISUAL ICONOGRAPHY OF ITS OWN

The most important impetus for intensive media discussion of the Holocaust thematic was the four-part American television series *Holocaust* in 1978. Marvin J. Chomsky's epic series follows the fortunes of the Jewish Weiss family and the German Dorf family, with each situated on opposing sides of the genocide. Whereas one family has to flee and is deported, Eric Dorf (Michael Moriarty) joins the SS and becomes implicated in organising the Holocaust. The series was criticised for its melodramatic and oversimplified structure, clearly following the format of the successful family epic *Roots* (1977), which told the story of slavery in the Southern states of the USA. Regardless of its trivial aspects *Holocaust* had a massive impact, comparable only to that of Spielberg's *Schindler's List*, and it must therefore be recognised as a milestone in Holocaust dramatisation.

Alan J. Pakula's *Sophie's Choice* is another film that makes use of the concept of 'meaningful montage'. It is a melodrama about Polish Catholic Sophie (Meryl Streep), who survived a concentration camp because she attracted the attention of an SS officer, who then asked her the question that destroyed her life: he asked her to choose which of her children should be spared death. The film tells of this harrowing event by way of long flashbacks from the midst of its melodrama structure. Pakula's film reconstructs the scenes taking place in the concentration camp in faded, monochromatic images, a style which in and of itself can be seen as iconographic and was later adopted by other productions, occurring sometimes as an empty quotation devoid of meaning e.g. more recently in Brian Singer's *X-Men* (2000).

In the wake of *Holocaust* a first wave of international TV series was produced. In France, Robert Enrico adapted the autobiography of

Fig. 5 *Au nom de tous les miens*

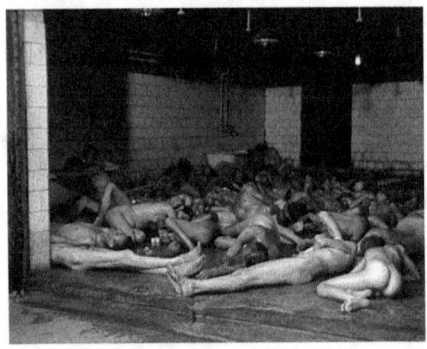

Fig. 6 *Au nom de tous les miens*

Martin Grey in *Au nom de tous les miens* (1985), starring Michael York. The series follows the Jewish main character on his odyssey through war-torn Europe, with a long episode taking place in a death camp where viewers witness the gassing of prisoners. Enrico is much more explicit in his depiction of the extermination than was the American prototype. But the iconography resembles the one established in the flashbacks of *Sophie's Choice*.

Dan Curtis adapted Herman Wouk's war opus *War and Remembrance* (1988) in a kaleidoscopic style and included equally explicit episodes of Nazi cruelty, sadism and war crimes. This sequel to the internationally successful series *The Winds of War* (1983) was never accepted by the audiences due to its extremely bleak view of the war (see Sharbutt 1987). Even in Germany, it was only shown once on public television. German series largely followed a different strategy and focused on everyday life under Nazi occupation. Egon Monk's family epos *Die Bertinis* (1988) was very successful, yet at no point was it as explicit as its international predecessors.

The biographical German series *Klemperer: Ein Leben in Deutschland* [*Klem-perer: A Life in Germany*] (1999) by Kai Wessel was meant to repeat the success of *Die Bertinis* on German TV, but it failed to find a huge audience. This portrayal of a well-known Jewish intellectual in Nazi Germany maintains an atmosphere of permanent menace, but the hero manages to escape deportation and execution on several occasions. The director cites well-established Holocaust images more than actually documenting events from the death camps. His protagonists suffer, but they often seem privileged and intellectually conscious, thereby introducing a new element.

In 2001, *Band of Brothers*, lavishly produced by Steven Spielberg and Tom Hanks, touched on the Nazi genocide in one episode, entitled 'Why We Fight', in which GIs discover a concentration camp in the woods. The imagery here is very close to earlier depictions of the camps in *Au nom de tous les miens* with its monochrome colour scheme and use of a hand-held camera. In Germany, the fictionalised history storytelling culminated in the major TV production of *Generation War* [*Unsere Mütter, unsere Väter*] (2013), produced by Nico Hoffmann. The deportation and execution of Jewish and other victims is touched on in a few scenes, but again is represented, at best, as a minor aspect of World War II. It seems that the Nazi genocide is now seen in this context rather than being an isolated topic like in *Holocaust*. A series like *War and Remembrance* proves to be ahead of its time in that respect. The following case studies will take a close look at the way staged images 'overwrite' actual documents from the war era.

AVOIDING GRAPHIC IMAGES: *KLEMPERER*

The most elaborate attempt at a fictionalisation of the Holocaust in German television is undoubtedly the twelve-part series *Klemperer: Ein Leben in Deutschland* by Kai Wessel and Andreas Kleinert from a screenplay by Peter Steinbach, freely based on the memoirs of writer and literary scholar Victor Klemperer. The original books were published posthumously in the 1990s: the diaries describe the increasing academic exclusion and disenfranchisement of Jews under the Nazi regime from a subjective point of view. Produced by the MDR in cooperation with the Konken Studios and Studio Babelsberg, the relatively high production cost for the series was then 20 million German marks. The film was shot on location in Dresden and in places in Prague that resembled the historical Dresden. For the first broadcast in 1999, ARD was hoping for a major audience share, but could only manage about 2.7 million viewers per episode (see fsz. 1999). *Klemperer* therefore did not reach the iconic presence and significance of such series as *Holocaust* or *Die Bertinis*, which may have been because of the now heavily modified and significantly differentiated television landscape in Germany. The series was hard to sell abroad; it was shown in Finland, but not in the USA.

Unlike *Die Bertinis*, *Klemperer* begins with Hitler's rise to power in 1933. Pressured by the SA hordes, Dresden calls for a boycott of Jewish businesses. Discrimination is piling up. At this time, professor of literature Victor Klemperer (Matthias Habich) and his wife Eva (Dagmar Manzel), a pianist, try to live their dream of owning a house in the countryside. When Victor is increasingly subjected to repression at the university, and when a much-needed loan for construction work is not granted, they react with defiance. Their friends Ellen and Henry Feller offer Klemperer a private loan. Other friends, Harry and Agnes Dember, meanwhile announce their plans of leaving Germany. The Klemperers never think of emigrating and escaping from the Nazis. Klemperer builds the house, passes his driving licence and buys a car, despite the ubiquity of the Nazis. But increasingly it is lonely at Victor and Eva Klemperer's home, as more and more Jewish families from their circle of acquaintances leave Germany.

During the burning of the synagogues throughout Germany, the Klemperers are surprised by the outbreak of Nazi terror in a small village. They experience the humiliation of Jewish families, see how shops are looted and set on fire. In such scenes, the subsequent events already are announced clearly in the image of book burning at the university. Victor Klemperer is less indignant than his wife, but the fear is spreading. While some community members help, others have already joined the SS and have become mortal enemies. They get a taste of the future when Obersturmführer Malachowski stands on their doorstep. Under the pretext of a search warrant for possession of firearms, he terrorises the two until the early morning hours.

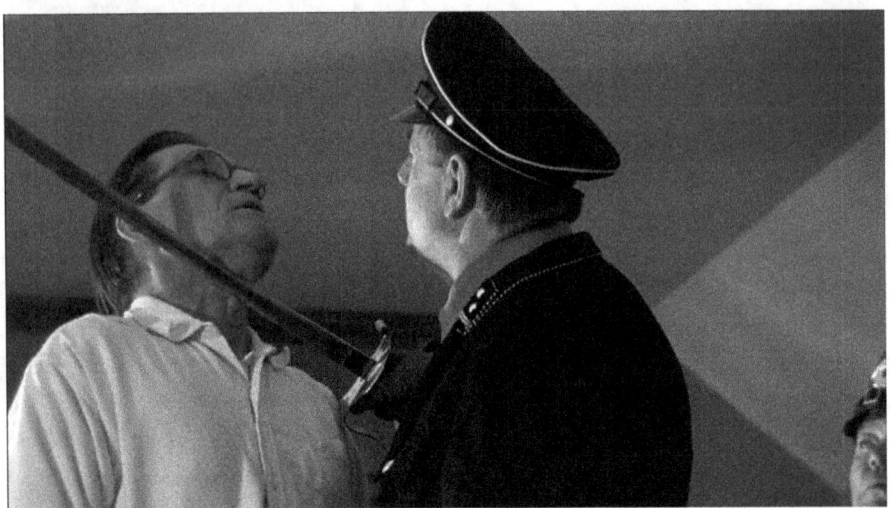

Fig. 7 *Klemperer*

In the summer of 1939, the war directly affects the couple. Victor is increasingly suffering from heart problems. Again he experiences courageous support, this time from a doctor who attends to Jewish patients in a secret compartment, called 'Hotel Aviv'. Since Eva ignores the German race laws by not seeking a divorce from Victor, they must live together in a dedicated 'Jewish house'. For violating the blackout rules Victor is sentenced to some time in jail, where he faces further humiliation.

Up to this point, the series has presented numerous situations that remind viewers of the concentration camps without being too explicit or moving beyond the biographical perspective. In this regard, *Klemperer* continues the tradition of German Holocaust series such as *Die Bertinis*, avoiding drastic re-enactments and consciously choosing a limited perspective that conveys a greater proximity to everyday experience. The deadly terror of the Nazis is staged sparingly and *pars pro toto* by Kai Wessel. Episode 8, however, introduces significant Holocaust iconography. Klemperer is almost deported, but is freed at the behest of his former driving instructor, SS-Müller. He sees cattle cars that serve the deportation and hears on an English news channel that the Nazis gas the deportees in their camps. The couple react to this news with disbelief and take it for enemy propaganda. When the SS storms the 'Jewish house', SS-Müller stops Obersturmführer Malachowski from raping a young woman. Klemperer is reassigned to forced labour, which is a further threat to his health. During his work on the railroad tracks Klemperer witnesses deportations in the mist – a dramatic representation convention that brings the title of Resnais' *Nuit et brouillard* to mind. Like a premonition in a long zoom-in, viewers see the black smoke from the train engine like the ashes from the concentration camp chimneys. Next to the train tracks, heaps of suitcases are left behind, evoking another iconic image.

Judged from Klemperer's stunned gaze it is clear that he now believes what he had previously dismissed on the radio. The series repeatedly alludes to images that viewers might know from international Holocaust films and series, and it is thus able to avoid being too explicit in its imagery. Wessel's mise-en-scène indirectly evokes the established world of images, without implementing them directly. Instead, he continues to build analogue and metaphorical motifs. In episode 10 Klemperer must take dead animals to the slaughterhouse, where they are gutted. The scene clearly shows the broken eyes, quick cuts and the intestines falling out. He manages to secure a beef tongue and distributes it to his group.

The loss of friends and relatives is now becoming more common, and thanks to the epic narrative of the series the audience is able to relate to this personal loss. In a striking scene the young Friedhelm (Fabian Busch) is shot by an SS man, when he refuses to stop playing his harmonica. After that incident, the 'Jewish house' is cleared, and the men and women are separated. With the dramatic view of Eva's and Victor's separation, the mise-en-scène comes closest to classical Holocaust iconography. Eva is interned with the other women in improvised camps. Prior to that, they have to be disinfected before the eyes of an SS guard. Later, Eva learns of Victor's imminent deportation. Again, she manages to save her husband from deportation at the last moment. Their reunion between the cattle cars aims at the style of classical iconography of the Holocaust with iconic images in night and fog.

The aim of the series *Klemperer* is clearly not to draw an explicit picture of the Nazi genocide, but to describe a subjective view of the growing suffering of the Jews under persecution and terror by the Nazis. To this, the series devotes a lot of time, and by

Fig. 8 *Klemperer*

doing so it reduces the shocking iconography to metaphorical images (the slaughtered animals) or analogous situations (the detention, the cattle cars), which reactivate the already established image archive of the audience. Yet the series encountered another problem: while *Holocaust* and *Die Bertinis* relied on a range of characters, *Klemperer* focuses on a rather self-pitying, initially privileged academic who needs to be rescued time and again by his wife or other people. As a character, he seems rather unable to captivate the interest of a large audience over a twelve-episode series. Also, by carefully avoiding explicit genocide imagery and by focusing on the daily lives of the protagonists, with *Klemperer* the tradition of dealing with the Holocaust in a more subtle manner had possibly come to a final stage. Other serial media simulacra had already established a dominant imagery of remembrance within popular culture. They were often spectacular and gave a transnational audience access to the topic; yet the privatized approach of this German TV series failed to gain significant attention.

THE REASON FOR FIGHTING: *BAND OF BROTHERS*

Fifteen years after *War and Remembrance*, Steven Spielberg and Tom Hanks teamed up for an ambitious semi-documentary television series that built on the success of their war film *Saving Private Ryan* (1998). *Band of Brothers* recounts in elaborate reconstructions the story of the Easy Company, a group of young American daredevils. At the beginning of the episodes, the real-life counterparts of the series' characters, US veterans of World War II, report on their experiences and legitimise the action series as a 'semi-documentary'. In episode 9, entitled 'Why We Fight', directed by David Frankel and written by John Orloff, the GIs discover an abandoned concentration camp in the woods. The perspective of the US Army here is implemented more consistently than in *War and Remembrance*, as viewers experience the events only from the perspective of young soldiers.

The story unfolds episodically and largely unpredictably. In April 1945, Easy Company is moved to Germany, where it encounters the German civilian population for the first time. During these meetings, they discover that the enemy is no different to themselves. They even begin to fraternise with the Germans (in the form of small affairs). In addition, they enjoy being able to sleep in real beds after a previous period of deprivation at the front lines. Major Winters (Damien Lewis) looks after his comrade Captain Nixon (Ron Livingston), who has become cynical of the war experience and slowly becomes an alcoholic. Rather abruptly the Holocaust breaks into these soldiers' everyday life. Shortly after President Roosevelt's death a security patrol reports an abandoned concentration camp in a remote forest populated by hundreds of emaciated prisoners. The American soldiers get closer and closer to this world of horror and destruction, whose real extent becomes visible only slowly. They free and feed the weakened prisoners, but then return the concentration camp survivors to the camp in order to record their rescue. The indigenous population, which denies that it was aware of the concentration camp near them, is given the order to bury the rotting corpses and clean up the camp. At this point, the ambiguity of the episode title is clear: *Why We Fight* was the title of the film series that Hollywood professionals like Frank Capra, John Houston and Samuel Fuller shot as directors and cameramen for the Propaganda Department of the US Army during World War II. The aim was to show the American people why it is necessary to engage in the war. Sam Fuller directed the now world-famous recordings of the liberation and clearance of the Bergen-Belsen concentration camp. In its penultimate episode, *Band of Brothers* revisits this series of historical propaganda films to a certain extent, addressing the legitimacy of the American presence in World War II. Here at last the need for the destruction of the Nazi regime is made obviously clear.

Increasing in intensity, the episode at first depicts the scene at the camp then supplements it with oral testimony. As GIs Winters and Nixon arrive at the camp barracks, they see firsthand the prisoners' terrible conditions. A German soldier translates the testimony by a prisoner who tells them that mainly Jews were interned and killed. In a cattle car, the GIs find piles of further bodies; another camp for women is located nearby. Through the eyes of the GIs, viewers become fellow witnesses. While *War and Remembrance* clearly follows the scenic tradition of *Holocaust*'s veridical style, the specific approach of *Band of Brothers* is rather based on later conventions. With films like *Saving Private Ryan*, the convention of black and white film as a sign of past events began to become outdated. The public learned to accept the washed-out, muted colour palette of films around the turn of the millennium as a method of historical authentification.

Fig. 10 *Band of Brothers*

Fig. 11 *Band of Brothers*

Thus the whole series *Band of Brothers* is marked by pale colours and a cloudy sky. This monochromaticism is now well-established in the collective archive as a code for the mythical model of tragic historicity. This convention goes so far that films that represent the setting of a concentration camp scenario with brilliant blue skies and green fields may immediately be perceived as 'inauthentic'. In 1955, *Nuit et brouillard* defined the public image archive for decades to come. Resnais distinguished between the present (not visibly manipulated in its colours) and the past (black and white photography). Resnais' approach was later followed by Spielberg in *Schindler's List*: colour is shown only in the semi-documentary footage at the beginning and at the end of the film, including images of the still-living Schindler Jews. The early films about the crimes of the Nazis preserved the black-and-white format known from the newsreels as a staging strategy. The images of the past corresponded to historical newsreel iconography. This changed in the 1970s: to display the events in Nazi concentration camps coloured material was reduced in its saturation (in a process called downgrading) so that mainly brown and blue tones dominated, which is intended to reinforce an oppressive and morbid atmosphere. This example shows that over decades, a partially conventionalised notion of historical events has been established, in effect creating medial simulacra of history. However, through this reliance on conventions, films and TV series contribute to popular modes of mythologising history. This process accepts only what adheres to the collective visual memory, and criticises forms of representation that look for other ways.

Band of Brothers strongly affirms the conventions established in the 1990s and thus creates, once again, a very satisfactory historical simulacrum for a large television audience. The muddy colour palette evokes the feeling of being in a drafty ditch or of roaming through frosty forests. These cinematic features confirm the viewers in the diffuse (and quite inappropriate) impression that they personally take part in the events portrayed.

CONSPIRACY THEORIES: *MADAR-E SEFR DARADSCHEH*

A counterpoint to the American approach just discussed can be found on television in the Middle East. There, too, the Holocaust as a media topic has not played a significant role in the early twenty-first century (except, of course, in Israel). In this context, the Iranian family series *Madar-e sefr daradscheh* [*Zero Degree Turn*] (2006–2007), created by Hasan Fathi, stands as a curiosity that at first sight hardly fits into Iran's anti-Semitic and anti-Israeli propaganda concept. Over 47 episodes the series tells the story of the Iranian diplomat Habib Parsa (Shahab Hosseini), who saves a Jewish family during World War II from the threat of deportation and falls in love with the young Jewish girl Sara Astrok (Nathalie Matti). In some scenes Holocaust iconography appears, but mostly the staging is limited to dialogue situations. In a much more dominant (though sometimes crudely staged) manner, the series employs stylistic references to the classic gangster film and the American film noir. In the end, the series is less concerned with a fictionalised rendition of historical events, as it is built on a conspiracy theory: the series shows the conflict between radical Zionists and peaceful Jews, and it plays on the extremely questionable conspiracy thesis that the Zionists had cooperated with Hitler to enforce the establishment of a Zionist state of Israel by the expulsion of Jews from Western Europe. The representative of the Zionist movement, named Theodore Stark and ostensibly linked to the historical Zionist Theodor Herzl, is contrasted with the peaceful Professor Weiss, who rejects the aspirations of the Zionists. The name of the latter establishes a clear reference to the Weiss family in the original *Holocaust* series. The Iranian series is clearly aimed at the formulation of a conspiratorial collaboration between Nazis and Zionists and thus follows the purpose of propaganda. *Madar-e sefr daradscheh* historically puts the creation of Israel in a criminal light since it is presented as the result of an internal Jewish conflict: a retired professor of history is in possession of documents that prove secret connections between the Jewish World Association and the National Socialists. This crude plot on the one hand corresponds well with the national discourse of Iran about Israel and the Holocaust; on the other, both the Holocaust subject and the conventionalised iconography are used and exploited to illustrate a propaganda message (see Kazemi 2007). To date, this must count as a unique move in fictionalising the Holocaust. And in the light of this perverse reversal, it makes perfect sense that the series generally avoids referring to the established Holocaust imagery and instead plays with genre stereotypes of epic melodrama, war film and thriller, embedded in the mise-en-scène of a soap opera.

FICTIONAL MEDIA AS A HISTORICAL ARCHIVE

The previous discussions have examined the staging of the Holocaust in American, German and international films and television series. They document the development from historical photographic documents to the origins of early cinematic Holocaust iconography and up to the popularisation of these images after the worldwide success of the US series *Holocaust*. As I have discussed at more length in my monograph *Auschwitz TV*, there is a permanent exchange between documentary, cinematographic and fictional TV representations of the Holocaust since 1945, culminating in the 1978 series *Holocaust* and then influencing all three formats (documentary, feature film, TV series). None of these formats can do without the others, and they are all transformed within the ever-changing media iconography. One can go so far as to refer to this process as a gradual replacement of real documentary images by staged pictures (see also Ebbrecht 2001: 313).

The fictionalised narratives overshadow the discourse by historians, and they establish not only the iconic images but also the terminology. Like the very term 'Holocaust', the medial iconography of historical events was transferred step by step into a popular mythology. In productions like *War and Remembrance, Band of Brothers* or *Klemperer* the imagery is not primarily based on historical documents, but rather on the audio-visual creations from previous fictionalisations. From this image archive both film-makers and audiences are fed alike – in this collective visual memory, which is stored within audiovisual media, a modern myth about history arose (see Barthes 1964). While movies, in their relatively dense (and shorter) narrative, aim primarily through 'meaningful montage' at a mingling of past and present, the epic narrative style of TV series is based more on a growing familiarity with the protagonists.

This phenomenology raises the question of whether this tendency establishes a homogeneous genre: the Holocaust film or series. The homogeneity of iconography, location and time as well as the standardised situations speak for it. The historically based elements mentioned above are clearly defined and recognisable. They usually correspond to the expectations and the pre-existing visual memory of the target audience. The intention of an illusionist reconstruction of the past is given in almost all examples. Holocaust films and series therefore comply with the topically named major genres (e.g. western, war movie, historical drama). However, the body of works, despite the accumulation in certain eras, remains relatively low in numbers, which suggests that it is one of the smaller genres that do not clearly correspond to subgenres of other major genres such as crime thrillers, melodrama or fantasy. Another possibility would be the discussion of Holocaust films and series as representations of a hybrid genre that combines elements of different genres. Thus we find elements of the war film (the era of World War II), including also the prisoner of war camp film (although the concentration camp's purpose is different to the mere detention of captured enemies). We also find numerous elements of melodrama, especially of the family melodrama: this is particularly noticeable in series like *War and Remembrance, Klemperer* or *Holocaust*, of course. Basically, one could speak of historical dramas that use a well-established iconography and combine it with individual plotlines.

Like feature films about the Holocaust, television series also tend to build a closed narrative form. In the series, the story is frequently more complex, but the family saga usually culminates in a final point of reunion of the survivors, which also represents the culmination of the fictionalised era. The open form of the popular series, developed over several seasons and years, seems complicated in this respect. This also explains the strong presence of miniseries (running 3-6 episodes) in this context. Internationally, the specific fictionalisations of the era of the Third Reich and the Holocaust are closely linked to the national discourse. The widely established iconography is then used for different ideological purposes. For instance, in series from the former GDR, despite clear evidence of war crimes and massacres by the Nazis, the specific persecution of Jews and other (non-political) groups of victims seems not to matter. The Jewish victims seem marginalised in favour of the anti-fascist prisoners whose resistance was compliant with the East German SED policy.

The West German TV series with Holocaust topics follow a model different from the US version: as described above, the pattern of a large-scale family narrative is left at the centre, but many series rather address the slow changes of everyday life under persecution by the Nazis, while the situation of deportees in the concentration camps is staged in a very explicit manner. A series such as *Heimat: Eine deutsche Chronik* [*Heimat: A Chronicle of Germany*] (1984) by Edgar Reitz focuses entirely on the daily lives of the rural population and mentions the deportations only briefly in the dialogue. In this way, each specific national discourse about the Holocaust and the historical era is depicted in the narrative patterns and productions. The actual film recordings from the concentration camps were done by Allied camera crews, and the most explicit re-stagings of historical events after 1978 were provided mainly by American productions in cinema and on television. The German productions here are working with a semantic reference system, in sequences like the one in *Klemperer* where Ms. Klemperer can save her husband in the last moment before the deportation – here the imagery of train cars against light and smoke refer exactly to that archetypical image from *Ostatni etap* and *Nuit et brouillard* (and therefore also to *Schindler's List*). German productions rather tend to reference internationally established iconography than reconstructing it within the mise-en-scéne. This phenomenon might be influenced by a fear of fictionalising the 'unimaginable': the arguments made by Claude Lanzman and Theodor W. Adorno about the need to avoid the staged images of the historical horror still seem dominant in German media productions.

While recent international TV series rarely reference the Holocaust explicitly – except as a side aspect in the historical context such as *Band of Brothers* – in German TV series the fate of the German population of the time is the focus. The persecuted and deported are present here in secondary roles (such as the Goldberg figure in *Dresden*). Nevertheless, the visually overwhelming effect of iconic fictionalisations of the Holocaust on TV is not broken: it lives on in countless documentary programmes (e.g. by the German TV historian Guido Knopp) where the iconography is appropriated to dramatise historical recordings in a melodramatic way. In this process, historical visual documents are overwritten by popular iconography: the medial simulacrum replaces the historical photographic archive.

Filmography

Am grünen Strand der Spree. Dir. Fritz Umgelter. West Germany, 1960
Band of Brothers. Produced by Steven Spielberg and Tom Hanks. UK/USA, 2001
Die Bertinis. Dir. Egon Monk. Germany, 1988
The Diary of Anne Frank. Dir. George Stevens. USA, 1959
Dresden. Dir. Roland Suso Richter. Germany, 2006
Das Haus in der Karpfengasse. Dir. Kurt Hoffmann. West Germany, 1963
For Those I Loved [*Au nom de tous les miens*]. Dir. Robert Enrico. France/Canada, 1985
Generation War [*Unsere Mütter, unsere Väter*]. Dir. Philipp Kadelbach. Germany, 2013
Heimat: A Chronicle of Germany [*Heimat: Eine deutsche Chronik*]. Dir. Edgar Reitz. West Germany, 1984
Holocaust. Dir. Marvin J. Chomsky. USA, 1978
Klemperer: A Life in Germany [*Klemperer: Ein Leben in Deutschland*]. Dir. Kai Wessel. Germany, 1999
The Last Stage [*Ostatni etap*]. Dir. Wanda Jakubowska. Poland, 1947
Night and Fog [*Nuit et brouillard*]. Dir. Alain Resnais. France, 1955
Roots. Dir. Marvin J. Chomsky. USA, 1977
Saving Private Ryan. Dir. Steven Spielberg. USA, 1998
Schindler's List. Dir. Steven Spielberg. USA, 1994
Shoah. Dir. Claude Lanzmann. France, 1985
Sophie's Choice. Dir. Alan J. Pakula. UK/USA, 1982
War and Remembrance. Dir. Dan Curtis. USA, 1988
Why We Fight. Dir. Frank Capra et al. USA, 1942–1945
The Winds of War. Dir. Dan Curtis. USA 1983
Zero Degree Turn [*Madar-e sefr daradscheh*]. Dir. Hasan Fathi. Iran, 2006–2007

Bibliography

Barthes, Roland (1964) *Mythologies*. Frankfurt: Suhrkamp.

Ebbrecht, Tobias (2011) *Images of History in the Medial Memory: Filmic Narratives of the Holocaust*. Bielefeld: transcript.

fsz. (1999) 'Frei nach Motiven: Klemperer – Ein Leben in Deutschland', *Hagalil*, 22 November. Online: http://www.hagalil.com/deutschland/sachsen/klemperer.htm

Insdorf, Annette (1983) *Indelible Shadows: Film and the Holocaust*. New York: Cambridge University Press.

Jackob, Alexander and Marcus Stiglegger (eds) (2005) *AugenBlick 26: Zur neuen Kinematographie des Holocaust – Das Kino als Archiv und Zeuge?* Marburg: Schüren.

Kazemi, Mohammad Reza (2007) 'Iranische Holocaust-Serie: Verschwörer als Betörer', Online: http://www.spiegel.de/kultur/gesellschaft/iranische-holocaust-serie-verschwoerer-als-betoerer-a-504864.html

Klemperer, Victor (1998) *I Shall Bear Witness: The Diaries of Victor Klemperer, 1933–1941*, trans. Martin Chalmers. London: Weidenfeld & Nicolson.

____ (1999) *To the Bitter End: The Diaries of Victor Klemperer, 1942–1945*, trans. Martin Chalmers. London: Weidenfeld & Nicolson.

Lanzmann, Claude (1988) *Shoah*. Munich: dtv.

Loewy, Hanno (2003) 'Fiktion und Mimesis: Holocaust und Genre im Film', in Margrit Frölich, Hanno Loewy and Heinz Steinert (eds) *Lachen über Hitler – Auschwitz-Gelächter? Filmkomödie, Satire und Holocaust*. Munich: text + kritik, 37–64.

Martínez, Matías (1997) 'Authentizität als Künstlichkeit in Steven Spielbergs Film *Schindlers List*', *Compass: Mainzer Hefte für allgemeine und Vergleichende Literaturwissenschaft*, 2, 36–40.

Sharbutt, Jay (2013) '"War" Proves a Ratings Misfire', *The Los Angeles Times*, 1 October. Online: http://articles.latimes.com/1988-11-29/entertainment/ca-525_1_premium-rates (7/30/2015)

Stiglegger, Marcus (2014) *Auschwitz TV: Reflexionen des Holocaust in Fernsehserien*. Wiesbaden: Springer.

____ ([1999] 2015) *SadicoNazista: Geschichte, Film und Mythos*. Rev. ed. Hagen-Berchum: Eisenhut.

INDEX

Abraham's Gold 147
Adorno, Theodor W. 15n.5, 257
Aftermath 3–5, 12, 88, 148, 154
Aimée & Jaguar 118
Albahari, David 9
America/United States 15n.2, 24–5, 30, 34–5, 41, 43, 45, 57n.7, 79, 89, 109, 111n.5, 130, 141, 147, 156, 163, 170, 190-1, 213–4, 216n.4, 217n.7, 226, 243, 252–6
amnesia 4, 11, 76–91, 92n.3, 146, 214, 216
Amorim, Vicente 14, 206
And Along Came Tourists 8
Anne Frank Remembered 136
anti-Semitism 34, 67, 78, 80, 129, 143, 146, 154, 229
Archeologia see Archeology
Archeology 106
Arendt, Hannah 4–5, 10, 25–7, 177n.6, 204–5, 216, 216n.2, 222, 238n.4
Arnold, Agnieszka 109–10
Assmann, Jan 1, 89–90
Auschwitz *see* concentration/extermination camps
auteur 48
avant-garde 8–10

Babi Yar (2002) 79
Babi Yar (2003) 79
Babi Yar massacre 79, 167, 226
Babi Yar (novel) 226
Babij Jar: Das vergessene Verbrechen see Babi Yar: The Forgotten Crime
Babi Yar: The Forgotten Crime 226
Bacon, Yehuda 66
Baier, Jo 234
Band of Brothers 248, 252–4, 256, 258

Bangert, Axel 6, 187, 195–6, 199n.3n.5n.8n.10, 200n.12, 223–4, 233
Baron, Lawrence 6, 15n.4, 192, 196
Barthes, Roland 37, 137, 256
Baudrillard, Jean 161, 168, 176–7, 213
Bauer, Fritz 4–5
Bełżec 64
Bertinis, Die 248–52
Big Red One, The 15n.11, 141–2
Birthplace 11, 64–9, 72, 73n.5, 110
Blake Nelson, Tim 5, 9, 186
Blobel, Colonel Paul 71
bloodlands 9, 238n.12
Boltanski, Christian 209–13, 217n.6
Boswell, Matthew 4, 186, 196, 199–200n.10, 217n.9
Boy in the Striped Pyjamas, The 13, 162, 167, 170–2, 176
Brasse, Wilhelm 11–12, 95–111, 111n.4, 162, 167, 170–2, 176
Brody, Richard 48, 51
Broken Silence 80
Browning, Christopher 217n.8, 228–9, 236, 238n.12
Brzozowski, Andrzej 106
Burning Land, The 79

Caché 215, 217n.10
caduta degli dei, La see Damned, The
Cannes Film Festival 47–9
Caruth, Cathy 3
Children from the Abyss 80
Chomsky, Marvin J. 144, 162, 226, 242, 247
Chronicle of the Warsaw Ghetto Uprising According to Marek Edelman 106
Churchill, Winston 24–5, 142

cinéma vérité 102
Cold War 24, 65, 142–3; and the Iron Curtain 65
Comedian Harmonists 118
Commissar 78
Communism 108–9, 144; post-war 153–5
concentration camps/extermination camps: Auschwitz 2, 5, 7–13, 15n.5, 16n.15, 29, 35, 56, 60, 70, 82–9, 91, 95–111, 125–9, 138n.4, 166, 173–4, 176, 183–98, 198n.1, 200n.16, 232, 245; and Auschwitz-Birkenau State Museum 95–6, 101, 104, 110; and Frankfurt Auschwitz trials 4; Bełżec 41, 45, 56n.1n.3, 63, 71, 126, 198n.1; Buchenwald 168, 173; Chełmno 56, 198n.1; Dachau 70, 127; Mauthausen 70; Rawa Ruska 70; Sobibór 5, 63, 126, 198n.1; Theresienstadt 42, 48–55, 169, 171; Treblinka 106, 126, 198n.1; Płaszów 7, 168–9; Westerbork 169; Zeitz 173; and gas chambers 9, 11, 13, 70, 86, 183, 186, 195–6, 198n.1, 203; and crematoria/crematorium 5, 13, 85, 107, 131, 167, 175–6, 183–4, 186, 188–9, 192–6, 198n.1, 199n.5
Cremator, The 14, 144, 205
Cry of an Owl 76–7, 81, 92n.2

Daddy 79
Damned, The 208–9
Damskii Portnoi see Ladies' Tailor
Dark Room, The (novel) 118, 130
David 80
Dead Snow 204
Defiance 5
Derrida, Jacques 43–4, 47
Desbois, Father Patrick 9, 69–72, 73n.6, 226, 236–7
Des Pres, Terrence 37, 105, 164
Destination Death 144
Deti iz bezdny see Children from the Abyss
Diary of Anne Frank, The 245
Diary of Mr. N, The 211–12

Dobrowolski, Irek 12, 17, 95, 96–111
docudrama 72–3, 120, 122, 233, 235
Død snø see Dead Snow
Downfall 122, 217n.7, 223
Dresden 118, 121–2, 234, 258
Durlacher, Gerhard 66
Dylewska, Jolanta 106, 109
Dziewczęta z Auschwitz see Girls from Auschwitz

Eaglestone, Robert 8, 107, 167, 173
Eastern Corridor 78
East of War 233
Edelstein, Jacob 49
Eichmann, Adolf 4, 49, 53, 55, 204, 204–5, 216, 216n.3
Eichmann in Jerusalem 204
Eichmann Trial 25, 52, 61
Elders 49–52
Elle s'appelait Sarah see Sarah's Key
empathy 10–11, 28, 32–5, 37–8, 51, 83, 88, 107, 224, 235–6
Ende kommen Touristen, Am see And Along Came Tourists
Eppstein, Paul 48, 52
European Union 12, 34, 145, 147
euthanasia programmes 9, 131, 206
Everything Is Illuminated 148
Everything Is Illuminated (novel) 226
Exile 78

Face of Our Time 103
Fair, The 144
Fam, Costa (Konstantin) 81, 86–7, 89, 91
Farocki, Harun 230
Fascism 4, 129, 223
Fateless 13, 161–2, 173–7
Fathi, Hasan 255
Ferencz, Benjamin 222, 225
Film Unfinished, A 14, 66
Final Solution 4, 49, 172, 214, 226, 235
Flucht, Die see March of Millions
forensic science 11, 59–62, 68–73
Forgács, Péter 211–13
Forgotten History, The 226

Fotoamator see Photographer
Frank, Anna/Anne   136–7, 169–70, 196
Frankfurter, Felix   42–6
French New Wave   228
Friedlander, Saul   25, 28, 38, 203–7, 216n.1
Führer Gives the Jews a City, The   48
Fuller, Samuel   141–2, 154–5, 157n.2, 253

Gadamer, Hans-Georg   210
Garfunkel, Leib   56
Generation War   12, 35, 118, 121, 224, 234, 248
genocide   6, 25, 27, 41, 44, 49, 55, 90, 117, 119–21, 126, 130–4, 137, 162, 164, 167, 171, 177n.8, 183–5, 192, 215, 227, 235–7, 243–8, 251–2
Germans, The   236
German German and non-German German   231–4, 237
Germany   10, 31–2, 34–5, 85, 97, 117–19, 121–2, 143, 147, 229, 249; Berlin   98, 125–6, 129, 170, 206, 233; and Holocaust memorial   31; Federal Republic of   146; GDR   31, 143, 257; Holocaust in   231, 243; Jews   123, 130, 135; post-unification 221, 223, 232–3; post-war generations 14, 30; *Wehrmacht*   225–6, 233–4; *Wehrmachtsausstellung*   234; West 143–4, 157n.4, 243; *see also* Nazism
Ghetto   79
ghettos   5, 48, 50, 52, 80, 119, 123, 226; model   48, 52; and Bełżec   45; Izbica Lubelska   41–2; Kovno   56; Łódź   109–10; Mizocz   71; Tulchin   79; Vilnius 79; Warsaw   30, 41–3, 106, 166, 169; and RSFSR (Russian Soviet Federative Socialist Republic)   84
Giraffe, The   147
Girls from Auschwitz   105
Goldhagen, Daniel J.   229, 234
Good   14, 204, 206–9, 216n.4, 217n.7
Grey, Martin   248
Grey Zone, The   5, 9, 13, 186–92, 196, 198, 199n.4n.5n.8, 200n.12
grünen Strand der Spree, Am   246

Grynberg, Henryk   64–70, 72, 73n.4n.5, 110
Gustloff, Die   234

Habermas, Jurgen   232
Haenel, Yannick   43, 45–8
Haneke, Michael   215, 217n.10
Hannah Arendt   4
Hartman, Geoffrey   36–7, 165
Haus in der Karpfengasse, Das   246–7
Heavy Sand   79
Heimat: A Chronicle of Germany   257
Heimat: Eine deutsche Chronik see Heimat: A Chronicle of Germany
heritage   26–8, 153, 211; Jewish   149; Soviet   77–81
Herman, Mark   167, 170–3, 177n.7
heroism: cinematic   197; collective   197; definition of   186; Holocaust   196–7; medical   188, 191, 197–8; narratives of 142–3; and doctor-hero   188–93, 197
Herrenpartie see Destination Death
Hersonski, Yael   4, 166
Herz, Juraj   14, 144, 205
Herz-Sommer, Alice   7
Himmler, Heinrich   52, 71, 97, 214
Hirschbiegel, Oliver   122, 217n.7
Hirsch, Marianne   7–8, 29, 36, 119–20, 134, 163, 166, 168, 176, 217n.6
Hitler, Adolf   5, 65, 76, 78, 123–4, 129, 143, 205, 209, 217n.7, 226, 232, 249, 255; Hitlerism   9
Hitler's Children   211
Hitler's Helpers   233
Hitler's Hidden Holocaust   226
Hitler's Willing Executioners: Ordinary Germans and the Holocaust (book)   229
Hoffman, Eva   2, 35, 147, 148, 150, 253
Hogan's Heroes   203
Holocaust: cultural aftermath of   1; denial of   59, 146, 164, 176, 215; discourse   11, 164, 172, 237; European memory of   12, 142, 145; Holocaust Remembrance Day   34; and Hollywood 10, 172, 186; legacy of   3, 223; meta-cinematic discourse in   5; narratives

of 3, 13, 127, 196; representation of 37, 79, 80–1, 169, 216n.1; in Russia 79–80, 85; visual representation of 4–5, 8, 14; YouTube 7, 8, 82, 86
Holocaust (tv series) 144, 243, 245, 247, 248, 257
Holocaust by Bullets 9, 11, 59, 64, 69–73, 226
Holocaust: Is it Wallpaper Paste? 11, 81–6
Holocaust Memorial Museum 15n.2, 41, 57n.7, 74n.8, 111n.5, 237
home-movies 211–12
human rights 14, 26–7, 32, 60, 62, 144, 213, 221, 232, 237

I am Looking at Your Photograph 106
Ida 13, 73n.5, 141, 153–7
Immersion 230
Inglourious Basterds 5, 15n.11, 203, 238n.8
Insdorf, Annette 6, 9, 246
Israel 29–30, 96, 143, 157n.5, 168, 177n.10, 213, 255; anti-Israeli propaganda 255
Izgoi see Exile

Jakubowska, Wanda 245
Jameson, Fredric 4
Jan Karski (novel) 43
Jedwabne massacre 3, 109, 110, 146, 147
Jenseits des Krieges see East of War
Jerusalem 4, 49, 55, 57n.7, 89, 204
Jewish War, The (novel) 65, 68
Jews: cemetery 3, 63, 66, 69, 142, 147–8, 155, 169; community 3, 25, 29–30, 34, 65, 69, 72, 129, 155; of Europe 1, 9, 29, 87, 126, 172, 221, 243; extermination of 9, 12, 56n.3; German-Jewish 118–20, 125, 129–30, 135, 137, 147; Jewish problem 45–6, 206; mass destruction of 9; non-Jewish partisans 80; privileged 105, 185–6, 194; Russian 80, 87; Singular Jew 12, 117–37; *Sonderkommando* 5, 13, 106–7, 183–98, 199n.n.7,8, 200n.n.n.11,13,14; victim 5, 11, 30–1, 34, 78, 90, 127–30, 143, 257; Zionists 255

Journey into Life 66

Kadelbach, Philipp 117–20, 122, 130–1, 133, 136
Kanew, Jeff 79, 226
Kaplan, Brett Ashley 7, 50, 205, 216n.5
Karski, Jan 11, 41–7, 51, 53, 56n.1n.3
Karski Report, The 10, 41–7, 53–6
Keenan, Thomas 60–2
Kertész, Imre 173–4, 176
Kholokost – Klei dlia oboev see Holocaust: Is it Wallpaper Paste?
Kill Team, The 214
Kirmes see Fair, The
Kiselev List 80
Kitty: Return to Auschwitz 65
Kleinert, Andreas 249
Klemperer: A Life in Germany 248
Klemperer: Ein Leben in Deutschland see Klemperer: A Life in Germany
Klüger, Ruth 24, 66
Knopp, Guido 233, 236, 258
Kola, Andrzej 63–4
Koltai, Lajos 173–4, 176
Kornblumenblau 9
Krik sovy see Cry of an Owl
Kronika powstania w getcie warszawskim według Marka Edelmana see Chronicle of the Warsaw Ghetto Uprising According to Marek Edelman
Kuznetsov, Anatoly 226

Labyrinth des Schweigens, Im see Labyrinth of Lies
Labyrinth of Lies 4
LaCapra, Dominick 2, 38, 141, 156–7, 216n.1
Ladies' Tailor 78
Lady in Number 9: Music Saved My Life, The 7
Langer, Lawrence 37
Lanzmann, Claude 4–11, 41–56, 56n.3, 57n.6, 61–6, 70, 72–3, 73n.1, 108, 154, 168, 236, 239n.19, 242
Last of the Just, The (novel) 47

Last of the Unjust, The 11, 41–2, 47–56
Last Stage, The 245
Last Witness, The 106
Lerner, Yehuda 5
Levi, Primo 23, 125, 183–7, 198n.1
Levy, Daniel 147, 15n.8, 36, 118, 147, 156–7, 165
L'histoire oubliée see Forgotten History, The
Liebe Perla 96
Life and Fate 81, 92n.7
Life Is Beautiful 15n.12, 173–4, 186, 196
Look of Silence, The 67
Lore 7, 12, 118–19, 130–6
Łoziński, Paweł 64–5, 68, 110
Lyotard, Jean-François 27

Madar-e sefr daradscheh see Zero Degree Turn
March of Millions 234
martyrdom 126; Polish 110
melodrama 79, 172, 207, 234, 243, 247, 255–8
memento mori 68–9
memory: collective 3, 16n.17, 77, 89, 166, 227, 234; communicative 1, 6, 30, 89; culture 3, 10, 26–8, 30–1, 33, 70, 77, 89, 110, 153, 163–5, 221, 225, 233; European 12, 142, 145, 155; Holocaust 1, 10, 23–38, 41, 77, 81, 89, 91, 118, 126, 137, 162–4, 166–9, 171–3, 176, 205, 224; national 14, 27, 121, 146, 221–37; negative 27–8, 30; postmemory/post memory 10, 29, 35–6, 37–8, 163, 166, 168, 176; public 9–10; structures of 7; transnational 34; visual 12, 254, 256; war 90; of World War II 89, 117n.9
Mengele, Dr. Joseph 13, 60–1, 83, 96, 98, 103, 184–5, 188–9, 192, 195, 198n.2
Meschugge see Giraffe, The
Miejsce urodzenia see Birthplace
mise-en-scène 49, 51, 55, 238n.3, 251, 255, 257
Mitscherlich, Thomas 66
Mörder sind unter uns, Die see Murderers Among Us

Morley, Peter 65
Moscovitz, Guillaume 64
Murderers Among Us 144
Murmelstein, Benjamin 11, 42, 47–56, 56n.5

Nasty Girl, The 147
Nazism 5, 13, 28, 70, 85, 87, 158n.8, 167, 205–6, 208, 209, 213, 215, 223, 237; Einsatzgruppen 59, 70, 167, 225–8, 231, 237, 238n.12, 239n.19; and reports 222, 230; Erkennungsdienst 96, 98–100, 102, 110; National Socialism 117–37, 183, 233; Nazi character 13, 177n.7, 203–5, 207, 213–14; Nazi collaborators 28, 77–8; Nazi crimes 9, 85, 130, 143, 236; Nazi evil 13; Nazi films 48, 215; Nazi genocide 164, 244–6, 248, 251; Nazi Germany 1, 14, 108, 151, 214, 221, 223, 225, 227, 248; Nazi hunter 5; Nazi ideology 225; Nazi monster 203, 209–10, 213; Nazi occupation 15n.3, 69, 77, 88, 149, 153, 168, 245, 248 ; Nazi party 5, 97, 205–6, 233; Nazi past 35, 144, 221, 223–5, 232–4; Nazi regime 3, 31, 119, 211, 229, 243, 245, 249, 253; Nazi rule 3, 53, 232; Neo-nazis 31; Nazi victims 51, 104; Nazi vocabulary 42; *see also* anti-Semitism
negative identity 232
Neighbors 109–10, 147–9
Nepokorennye see Unvanquished
New York Times (newspaper) 60, 207
Nicht alle waren Mörder see Not All Were Murderers
Night and Fog 14, 74n.8, 144, 169, 204, 245
Night Will Fall 4, 166
nom de tous les miens, Au 247–8
No Place on Earth 72
Not All Were Murderers 234
Nuit et brouillard see Night and Fog
Nuremberg Trials 157n.3, 222
Nyiszli, Dr Miklós 13, 184–98, 198n.2, 199n.7, 200n.13

Obchod na korze see Shop on Main Street, The
Obyknovennyi fashizm see Ordinary Fascism
Of Grammatology (book) 43–4
Operation Reinhard 59, 63, 71, 126
Oppenheimer, Joshua 67, 230–1
Oppenheim Family, The 78
Ordinary Fascism 78
Ordinary Men: Reserve Police Battalion 101 and the Final Solution in Poland (book) 228
Ostatni etap see Last Stage, The
Ostatni świadek see Last Witness, The
Otche Nash see Our Father
Our Father 78

Pakula, Alan J. 244, 247
Papa see Daddy
Paquet-Brenner, Gilles 12, 151, 153
Pasikowski, Władysław 3, 12, 88, 148–9, 150, 154
Patrzę na Twoją fotografię see I am Looking at Your Photograph
Pawlikowski, Paweł 13, 73n.5, 153
Phelan, James 3, 227, 231
Photographer 109
Pianist, The 166, 186
Pogodin, Oleg 76
Pokłosie see Aftermath
Poland: anti-Polish sentiments 3; Polish army 96; Polish filmmakers 109; Gentile Poles 3; Holocaust 97, 106, 109; Polish Jewish 41, 106, 109–10, 154; Past 12, 154; Polish nationalism 3, 103, 109; Polish resistance 41, 153; *see also* Jedwabne massacre
Polin: Okruchy pamięci see Polin: Scraps of Memory
Polin: Scraps of Memory 109
Pollock, Griselda 136–7, 138n.5
popular culture 2, 36, 226, 252
Portraitist, The 6, 12, 95–111
Portrecista see Portraitist, The
Professor Mamlock 78

propaganda: anti-Israeli 255; anti-Semitic 230; Communist 103; movie/film 5, 48, 166, 171, 253; Nazi 133

Radical Evil 7, 9, 14, 73n.6, 221–37
radikal Böse, Das see Radical Evil
Rafle, La see Roundup, The
Red Cross 48, 52
Reisen ins Leben see Journey into Life
Resnais, Alain 14, 74n.8, 144, 169, 204, 245–6, 250, 254
Ricciarelli, Giulio 4
Roosevelt, Franklin D. 42–6, 252
Rose, Gillian 4–5, 167, 217n.9, 223
Rosen für den Staatsanwalt see Roses for the Prosecutor
Roses for the Prosecutor 144
Rothberg, Michael 2, 8, 27, 90, 118, 120, 163–5, 217n.9
Roundup, The 151
Ruzowitzky, Stefan 9, 14, 73n.6, 221–31, 235–7, 238n.8

Safran Foer, Jonathan 73n.3, 148, 226
Sander, August 103
Sans Souci 209–11, 217n.6
Sarah's Key 12, 141, 151–3, 156–7
Sąsiedzi see Neighbours
Saving Private Ryan 252–3
Schindler, Oskar 172, 193, 204, 207
Schindler's List 7, 14, 62, 73, 73n.1, 88, 166, 168–70, 172–3, 186, 196, 198, 204, 207, 233, 242, 244–5, 247, 254, 257
schreckliche Mädchen, Das see Nasty Girl, The
Schreiber, Liev 148, 238n.15
Schwarz-Bart, André 47
secondary witness 10, 35–8
Seiffert, Rachel 118, 130, 132
self-reflexivity 5–6, 223
Sem'ia Oppengeim see Oppenheim Family, The
Shakirov, Mumin 81–6, 91
Shoah 4, 6, 8, 10–11, 38, 41–56, 61, 64, 69–70, 84–5, 144, 154, 216n.1, 236, 239n.19, 242

Shoah par balles: L'histoire oubliée, La see
   Holocaust by Bullets
Shoes 11, 81, 86–9
Shop on Main Street, The 144
Shortland, Cate 118–20, 130–4, 137
Singer, Andre 4, 166
Snow, Clyde 60–2, 69
Snyder, Timothy 9, 15n.3, 90, 126, 138n.4, 162, 238n.12
Sobibór, October 14, 1943, 4pm 5
Sons of the Fatherland 78
Sontag, Susan 214
Sophie's Choice 166, 244, 247–8
Sophie Scholl: Die letzten Tage see *Sophie Scholl: The Final Days*
Sophie Scholl: The Final Days 223
Sorstalanság see *Fateless*
Soviet Union 11, 79, 84, 86–7, 89, 143; censorship 78, 80, 88; films 77–8; Holocaust 77–8, 88; post-Soviet audiences 226; post-Soviet cinema 79
Spalovač mrtvol see *Cremator, The*
Spiegel, Der (newspaper) 8, 121
Spielberg's Shoah Foundation 166
Spielberg, Steven 7, 14, 88, 144, 161–2, 166, 168–70, 173, 176–7, 177n.9, 186, 196, 204, 233, 242, 245, 247–8, 252, 254
Spisok Kiseleva see *Kiselev List*
Stalin, Joseph 76, 87, 90, 143; anti-Semitic policies 78; KGB 76–7, 81; post-Stalin 76, 78; Stalinism 9, 76, 153
Staudte, Wolfgang 144
Stermer, Esther 72
Stevens, George 245
Struk, Janina 95, 98
Svideteli see *Witnesses*
Syny otechestva see *Sons of the Fatherland*
Sznaider, Natan 15n.8, 36, 156, 157, 165

Tarantino, Quentin 5, 186, 203, 238n.8
Terezin: Il Ghetto-Modello di Eichmann (book) 51
Thalheim, Robert 8
Third Reich 101, 118, 223, 225, 232, 243, 257

Tiazhelyi Pesok see *Heavy Sand*
Tobias, Janet 72
totalitarianism 25, 79; and memory 2
traumatic realism 2, 120
Triumph of the Spirit 166
Tufel'ki see *Shoes*
2G (second generation) 29, 31

unbekannte Soldat, Der see *Unknown Soldier, The*
United Nations 27, 34
Unknown Soldier, The 233
Unsere Mütter, unsere Väter see *Generation War*
Untergang, Der see *Downfall*
Unvanquished 78
Ursuliak, Sergei 81

V Iiune 41 see *Burning Land, The*
victimhood 27, 78, 110, 119, 130, 143
vita è bella, La see *Life Is Beautiful*
vivant qui passe, Un 49
Volk und Rasse (magazine) 97
von Trotta, Margarethe 4
Vostochnyi koridor see *Eastern Corridor*

Waller, James 235
Walser, Martin 38–39n.2, 232
War and Remembrance 248–9, 252–3, 256–7
War and Remembrance (book) 248
We Fight to Survive (book) 72
weiße Band: Eine deutsche Kindergeschichte, Das see *White Ribbon, The*
Weissmandl, Rabbi Michael 56
Weizman, Eyal 60–2
Wessel, Kai 248–51
White Ribbon, The 215–16
Wiesel, Elie 2, 23, 162, 170, 172, 177n.2
Wiesenthal, Simon 5, 60
Wieviorka, Annette 25, 46
Wildmann, Daniel 47, 53, 55, 56n.1
Winds of War, The 248
Wirkola, Tommy 204

Witnesses 89
Wołoszyn-Świerk, Kinga 105
World War I 49, 212
World War II 1–4, 15n.11, 23, 25, 27, 30, 42, 90, 95, 117, 145, 177n.9, 191, 207, 211, 232–4, 237, 248, 252–3, 255–6; narrative 12; post-war 4, 14, 15n.3, 44, 63, 68, 89, 101, 103–7, 118–19, 124, 128–32, 135, 142, 144, 153, 157n.3, 185, 190, 229, 232, 245–7; post-war amnesia 4; post-war Europe 12, 142–3

Wosiewicz, Leszek 9
Wouk, Herman 248

Yerushalmi, Yosef H. 25

Zaseev-Rudenko, Nikolai 79
Zeevi, Chanoch 211
Zero Degree Turn 255
Zhizn' i Sud'ba see *Life and Fate*
Ziarnik, Jerzy 106
Zwick, Edward 5

GPSR Authorized Representative: Easy Access System Europe, Mustamäe tee 50, 10621 Tallinn, Estonia, gpsr.requests@easproject.com